Lives of the Great Modern Artists

Lives of the Great Modern Artists

EDWARD LUCIE-SMITH

With 290 illustrations, 111 in color

Thames & Hudson

First published in 1999 in hardcover in the United
States of America, under the title *Lives of the Great
20th-Century Artists*, by Thames & Hudson Inc.,
500 Fifth Avenue, New York, New York 10110

thamesandhudsonusa.com

Revised and expanded edition 2009

Library of Congress Catalog Card Number
2008908372

ISBN 978-0-500-28191-8

Printed and bound in Singapore by
CS Graphics Pte Ltd

Contents

Introduction

We live in an age when creative personalities of all kinds are of great public interest. That is one, perhaps the chief, reason for the existence of this book, which is rather impertinently modelled on the greatest classic of Renaissance art history, Giorgio Vasari's *Lives of the Artists*, the indispensable narrative source upon which all subsequent historians of Renaissance art have relied, at least for basic biographical information. Published in 1550, it was the first in a long tradition of biographical collections featuring artists. It is a bold author who tries to rival Vasari's quirky vividness, his gift for the telling anecdote; nevertheless, our views both of art itself and of the nature of the human personality have changed radically since the sixteenth century.

Vasari based his book on the idea that art is perfectible – that each successive generation of artists could build upon the achievements of its predecessor. For Vasari, true art consisted in the devoted imitation of nature, but this imitation had to correspond with an ideal form which was already to be found in the artist's mind. The final result must, moreover, be imbued with grace, 'an indefinable quality dependent on judgment and therefore on the eye'. And it must have a quality Vasari called 'decorum' – that is, appropriateness to the task in hand. These beliefs gave his collection of lives a logical shape and structure which it is difficult to discover in the conflicting -isms that are characteristic of the history of the Modern movement and its Postmodern successor. Two reasons may account for this difference. One is the fact that the early interpreters of Modernism placed almost exclusive emphasis on the formal aspects of what they were dealing with, at the expense of personal content. The other, and perhaps more important, is that the actual dialectic of styles within the development of twentieth-century art seems to be entirely different from anything envisaged by Vasari. Speaking of Abstract Expressionism, the American critic Jacques Barzun remarked that it was an 'abolitionist' style, which sought to efface all memory of the achievements that had preceded it – to create a *tabula rasa* and start entirely anew. Other Modernist styles have had the same ambition, and I am forced to rebuild what their partisans have tried to demolish.

It is for this reason, among others, that the book contains rather more scene-setting than Vasari was prepared to allow himself. Another reason is that Vasari shared both a common background and a common culture with his prospective readers. This is an assumption no historian can afford to make today. In any case, historical method has greatly changed since the time Vasari undertook his task. One can generalize by means of a paradox. Vasari thought of art as quasi-scientific, it being the essence of science that one man can build on the discoveries of others. Until recently, the twentieth-century view of artistic creation was that every truly original artist was forced to begin anew, and forge, as far as possible, a completely original artistic language, with no relationship to anything that had preceded it. Only with the coming of Postmodernism in the 1970s did this attitude begin to change. It began to be felt that the artist was now confronted with a problem not of language, but of languages (in the plural) and that his task was not to invent but simultaneously to use and subvert the multiple formulae which already existed.

When we look back to the Renaissance, we realize not only how much our view of art has changed, but how fundamentally our view of human beings has altered. For Vasari, an adult possessed a relatively fixed 'character' which could be appropriately illuminated by means of striking anecdotes. The memorability of these anecdotes, and the fact that they had stuck in people's minds, served almost as a guarantee of the fact that they illuminated some important facet of what a person was like. This attitude helps to give his biographies their cutting edge, the clear, defined contour which is the equivalent of the Florentine artistic tradition of *disegno* – a word which, in Italian, means so much more than either 'drawing' or 'design'.

Writing in a post-Freudian epoch, when personality is essentially seen to be mutable throughout the whole course of a person's life, one must find other ways to seek Vasari's concision and his vividness. However, the enterprise is worth undertaking for one reason, and that is the central place which the personality of the artist now takes in the judgments which we make about twentieth-century art. In fact, in much of the writing devoted to the Modern movement and its products, there is an unresolved tension. On the one hand, we have a feeling that artworks ought to be admired in isolation, cordoned off from the circumstances which surrounded their creation. With the whole contents of André Malraux's *musée imaginaire* at our disposal, for instance, we feel that we ought to be able to judge an Egyptian statue of the Old Kingdom, about whose maker we know nothing, on exactly the same basis as a carving by Brancusi, about whom we happen to know a great deal. On the other hand, there is an increasing tendency, not merely to see works of recent art as being extensions of the personality which created them, but to see that personality as the dominant element, to which all physical objects remain subsidiary. W. B. Yeats, in his poem 'Among Schoolchildren', memorably posed the question: 'How can we know the dancer from the dance?' One might easily reverse the proposition and ask, how can we distinguish the dance from the person who performs it? The tendency of early Modernist critics was to privilege formal values as if these were immutable Platonic forms, and to ignore personality. As the prominent Postmodern critic Paul de Man wrote, what now concerns us is 'the potential unity between form and experience, between creator and creation'. Postmodernism reminds us that artists' personalities, as well as works of art, appear most revealingly in contextual terms: that is, taking into consideration all the factors – social, political, sexual, etc. – that happen to surround them.

Modern and contemporary artworks cannot be understood fully in total isolation. This book demonstrates the artist's life as one of the most obvious, if not always the only, key to creative achievement. If it concentrates largely on artists who are already dead, this is because it is difficult to see the true shape of any life until it has completed itself. Nonetheless, like Vasari in his second edition, I have written about some living artists whose work and career to date are of such importance that they deserve to be included in a book about the lives of the great modern artists.

Above: EDVARD MUNCH,
photographic self-portrait, 1906
Right: EDVARD MUNCH, *Jealousy*, c. 1895

1 Towards the Modern

Two very different artists share this section which serves as a prelude to the main series of biographies that follows. The work of each contains Modernist elements, but neither seems fully Modern. Munch is a confessional painter – his work is almost entirely autobiographical. In his work we find a candour missing from that of both contemporaries and predecessors, with the exception of Van Gogh. It is Munch, in fact, who forms the bridge between the European Symbolist movement and German Expressionism – that is to say, between the creative milieu of the late nineteenth and early twentieth century.

Käthe Kollwitz, one of the two or three most powerful women artists of the century, and one who came close to producing art which is truly feminist, in the sense in which we now use that term, nevertheless uses forms which are still rooted in the nineteenth century. The comparisons which most easily spring to mind are not with her German contemporaries Grosz and Dix, but with Honoré Daumier and J. F. Millet.

EDVARD MUNCH

Edvard Munch's influence on the Modern movement is the more extraordinary because he came from such a remote and provincial milieu. He was born in December 1863 at Løten, Hedmark, in Norway, the second of five children. His father was an army doctor who later became a district physician in Christiania (renamed Oslo in 1924). Munch's mother died of tuberculosis when he was five. This had a strong effect on his father, who retired into a life of seclusion and began to suffer from bouts of religious anxiety bordering on insanity; Munch long afterwards remembered his outbursts of violence. The situation grew still worse in 1877, when Munch's elder sister died, an event which made an indelible mark on his imagination:

> Disease, insanity and death were the angels which surrounded my cradle, and since then they have followed me throughout my life... In my childhood I always felt I was treated unjustly, without a mother, sick, and with the threat of punishment in Hell hanging over my head.

There was, however, one compensating factor. After the death of his mother, the Munch household was run by a devoted aunt who was herself a painter and who recognized and encouraged Edvard's gift as an artist.

In 1879 Munch was sent to a technical college to study engineering, but poor health prevented him from attending classes regularly. In November 1880, after many hesitations on both moral and practical grounds, his father finally agreed that he could study art. He entered the Royal School of Design in Christiania in 1881. His gifts were soon recognized and he was allowed to skip all the elementary classes. In 1882 he rented a studio with a group of six other young artists, and the next year he exhibited for the first time in a group show.

The mid-1880s brought many important events for Munch. In 1885 he made his first visit to Paris where he studied the pictures in the Louvre and in the official Salons, and saw and was deeply impressed by the work of Manet. He painted *The Sick Girl*, his first major work, which was seen and praised by the leading Norwegian artist of the time, Christian Krohg, who had taught Munch in 1882. He fell in with a set called 'the Christiania Bohemians', led by the writer Hans Jaeger, whose wild ways and the fact that they defended free love shocked the staid citizens of the town. It was in this circle that Munch had his first love affair, with Milly Thaulow, the wife of a friend:

> I was made to feel the entire unhappiness of love ... and for several years it was as if I were nearly crazy. The horrible face of mental illness then raised its twisted head. ... After that I gave up the hope of being able to love.

In 1889 Munch organized his first one-man show, which was also the first one-man exhibition held in Norway. He was given a state grant to travel, and in October he set out once more for Paris, where he enrolled under the academic artist Léon Bonnat. While he was absent his father died. He returned home in May 1890, succeeded in having his grant renewed and set out again the following winter. Munch's second trip was not so successful: he caught rheumatic fever and spent two months in hospital in Le Havre. He returned to Christiania once more in May 1891 and succeeded in getting his travel grant renewed for a third time, which excited a certain amount of controversy. The controversy was revived when he held a second one-man show in Christiania in 1892 which caused an uproar among the local critics. The show did, however, attract the attention of a fellow Norwegian, Adelsten Normann, who was the Director of the Berliner Künstlervereinigung (Berlin Artists' Union). Acting on his own authority, Normann invited Munch to exhibit in Berlin. The result was a famous scandal, as the work was too radical for the taste of the organization's membership. The show was closed after a week, having caused a heated debate in the Kunstlervereinigung which ended in a vote unfavourable to Munch. The final outcome of the affair was the foundation of the Berlin Sezession under Max Liebermann, when the defeated faction withdrew from the organization.

Munch did his best to take advantage of the publicity. He rented a gallery in the Friedrichstrasse, draped a large Norwegian flag above the entrance and showed his pictures there independently. He now decided to base himself in Berlin, though he also travelled restlessly throughout Germany and Scandinavia. At this time he was often very poor: in November 1894 he was discovered wandering the streets of Berlin, having been turned out of his room for non-payment of rent, and not having eaten anything for three days. But he was beginning to find patrons, chief among them Walter Rathenau, the great industrialist, director of Allgemeine-Elektrizitäts-Gesellschaft (AEG) and later Foreign Minister of the Weimar Republic. He had also found an even wilder circle of bohemian friends than that in Christiania. The Berlin circle centred on the Polish writer Stanislas Przybyszewski and his wife Dagny Juell. Przybyszewski suffered from hallucinations which sometimes took on an uncomfortably prophetic tinge, and Dagny, a young music student whom Munch had himself introduced into the circle, was a *femme fatale* who was to die violently – she was shot in Tiflis in 1901 by a crazy Polish student whom she had provoked. At one time Przybyszewski, the playwright Strindberg, the art critic and historian Julius Meier-Graefe and Munch himself were all simultaneously in love with her.

This was not Munch's only amorous entanglement at this time. In 1893, or perhaps a little earlier, he had just ended an affair with the rich and beautiful daughter of a Christiania wine-merchant, and was living outside Christiania at Åsgårdstrand. One stormy evening a boat full of friends arrived from a neighbouring village to tell him the girl was now dying, and wanted to see him one last time. Munch agreed, and arrived to find her lying in bed between two lighted candles. As soon as she saw him she rose and revealed that the whole thing had been a hoax. She then produced a revolver and threatened to kill herself if he did not return to her. Munch struggled to take the gun from her (believing that in any case it must be unloaded). It went off and shot away the top joint of the middle finger of his left hand.

In 1895 Munch was twice in Paris, and in December of that year *La Revue blanche* published his famous composition *The Scream* as a lithograph. He returned to Paris for a longer stay in 1896–97, and formed part of the Symbolist circle round the poet Stéphane Mallarmé, of whom he made two portrait prints. In 1897 a painting from his *Frieze of Life* series, which he had been elaborating since about 1889, was given a place of honour in the main hall of the Salon des Indépendants. But having established a useful foothold in Paris he promptly abandoned it, and once more started spending most of his time in Germany, and summer months at a little house he had bought at Åsgårdstrand. His output and his energy in promoting himself were prodigious. Between 1892 and 1909 he exhibited no less than 106 times in Scandinavia, Germany, France, Belgium, Austria, Italy, Russia, Czechoslovakia and the United States (once in Chicago and once in New York). Important stages in the growth of his reputation were the purchase of two paintings by the National Gallery in Christiania in 1899, a sign of recognition from his own countrymen; the exhibition of a series of pictures from *The Frieze of Life* at the Berlin Sezession in 1902; and his first real retrospective, held in Prague in 1905. In 1908 he was made a Knight of the Royal Norwegian Order of St Olav.

By this time Munch's health was suffering from the effects of alcohol and overwork. In 1908 he had a nervous breakdown in Copenhagen: he committed himself to a psychiatric clinic, after an uncontrollable drunken binge. He was under treatment for eight months and was given massage and electric shock. He emerged a teetotaller, and in May 1909, after his release, he decided to settle permanently in Norway.

The first years after his return were dominated by the controversy over the murals for the new Christiania University Hall. Munch was the obvious candidate, but the Building Committee of the University Senate were very reluctant to give him the job, even after a competition jury had declared in his favour. A counter-committee was formed to agitate on Munch's behalf, and eventually in 1914 the University Senate agreed to accept Munch's canvases, which he had in any case begun to paint, as a private gift. The paintings were installed in September 1916.

In 1916, after several changes of address, he bought the house and estate of Ekely, in Skøyen, just outside Christiania, and lived there for the rest of his long life. Munch continued to be hugely prolific, often making new versions of motifs he had already used, but also tackling fresh ones. Not all the new pictures are as intense as those he painted earlier, but some of his finest work can be found in the desolate self-portraits he painted at the very end of his life.

A number of Munch's paintings were removed from German museums as a result of the Nazi campaign against 'Degenerate Art', and during the wartime German occupation of Norway he refused to have any contact either with the Germans themselves or their Norwegian collaborators. On 19 December 1943 the windows of his house at Ekely were blown out when a German ammunition dump on the Filipstad Quay in Oslo was sabotaged. Munch spent some time walking restlessly up and down his garden in freezing weather, and caught a cold which he was unable to shake off. He died of bronchitis on 23 January 1944.

KÄTHE KOLLWITZ

The work of Käthe Kollwitz foreshadowed that of the artists of the Neue Sachlichkeit in Weimar Germany, and though she was in fact considerably senior to Grosz and Dix, she ranks as their colleague. She was born in July 1867, in Königsberg, East Prussia, and grew up in an atmosphere of intense religious feeling, which continued to mark her work even after she abandoned formal religious belief. Her maternal grandfather was Julius Rupp, an ordained Lutheran pastor, who was expelled from the Church because of his scruples regarding the Athanasian Creed, and who then founded the first Free Religious Congregation in Germany. Kollwitz later said: 'A loving God was never brought home to us.'

Her father, Karl Schmidt, was equally remarkable. He studied law and gave it up when he was about to

KÄTHE KOLLWITZ, *Self-Portrait*, 1910

KÄTHE KOLLWITZ at work on a plaster model for her sculpture *Mother with Her Two Children* (1932–37), *c.* 1932

qualify as a professional lawyer because he felt that his radical views would prevent his advancement in the legal profession. He then learned the trade of mason from the bottom up, and became a master mason. On the death of his father-in-law in 1884 he succeeded him as head of the Free Religious Congregation.

At the age of thirteen Kollwitz received her first instruction in art, from a teacher named G. Naujok and the engraver Rudolf Mauer. Mauer taught her etching and intaglio printing, and this oriented her from the beginning towards the graphic arts rather than painting. In 1885 she went to Berlin with her brother, who was studying at the University, for a year's trial at art school. She returned home for two years then went to Munich, where the artistic atmosphere was much livelier than in Berlin. She continued her artistic studies and discovered

contemporary literature, particularly the work of Zola, Ibsen and Bjornson. She attended a lecture by August Bebel which aroused her interest in social democracy and in the related feminist movement.

In 1891 she married Dr Karl Kollwitz who was a *Kassenarzt*, maintaining a kind of clinic or dispensary open to subscribers for a small weekly sum. These clinic were a first step towards socialized medicine. They had two sons, born in 1893 and 1896. Kollwitz exhibited her work in public for the first time in 1893. At this time she encountered Gerhart Hauptmann's play *The Weavers*, which was based on the revolt of the Silesian handloom weavers in 1840, when their livelihood was threatened b mechanization. The play prompted Kollwitz to produce a dramatic sequence of six prints which occupied her continuously from 1894–98. These were shown in 1898 and caused sensation and scandal because of the politically radical nature of their subject-matter. The jury wanted to give her a gold medal, but the Emperor personally vetoed the award. The sequence subsequently won awards at Dresden in 1899 and in London in 1900.

In 1902 Kollwitz embarked on another major cycle of prints, based on the sixteenth-century Peasants' War in Germany. This won her the Villa Romana Prize in 1908, and she duly spent a year in Italy. But the visit made little difference to her art, and may even have checked its development, as she was always a quintessentially northern artist, with her roots deeply in the German Gothic. In this she resembled Ernst Barlach.

The years 1910–19 were relatively unproductive, and were marked by personal tragedy. Kollwitz's younger son volunteered when war was declared in 1914, and was killed the following October at Diksmuide in Flanders. But this was also a period in which her reputation continued to grow. In 1917 her fiftieth birthday was celebrated with an exhibition at the Paul Cassirer Gallery in Berlin, and in 1919 she was elected to the Berlin Academy of Art and given the honorary title of Professor. She was the first woman to be elected to the Academy.

Kollwitz had moved away from etching and had begun to explore woodcut and lithography, which became her preferred media during her later career. She also started to experiment with sculpture, beginning work on a sculptured memorial to fallen war volunteers and to her son, which at first she was unable to bring to completion. It was only when she began a new version in 1924 that she was able to achieve what she wanted. The sculpture was finally completed in 1932 and set up at Diksmuide.

Once the war was over Kollwitz felt a rekindling of the creative urge. Her work became more abstract and universal, and at the same time provided an accurate reflection of the social stresses which would eventually tear the Weimar Republic apart. She became identified with the left and with pacifism – she produced a poster-print as a memorial to the murdered co-founder of the German Communist Party Karl Liebknecht and paid a visit to Russia. Her profoundest feelings were, however, expressed in another deeply moving sequence of images, published in 1923 and entitled simply *War*.

Kollwitz's work was offensive to the Nazis for its content as much as for its style. She was expelled from the Berlin Academy of Art in 1933, and had to face increasingly tight restrictions on the exhibition and publication of her work. She was nevertheless able to continue and in 1934–35 produced a last great print sequence on the theme of death, which consisted of eight large lithographs. She created only four more prints after 1935, turning instead to making small sculptures.

In 1941 Kollwitz's husband died, and her studio, which contained many unique proofs and much other material, was destroyed in the wartime bombings. The last year of her life, 1944–45, was spent as the guest of Prince Ernst-Heinrich of Saxony at his ancestral castle, the Moritzburg, near Dresden. She died in April 1945. In old age she was a figure of serene dignity. George Grosz, who met her only once, gives a vivid snapshot impression of Kollwitz at the period when she was most celebrated. He recalled 'a certain aura of melancholy about her – far from talkative, rather moody.'

KÄTHE KOLLWITZ,
Losbruch, 1907,
from *The Peasant War* series,
1902–8

Fauvism is generally regarded as the first coherent Modernist movement, but its period of dominance, before it was overtaken by Cubism, was brief, and the artists connected with it soon went their separate ways. Matisse, the most original, continued his search for a decorative idiom which would genuinely reflect a twentieth-century sensibility; Derain tried to legitimize a return to classic values; Vlaminck became a kind of Expressionist. Matisse's political passivity, despite the urging of his fiercely patriotic wife, and the fact that both Derain and Vlaminck came close to collaboration with the occupying German forces during the War, are indications that the artists who made Fauvism were revolutionaries almost by accident and retired from the role with some alacrity once they were established.

HENRI MATISSE

Matisse was the unlikely leader of the small force of shock troops which created Modernism in painting. Cool by temperament, he painted pictures in fervent colours which altered sensibilities overnight. In his later years, Matisse came to be regarded as someone who had betrayed his original avant-garde principles – until the flowering of his astonishing late phase. His reputation for aloofness is belied by the practical friendship he gave to many of his fellow artists, including men otherwise as different from one another as Pierre Bonnard and André Masson.

He was born on the last day of 1869, the son of a grain merchant who lived near Saint Quentin. After going to school in Saint Quentin he studied law in Paris, a training which led to a dead-end job as a lawyer's clerk in his home town. His chief occupation was to copy out the *Fables* of La Fontaine, so as to use up the required quantity of stamped legal paper. At this time he was also attending early morning classes in drawing at the local art school.

In 1890, when he was convalescing from appendicitis, his mother gave him a box of oil paints, and he started to paint. It took him nearly two years of badgering to overcome his father's objections to his studying art professionally. He enrolled at the Académie Julian in Paris, under Bouguereau, and discovered that the instruction offered was not much better than having to copy La Fontaine. The Symbolist painter Gustave Moreau, the best teacher of his time, rescued Matisse by giving him unofficial admission to his own studio in the Ecole des Beaux-Arts in 1895. Here he met Georges Rouault, Moreau's favourite disciple, and Albert Marquet, who became a close friend. At this time he made numerous copies in the Louvre, not merely to learn, but as items for sale to supplement his father's allowance. Most of the pictures he chose were French eighteenth-century – Matisse's characteristic hedonism thus showed itself early.

Left: HENRI MATISSE in his studio, Hôtel Régina, Nice, 1950, working on *Virgin and Child* for the Chapel of the Rosary in Vence. Photo Hélène Adant. Right: HENRI MATISSE and model in his studio, 1 place Charles-Félix, Nice, c. 1927–28. Photographer unknown

In 1896 he made a belated début as a professional, sending four pictures to the supposedly 'liberal' Salon de la Société nationale des Beaux-Arts. He had a modest success, selling two works, one to the French state, and was elected an associate member of the group which ran the Salon, proposed by its president, Puvis de Chavannes. This meant that in future he could exhibit there without submitting his work to a jury. In 1898 he married Amélie Parayre, a woman of strong character, who was to be a great help to him during the early, difficult years of his career, and supported the household for some years by keeping a milliner's shop.

Her assistance was needed, since in 1899 Matisse's affairs took a turn for the worse. Moreau had died, and his successor, Cormon, turned Matisse out of the studio. He attended classes at the Académie Carrière (where he met Derain) but in effect his student days were over. Artists younger than himself had already begun to regard him as a leader, and, impressed by his sober demeanour and red beard, insisted on nicknaming him 'the Doctor'.

The next years were difficult. In 1900 Matisse was so hard up that he was forced to join the team of decorators who were preparing the newly built Grand Palais for the Exposition Universelle of 1900. He and Marquet painted yards of laurel leaves round the cornice. In 1901 his father cut off his allowance. Gradually, however, he was becoming better known. In 1903 he was one of the founders of the new Salon d'Automne, and the following year he had a one-man show with Ambroise Vollard. He spent the summer of 1904 with Signac in St Tropez. The year 1905 was his *annus mirabilis*. He and his friends were allowed to show as a group at the Salon d'Automne, and the effect was electric. The critic Louis Vauxcelles dubbed them the Fauves, or 'wild beasts', and Matisse, as their leader, became *le roi des fauves* – the 'king of the beasts'. For someone like Fernande Olivier, Picasso's mistress at that time, Matisse became a man who 'shone imposingly'. Important collectors began to buy his work – first the Stein family, then the Russian millionaire Sergei Shchukin. In 1907 he set up a school which attracted many pupils, chiefly Scandinavians and Germans, and many of his financial worries were removed by a contract with the Bernheim-Jeune Gallery, to take his entire production, which he signed in 1909. He travelled to Munich to see an exhibition of Islamic art, visited Spain, Moscow (where he studied the icons), and Morocco.

During this period of his first major success, Matisse wrote a kind of credo. Called 'Notes of a Painter', it appeared in *La Grande Revue* at the end of 1908:

> What I am after above all is expression. ... Expression to my way of thinking does not consist of the passion mirrored upon a human face or betrayed by a violent gesture. The whole arrangement of my pictures is expressive. ... Composition is the art of arranging in a decorative manner the various elements at a painter's disposal for the expression of his feelings.

But Matisse's position of leadership among the younger painters was soon challenged by the emergence of Cubism and the growing reputation of Picasso. When the First World War broke out, he was already over military age. He remained in Paris until 1916, painting some of his greatest pictures, but the wartime cold defeated him. He retired to Nice, at first as a temporary arrangement, and his family visited him, but did not stay – one reason may have been the well known fact that he slept with his models. He now gradually evolved a way of life devoted to painting. He was perhaps encouraged in this by a series of visits he made to Renoir, then crippled by arthritis and coming to the end of a long life. Certainly there is something rather Renoiresque about the many odalisques and glowing interiors which Matisse produced during the first half of the 1920s.

In the 1930s Matisse was more restless: he travelled, and he accepted new challenges. He want as far as Tahiti and he agreed to paint a mural on the theme of dance for the Barnes Foundation in Merion, Pennsylvania. Because he was sent the wrong measurements he painted the vast composition twice over, a practical demonstration of his belief that the slightest change in proportion altered the composition in a fundamental way.

The Second World War came, and Matisse prepared to emigrate to Brazil. But, after leaving Paris for Bordeaux and witnessing the mad scramble of refugees, he decided not to go. 'If anyone who has any value leaves France,' he wrote to his son Pierre, a dealer in America, 'what remains of France?' Nevertheless, his formidable wife seems to have found his attitude too passive, and demanded a legal separation. Both she and his daughter Marguerite joined the Resistance, and both were eventually arrested. Marguerite was tortured, but escaped from the train taking her to Ravensbruck thanks to an air-raid

Meanwhile, Matisse himself had begun to suffer the misfortunes of old age. In 1941 he underwent an operation for an internal occlusion. A post-operative infection followed and a second operation was performed which permanently damaged the muscles on one side of his stomach, and from now on he could only hold himself upright for short periods. Wryly he referred to himself as being not *malade* (sick) but *mutilé* (maimed) – alluding to the French bureaucratic expression *mutilé de guerre* (disabled war veteran). His ill health and residence in the Unoccupied Zone enabled him to keep himself apart from politics, though he did make two non-political broadcasts on the Vichy radio. The second of these contained a savage attack on the academic Beaux-Arts system of training artists from which he had suffered in his youth. He was not asked to perform again.

The chief enterprise of his last years was for many people a surprising one. Between 1948 and 1951 he decorated a chapel in Vence for a convent of Dominican nuns, one of whom had nursed him during his convalescence after his operation before she herself took the veil. Matisse belonged to a generation which consisted either of militant believers, like the writer Paul Claudel, or else of sceptics; in undertaking the chapel decoration, he was wary of giving the impression that he had undergone any kind of conversion. In his letter to the bishop who performed the dedication he merely said: 'In my own way I have always sung the glory of God and his creation.' He did not attend the dedication ceremony on the grounds of ill health and he also, rather cannily under the circumstances, saw to it that the preliminary designs were exhibited with an organization which was well known to be a Communist front. Matisse seems in fact to have considered the chapel chiefly as a monument to himself, a complete statement of his aesthetic credo. He made sure that if the nuns should ever be dispossessed, the building would be protected as a historic monument.

Apart from its stained-glass windows, the decorations in the chapel are austerely black and white. Their boldness of line, however, makes them completely congruous with the brilliantly coloured large-scale paper cut-outs which were the chief products of Matisse's last years, and which represent some of his finest achievements. The method was originally adopted as a way of positioning the figures in *La Danse*, but then became a concession to increasing physical weakness; it developed a rationale of its own in the artist's mind. Lying in bed, Matisse would scissor bold shapes from sheets he had coloured himself: he compared the process to the way a sculptor carves a form from the block prepared for him. These shapes were moved around on a canvas by assistants at the artist's direction until he got the configuration he wanted. Colour had always been the central theme of Matisse's art, and this technique allowed him to produce some of his strongest colouristic effects. His doctors even told him to wear dark glasses in the studio when not actually working, for fear that the optical vibrations would injure his already failing eyesight. Matisse was still working energetically on his cut-outs when he died in 1954. He is buried in a grave which is now shared by his estranged wife.

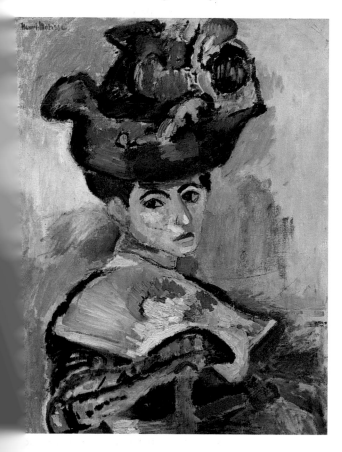

Henri Matisse,
The Woman with the Hat, 1905

MAURICE DE VLAMINCK

Now remembered chiefly for his brief association with the Fauves, Maurice de Vlaminck is better categorized as a kind of Expressionist. He rapidly abandoned the revolutionary stance he adopted before the First World War, and his later work is repetitious and generally of much lower quality than that produced at the beginning of his career.

He was born in the Les Halles quarter of Paris in 1876; his father was Flemish and his mother came from Lorraine. The family background was a musical one – his father, who had been a tailor, became a teacher of music, and his mother, who also taught music, had in her youth received second prize for piano at the Paris Conservatoire. When Vlaminck was three the family moved from Paris to live with his grandmother at the nearby town of Le Vesinet. The young Vlaminck received a somewhat rudimentary education which included some painting lessons between 1888 and 1891 from an academic artist who was a friend of his family.

In 1892 he left home and went to live independently at Chatou. The great bicycling craze had just begun, and Vlaminck, who was tall and powerfully built, became an adept cyclist. In 1893 he turned professional cycle racer, supplementing his income from this source by working in a bicycle factory. He hugely enjoyed the attention he attracted when he raced:

> The admiring looks of the girls and women, the bravos and cheers of the excited spectators ... never, anywhere, had I felt such utter and complete satisfaction as I did in the days when I was nothing more than the winner of a simple bicycle race. At that time women admired us in the same way as today they admire an airman.

Vlaminck married young, in 1894, and the following year his daughter was born. In 1896 he was forced to withdraw from an important race because he suffered an attack of typhoid fever, and this marked the end of his career as a professional cyclist. Four months after he had recovered he was summoned for military service. He found the military atmosphere stultifying, but was more fortunate than most of his comrades since, thanks to his musical skills, he was allowed to serve as a regimental

bandsman. His barrack-room friends were all radicals – 'Dreyfusards, anti-militarists, anti-religious'. He read widely (his preferred authors included Zola, Flaubert, Alphonse Daudet and Guy de Maupassant), and began to write, contributing to radical magazines such as *Fin de Siècle* and *L'Anarchie*. He had very little opportunity to paint, though his earliest surviving work is a decoration made in 1899 for the regimental fête.

In 1900 Vlaminck met Derain, when they were both involved in a minor railway accident during his last leave before the end of his military service. They rapidly became close friends and agreed to share a studio in Chatou. After his release from the army Vlaminck painted by day, and by night worked as a musician in various Montmartre nightclubs and restaurants.

> The performances which, unwillingly, I was forced to attend, troubled my senses. From the orchestra pit my eyes were free to explore beneath the skirts of the comediennes and note the curly black or blonde hair under their armpits.

He also won prizes at billiards and rowing, and pursued a career as a writer, in collaboration with a friend he had met in the army. His first book, a sentimental novel called *D'un Lit dans l'autre* (From One Bed to Another), was published in 1902, with illustrations by Derain. It was to be followed by several other books of the same type, one of which only narrowly missed nomination for the Prix Goncourt. In 1904 he showed a painting in public for the first time, in a mixed exhibition at the Galerie Berthe Weill. At about the same time he got to know Apollinaire and also gave up playing in nightclubs.

> In order to find more time for painting I left Paris and my work with orchestras. I became a poor music teacher in a family. This was the hardest period of my life. I started all over again. For my own benefit and that of my pupils I taught the methods of Mazas and Kreutzer, together with classical music, Bach, Haydn Beethoven and Mozart.

In 1905 Vlaminck showed four paintings in the Salon des Indépendants which attracted some attention. Later in the year he exhibited eight canvases at the Salon d'Automne, and found himself hailed as a member of a new and exciting radical group – the Fauves.

The Vlaminck fam
at home in Paris, 19
Photo André Ker

In April 1906, the dealer Ambroise Vollard bought the complete contents of his studio, as he had done previously with Derain, and in 1907 he gave Vlaminck his first one-man show.

This was a time of transition in the painter's life. His first marriage was in the process of breaking up after the birth of a third daughter in 1905. One of his last pupils, before he was able to give up teaching music for good, was a fashion designer named Berthe Combe who subsequently became his second wife and indispensable helpmate. He described her later as 'more than a wife – a friend who understands what is in my mind before I've expressed it.'

In 1908 he abandoned the primary colours characteristic of Fauvism and his palette began to grow darker. In 1911 he went to London at Vollard's insistence, and stayed for a fortnight; he did not enjoy his visit. All his life, despite his love of locomotion – bicycles, motorcycles and, later, fast cars – he was a deeply reluctant traveller. Two major essays on his work were published in 1913, one by Gustave Cocquiot and one by Daniel-Henri Kahnweiler. Kahnweiler was the promoter of the Cubists, but Vlaminck, after a brief flirtation with Cubism, found himself unable to come to terms with the new movement. Indeed, he later denied that he had found any attraction in it at all, his version of the matter being that he was suddenly confronted with a Cubist painting at Paul Guillaume's gallery as late as 1914 and 'felt I was no longer on my own ground – as though I was on the brink of an abyss'. He subsequently developed a lifelong grudge against Picasso, whom he saw as a trickster and an imposter.

At the outbreak of war Vlaminck was mobilized, but, thanks to the influence of his brother-in-law Elie Bois, the editor of *Le Petit Parisien*, he was soon released from the army to serve in the war industries in and near Paris. He held his second one-man show just after the war, in 1919, and was lucky enough to attract the attention of a rich Swedish businessman, who bought ten thousand francs' worth of pictures. This windfall enabled him to buy a small country house in the Vexin, 40 kilometres from Paris. This purchase marked his virtual retirement from Montmartre and Montparnasse. In 1925 he acquired a larger house, a farm called La Tourillière near Reuil-la-Galadière, in the Eure-et-Loire. This was further from the capital – 125 kilometres rather than 40 – and his isolation from the artists increased. The surrounding countryside was to supply Vlaminck with most of his subject-matter for the rest of his career.

MAURICE DE VLAMINCK,
Street in Marly-le-Roy,
1905–6

MAURICE DE VLAMINCK,
Banks of the Seine at Chatou,
1905–6

The inter-war years saw a steady growth of his reputation both at home and abroad. Several books were published about him; in 1933 he had a retrospective at the Palais des Beaux-Arts in Paris; and in 1937 a substantial body of his work was included in the Exposition des Artistes Indépendants held at the Petit Palais in connection with the Paris Exposition Universelle. Vlaminck made the political gestures standard at the time: he was, for example, a member of the League of International Solidarity against Fascism, but his aesthetic views were growing steadily more conservative. Modernism he now considered to be 'an art made of theories, metaphysical painting and abstraction replace sensibility, an art which lacks moral health.'

When the Germans invaded France in 1940 Vlaminck took refuge at Fromentine, a small port in Normandy, but he soon returned to his farm. Like Derain, he found himself being assiduously courted by the Germans, and in 1941 he agreed to join an official party of French artists who would visit the Reich under German auspices. Other members of the group included his old friend Derain, with whom he had quarrelled. Van Dongen, Othon Friesz, André Dunoyer de Segonzac and the sculptor Charles Despiau. The visit was highly publicized by the German propaganda machine. In 1943 Vlaminck compounded his offence by publishing a book entitled *Portraits avant Décès* (Portraits Before Death), which gave free rein to his now extremely critical view of modern art. Most of the text had been written as early as 1937 but its publication, when some of the artists Vlaminck criticized so harshly were under direct threat from the Nazis, seemed extremely inopportune. Immediately after the Liberation, in August 1944, he was arrested, held for forty-eight hours and interrogated before a tribunal about his conduct. Nothing serious was proved against him, but the whole business left a question mark against his name.

It was a decade before his reputation recovered even partially – in 1954 he was invited to show at the Venice Biennale, and in 1956 he was elected a member of the Académie des Beaux-Arts in Belgium. This was also the year in which he had a major retrospective. Significantly it was held at a private gallery, the Galerie Charpentier, and not under official auspices. Vlaminck died in 1958.

ANDRÉ DERAIN

Of all the major figures in the Ecole de Paris, André
Derain's reputation has sunk into the deepest trough.
It is doubtful if it will ever again stand as high as it did
between the two World Wars.

Derain was born in 1880 at Chatou, which was then a
kind of artists' colony at the gates of Paris. His father was
a successful *patissier* (pastry chef) and a town councillor
and Derain was given a middle-class education. He
disliked school – much later, he said that 'the teachers,
ushers and pupils were a far more bitter memory for me
than the darkest hours of my military career.' He left
'with few regrets and the reputation of being a bad, lazy
and noisy scholar', but with a prize for drawing. He took
his first lessons in painting in 1895 from an old friend of
his father's and of Cézanne's (but who nevertheless
thoroughly disliked Cézanne's work), and in 1898 he
went to the Académie Carrière in Paris, where he met
Matisse. In June 1900 he met Maurice de Vlaminck,
and formed a close friendship with him. The two young
artists rented a disused restaurant in Chatou which they
used as a studio, and often shocked their neighbours with
their antics. Meanwhile, Derain pursued his studies,
copying in the Louvre and visiting exhibitions of
contemporary art. In 1901 he was extremely impressed by
the Van Gogh retrospective at the Bernheim-Jeune
Gallery, and it was here that he introduced his two
friends, Vlaminck and Matisse, to one another.

In the autumn of that year Derain was called up for
military service. He could do little work, but carried on a
lively correspondence with Vlaminck until his release in
September 1904. He returned to Chatou, and it was at
about this time that he got to know the poet Guillaume
Apollinaire. The following year, 1905, was an important
one for him. The dealer Ambroise Vollard, to whom he
had been introduced by Matisse, bought the entire
contents of his studio (he did the same with Vlaminck).
Derain exhibited at the Salon des Indépendants and sold
four pictures, and then at the Salon d'Automne where he,
Matisse, Vlaminck and others were hung together as a
group, in a space which was promptly dubbed the 'Cage
aux Fauves' ('Cage of Wild Beasts') by a facetious critic,
and Fauvism was officially born.

Following his success at the Salon d'Automne, Vollard
commissioned some views of London from him, and he
visited England for the first time, returning in 1906. The

ANDRÉ DERAIN, *Henri Matisse*, 1905

summer of 1906 was spent painting at L'Estaque, where
he met Picasso, and in the next year he signed a contract
with Daniel-Henri Kahnweiler, Picasso's dealer. He
married on the strength of this new financial security,
and with his wife, Alice, went to live in Montmartre,
where his friendship with Picasso continued. Fernande
Olivier, Picasso's mistress at that time, has left a vivid
description of him:

> Slim, elegant, with a lively colour and enamelled black
> hair. With an English chic, somewhat striking. Fancy
> waistcoats, ties in crude colours, red and green.
> Always a pipe in his mouth, phlegmatic, mocking,
> cold, an arguer.

Alice Derain at this period was so calm and beautiful
that she was nicknamed 'La Vierge' – 'the Holy Virgin'.
Her husband's ties with Picasso and his circle were

André Derain in fancy dress as Louis XIV, 1935. Photo Papillon

strengthened when he supplied the illustrations for Apollinaire's first book of poetry, *L'Enchanteur pourissant* (1909), and illustrated a collection of poems by Max Jacob in 1912.

With the outbreak of war in 1914, Derain was mobilized and remained in the army throughout the conflict, fighting on the Somme, at Verdun and in the Vosges mountains. There was little opportunity to paint, but his career did not come entirely to a halt. The dealer Paul Guillaume gave him his first one-man show in 1916, with a catalogue preface written by Apollinaire; and he provided another set of illustrations, this time for André Breton's first book, *Mont de Piété*. He was forced to remain in the army until 1919, serving with the French occupation forces in Mainz, but when he was finally released the French art world received him with open arms. In 1919 he designed the ballet *La Boutique fantasque* for Diaghilev (the first of many ballet designs), which scored a major success, and in 1920 he signed

another contract with Kahnweiler, replaced by a contract with Paul Guillaume in 1923. Four books were published about his work between 1920 and 1924, and he began to move in fashionable circles. The aristocratic patron Count Etienne de Beaumont, who had set himself up as Diaghilev's rival, offered him further theatrical commissions in 1924 and 1926. His reputation rose to new heights when he was awarded the Carnegie Prize in 1928 and began to exhibit extensively abroad – in London in 1928; in Berlin, Frankfurt and Düsseldorf in 1929; in New York and Cincinnati in 1930; and once again in London and New York in 1931.

By now, Derain's art had evolved considerably since his Fauve days. First, he had passed through a period when he showed the influence of African art (of which he was a pioneer collector), and also of Picasso's Cubism. After the war, like many other artists, he felt the renewed appeal of Classicism. He went to Italy in 1921, for the Raphael centenary celebrations held that year, and was deeply impressed by High Renaissance painting. He also drew on more directly 'classical' sources, such as Fayum portraits and Roman mosaics. The increasing conservatism of his work was not challenged until 1931, when a book called *Pour et Contre Derain* (For and Against Derain), containing essays by various hands, was published. A particularly damaging verdict came from the veteran painter and critic Jacques-Emile Blanche, who wrote: 'Youth has departed; what remains is a highly cerebral and rather mechanical art.'

Derain's work now divided informed opinion – and those who defended him began to make him the pretext for a general condemnation of Modernism. During the 1930s he gradually lost touch with many of his old friends. He bought a large house at Chambourcy near Saint Germain-en-Laye, though he also maintained a *pied-à-terre* in Paris. The latter served several purposes: he found it difficult to find good models at Chambourcy, where he lived with Alice, his wife, her sister, and the latter's daughter; it also provided a convenient place to meet his mistresses.

Despite the animosity which some of the avant-garde now displayed towards him, he continued to receive plenty of official recognition. He was given a retrospective at the Kunsthalle in Bern in 1935, and was included in the important 'Exposition des Artistes Indépendants' held at the Petit Palais in connection with the Paris Exposition Universelle in 1937.

The Second World War was the beginning of Derain's long catastrophe. In 1940 he fled from his house in Chambourcy and returned to find that it had been requisitioned by the Germans; 1941 saw the birth of an illegitimate son, the child of a favourite model. During the Occupation he lived mostly in Paris, dividing his time between several households – his own studio, the house he had provided for his wife, and the apartment of his mistress. He was much courted by the Germans, since he belonged to a group of artists who could not be dismissed by Nazi theoreticians as 'degenerate' (as was the case with the Cubists and Surrealists), but who, on the contrary, represented the prestige of French culture, with which the Nazis wished to identify themselves. Hitler's Foreign Minister Ribbentrop wanted him to come to Germany and paint his whole family: Derain rejected this offer, but accepted an invitation to make an official visit to Germany in 1941. Vlaminck also agreed to accompany the party, and the tour was preceded by a series of official receptions designed to reconcile the two men, who had quarrelled some time previously. The German propaganda machine naturally made much of Derain's presence in the Reich, and after the Liberation he was branded as a collaborator and ostracized by many people.

Derain continued his public activity as an artist to some extent: he did book illustrations, including a splendid series for an edition of Rabelais's *Pantagruel* published in 1944. He executed more theatre commissions, notably the ballet *Mam'zelle Angot* for the Royal Opera House, Covent Garden, in 1947; Mozart's *Seraglio* for the Aix-en-Provence Festival in 1951; and Rossini's *Barber of Seville* for the same festival in 1953. But gradually he became more and more reclusive. He, his wife and her relations had returned to Chambourcy, together with his illegitimate son, whom he had now formally adopted. His wife gave the necessary consent for this, but the relationship between the couple was otherwise very bad; they were reputed to speak to one another only on rare occasions, and then about money (they had married under the French law of 'community of property' and Alice Derain was determined to protect her financial interests). He had another affair with a model, and a second illegitimate child was born, whom he dared not acknowledge. Derain was now increasingly filled with doubts about his own art. He once said ruefully:

I concentrate too much and too effectively on my painting and am in too close contact with it. I can visualize the shapes I want to portray and it is these shapes that are killing me. When I try to disengage myself from a choice between two known shapes, everything falls apart.

In 1953 Derain fell ill, and his sight was seriously affected. His wife made an attempt to seize control of his affairs and to keep certain old friends (and the mothers of his two children) apart from him. As soon as he was well again he and Alice separated. But he was not to enjoy his freedom from her for long. In 1954 he was knocked down by a truck in Chambourcy. He was taken to hospital, and at first it was thought he was not seriously injured, but the shock was too much for a man now in his seventies. He failed to recover, living only long enough to effect an official reconciliation with his wife.

ANDRÉ DERAIN with Geneviève,
rue Bonaparte, *c.* 1925.
Photographer unknown

Nabi, the Hebrew word for prophet, was the name that a group of young French artists took half-jokingly. This name was originally inspired by a brief contact between Gauguin and a young painter called Paul Sérusier (1865–1927) in Brittany in 1888.

Sérusier painted a small landscape under Gauguin's tuition, which employed the new 'synthetist' principles – an intensification through radical simplification of form and colour, and the organization of colour into flat, highly contrasted areas. Sérusier took his little painting back to Paris (where the work was promptly dubbed *The Talisman*), and preached Gauguin's doctrines to a group of friends of his own generation. These formed the nucleus of the Nabi group. Most of the Nabis, like Sérusier himself and his friend Maurice Denis (1870–1943), were mystical and philosophical by inclination, closely allied to the Symbolist movement, then dominant in both literature and the arts throughout Europe. The two most gifted members of the circle, Pierre Bonnard and Edouard Vuillard, were rather different. Both had a gift for depicting the intimacies of bourgeois life – Vuillard in fact preferred to describe himself as an 'intimist' – and their sumptuous orchestrated canvases, characterized by an eye for telling shapes as well as by the skilful use of pattern-on-pattern, offer a bridge between the art of Gauguin and that of the Fauves. Their work took the essential first step towards Modernism. Bonnard was to develop into one of the greatest painters of the twentieth century.

Above: PIERRE BONNARD,
Le Cannet, 1944.
Photo Henri Cartier-Bresson
Right: PIERRE BONNARD,
Large Nude in Bath, 1924

PIERRE BONNARD

It is inaccurate to dismiss Bonnard as a mere intimist, stranded by the onset of Modernism. He is in fact one of the most powerful artists produced by France this century, and Matisse, a shrewd judge of other painters' merits, regarded him with a respect he accorded to no other artist of the same generation as his own.

Bonnard was born in 1867, at Fontenay-aux-Roses near Paris. His father was Head Clerk at the French War Ministry, and he had an older brother and a younger sister. He was sent to boarding school at the age of ten, and subsequently attended various schools in Paris, including the famous Lycée Louis-le-Grand near the Sorbonne. When he passed his *baccalauréat* in 1885,

his father insisted that he study law, though he had already shown a strong propensity for art.

Bonnard had other ideas, and without completely abandoning his studies as a law student he registered at the Académie Julian, where he met Paul Sérusier, Maurice Denis, Gabriel Ibels and Paul Ranson. In July 1888 he took his law degree, and failed the oral examination. He was forced by his father to take an administrative post at the Registry Office, and later worked for the Public Prosecutor of the Seine District. While working unenthusiastically at these jobs, he also managed, in 1889, to get himself accepted by the Ecole des Beaux-Arts, where he met Edouard Vuillard and Xavier Roussel. The previous autumn, Sérusier had returned from Brittany, full of enthusiasm for Gauguin's teaching, and as a result he and his friends had formed themselves into a group which they called 'the Nabis' – *Nabi* is the Hebrew word for 'prophet'. Now, in June 1889, Gauguin and a group of followers showed at the Café Volpini, and his young admirers were filled with renewed admiration for his work.

In 1891, after his military service, Bonnard had his first public success: he won a competition for a champagne poster, which convinced his father to let him paint full time. The poster also attracted attention in other quarters. It was praised by Félix Fénéon, later to become a very important supporter of Bonnard's work, and it prompted an approach from Toulouse-Lautrec, who started designing posters in Bonnard's wake. The two men became good friends, despite the wide difference in temperament. In December Bonnard and his colleagues organized a Nabi show at the Galerie La Barc de Boutteville, their first public appearance as a group.

In 1893 Bonnard met Maria Boursin. Maria, who preferred to be called Marthe, became his constant companion, and her quirks of character were later to exercize a great influence over his work. Bonnard was now being drawn into the circle which surrounded the prestigious *Revue blanche*, then reckoned to be the best independent review in Paris. He held his first one-man show at Durand-Ruel in January 1896. It was praised by the important critic Gustave Geffroy, but Camille Pissarro, uncharacteristically malicious, wrote gleefully to his son that it was a complete fiasco: 'All the painters worth anything, Puvis, Degas, Renoir, Monet and your humble servant, unanimously term hideous the

exhibition held at Durand-Ruel's of the young Symbolist named Bonnard.' Later he was to change his mind, as were most of the other painters whom he mentioned. Bonnard also showed a few works in Brussels that year, at the Salon de la Libre Esthétique, and began his association with Lugné-Poë's experimental Théâtre de l'Oeuvre, by designing a programme for them. His most surprising connection with this theatre was to be the help he gave with the production of Alfred Jarry's explosive play *Ubu Roi*, which was given its premier in December 1896.

The dealer Ambroise Vollard, who had an almost infallible instinct for new artists, had for some time been commissioning prints from Bonnard, who at this stage was perhaps better known for his graphic work than his paintings, and these were shown with success in a mixed exhibition in 1899. But it was not Vollard who finally took him on: from 1900 the prestigious firm of Bernheim-Jeune were to be his dealers, and Bonnard's link with them was to be considerably strengthened after 1903, when *La Revue blanche* ceased publication, and Fénéon, who had been its secretary, moved over to Bernheim's. His first one-man show with Bernheim-Jeune did not, however, take place until November 1906.

By this stage Bonnard could think of himself as being an established artist. He travelled a good deal, going to Spain in 1905, to Belgium and Holland in 1906, to Algeria and Tunisia in 1908, and to Hamburg in 1913. He also travelled restlessly within France, spending increasing amounts of time in the South, on the Mediterranean coast. In 1912 he bought a country house called 'Ma Roulotte' ('My Caravan'), at Veronnet, near Vernon in Normandy, and this was to be his real base for more than a decade, though he also maintained a foothold in Paris.

When the First World War broke out Bonnard was already too old to be called up, and the main effect of the war was to put a stop to most of his travels. He remained very much in fashion, perhaps more so than ever. Diaghilev, who had commissioned a poster from him for *La Légende de Joseph*, his last big pre-war production, now asked him to do the sets for *Jeux*, Nijinsky's second show as a choreographer. The ballet was a failure, but the set is remembered as being mysteriously beautiful, and perfectly matched to the mood of Debussy's score.

In 1925 there was another shift in Bonnard's life. He continued to feel drawn by the South, and now, in 1925, he bought a house at Le Cannet. In the same year he finally married Marthe. At first they divided their time between Le Cannet and the house at Veronnet, which was not sold until 1938. Bonnard continued to do what was expected of a successful painter in mid-career. In 1926, for example, he was a member of the jury for the Carnegie Prize, and travelled to the United States, visiting Pittsburgh, Philadelphia, Chicago, Washington and New York. In the mid-1930s he frequently deserted the South for the Channel coast, particularly Deauville, where he found the changeable light more interesting. But Marthe's neurasthenia encouraged him to spend more time at home. She had an obsession with bathing, and spent many hours a day in the bathroom, and scenes showing her in the bath or at her toilette came to play a larger and larger part in Bonnard's oeuvre.

The outbreak of war in 1939 confined the Bonnards entirely to Le Cannet, and they now saw only a small circle of people. One important friendship was with Matisse, also living in the South, with whom Bonnard had a regular exchange of letters. It was Matisse who tried to give him some consolation when Marthe died in January 1942. Bonnard survived the War, and lived on until January 1947, cared for by his niece, Renée Terrasse, who came to live with him in 1945.

Some extraordinary late self-portraits show the extent of his desolation in these final years. It was not merely that Marthe was dead; he had outlived all his old friends. Yet the late paintings are also among his strongest and most radical works.

EDOUARD VUILLARD sitting on a wicker chair, Villeneuve-sur-Yonne. Photographer unknown

EDOUARD VUILLARD

In his lifetime Edouard Vuillard was briefly considered important both historically and aesthetically, but his reputation then diminished. Born in 1868, at Cuiseaux, a small town in the Jura, Vuillard moved with his family to Paris in 1877. Here he attended the Lycée Condorcet, one of the best schools in the city, and made friendships which were to last for the rest of his life. Vuillard's father, a soldier turned tax-collector, was much older than his mother, and died in 1884. Madame Vuillard had already, by this time, set herself up as a professional corsetière, and her son was brought up in a household of women, since the work was done at home. His family had originally assumed that he would, like his father, pursue a military career, but by the late 1880s, perhaps under the influence of his classmate Ker-Xavier Roussel (who was to marry Vuillard's older sister Marie), he decided to follow his vocation to be a painter.

By 1887 he was taking day-classes in art at Delacroix's old studio in the Place Furstenberg on the Left Bank. He tried the Ecole des Beaux-Arts but disliked the rigid curriculum, so in 1888 he moved to the Académie Julian, the most celebrated of the 'free studios' where artists

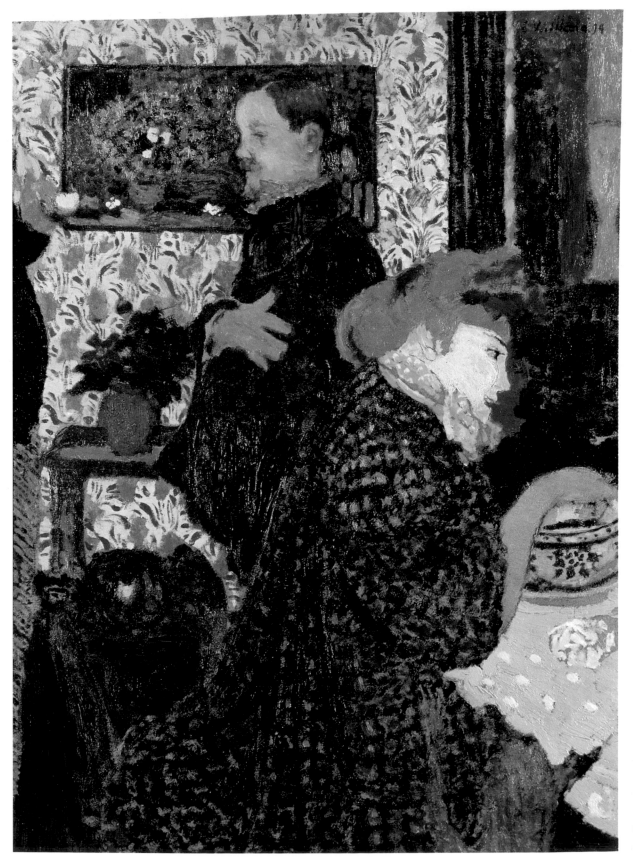

EDOUARD VUILLARD, *Misia and Vallotton*, 1894

could practise life drawing. In 1889 he had a drawing accepted for the Salon – a portrait of his grandmother. It was the only time he exhibited there. Meanwhile his circle of artistic friends was widening. It now included not only Roussel and Maurice Denis (both from the Lycée Condorcet), but also Pierre Bonnard, Paul Ranson, Henri-Georges Ibels and Paul Sérusier. These were leading members of the Nabis Group, formed in 1888 as an expression of the ethos of the Symbolist movement in art and literature, and in response to the influence of Gauguin, whom Sérusier had met in Brittany, at Pont-Aven.

These friends had an important influence on Vuillard's attitudes to art, as did another school-mate, the actor-director Aurélien-Marie Lugné-Poë, the greatest theatrical innovator of the time. Vuillard designed programmes for the Théâtre Libre, where Lugné-Poë was an actor and assistant-director, and later both programmes and scenery for Lugné-Poë's own Théâtre de l'Oeuvre, which put on productions of all the most innovative dramatists of the time, chief among them Maeterlinck and Ibsen. Painting scenery taught Vuillard how to work with distemper. It also gave him the ambition to paint large-scale decorations; the preference for decorative works which filled whole walls, as opposed to easel paintings, was a part of Symbolist doctrine.

Despite this, the majority of the paintings which he produced in the 1890s, the most innovative decade of his career, are quite small in scale. Vuillard described himself as an 'intimist': many of the works he produced at this time show life in the Vuillard household, and feature his mother, his sister Marie, his grandmother, and his mother's employees. The most intense feature family occasions, such as meals, and seem to suggest that a considerable degree of tension existed between Marie Vuillard and her mother. Vuillard made skilful use of dense pattern-on-pattern to create a feeling of emotional claustrophobia. The Vuillards were not rich, but Edouard gradually moved into a more prosperous milieu, that of the Natanson brothers and their luxurious Symbolist periodical La Revue blanche. Other habitués of this circle included Toulouse-Lautrec, the critic Félix Fénéon – perhaps the best writer on art of his time – and the great Symbolist poet Stéphane Mallarmé. Mallarmé, who advocated suggestion rather than description, wanted Vuillard to illustrate his most important poem 'Hérodiade', but Vuillard, thinking the subject-matter

not domestic enough for him, avoided the commission.

Vuillard paid more attention to Misia Natanson, the wife of Thadée (another school-fellow from the Lycée Condorcet). Of Polish descent, and a gifted pianist – she was the pupil of Gabriel Fauré – Misia mesmerized many men. Her niece by marriage, Annette Vaillant, later described her as having 'the swagger of a low-life princess'. The shy Vuillard was secretly in love with her, and Misia, in her own notoriously unreliable memoirs, published long after the event, describes how once, as they walked in the woods, she stumbled, he took her arm – but then the moment for a declaration of love passed.

However, the paintings Vuillard made of life in the Natanson household, both in Paris and in various places they rented in the country close to Paris, have a hushed magic which is in itself equivalent to a declaration of love. The Revue blanche circle broke up at the end of the decade, and Vuillard, by this time a well known artist, passed into a more conventional circle, that of Lucy Hessel, wife of the immensely successful art-dealer Jos Hessel. Lucy was to guard his interests for the rest of his long career and became his sole emotional focus after the death of his mother. The intensity of his work faded, though he produced some telling portraits, and the new generation of Modernists did not consider him to belong to their group, though they still made a place for Bonnard, his colleague and contemporary. Vuillard died in 1940.

C ubism had two identities, one public and one private. The style was jointly evolved by Picasso and Braque, on the basis of observations derived from Cézanne, and also, to some extent, from ethnographical art. It made its public début with Braque's one-man exhibition organized by the dealer Daniel-Henri Kahnweiler in November 1908. But after this both he and Picasso more or less went to ground, and the Cubist banner was upheld by others, notably Robert Delaunay, Fernand Léger, Henri Le Fauconnier, Albert Gleizes and Jean Metzinger at the Salon des Indépendants in 1910; and by these and others at the same Salon in 1911.

In 1912 a group of Cubists with Delaunay at their head exhibited at the Galerie La Boëtie, now calling themselves the 'Section d'Or' (Golden Section). When he reviewed this show, Apollinaire coined the term 'Orphism', applying it to Delaunay in particular. The first published statement of Cubist theory was *Du Cubisme*, by Metzinger and Gleizes, published in 1912; this was followed by Apollinaire's *Les Peintres cubistes*, published in 1913.

The internal logic of Cubist development led Picasso and Braque from the Analytic Cubism with which they started to the Synthetic Cubism of 1912, which sprang from the new technique of collage. At this point they were joined in their explorations by Juan Gris. Cubism had a widespread and persistent influence, and affected artists generally classified as Expressionists (Marc), Futurists (Severini), and even Dadaists (Picabia and Duchamp).

Above: FERNAND LÉGER, 1954.
Photo Ida Kar
Right: FERNAND LÉGER, stage model for *La Création du Monde* (The Creation of the World), 1923

FERNAND LÉGER

Fernand Léger still ranks as an under-appreciated artist, on the whole more respected than loved. His work has a deliberate harshness which repels many spectators.

He was born in Argentan in Normandy in February 1881. His father was a stock-raiser of combative temperament who died before Léger was sixteen. His mother was gentle and pious, with little head for business; after his husband's death she frittered away most of the family inheritance. From 1890–96 Léger studied at the municipal school in Argentan, and then at a religious school in the small town of Tinchebray. Later when he announced his intention of becoming a painter his mother and uncle sent him to a school of architectu in Caen – in their eyes, architecture was a more serious profession than painting.

In 1900 he went to Paris, where he found employment as an architectural draughtsman, but within two years he had to do his military service. When he was released he applied to the Ecole des Arts Decoratifs in Paris, and was accepted, but did not find the curriculum interesting enough to attend classes regularly. He failed the entrance examination for the Ecole des Beaux-Arts but entered Gérôme's studio as a 'free [independent] pupil', then moved to that of Gabriel Ferrier. Surprisingly, Gerôme, the arch-conservative and opponent of Impressionism, proved the more liberal master of the two. He called his avant-garde pupils 'the red and green gang' because they liked brutal oppositions of complementary colours. Léger probably inherited from Gérôme his deep respect for the great academic J. L. David. Later he went so far as to say: 'I love David because he is anti-Impressionist'.

From 1903–4 Léger once again did routine work in an architect's office; he also worked as a photographic retoucher to earn some extra money. He found himself a studio, which he shared with a boyhood friend from Argentan, and began painting. But eventually poverty and overwork wore him down. He fell ill in 1906 and was forced to spend the winter in Corsica. Some months after his return he was vastly impressed by the great Cézanne retrospective held in 1907 as part of the Salon d'Automne. 'I had to spend years getting rid of Cézanne's influence,' he complained later. 'He had such a hold on me that, to get rid of it, I had to go all the way to abstraction.' In the same year he went to live in La Ruche, and residence in this famous group of studios, nicknamed for its resemblance to a beehive, brought him into contact not only with numerous other artists, but with a number of strange characters who had only a peripheral relationship to art:

> I recall there among the rest four Russians, nihilists. I was never able to understand how they lived in a single room three metres square and I never understood how it was that they always had vodka. Vodka was expensive, but of course it helped one to live...

He also got to know the Cubists and their advocate, Apollinaire, as well as Apollinaire's undeclared rival, the poet Blaise Cendrars:

Apollinaire never liked my painting despite what he wrote. At the same period I also knew Cendrars, but it was completely different with him, we had the same antennae. Like me, he picked things up in the street. We were both fascinated by modern life, we rushed towards it. But I've never read his books – it isn't books that interest me.

Notwithstanding this final declaration, Léger did become one of Cendrars's chief illustrators.

Despite Apollinaire's hidden hostility to Léger's painting, the dealer Daniel-Henri Kahnweiler began to show an interest in his work. In 1910 he was given space at Kahnweiler's gallery, where Picasso and Braque were exhibiting. He was now associating with the dissident Cubists who were to form the Section d'Or group. Delaunay was one of the most vocal members of this group and it is clear that Léger agreed with his complaint about the Cubism of Braque and Picasso: 'It looks as if they paint with spiders' webs.' The Section d'Or held its first exhibition in 1911, and in the same year Léger made considerable impact at the Salon des Indépendants with *Nudes in the Forest*. By 1912 Kahnweiler felt sufficient confidence to buy all the pictures in his studio, and to give him a one-man exhibition, and in 1913 he offered Léger a contract. Léger's reputation was also beginning to spread abroad – he was invited to show at the First Autumn Salon organized by *Der Sturm* in Berlin.

All these promising developments were cut short by the war. Léger was mobilized on 2 August 1914, and fought in the Argonne and then served as a stretcher-bearer at Verdun until he was gassed in September 1916:

The war was a major event for me. At the Front there was a hyper-poetic atmosphere which excited me greatly ... the war brought me down to earth ... I left Paris when I was painting entirely abstract work ... suddenly I was at the level of the whole French people.

He was in hospital for more than a year, and was finally discharged at the end of 1917. In December 1919 he married Jeanne Lohy.

During the inter-war period Léger's activity was particularly complex. In 1920 he met the architect Le Corbusier, and became associated with the magazine *L'Esprit Nouveau*, directed by Le Corbusier and Amadée Ozenfant. *L'Esprit Nouveau* was founded to defend the machine aesthetic, and much of Léger's work at this period shows a preoccupation with machines. In 1925, at the Exposition des Arts Décoratifs, he supplied murals (his first attempts in the genre) for the Pavillon de l'Esprit Nouveau by Le Corbusier. He collaborated with Delaunay in decorating the entrance hall of a 'French Embassy' designed by Mallet-Stevens and did a good deal of work for the theatre and the cinema, growing increasingly sceptical about the future of easel painting. For the Ballets Suédois of Rolf de Maré (the chief rivals of Diaghilev's Ballets Russes) he designed a set for the ballet *Skating Rink* in 1921, and in 1922 the important *La Création du monde* with a book by Cendrars and music by Darius Milhaud. In 1924 Léger created the first 'abstract' film, *Le Ballet mécanique*, with cinematography by Man Ray and Dudley Murphy and music by Georges Antheil. A decade later, no doubt on the strength of this, Alexander Korda invited him to come to London to design the sets for *The Shape of Things to Come*, his film based on the book of the same title by H. G. Wells.

Léger was at this time active as a teacher in the Académie Moderne, which had been founded by Othon Friesz in 1912. He began giving classes there in late 1923 or at the beginning of 1924. When Léger left the Académie Moderne in 1931, he transferred for a while to the Académie de la Grande Chaumière, and then opened an atelier of his own in the rue de la Sablière. The school subsequently moved premises twice, but, under the title Académie de l'Art Contemporain, it survived until 1939.

Léger regarded himself as a man of the Left, and presented one of his own paintings to the Pushkin Museum in Moscow in 1927. Throughout the 1930s he remained a close friend of the Communist deputy and poet Paul Vaillant Couturier, who set up the Association d'Ecrivains et d'Artistes Révolutionnaires in 1932 – Léger was a founder member. He hastened to put himself at the disposal of the French Council of Trade Unions, dominated by the Left, and in 1937 planned the décor for their Congress, held in the Vélodrome d'Hiver in Paris.

During the 1930s Léger travelled widely, spending much time in America. His first visit took place in 1931, and he returned in 1935 with Le Corbusier, when he had exhibitions at the Museum of Modern Art in New York and at the Art Institute of Chicago, and in 1938–39. On this third occasion he decorated an apartment for Nelson Rockefeller in New York, stayed at Provincetown with John Dos Passos, and lectured at Yale.

When the Germans invaded in 1940, Léger first took refuge in Normandy, then in Bordeaux, and afterwards made his way to Marseilles. From Marseilles, in October 1940, he was able to sail to the United States. The connections he had already made there stood him in good stead: he taught at Yale, and at Mills College in Oakland, California, and he had exhibits at the Paul Rosenberg Gallery in 1942, at the Fogg Art Museum, and then with the Valentine and Sam Kootz galleries in New York in 1945, before returning to France that December.

During his American exile Léger made a significant new friendship, with the progressive Catholic priest Father Couturier, who in 1946 commissioned him to design a mosaic at the church of Assy (Haute-Savoie). This was the first of a series of church commissions, the most important of which came in 1951: he was asked to design stained glass and tapestries for the church at Audincourt (Doubs). Léger cherished his left-wing connections (he attended the Communist Front Peace Congress at Wroclaw, Poland in 1948), and defended himself somewhat uneasily for his service to the Church:

> I was not double-faced. For me it was not an evasion to glorify sacred symbols – nails, or ciboria, or the Crown of Thorns; or to make my subject Christ's Passion. I am perfectly sound and healthy; my spirit has no need of crutches. It was quite simply that I was given an unhoped for opportunity to decorate vast surfaces, following my own artistic ideals.

At the time when he was carrying out these church commissions, Léger was busy painting the huge (proletarian) figure-compositions which are the culmination of his late style. *Les Constructeurs*, which is perhaps the best known of them, dates from 1950, which was also the year in which his wife died.

In 1952, Léger married again. His second wife, Nadia Kodessevitch, was a long-time associate who had been with him since 1924 when she enrolled as a pupil at the Académie Moderne, and who had run his school during his frequent absences. They settled at Gif-sur-Yvette, Oise. Léger was now receiving commissions commensurate with his status as one of the Grand Old Men of the Modern movement. In 1952 he was asked to paint a mural panel for the new United Nations Building in New York. Honours came to him too: in 1955 he was awarded the Grand Prix at the Bienal in São Paolo. He made a final trip to Eastern Europe, to attend a congress in Czechoslovakia, and returned home where he died suddenly on 17 August 1955.

PABLO PICASSO

Pablo Picasso is the most important artist of the Modernist epoch, but much of his achievement remains controversial. The many authors who have written about him characteristically seek to discard one or another aspect of his enormous œuvre, to concentrate upon some central core, which, however, seems fated to remain undefinable. The same thing can be said of Picasso's biography, which is full of shifting perspectives.

Though closely associated with Catalan culture in his youth, Picasso was not born in Catalonia but in Málaga, in 1881, and lived there until he was ten. The name Picasso came from his mother, not his father, Don José Ruiz Blasco, an academic painter of mediocre gifts and a professional teacher of art. After leaving Málaga the family spent four years in Coruña, until Picasso's father was appointed Professor at the School of Fine Arts in Barcelona, culturally the liveliest city in Spain.

Picasso's artistic talents were already developing at prodigious speed – he seems never to have been a 'child artist' – and he rapidly achieved a mastery of the approved academic style of the day. Since his father was already a professional painter, he met with no discouragement in following an artistic career: one story has it that Picasso's father was so impressed by his son's talent that he ceremoniously resigned palette and brushes to him. Picasso studied at the Academy in Barcelona, and also, briefly, at the Royal Academy of San Fernando in Madrid, but neither institution had much to teach him. In Barcelona, as a young man, he formed part of a circle of *fin de siècle* artists and intellectuals who gathered at a tavern called 'Els Quatre Gats' ('The Four Cats' in Catalan). Picasso's work at this time was influenced by French painters of urban life such as Steinlen and Toulouse-Lautrec.

In 1900 Picasso paid his first visit to Paris, in the company of Carlos Casamegas, another young painter from the same group in Barcelona. Casamegas's suicide (due to his impotence and unrequited love) supplied much of the inspiration for the paintings of Picasso's Blue Period, which was his declaration of artistic independence. In the opening years of the century he went back and forth between Paris, Madrid and Barcelona. He had an exhibition with the perceptive dealer Ambroise Vollard in 1901, which brought him the friendship of the poet Max Jacob (until then his Parisian

PABLO PICASSO in his Vallauris studio, 1965. Photo Alexander Liberman

circle had consisted almost entirely of emigré Spaniards). Jacob introduced him to other writers, notably Guillaume Apollinaire. Finally, in 1904, Picasso settled in Paris in the dilapidated studio building known as the 'Bateau-Lavoir' because of its fancied resemblance to the boats then used for washing laundry on the Seine, and soon became the centre of a circle of avant-garde artists and poets. He found a mistress, Fernande Olivier, who later wrote a book of memoirs recording this era, and he gained the friendship of the American writer and collector, Gertrude Stein. Olivier provided a description of Picasso's appearance at this time:

> Small, black, thick-set, restless, disquieting, with eyes dark, profound, piercing, strange, almost staring. Awkward gestures, the hands of a woman, poorly

dressed, badly groomed. A thick lock of hair, black and shining, slashed across his intelligent and obstinate forehead.

The Blue Period evolved into the less doleful but still melancholy Rose Period, and this gave way to a series of *Saltimbanques* – delicate paintings of circus performers and itinerant entertainers, with an echo of the academic Symbolist Puvis de Chavannes. In 1906 Picasso abandoned these, to paint some pictures marked by a heavy primitivism. These led, in the following months, to an extraordinary creative explosion. In 1906–7 Picasso produced what is still perhaps his best-known painting, *Les Demoiselles d'Avignon*. This ferocious group of female nudes was jokingly christened by the poet André Salmon for its pretended likeness to the inmates of a particularly low-class brothel in Barcelona. It shocked the few people who saw it in Picasso's studio: Braque, for instance, said that Picasso wanted people to exchange a normal diet for one of tow and flax (although soon afterwards he himself painted a similar picture of a single nude).

One of the ingredients in *Les Demoiselles* was the late work of Cézanne. Another was the art of black Africa. For the moment it was Africa which triumphed, and Picasso moved into what has been called his Negro period. This was followed by another, and decisive, shift, the evolution of Analytical Cubism, which Picasso created in collaboration with Braque. Cubism was different from the previous styles Picasso had used because it had an intricate formal grammar, a way of coding appearances which became a new language for a whole generation of artists. For a long time it was these followers who were the public representatives of Cubism, as Picasso and Braque were reluctant to exhibit their work in the big Salons where new stylistic experiments generally made their début.

Picasso nevertheless built a powerful reputation amongst the small circle of people who mattered – dealers, collectors and critics – and by 1909 was doing well enough to move into a new and more comfortable studio in the boulevard de Clichy. In 1912 he left Fernande Olivier for a new mistress, Eva (Marcelle Humbert). She is the only one of Picasso's companions who did not inspire a series of portraits, though her name, or the phrase 'Ma Jolie' which refers to her, can be found inscribed on a number of Cubist paintings.

In August 1914 Picasso's link with Braque was severed when war broke out. Picasso, as a Spanish citizen, was not required to serve, and he remained in grey and dispiriting Paris. In the autumn of 1915 Eva died of cancer, and a little later Picasso moved out to Montrouge in the suburbs. Diaghilev rescued him from his depression by inviting him to Rome at Cocteau's suggestion, to collaborate on the new ballet, *Parade*. Once he had arrived Picasso associated closely with Diaghilev's company, which formed a small world of its own, and soon fell in love with a member of the *corps de ballet*, Olga Kokhlova, the daughter of a Russian general. In 1917 he accompanied the ballet to Spain; and in 1918 he and Olga returned to Paris, while the rest of the Ballets Russes went on to South America. In July they married. Olga had conventional bourgeois tastes, and they took a smart apartment in the rue de la Boëtie. For a while Picasso

sampled fashionable life in Paris and on the Riviera. In 1921 his first child, a son named Paulo, was born.

Picasso was now in the midst of a new stylistic phase, the Neo-Classical Period, a reversion to the antique world which had fascinated Poussin and Ingres. It shocked some of his former friends in the avant-garde, who attributed it to his association, through Olga, with the fashionable world. But he was also keeping a shrewd eye on the antics of the Dadaists, and then on the development of Dada's successor, Surrealism. The kind of life Olga liked soon began to pall, and so did her obsessive jealousy. In the late 1920s Picasso's work became increasingly savage and misogynistic, and the mood did not change until he fulfilled Olga's worst fears and found a new mistress, a placid seventeen-year-old girl called Marie-Thérèse Walter whom he met in 1932. Her calm beauty made her the inspiration for a number of paintings, and also for a series of large sculptured heads. The latter were made in a new studio at the seventeenth-century Norman Château of Boisgeloup – Picasso was now wealthy enough to begin the process of accumulating property which continued for the rest of his life.

In 1935 he obtained an official separation from Olga, who continued to haunt him when she could; and in 1936, soon after Marie-Thérèse had borne him a daughter, Maia, he found another companion, a Yugoslav photographer named Dora Maar. A more intelligent woman and a far more complex personality than Marie-Thérèse, she gradually displaced the latter in Picasso's affections. He still possessed his apartment in the rue de la Boëtie, but it now seemed cluttered and inadequate, and it was Dora who found him vast new studios in an ancient building in the rue des Grands Augustins.

During the early 1930s Picasso renewed his ties with Spain. He visited his family in Barcelona in 1933, and made a longer visit in 1934. In 1936, the year the Civil

Pablo Picasso,
The Scallop Shell, 1912

Pablo Picasso in his studio, boulevard de Clichy, Paris, 1909.
Photographer unknown

War broke out, a group of young admirers organized an exhibition for him in Barcelona – the first he had had in Spain for a quarter of a century. During the war his sympathies were vehemently with the Republicans, and the Republican Government was well aware of his value to them. They stressed the link by giving him the Honorary Directorship of the Prado Museum. Picasso reciprocated by painting the huge canvas *Guernica*, which was shown in the Spanish Pavilion at the Paris Exposition Universelle of 1937 and was afterwards sent on tour. The composition is a bitter and effective condemnation of the bombing of the Basque capital by Franco's German allies.

During the late 1930s Picasso continued his habit of visiting the Mediterranean every summer, and when war broke out in 1939 he was staying at Antibes with Dora Maar and his devoted secretary and court-jester, Jaime Sabartés. He went to Paris and put his affairs in order, then retired to Royan on the coast near Bordeaux and

remained there until October 1940, when he returned to Paris for the rest of the war. The apartment in the rue de la Boëtie was definitively abandoned, and he went to live in the cavernous spaces of the rue des Grands Augustins, which he turned into a private world. He kept himself strictly apart from the occupying German forces, but does not seem to have been much troubled by them, both because he was not French and because his art was not to their taste. The subject-matter of the paintings he produced, such as the series of still lifes with a skull and a candle, echoes the all-prevailing gloom of those years.

With the Liberation, Picasso suddenly found he had become one of the sights of Paris, the symbol of a new epoch of freedom. To some extent he accepted the role of public figure. He joined the Communist Party, and for the next few years was a regular attender at Peace Congresses held in Paris, Rome, Wroclaw and Sheffield. The Party made good use of this eminent recruit – his drawing of a dove became one of its emblems. He painted a number of ambitious political works which can be thought of as successors to *Guernica*, though they failed to win the same universal acceptance. They include *The Charnel House* (1944–45), a commemoration of the concentration camps, and *Massacre in Korea* (1951).

After the war Picasso went to live on the Riviera. Dora Maar had been displaced by Françoise Gilot, whom he had met just after the Liberation. She was celebrated in a new group of portraits, often as 'femme fleur'. During their period together Picasso lived in Vallauris – he became interested in the local potteries and revivified the industry by collaborating with the local artisans.

In 1955, after separating from Françoise, he moved to La Californie, a pompous turn-of-the-century villa overlooking Cannes. His new companion, Jacqueline Roque, was eventually to become his wife in 1961. La Californie has been the subject of many descriptions, which celebrate the pell-mell accumulation of objects with which Picasso filled its rooms. He remained there until the development of the Riviera coastline began to encroach upon the property and spoil its view. He then transferred himself to the vast seventeenth-century Château de Vauvenargues near Aix, which he bought in 1958 and moved into fully in 1961. Finding that this had the opposite defect of being too isolated, he returned to the coast, purchasing an old Provençal manor house called Notre-de-Dame-de-Vie, overlooking Mougins.

Picasso enjoyed an extraordinarily vigorous and creative old age, but in 1965 he was forced to undergo a prostate operation and after this there was always a note of desperation in the ceaseless production of his work. More and more it became a sardonic commentary on the inevitable process of physical degeneration. Though his prestige remained immense, he had started to lose touch with the avant-garde art world and the respect of the ruling junta of theoreticians and critics. His last major exhibition in his own lifetime was held at the Palais des Papes in Avignon in 1970. It consisted of a vast mass of new work, headlong and brutal in style, which alarmed the public and alienated the reviewers. It is only more recently that these works have come to be seen as precursors of the Neo-Expressionism which dominated the art of the first half of the 1980s. A series of no less than 347 prints executed in the space of seven months in 1968 was better received, though their content was often harsh: they jeered sardonically at the illusions of youth and were equally fierce in their condemnation of the impotence of old age. Their undisguised eroticism delighted some and offended others, but Picasso had gone a long way beyond caring what anybody thought of him. He died in 1973, and his departure brought a whole epoch to a close.

GEORGES BRAQUE

Georges Braque was simultaneously a revolutionary and a conservative: his paintings were an evolving, constantly revised statement of his ideas concerning the nature of art. Though he remained fiercely anti-academic throughout his career, he was one of the leading modern advocates of the value of craftsmanship in painting. It was a symptom of this that he even ground his own colours.

Many of his attitudes were inherited, and came from his family background. His father and his grandfather were master house-painters, with the specialized skills demanded by the elaboration of late nineteenth-century interior decoration. Braque was born in 1882 at Argenteuil, just outside Paris, but in 1890 his family moved to Normandy and settled in Le Havre, and he always remained more Norman than Parisian. From 1897 onwards he attended evening classes at the local Ecole des Beaux-Arts, and the following year he left school and was apprenticed to a house-painter, with the idea that he should eventually take over the family business. His apprenticeship was completed in Paris under another house-painter, a friend and former employee of his father, and while he was doing this he also continued to study drawing and painting at evening classes.

Above: GEORGES BRAQUE,
Bottle and Fishes, 1910
Right: GEORGES BRAQUE
in his studio at 5,
Impasse de Guelma,
Paris, *c.* 1911.
Photographer unknown

After his military service his parents agreed that he should train to be an artist, and in the autumn of 1902 he returned to Montmartre, where he had lived previously. He enrolled at the Académie Humbert, where he met Marie Laurencin and Francis Picabia, and tried Léon Bonnat's classes at the Ecole des Beaux-Arts, which he abandoned after two months because he found them impossibly rigid and conservative.

In 1904 Braque decided that he had had enough of academic instruction and set up in a studio of his own. His first public appearance was at the Salon des Indépendants in March 1905, with seven paintings which he afterwards destroyed as being immature. Through his friendship with Othon Friesz, who had attended the same *lycée* in Le Havre, he was gradually being drawn into the ranks of the Fauves. In 1907 he met Matisse, Vlaminck and Derain and his style became fully Fauvist. His work was now attracting favourable attention, and he was able to sign a contract with the dealer Daniel-Henri Kahnweiler, who introduced him to the poet and critic Guillaume Apollinaire. It was Apollinaire who took Braque to Picasso's studio in the Bateau-Lavoir in Montmartre, where he saw the great canvas of *Les Demoiselles d'Avignon* which Picasso had just abandoned. According to Fernande Olivier, Picasso's mistress at that time, Braque reacted against it sharply; in December 1907, however, he painted a large female nude in the same style.

By 1908 Braque was producing his earliest Cubist canvases, the L'Estaque landscapes, heavily influenced by Cézanne. A group of these new paintings was rejected by the jury of that year's Salon d'Automne, even though Matisse was one of its members. In compensation for this, and also to protect his investment, Kahnweiler gave Braque a one-man show in November. Reviewing the exhibition, the art critic Louis Vauxelles rather condescendingly remarked: 'M. Braque is an exceedingly bold young man. ... He despises form and reduces everything, landscapes and figures and houses, to geometrical patterns, to cubes'. Thus the term 'Cubism' was born.

By 1909 Picasso and Braque had formed not only a close friendship but also an artistic alliance – Braque described them as being, at this period, 'like two mountaineers roped together'. In 1911 numbers and letters began to appear in Braque's canvases, and in the next year he made his first collages, inspired by scraps

GEORGES BRAQUE, *Fruit Dish, Ace of Clubs*, 1913

of wood-grained wallpaper which seemed to introduce a necessary element of reality into compositions which had now become puzzlingly hermetic in their search for every possible nuance of form. A little later he began to make good use of the techniques he had learned during his apprenticeship as a house-painter – the various tricks used to produce imitation wood-grain and marble in paint.

In the summer of 1914 Braque was at Sorgues near Avignon, where he and his wife had rented a house for the summer (he had married Marcelle Laprés in 1912). At the outbreak of war he was immediately mobilized, and it was Picasso, living nearby, who saw him off at Avignon railway station. The war put an end to their collaboration, which was never renewed.

In May 1915 Braque was severely wounded in the head; he had to be trepanned and a long convalescence followed. In April 1916 he went to Sorgues on sick leave, and after this was discharged from the army as

GEORGES BRAQUE in his studio, Impasse du Douanier, Paris, *c.* 1935–36. Photo Brassaï

permanently unfit. His friends threw a banquet for him in Paris the following January, to celebrate his recovery. During the last year of the war Braque moved into a phase of Synthetic Cubism, with planes arranged decoratively, which paralleled Picasso's work of the past three years. In 1919 he held a successful exhibition at L'Effort Moderne, the gallery run by Léonce Rosenberg, who had replaced Kahnweiler as his dealer – the latter counted as an 'enemy alien' and had retired to Switzerland. This show served to confirm Braque's reputation as a leading Modernist; but, like many of the leading avant-garde artists of the time, chief among them Picasso, he moved into a 'classical' phase in the early 1920s. Good examples of this are the *Canephorae*, a series of paintings of Greek-inspired female figures bearing flowers and fruit. This stylistic shift coincided with a change of residence, from Montmartre to Montparnasse. By 1925 Braque was prosperous enough to move again, this time to a house built for him by the leading architect Auguste Perret, near the Parc Montsouris. This was to be his Paris residence for the remainder of his life.

He was still attracting the attention of the fashionable art world. Both Diaghilev and Count Etienne de Beaumont commissioned ballet décors from him, and a special room was devoted to his work in the Salon d'Automne of 1922, in honour of his fortieth birthday. In the 1930s his reputation had become international. His first large-scale retrospective was staged at the Kunsthalle, Basle, in 1933: in 1937 he was awarded first prize at the Carnegie International, Pittsburgh; and in 1939–40 he had retrospectives in Chicago, Washington and San Francisco.

Braque was now dividing his time between his house in Paris and one he had had built in 1930, at Varengeville on the coast of Normandy, in traditional Norman style. The German invasion forced him to take refuge in the Limousin, and then in the Pyrenees, but in the autumn of 1940 he moved back to Paris and remained there undisturbed throughout the German Occupation. In 1943, for the second time, a special room was devoted to his work at the Salon d'Automne.

In 1945 and 1947 his routine was interrupted by two serious illnesses, but he made a good recovery, and in 1948 exhibited at the Venice Biennale where he was awarded the First Prize for painting. The following year he began work on the paintings of *The Studio* series, the culmination of the last phase of his work. The series was completed in 1956. After this, Braque's health began to fail and the physical effort of making paintings became increasingly onerous. Much of his creative energy was now diverted into making colour lithographs. He had executed the first of these with the master printer Mourlot soon after the war, and now his use of the technique took on a simplicity and directness reminiscent of the paper cut-outs which Matisse made at the end of his life. Braque also simplified the imagery in his paintings, using in particular the silhouette of a bird in flight which had first made its appearance in the various representations of his studio. He also painted abandoned agricultural machines and implements, producing images which are strangely reminiscent of Van Gogh's last painting, *The Cornfield*. With these works Braque seemed to return to a version of the Fauvism with which he had begun his career. He died in 1963.

ROBERT AND SONIA DELAUNAY

The liberation of colour in twentieth-century art owes much to the two Delaunays, yet there is also a feeling of lack of fulfilment about their careers, especially Robert's.

They were both born in 1885, but in very different circumstances. Robert was French, and came from an aristocratic background. His father was an engineer, and was divorced from his mother, Countess Berthe Félicie de Rose, soon after Robert's birth. Robert was brought up largely by his uncle by marriage, Charles Damour, who had a handsome property near Bourges. He was educated first in Paris, then at a boarding school in Bourges, then once again in Paris, at the Lycée Vanves. He was a poor scholar, and his spelling remained atrocious all his life. At the age of seventeen he declared his intention of becoming an artist, and was apprenticed to the Rosin Decorative Studio in Paris, which specialized in producing theatrical backdrops. From here he seems to have derived his lifelong taste for large canvases, and his confidence in tackling them. His earliest work was Impressionist in style, and later he became enamoured of the Neo-Impressionists, especially the coarse, bold version of the style used by Henri-Edmond Cross. He first exhibited his work in public at the Salon des Indépendants of 1904, and he also showed in the Salon d'Automne in 1904 and 1906. His earliest important artistic friendships were with 'Le Douanier' Rousseau and with Jean Metzinger, later to be a leading theoretician of Cubism. In 1907 he was summoned for compulsory

military service, but after six months was transferred to the reserves on the grounds of ill health and given a job as regimental librarian. He took the opportunity to catch up on the reading he had neglected at school. After a further six months of this he was excused the rest of his service and discharged.

Sonia Delaunay was born Sonia Stern, the third child of a Jewish factory worker in the Ukraine. At the age of five she was adopted by her uncle, Henri Terk, a prosperous lawyer in St Petersburg. Henceforward she was provided with every advantage, learning French, German and English from different governesses and travelling to Germany, Switzerland and Italy. She was first encouraged to paint in 1899 by the German Impressionist Max Liebermann, a friend of the family. From 1903 she attended the university at Karlsruhe, where she studied drawing and anatomy, and was introduced to the work of the French Impressionists. In 1905 she moved to Paris, sharing a lodging in the Latin Quarter with a group of other Russian girls and studying at the Académie de la Palette. She was soon producing figurative works in intense colour which owed a great deal to the Fauves, and had found her way into avant-garde circles. In 1907 she had her first encounter with her future husband, at the house of the German critic,

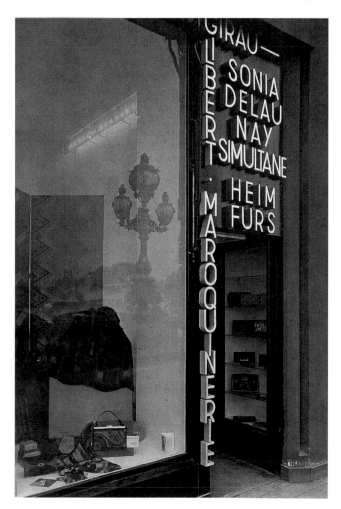

Above: SONIA AND ROBERT DELAUNAY,
in front of *Hélice* (1923) by Robert Delaunay.
Photographer unknown
Right: Boutique Simultanée,
at the Art Deco exposition in Paris, 1925.
Photographer unknown

dealer and collector Wilhelm Uhde, but they do not seem to have paid much attention to each other. The following year, when she had come under pressure from her family to return home, she entered a marriage of convenience with Uhde. She also had her first solo exhibition at his Galerie Notre-Dame-des-Champs.

In 1909 she and Delaunay met again, and their relationship blossomed. 'He was like a whirlwind,' she recorded. 'His eagerness for life, his aggressiveness, filled me with delight.' The following year she asked Uhde for a divorce, which he granted quite willingly, and married Delaunay. Their son Charles was born in January 1911.

At this time Robert was entering his most productive period as an artist. In the spring of 1909 he produced the

Robert Delaunay,
c. 1930.
Photo Man Ray

first of the interior views of the Gothic church of Saint-Séverin in Paris, which were his earliest mature works, and these were followed by his *Eiffel Tower* series, mostly painted in 1910–11. In late 1911, Kandinsky, who had got to know of his work, asked him to exhibit at the first Blaue Reiter exhibition in Munich, which opened in December. Three of the four pictures Delaunay sent sold within the first two days. In February 1912 he had his first one-man show at the Galerie Barbazanges in Paris, and this was followed by the success of his huge canvas *La Ville de Paris* (The City of Paris) at the Salon des Indépendants. Delaunay painted this in fifteen days especially for the occasion and Apollinaire, who had become a close friend, proclaimed it to be 'by far the most important painting' on view. In April 1912, Delaunay, hitherto classified as a dissident (because more colourful) Cubist, moved close to total abstraction, with a series called *Les Fenêtres* (The Windows), and Apollinaire gave his new style a separate identity as 'Orphism', to the jealous disgust of the orthodox Cubists.

Delaunay was notoriously competitive. Gertrude Stein, in *Autobiography of Alice B. Toklas*, describes him:

Fairly able and inordinately ambitious. He was always asking how old Picasso had been when he painted a certain picture. When he was told he always said, oh I am not as old as that yet. I will do as much when I am that age …

Stein's implied character judgment is apparently supported by the fact that on one occasion before the First World War Delaunay actually drew up a list of every artist, however minor, he believed himself to have influenced.

Because of this aspect of her husband's personality, Sonia for a while gave up painting and moved into decoration and handicraft. Almost her first product in this field was an appliquéd crib blanket for her infant son:

The mosaic of material was a spontaneous creation, and nothing more. I continued to use this process on other objects – some art critics have seen this as a geometrization of shapes and a celebration of colours which foreshadowed my work in the years to come.

Meanwhile, the Delaunays had become the centre of a large circle of artists and writers. They had enough

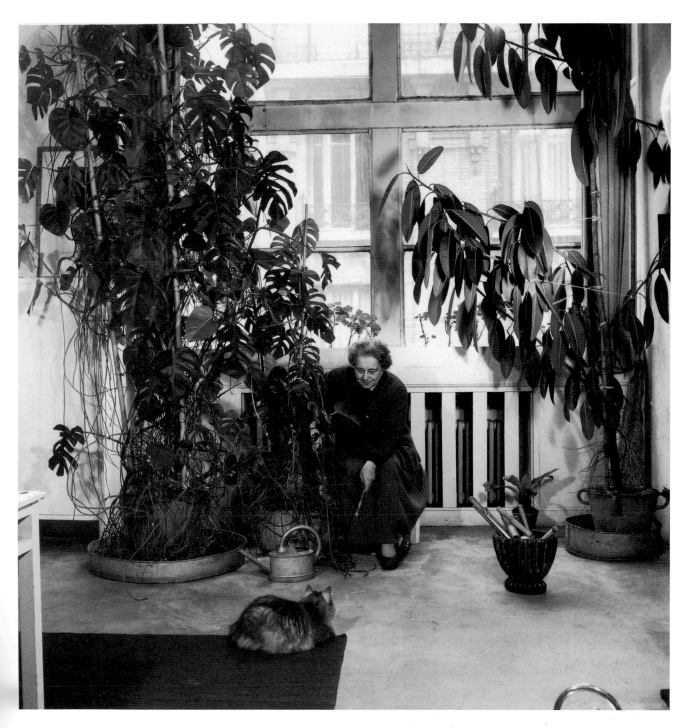

Sonia Delaunay, Paris, 1954. Photo Denise Colomb

money already from Sonia's family in St Petersburg to live well and to entertain fairly lavishly, though some of their amusements were distinctly proletarian. A favourite spot was a working-class dance-hall called the Bal Bullier, where a group of them went every Thursday. Sonia said: 'The Bal Bullier was for me what the Moulin de la Galette

had been for Degas, Renoir and Lautrcc.' In the summer of 1913 she created the first 'simultaneous clothing', covered with enormous jazz patterns and inspired by Robert's new, near-abstract work, to wear on their evenings out. Another amusement was going to the new airport at Saint-Cloud to watch the aeroplanes: 'We were on the verge of a new vision which, in the visual and poetical world, was going to throw out all the old conceptions.'

Meanwhile, Robert's connections with Germany remained strong. Franz Marc and August Macke had come to visit him in 1912, as had the still almost unknown Paul Klee. In January 1913 he went to Germany with Apollinaire for an exhibition of his work at *Der Sturm* Gallery in Berlin, and in the autumn of the same year there was a large group of his paintings in *Der Sturm*'s Autumn Salon. But in 1914 his friendship with Apollinaire began to cool, and they conducted a sharp exchange of views in print when Apollinaire implied that Robert was no more than a French Futurist. One reason for the estrangement may have been Sonia's close alliance with another poet, Blaise Cendrars, with whom she was now collaborating on various projects.

In the summer of 1914 the Delaunays went to Spain – their son had been seriously ill and needed to convalesce. When war broke out they decided to remain in the Iberian peninsula. In 1915 they visited Lisbon, then moved on to Vila do Conde in Portugal. Their life for the most part remained pleasant, though Sonia was at one time detained for several weeks on espionage charges. But the Russian Revolution faced them with an immediate crisis as it cut off their income. Sonia afterwards reflected philosophically that: 'It was a good thing ... Before, we lived like children ... After the Revolution, we had to make our own way.'

The first thing that happened was that they moved to Madrid, where they met Diaghilev whose plight was rather similar to their own. Nevertheless, he commissioned Sonia to do the costumes and Robert the sets for a revival of his ballet *Cléopâtre*. They carried out the task extremely successfully and became part of the Ballets Russes circle. Diaghilev introduced Sonia to all his grand Spanish acquaintances. She presented a fashion show at the Hotel Ritz in Madrid, and opened a successful boutique there, the Casa Sonia, to market her designs. In the two years that followed, 1919 and 1920, she carried out a number of commissions in Spain, designing interiors, costumes and décors for the theatre.

They decided to return to Paris after coming into contact with a new art movement, Dada. Robert was a contributor to the second issue of the magazine *Dada* published in Zurich, and he remained in touch with Tristan Tzara when the latter moved to France. In Paris the Delaunays immediately became part of a circle which included both the Dadaists and those who were to become Surrealists. Their real contact was through poetry, as in art their stylistic principles remained very different from those professed by the newcomers. Sonia adapted more readily. In 1922 she was busily designing what she called 'curtain-poems', 'dress-poems' and 'vest-poems' covered with lettering, and even 'simultaneous' scarves. Robert had an exhibition the same year at the fashionable Paul Guillaume Gallery which was a failure. It became clear that their income must continue to come from Sonia's activities as a designer. In 1924 she established the Atelier Simultané to market her designs in soft furnishings and clothing, and the following year she and the furrier Jacques Heim created a Boutique Simultanée for the Exposition des Arts Décoratifs which was a great success. In the late 1920s Sonia also carried out numerous theatrical projects. Her husband was less active, though he did produce a large decorative panel for the 1925 Art Deco exhibition.

The Depression caused another change in their fortunes. Sonia, who was now employing thirty workers, was forced to close her workshops and decided to return to painting. Her style was now more closely linked to Robert's than ever before. In 1930 he made a definitive commitment to abstraction and embarked on a series which he called *Rythmes sans fin* (Rhythms Without End). There was now a gradual return of interest in his work, both past and present, but he was not the aggressively self-publicizing force he had been previously. In 1936 the Delaunays received their last major joint commission: they were asked to produce decorations for the Pavillon de l'Air and the Pavillon des Chemins de Fer at the Exposition Universelle of 1937. With the help of a team of sometimes quarrelsome and obstructive unemployed artists, they produced 25,000 square metres of murals. These were well received, though the pavilions opened late and thus lost part of their impact.

In 1939 Robert began to show the first signs of failing health. The couple went to the Auvergne for four months, and then, because of the war, decided to move to the Midi. They joined forces with Hans Arp and Sophie Taeuber-Arp, and with the Italian painter Magnelli and his wife. In 1941 Robert underwent an operation for cancer in Clermont-Ferrand, and died soon after in Montpellier. His widow rejoined the Arps and the Magnellis, who were now living in Grasse, and remained there alone after the others departed. In 1943 Italy surrendered and the Italian forces who had been occupying the town were rounded up by the Germans. In the summer of 1944, prior to the Allied invasion of the South of France, Sonia went to Toulouse, where she remained for three months, finally returning to liberated Paris at the end of that year.

Her first concern was with her late husband's reputation. The first major Robert Delaunay retrospective took place in Paris in 1946. This was followed in 1953 by Sonia's first solo show since she had exhibited with Uhde in 1908. In 1963 she gave forty of her husband's paintings and fifty-eight of her own to the Musée National d'Art Moderne in Paris, and the following year the donation was exhibited in the Salle Mollien in the Louvre, making Sonia Delaunay the first living woman artist to have an exhibition in the museum. Other major retrospectives followed, and, additionally, many of Sonia's designs were issued in large editions by her dealer and close friend, Jacques Damase. This was in keeping with her constant wish throughout her career to democratize art and make it accessible to ordinary people. In 1968 she summed up her career by saying:

I have led three lives: one for Robert, one for my son and grandsons, a shorter one for myself. I don't regret not having given myself more attention. I really did not have time ...

Sonia Delaunay died in Paris in December 1979.

JUAN GRIS with his wife Josette in his studio at the Bateau-Lavoir, Montmartre, 1922. Photo Daniel-Henry Kahnweiler

JUAN GRIS

Juan Gris was a quietist, whose life was ostensibly marked by few major incidents. Though not the inventor of Cubism, he was one of its most able practitioners and evolved a very personal variety of it, combining elements which he had learned from Braque and Picasso with others which were his own personal invention. Typical of his approach was his remark about Cézanne, the universally acknowledged father of Cubism: 'Cézanne made a cylinder out of a bottle. I start from the cylinder to create a special kind of individual object. I make a bottle out of a cylinder.' A highly intelligent man, he had a marked impact on other painters – not only on the artists of the Section d'Or, the group with whom he identified himself, but also on senior members of the Ecole de Paris, such as Matisse, with whom he spent the summer at Collioure in 1914. He had a special sympathy for poets, and collaborated with a number of distinguished writers, among them Pierre Reverdy, whose *Guitare Endormie* he illustrated, Gertrude Stein and Raymond Radiguet.

Gris was a pseudonym: he was born José Victoriano González in 1887, in Madrid, the thirteenth child of a rich Castilian merchant. He studied first to be an engineer at

JUAN GRIS, *The Siphon*, 1913

the School of Arts and Manufactures in Madrid, which he entered in 1902. By the time he abandoned this for an artistic career he was already contributing illustrations to the reviews *Blanco y Negro* and *Madrid Comico*.

Madrid at this time was an extremely provincial milieu, much more so than Barcelona, and as soon as he could Gris abandoned it for Paris, arriving there in 1906 at the age of nineteen. He found himself a studio at the famous Bateau-Lavoir in Montmartre, and was soon in contact with his compatriot Picasso, who also lived and worked there, and with the poets Guillaume Apollinaire, Max Jacob and André Salmon, who formed part of Picasso's circle. At first he supported himself by making humorous drawings for papers such as *L'Assiette au beurre* and *Le Charivari*, but in 1910 he began his career as a serious artist by making a series of large watercolours. In the following year he started to paint. Gris's subject-matter was always his immediate surroundings: he produced still lifes composed of simple, everyday objects, portraits of friends, and occasionally landscapes or cityscapes.

In 1911 (the year in which he spent time with Picasso at Céret) he held his first exhibition, showing fifteen paintings at the little gallery run by Clovis Sagot. This was well received by those whose opinion he respected, and he was sufficiently encouraged to send three paintings to the Salon des Indépendants in the spring of 1912. In October of the same year he showed his work in the Section d'Or exhibition, with Marcoussis, Gleizes and Metzinger. Since Braque and Picasso were not at this time showing their work, the Section d'Or was the public face of Cubism. Gris was clearly the most gifted of the group, and he attracted the attention both of dealers and of well informed collectors. Gertrude Stein and Léonce Rosenberg bought paintings, and in 1913 Daniel-Henri Kahnweiler offered Gris a contract, which he accepted. His work was evolving rapidly; he had grasped the significance of collage almost as soon as it was invented by Braque and Picasso in 1912. This liberated his compositional sense enabling him to evolve the subtler patterns of overlapping planes characteristic of his mature work. At this time he was friendly with the Delaunays. Sonia recalled that he spent so much time at the Bal Bullier, their favourite night-spot, that they wondered that he still had enough energy left to work.

The outbreak of war brought a momentary check, since Kahnweiler was an enemy alien and was forced to

leave Paris. Gris's contract with him lapsed, but in 1917 he was able to make another with Léonce Rosenberg which tided him over until Kahnweiler's return to France, when he renewed his former allegiance. But in 1920, just after his new contract was signed, Gris suffered a serious attack of pleurisy, and his health was never to be strong again.

Diaghilev was now taking an interest in Gris, having recognized in him a kind of classicism in tune with postwar taste. A first project, for *Cuadro Flamenco*, did not come to fruition, but in November 1922 Diaghilev commissioned Gris to design sets and costumes for *Les Tentations de la Bergère*, which was premièred in 1924. In 1925 Gris had his first exhibition – and the only one in his lifetime – outside France, at the Flechtheim Gallery in Düsseldorf. His health was now very poor: bronchitis was succeeded by asthma and finally by uremia. Gris died on 11 May 1927 at the age of forty, leaving a wife, Josette, and a son, Georges.

JUAN GRIS,
Woman with a Mandolin
(after Corot), 1916

uturism, like Surrealism, was initiated by a writer rather than an artist. He was Filippo Tommaso Marinetti (1876–1944), whose First Futurist Manifesto was published in the French newspaper *Le Figaro* on 20 February 1909. It was symptomatic of the Italian provincialism of the day, and in particular of the sense of inferiority then felt by Italian avant-gardists, that the movement should feel compelled to launch itself in Paris in preference to Milan or Rome.

Futurism found a warmer welcome among artists than it did among Marinetti's fellow-writers, and the Manifesto of Futurist painting signed by Umberto Boccioni, Carlo Carrà, Luigi Russolo and others was launched in Turin in February 1910. Futurism's main concern was to reject the burden of the Italian past by exalting what was new for its own sake. Its membership hastened to associate themselves with objects and activities which seemed quintessential expressions of modernity – hence the famous polemical phrase in the First Futurist Manifesto: 'A racing automobile is more beautiful than the Victory of Samothrace!' It was nevertheless also the most misogynistic of the early modernist art movements, with little place for the creative activity of women, which the Futurist associated with the 'moonshine' of Symbolism. The first and most creative phase of Futurism ended with the death of Boccioni in 1916, but the movement continued between the wars.

Top: GIACOMO BALLA,
Flags at the Country's Altar, 1915
Bottom: (left to right) Luigi Russolo,
Carlo Carrà, Filippo Marinetti,
Umberto Boccioni and
Gino Severini, Paris 1912.
Photographer unknown
Right: GIACOMO BALLA
Speeding Automobile, 1912

GIACOMO BALLA

Giacomo Balla was the oldest of the leading Italian
Futurists, and was more timid and essentially more
provincial than either Boccioni or Severini, who were his
pupils. He embarked on the Futurist experiment rather
cautiously, drawn into it by his juniors, and was prompt
to abandon it once he thought its moment was over.

He was born in Turin in 1871. His father was a
chemist whose hobby was photography, and who also
had an interest in art. Despite his father's early death, in
1878, when Balla was only seven, these interests seem to
have made a great impression on him, though his artistic
studies only started after his father died: Balla senior had

wanted his son to be a musician, insisting that he
study the violin.

As a painter Balla was largely self-taught, though
he followed an art course at night school during his
adolescence while working by day at a lithography shop.
This double life came to an end when he was stricken
by a depressive illness. In 1891 he had sufficiently
recovered to study full-time for two months at the
Accademia Alberti in Turin, and at the same time
studied photography in the studio of a professional.
This was also the year in which he exhibited for the
first time – he showed a small landscape in a mixed

show in Turin, and was bitterly disappointed when it was passed over because of its size. At this time his production consisted mostly of portraits and of sketches of street-types.

In 1895 Balla moved to Rome with his mother, and in the following year he set up in a studio of his own. He continued his production of caricatures and also began to study problems of light. He was not yet established as an artist, and at one stage was reduced to making designs for chocolate boxes to earn money. In 1900 he found the funds to go to Paris and remained there for six months, working with a compatriot who was an illustrator and poster designer. He seems to have been more struck by the exaggeration of Paris fashions than he was by the local art scene – he took a keen interest in clothes throughout his life. While in Paris he continued his investigations of the effects of light, exploring the visual properties of artificial illumination.

After he returned home to Rome he built up a successful practice as a portraitist and also continued to paint nocturnes. He was now exhibiting fairly frequently: his work was seen in the Turin Quadriennale in 1902 and at the International Exhibition in Venice in the following year. It was during this period that Boccioni and Severini became his pupils. He was at last sufficiently established to marry: he had been engaged to Elisa Marcucci since 1897. Significantly, the year in which he married, 1904, was also the year in which an important magazine, *Italia Moderna*, devoted a whole article to his work, headed 'Giacomo il Notturno'. Photography continued to exert an important influence over his painting: at this time some of his portraits were entirely in black and white, and he was using compositional devices which showed the clear influence of the camera.

In 1905 Balla was a member of the jury for an exhibition organized by the chief Roman exhibiting society. He seized the chance to place one of his own works next to a portrait by Mancini, then one of the most fashionable Italian painters. This was considered hubristic and caused a certain amount of mocking comment. His influence over his fellow jurors was nevertheless insufficient to secure the acceptance of works by Boccioni and Severini, who were as a result the moving spirits in organizing the first Italian Salon des Refusés. At this time Balla's work seemed to be moving towards Social Realism mixed with Symbolist elements, in the manner of Pellizza da Volpedo. Boccioni, always

the most advanced of the Futurists, was becoming somewhat disillusioned with him. In 1909 he wrote to Severini: 'For me Balla is a reminder of a kind of energy which helped me enormously. I admire him too, but I think that all that energy is going for nothing.' According to Boccioni, Balla was at this moment having little professional success: 'He hasn't sold a picture for three years, and is obliged to give lessons.'

The year 1910 brought with it the beginnings of a major change of direction. In February Balla was one of the signatories of the Manifesto of Futurist Painting, together with Boccioni, Carrà, Russolo and Severini, although for the moment this aggressive text had little to do with his own work. One of the things which may have attracted him to the Futurists was a hitherto suppressed streak of exhibitionism. In the early 1930s Marinetti remembered watching Balla unobserved, in the streets of Rome twenty years before: 'Upright, immobile, wearing a bright blue jacket of asymmetrical cut, his arms crossed over a cravat decorated with little bits of glass, tiny bells and pieces of gilded wood.'

For a while Balla remained extremely cautious about his commitment to the new movement. He was not represented in the first two Futurist exhibitions held in Milan in 1911, and though his painting *Lampada Studio di Luce* was included in the catalogue of the first Futurist Exhibition in Paris, it was not in fact shown. He did not appear in a Futurist group show until 1913, at the Teatro Constanzi in Rome. In April of that year he officially abandoned his pre-Futurist work, offering to sell it off at bargain prices (though it seems from subsequent events that in fact he kept much of it). He changed his appearance by cutting his hair and shaving off his beard, and appeared 'freshly shaved, with starched collar and cuffs and a fashionably cut suit.'

In September 1913 he participated with the other Futurists in a group show at the *Der Sturm* Gallery in Berlin, and in November he exhibited his studies of an automobile in movement (a quintessentially Futurist subject) in Florence. Yet the next year he was still showing works of his early, more conventional period in official exhibitions while continuing to take part in Futurist shows. He developed a taste for appearing in the nonsense playlets (an early version of the 'Happenings' of the 1960s) that the Futurists liked to put on. In one he impersonated a character called 'Monsieur Putipu', with a multicoloured pot on his head. He also experimented

GIACOMO BALLA, 1912. Photo Bragaglia

with Futurist sound poetry and with onomatopoeic compositions on the guitar. Like the other Futurists he was a strong nationalist, and in February 1915 was arrested, with Marinetti and others, for taking part in a demonstration in favour of Italy's entry into the war. This was probably the year in which his art reached its most experimental point. He had joined forces with a youthful recruit to Futurism called Fortunato Depero, and in collaboration they produced what they called 'Plastic Complexes', constructions of wire, cardboard, cloth and paper which could be set into motion. One such was described as a 'futurist toy – artificial landscape – metallic animal'.

During the war Balla's studio in Rome became a meeting place for the artists of the avant-garde. Balla presided in one of his extraordinary costumes, wearing 'a scent devised by his wife especially for afternoon and Sunday wear'. His prestige was now such that Diaghilev, who had taken refuge in Rome, turned to Balla to provide a décor for Stravinsky's *Fireworks* to be presented at the Teatro Constanzi.

From 1919 onwards Balla began to devote much attention to the design of utilitarian objects. He opened his house to the public in order to exhibit his Futurist furniture and bibelots. He even designed hats, which were shown in the 'Futurist Fashion' section of the exhibition held in Milan to relaunch Futurism immediately the war was over. A little later he designed a striking décor for a cabaret in Milan. He was one of the exhibitors in the great Exposition des Arts Décoratifs Industriels et Modernes held in Paris in 1925.

By 1928 the Futurist adventure was over as far as Balla was concerned, and he had returned to a more conventional kind of figuration. He was, however, reluctant to sever his connections with Futurism altogether, and in 1929 he signed the Manifesto of Aeropittura which launched the final phase of the movement. Yet by 1937, he was ready to deny almost all connection with what he now felt was a miserable remnant:

I am ready to declare that my art has nothing in common with theirs and that for several years I have had no connection with any Futurist manifestation. In all sincerity I dedicated all my energies to the search for the new, but then, at a certain moment, I found myself surrounded by opportunists and arrivistes who were more interested in making money than they were in art; I am convinced that pure art is to be discovered in absolute realism, without recourse to decoration, and this is the reason why I have returned to my earlier style: a pure interpretation of reality, which, when apprehended through the sensibility of the artist, seems always infinitely novel and convincing.

This did not prevent him from feeling some loyalty to his own past. In 1947 his one-man show at the Accademia di San Luca in Rome (of which he had been a member for more than a decade) was cancelled because of a disagreement with his fellow Academicians, who wished to show only his non-Futurist works.

This incident took place on the eve of a revival of interest in at least the earlier history of Futurism. Balla once again allowed himself to be convinced by the force of public opinion. In 1951 he said:

Today I am pleased, and perhaps a little astonished when I take out again the old Futurist canvases which I put aside twenty years ago. I thought that these works concerned only myself; I now see that they also belong to history.

He basked in the renewal of his artistic glory as the senior surviving Futurist, until his death in 1958 at the age of eighty-seven.

UMBERTO BOCCIONI,
The City Rises, 1910

UMBERTO BOCCIONI

Umberto Boccioni was perhaps the most gifted of the Italian Futurists, and the movement suffered greatly from his untimely death in 1916.

He was born in 1882 at Reggio Calabria, but his family moved often during his childhood and adolescence because of his father's work as a government employee. In 1897 he was sent to school in Padua, and later continued his education at the Technical Institute in Catania. At this period he was equally attracted to art and literature, and in 1900 he wrote a novel, which was not published. In 1901, after falling out with his family, he moved to Rome, where he lived with an aunt. During this period he learned the rudiments of drawing from a poster designer – according to Boccioni's own account he was forced into this apprenticeship by his father, and his instruction consisted chiefly in making faithful copies of his employer's designs, which he considered hideous. Soon after he moved to Rome, he met a kindred spirit, Gino Severini, at a concert on the Pincio, and it was Severini who, though almost as ignorant as himself, imparted to him the first rudiments of academic drawing. A little later both young artists became the pupils of Giacomo Balla, then one of the few progressive artists in Rome.

In 1906 Boccioni departed abruptly for Paris, without informing his friends. Severini says in his memoirs that this was because of one of the sentimental entanglements which were common in Boccioni's life (although his main emotional attachment seems always to have been to his mother). From Paris he travelled to Russia as the guest of a Russian noble family before returning to Italy in November 1906. From 1906–7 he lived in Padua, and then moved to Venice where he enrolled for a while at the Academy. In 1908 he made his way to Milan, culturally the liveliest city in Italy. He lived with his mother and sister, and sketched for various magazines, in particular for *Illustrazione Italiana*, and painted urban and industrial subjects.

He was now able to widen his range of artistic contacts. He got to know the Italian Symbolist painter Gaetano Previati, and, more important, became friends with the poet and polemicist Filippo Tommaso Marinetti, who was evolving the theory of Futurism. Boccioni was already sympathetic to certain basic Futurist ideas. One entry from the diary he kept in Padua, dated March 1907, reads: 'I want to paint what is new, the product of our industrial epoch.'

In February 1910 Boccioni drafted the Manifesto of Futurist Painting as the successor to the Futurist Manifesto which Marinetti had issued in 1909. In July of the same year he showed a large group of works at the Summer Exhibition held at Ca' Pesaro in Venice, but did not yet appear openly as a Futurist. His new artistic identity was given substance in two group exhibitions, shared with Carrà and Russolo, held in Milan in 1911. In September of that year virtually the whole Milanese Futurist group departed for Paris, where a Futurist Exhibition was planned at the Bernheim-Jeune Gallery, under the aegis of the distinguished French critic Félix Fénéon. The show was put off for some months because of the war between Turkey and Italy, but opened to the public in February 1912.

Boccioni seems at first to have been knocked off balance by the Paris art world, in which so much that was new was appearing. He wrote to Severini:

Within me everything is in a state of chaos – men, women and objects. I'm nearly thirty years old, and I'm still in the dark! Yes, and I thought I knew so many things ...

The Futurist Exhibition was not the immediate triumph which Marinetti afterwards claimed – Apollinaire, for example, reviewed it condescendingly, dismissing most of the work on view as rather provincial. But the show caught on and began a long tour which was to establish the European reputation of the new movement. Its second showing was in London, where the composer Busoni bought an important painting by Boccioni, *The City Rises*; the purchase marked the start of a friendship which lasted until the end of Boccioni's life. The next stop was Berlin, where a collector named Borchardt bought the remaining pictures almost *en bloc*.

Boccioni was now beginning to be interested in sculpture: in April 1912 he issued the Futurist Manifesto of Sculpture, and during the summer he made an intensive study of the sculptors connected with Cubism, particularly Archipenko, Brancusi and Duchamp-Villon. He was ready to show his own efforts in this line at that year's Salon d'Automne. In 1913 Boccioni took part in the exhibition of Futurist painting in Rome which marked Balla's début with the group, and in June exhibited work at the First Exhibition of Futurist Sculpture at the Galerie La Boëtie in Paris. In December an exhibition of his sculpture initiated the new permanent Futurist Gallery in via del Tritone in Rome.

UMBERTO BOCCIONI's studio with versions of *Unique Form of Continuity of Space*, 1913. Photographer unknown

Like other artists of the period, he was affected by the menacing political atmosphere. In October he published a 'Futurist political programme' in the magazine *Lacerba* which indicated his wish to unite the ferment of Italian nationalism with the transformation of the world through the use of technology.

The publication of this programme marked a psychological shift. Boccioni was now more inclined to organize and agitate than to paint. In 1914 he took part in demonstrations in favour of Italy's entry into the war, and in September of that year he was one of the signatories of a new political manifesto, *Sintesi futurista della guerra*. In July 1915, when Italy joined the war, he enlisted in a battalion of cyclist volunteers.

Confronted by the reality of war, he soon found he could no longer think of it as 'the only hygiene of the world', as he and his fellow Futurists had once proclaimed it. He recognized its squalor and misery and more and more tended to retreat into himself, breaking off a number of friendships as a result. A letter of this period expresses his feeling of alienation. 'War,' he wrote, 'when one is waiting to fight, consists of just this: insects, boredom, obscure heroism ... one thinks of life ... past and of so many things which are now far away.'

In November 1915 his battalion left the Front; he was on leave for a long period in Milan and was also able to spend time with the Busoni family at San Remigio. This interlude enabled him to return to painting, and he completed a final group of work. In July 1916 he was recalled, and posted to an artillery regiment stationed at Verona. He was offered a place in the battalion offices, but said that he would prefer to remain with his battery – 'I said in addition that when we next go into action (which everyone dreads) they could count on me. ... My declaration aroused wonder and admiration. I did well.' But Boccioni was not called upon to fight again. On 16 August, during normal exercizes, he was thrown from his horse and trampled. He died the following day.

UMBERTO BOCCIONI (left) and Filippo Marinetti at the Salon des Futuristes in Paris, *c.* 1912. Photographer unknown

The word 'Expressionism' has often been extremely loosely used – at one time it was employed as a kind of synonym for Modernism. As a term which specifically designated a style or school it was first applied to French artists, but in about 1910 it was transferred to developments in Germany.

The precursor of German Expressionism, who herself belonged to no group, was the important but short-lived Paula Modersohn-Becker, who was influenced both by the great French Post-Impressionists and by contacts with the German poet Rainer Maria Rilke.

The other artists whose lives are grouped together here belong to three different aspects or sections of the Expressionist Movement in Germany: members of 'Die Brücke' (The Bridge), founded in 1905 in Dresden (Kirchner and Nolde); a member of 'Der Blaue Reiter' (The Blue Rider), founded in 1911 in Munich (Gabriele Münter), and a major artist who continued the Expressionist tradition after the First World War (Max Beckmann). This tradition was basically one of obedience to the dictates of inner feeling. Other artists who could plausibly be placed here include Kandinsky and Klee, both members of Der Blaue Reiter, but also active later in the Bauhaus (see pp. 170–87).

Above: EMIL NOLDE,
Still Life of Masks, 1911
Right: EMIL NOLDE,
*The Dance Round the
Golden Calf*, 1910

EMIL NOLDE

Emil Nolde added a special, mystical dimension to German Expressionism, and his career illustrates a number of the moral dilemmas which faced German Modernists of the first generation, since his instincts were nationalist and conservative even though his art was regarded as experimental.

His real name was not Nolde but Hansen; his parents were Frisian peasants. He was born in 1867 and grew up on the farm which had belonged to his mother's family for nine generations. Even as a boy Nolde was different from his three brothers: he drew, modelled and painted, and covered boards and barn doors with drawings in chalk. Some aspects of the family background, however, affected him deeply. The family were Protestants, steeped in religion, and in his youth Nolde read the Bible a great deal – its images were to return to him later in life.

It was clear that Nolde was unsuited for farm work, and in 1884 he took a job as an apprentice carver in a furniture factory in Flensburg. Here he stayed for four years, drawing and painting in his spare time. In 1888 he went to Munich, to see an exhibition of industrial arts, and managed to stay on by finding a job in a furniture factory. After only a few weeks he moved to Karlsruhe, where he found a similar job and attended classes in a school of industrial arts in the evenings. Eventually he gave up his job and enrolled in day classes at the same school, drawing from plaster casts and studying perspective and anatomy. He was unable to stay more than two semesters, as his savings ran out. In the autumn of 1889 he moved to Berlin, where he took a job as a furniture designer and spent his leisure time studying Old Master paintings in the magnificent Berlin museums; he also had his first encounters with Ancient Egyptian and Assyrian art in the archaeological collections there. In 1890 he fell ill, and spent the summer on his parents' farm.

The autumn of 1891 marked a change of direction, when Nolde saw an advertisement for a teaching post at the Museum of Industrial Arts at St Gallen in Switzerland. He applied for the job and was accepted, moving to St Gallen in January 1892. His duties were to teach industrial and ornamental drawing. The job was demanding, and he could paint only in the vacations;

nevertheless, the fact that Switzerland was at the crossroads of Europe enabled him to travel. He went to Milan and saw Leonardo's *Last Supper*, some aspects of which were to haunt him for long afterwards, and to Vienna, where he saw Dürer's prints in the Albertina. Though he was a reluctant reader, his intellectual horizons were expanding. He discovered the Symbolists and Nietzsche, and he was deeply impressed by a performance of Ibsen's *The Wild Duck*. Like many half-educated men, he started to feel that he was alone, misunderstood and persecuted – he was to suffer from these feelings for the rest of his life, latterly with some reason.

In 1893 Nolde embarked on an artistic enterprise which he at first treated only half-seriously. He made a series of humorous postcards in which he represented the most famous of the Swiss mountains in semi-human form as a race of giants. The periodical *Jugend* reproduced two of these in 1896, and the proprietor of the magazine was sufficiently impressed to invite the artist to his home in Munich. Thus encouraged, Nolde borrowed enough money to issue a large edition of the postcards. They appealed to popular taste, and 100,000 copies were sold within ten days. Nolde made 25,000 gold francs, and, freed from financial worries for the time being, gave up his job and went to live in Munich. He wanted to study at the Munich Academy under the most celebrated painter in the city, Frans von Stück, but was not accepted, and instead attended two private academies. In the autumn of 1899 he moved to Paris for nine months where he worked on and off at the Académie Julian, but spent most of his time in the museums and studying the special exhibitions put on for the Paris World's Fair of 1900. He was already an admirer of Daumier's lithographs and was now impressed by Manet, but not by the other, younger Impressionists.

Nolde returned to northern Germany in 1900, and embarked on a tormented search to discover his own artistic personality:

I had an infinite number of visions at this time, for wherever I turned my eyes nature, the sky, the clouds were alive, in each stone and in the branches of each tree, everywhere, my figures stirred and lived their still or wildly animated life, and they aroused my enthusiasm as well as tormented me with demands that I paint them.

Despite these feelings, Nolde painted very few visionary pictures during this period – they were to come later – but instead painted mainly landscapes and portraits.

In 1900 he moved to Copenhagen, where he met and married Ada Vilstrup. They soon began to be dogged by financial problems, and in addition Ada was repeatedly ill. In the spring of 1903 the couple moved to the remote island of Alsen. In 1904 they went to Berlin, where Ada made an ill-fated attempt to make some money by singing in nightclubs. This led to a serious breakdown, so Nolde took her to Taormina in Italy to convalesce, moving afterwards to Ischia. The Italian scene, for all its beauty, did not move him as his native Germany did, and in 1905 they returned. Ada was in and out of one sanatorium after another; Nolde based himself in his lonely fisherman's cottage in Alsen. His visionary feelings were stronger than ever, the calls of animals at night had the power of suggesting colours: 'The cries appeared as shrill yellows, the hooting of owls in deep violet tones.'

He was rescued from his isolation by the young artists of Die Brücke, who recognized in him a kindred spirit. Schmidt-Rottluff saw some paintings Nolde was exhibiting in Dresden, and wrote inviting him to become a member of their group. He followed up his letter with a visit to Alsen, and in 1907 Nolde moved to Dresden, putting Ada into yet another sanatorium there. His official membership of Die Brücke did not last long – Nolde was essentially not gregarious and soon withdrew, though he maintained friendly relations with individual members. His young colleagues had an important influence on his work: in particular, he followed their example in making woodcut prints, and in addition they encouraged him to return to lithography, which he had tried in Munich.

Nolde's art became much freer: he began to see that 'dexterity is also an enemy' and he allowed himself to create fantastic paintings 'without any prototype or model, without any well defined idea ... a vague idea of glow and colour was enough. The paintings took shape as I worked.' The fantasies and the Biblical paintings he created at this time are generally considered his greatest works.

He was becoming a well known and controversial figure in the German art world of the time. In December 1910 he wrote a violently critical letter, with nationalist and racist overtones, to Max Liebermann, the greatly respected President of the Berlin Sezession, who happened to be a Jew. As a result he was expelled from the Sezession. When Max Pechstein and other Expressionists formed the Neue Sezession in the following year, Nolde duly joined, and helped to give the new organization much of its aggressive character. He was invited to take part in the second Blaue Reiter show in Munich, and also in the 1912 Sonderbund exhibition in Cologne, which brought together all the avant-garde painters in Germany. In the same year the museum in Halle acquired his painting of *The Last Supper* despite the violent opposition of Dr Wilhelm von Bode, the great savant who had been largely responsible for building up the magnificent collection of Old Masters in Berlin.

In 1913, for reasons which remain somewhat mysterious, Nolde was offered a unique opportunity to expand his horizons. The German Colonial Office invited him to take part in an expedition to the German territories in the South Pacific. Its main purpose was medical – to study health conditions among the natives – but Nolde, who had no professional qualifications for the task, was asked to research the racial characteristics of the population. He and Ada travelled via Moscow, Mukden, Seoul, Tokyo, Peking, Nanking, Shanghai, Hong Kong, Manila and the Palau Islands to Rabaul, in German New Guinea. In 1914 he made trips to Neu-Mecklenburg (now New Ireland) and the Admiralty Islands, before setting off again for home, travelling via the Celebes, Java and Aden. When Nolde and his wife arrived at Port Said they found that the First World War had broken out, and were only able to make their way home by obtaining Danish passports. On this journey Nolde noted the damage done by Europeans, even in China, which possessed such an ancient civilization of its own. 'We live in an evil era,' he said, 'in which the white man brings the whole earth into servitude.'

On his return he resumed what had now become a customary pattern, which was to spend the spring, summer and autumn in the countryside, and the winter in Berlin, where he drew rather than painted. He gave up his house on Alsen in 1916, and returned to his native Schleswig, living first at Utenwarf, which became Danish after the war. In the immediate post-war years he travelled quite widely, going to England, France and Spain in 1921, and to Italy in 1924. In 1927 he settled on the German side of the frontier, building a house to his own design on the site of a disused wharf which he named 'Seebüll'. His reputation now stood very high in Germany. In 1927 his sixtieth birthday was celebrated with an official exhibition in Dresden; in 1931 he became a member of the Prussian Academy of Fine Arts, and in 1933 he was offered the presidency of the State Academy of Arts in Berlin.

The Nazi takeover did not effect Nolde immediately, but he had other troubles to think about. In 1934 it was discovered that he was suffering from stomach cancer. He had a successful operation in Hamburg in 1935 which was followed by a long convalescence in Switzerland, during which he met Paul Klee, who was also in poor health. The two men genuinely admired one another. Nolde once described Klee as 'a falcon soaring in the starry cosmos', and Klee reciprocated by calling him 'the mysterious hand of the lower region'.

Despite ominous signs to the contrary, Nolde had assumed that he would be immune from the Nazi campaign against Expressionism and other forms of modern art. In a certain sense the Nazi philosophy resembled his own, which continued to owe a debt to Nietzsche. He was stripped of his illusions by the events of 1937, when his work was included in the Degenerate Art Exhibition in Munich (his protests to the authorities went unheeded); when more than a thousand of his works were removed from German museums; and when the official celebrations for his seventieth birthday were cancelled. Worse was to follow. In 1941, the Reichskammer der Bildenden Kunste demanded that he send in his entire production for the past two years. Fifty-four of the works he sent were confiscated, and he was forbidden to practise his vocation as an artist. Later Nolde went to Vienna to appeal personally to the Nazi gauleiter Baldur von Schirach – in vain.

He had already given up his apartment in Berlin, and had begun to produce what he called his 'unpainted pictures' – hundreds of small watercolours which he hid in a secret cache in his isolated house. He was very much alone. His wife became ill again in 1942 and was taken to hospital in Hamburg. The opportunity to leave Germany was long past – at one stage Nolde could have done so easily, by crossing the nearby Danish frontier, but apparently he never entertained the idea.

EMIL NOLDE with Ada, wedding photograph, 1902. Photographer unknown

He survived the war, as did his invalid wife, who died in November 1946. As the grand old man of German art, Nolde now enjoyed a new lease of life. In 1947 there were exhibitions in Kiel and Lübeck to celebrate his eightieth birthday. In 1948 he married a twenty-eight-year-old woman, the daughter of a friend. In 1952 he was awarded the German Order of Merit, his country's highest civilian decoration. He continued to work with tremendous energy, producing oils based on the watercolours he had created during the years of persecution. His last oil painting was done in 1951, and he was able to make watercolours late in 1955. Nolde died in April 1956, aged eighty-eight.

PAULA MODERSOHN-BECKER

Paula Modersohn-Becker, despite the brevity of her career, was the most important female artist of the early Modernist epoch. Though she was never a member of any Expressionist grouping, it is in her work that we can see the beginnings of German Expressionism. Paula Becker, the third of seven children, was born in Dresden in 1876. Her mother was a German aristocrat, her father was Russian. The family moved to Bremen in 1888, and it

was here that Paula received her first lessons in art. From the first, she never seems to have doubted that art would be her profession. After placating her parents by training to be a teacher in Bremen, in 1896 she moved to Berlin to live with an uncle while studying at the Berlin School of Art for Women. The instruction was conventional, but she was impressed by the Holbeins and Rembrandts she saw in the rich collections of the Berlin museums, and also by the drawings of Michelangelo and Botticelli.

In 1897 she paid her first visit to the artist's colony at Worpswede, twenty miles from Bremen, and in 1898, after graduating, she rented a studio there. Worpswede was one of a number of rural artists' colonies which sprang up in Germany around the turn of the century, in reaction against the late but now very rapid industrialization of the country. They embodied not merely a revolt against the evils of industry but against the prevailing academic style of art. There was a search for the roots of German culture, and a cult of nature and natural things. The inhabitants of these colonies were anti-bourgeois, but at the same time elitist. Their attitudes were formed in particular by the writings of Friedrich Nietzsche – Modersohn-Becker praised Nietzsche's *Also Sprach Zarathustra* (Thus Spake Zarathustra) in diary entries of 1898 and 1900, calling him 'a man of gigantic stature'.

Among those Modersohn-Becker met at Worpswede were the poet Rainer Maria Rilke, Rilke's wife-to-be the sculptor Clara Westhoff, and the painter, Otto Modersohn, whom she married in 1901. Modersohn had been one of the founders of the Worpswede colony and was already on his way to becoming well known, painting in a slightly backward-looking pre-Impressionist manner which derived from the Barbizon landscapists in France. Nevertheless, in Germany itself the artistic conservatives continued to denounce the Worpswede style as revolutionary.

Worpswede was remarkable for the number of women artists who had settled there. They met to discuss ideas, but also worked and exhibited alongside the male members of the colony, and in general received more respect than was usual for women painters and sculptors at this time. Modersohn, who was eleven years older than Paula, was to begin with one of her mentors, and they married after the sudden death of his first wife.

Paula soon began to feel increasingly oppressed both by the demands of marriage and by the narrowness of

PAULA MODERSOHN-BECKER with her husband Otto and step-daughter Elsbeth, Worpswede, *c.* 1904. Photographer unknown

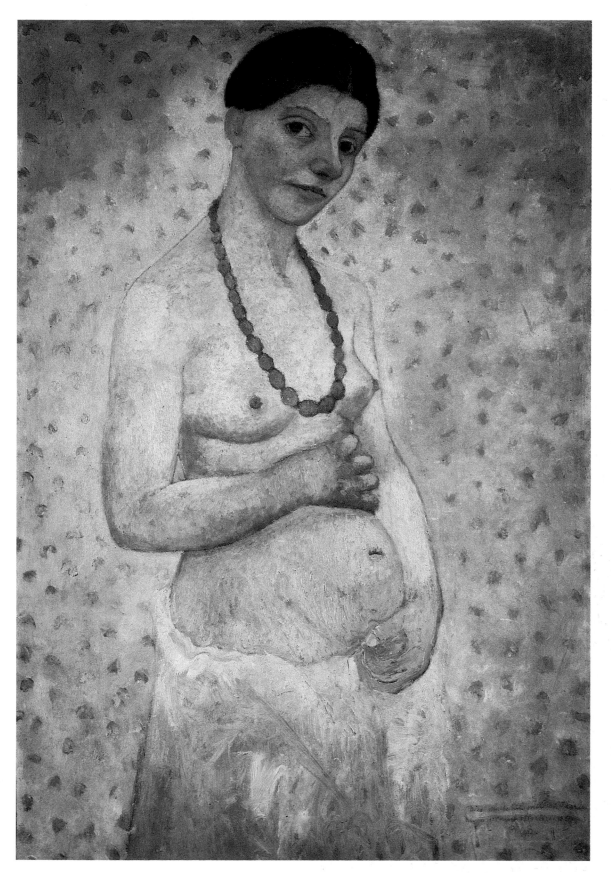

PAULA MODERSOHN-BECKER, *Self-Portrait on her Sixth Wedding Anniversary*, 1906

the Worpswede environment. She nevertheless received much encouragement from her husband, who admitted that he in turn had been influenced by the freer, more monumental style of painting she was now developing. But Paula longed for a more challenging environment, and in 1903 she made a long visit to Paris. It was not the first time she had been there – her first trip, made in 1900, had enabled her to see the great International Exhibition of that year, and to study life drawing at the Académie Colarossi, one of the famous 'free academies' in the city, where well known artists instructed all-comers. These institutions provided special studios for women, and attracted students from all over the world.

Modersohn-Becker's return to Paris in 1903 marked a more systematic and determined effort to free herself from the constraints of her life in Germany, and at the same time to liberate her art. Like the majority of the women students who frequented the free academies, she lived very simply, renting a single small room which she also used as her studio, and making daily visits to her classes. She remained in touch with Rilke, who was now employed by the sculptor Rodin as his secretary, and with fellow artists from Germany. For Rodin she had a profound admiration. Other artists who impressed her were Cézanne, Gauguin, Van Gogh (all of whom influenced her work), and the newly emergent Nabis – in particular Vuillard, Denis and Bonnard. She was also deeply impressed by the Ancient Greek, Ancient Egyptian and Gothic works she saw in the Louvre.

It was during her months in Paris in 1903 that she began to see particular symbolic importance in the naked human body, most of all her own. Her series of nude self-portraits begins at about this time, and in a letter written to her husband in February 1903 she compared her own naked body to the idea of her soul laid bare.

Modersohn-Becker now established a pattern of trips to Paris of increasing length – she returned there in 1905 and again in 1906 – interspersed with periods in Worpswede, where she continued to admire the 'biblical simplicity' of peasant life. Worpswede supplied her with material for numerous studies of old men and women, and also of children. The mother-and-child theme played a prominent part in her subject matter.

Her later trips to France were marked by increasing intimacy with Rilke (until the latter's departure from Paris in July 1906), and renewed intimacy with Rilke's wife Clara, even though Rilke and Clara were now

drifting apart. Rilke's biographers have sometimes spoken of his 'double romance' with the two women, and Paula's diary entries show that her own feelings for Clara verged on the erotic. Otto Modersohn, meanwhile, was increasingly distressed by his wife's apparently firm determination not to settle permanently in Worpswede. During her longest stay in Paris, which lasted a year, he visited her twice, but she resisted his entreaties until the spring of 1907. When she returned she was pregnant. The baby was born on 2 November 1907, and less than three weeks later Paula Modersohn-Becker died of an embolism. As early as 1900, as a diary entry shows, she had had a premonition of her own early death. 'If I have painted three good pictures,' she wrote, 'I shall leave gladly with flowers in my hair.' She had worked largely in isolation, and without attracting much critical attention. Even her husband was astonished by the sheer quantity of work she left behind her.

GABRIELE MÜNTER

Gabriele Münter is now best remembered for her association with Vasily Kandinsky, and in particular for her role in the foundation of the Blaue Reiter group. In fact she had a long career as an independent artist, and her period with Kandinsky formed only a part of this, though undoubtedly the most important part. She was born in Berlin in 1877, and studied art first in Düsseldorf and then in Munich. She met Kandinsky in Munich at the beginning of 1902, when she enrolled at the Phalanx art school, founded by him and a number of other progressive artists. In the summer of that year, Kandinsky took a small group of pupils on a painting expedition to Kochel, in the foothills of the Bavarian Alps, and he and Münter began to be emotionally involved. He was, however, already married to a fellow Russian, his cousin Anja Chimiakin. Kandinsky finally left his wife in September 1904, but a divorce, which could only be granted in Russia, could not be arranged until 1911.

Kandinsky and Münter now embarked on a period of unsettled wandering, made possible by the fact that they both had small private incomes. They visited Tunisia, Belgium, Italy and Austria. In June 1908, they discovered the small town of Murnau, at the foot of the Bavarian Alps near Munich, and there, at Kandinsky's urging, Münter bought the modern villa which was to be her base, despite frequent absences, for the rest of her life.

It was in Murnau that Münter made a discovery of significance to both Kandinsky and herself – the folk-paintings on glass which were a regional speciality. Study of these helped her to clarify her use of colours and simplify her forms. Her work had always been bold and instinctive, and the glass-paintings, together with Kandinsky's encouragement, helped her to focus the qualities which are the essential features of her best work.

In January 1911, Münter and Kandinsky met Franz Marc, and in the middle of the same year they got to know August Macke, events which led directly to the formation of the Blaue Reiter group, which held its first exhibition at the Thannhauser Gallery in Munich. By this time, however, their own paths were beginning to diverge. The years 1911–13 were immensely productive for Kandinsky – it was the period when he made his breakthrough into abstraction. Münter was not as boldly experimental by temperament, and though she made a few abstract studies in the period 1912–15, she found

difficulty in following him into this unexplored area. Her output declined, as his increased. Kandinsky was often away in Russia on family business, and her letters to him show that she had a knack of falling out with friends and colleagues in his absence. She quarrelled with both Marc and Macke in 1912 – irreparably with the latter, though her differences with Marc were patched up. Their correspondence makes it clear that she was finding Kandinsky increasingly withdrawn and inaccessible. He, it seems, had already begun to think of putting an end to the relationship.

On the outbreak of war in August 1914, Kandinsky, like many other Russians in Germany, had to leave the country immediately. He and Münter went to Switzerland, where they separated – Kandinsky took a circuitous route back to Russia. He made it clear to Münter by letter, after his arrival, that their alliance was effectively at an end.

Reluctant to accept this, she persuaded Kandinsky to meet her on neutral territory, in Stockholm in 1915.

GABRIELE MÜNTER,
Boating, 1910

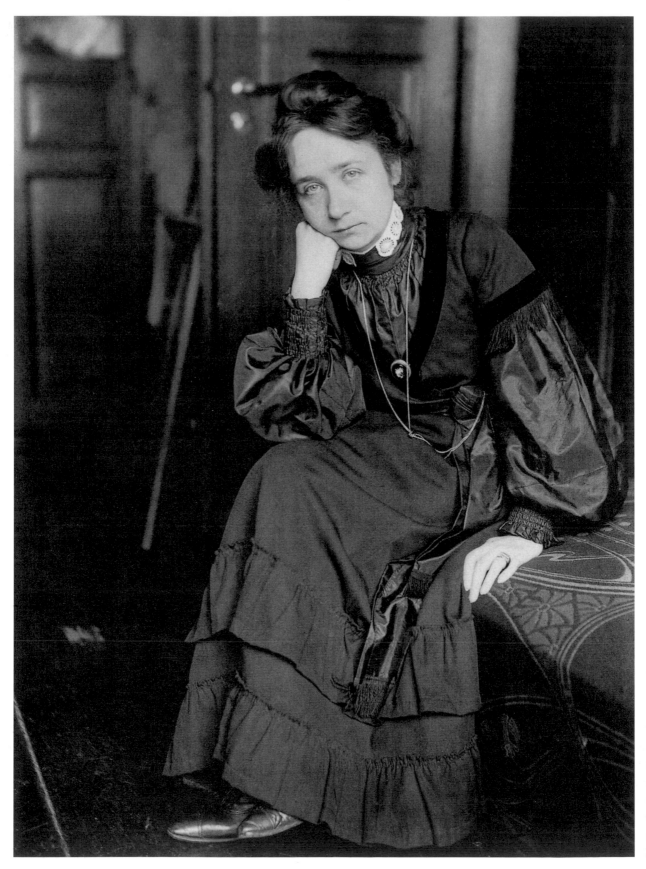

GABRIELE MÜNTER, Dresden 1905. Photo Vasily Kandinsky

Kandinsky still did not have the courage to make the final break, but returned to Russia the following year, promising to return when he could. He never did so, and this was their final meeting. Münter lingered in Sweden, then in Denmark until 1920, when she returned to Germany. The first part of the 1920s was a period of deep depression and little productivity. Kandinsky had also returned to Germany, disillusioned with the new Soviet regime, and she engaged in a legal battle with him over the paintings and other possessions he had left at Murnau. This was not finally settled until 1926, largely in her favour. In that year she marked her return to productive life with a major solo exhibition in Braunschweig.

In 1927 Münter formed a new alliance with the art historian and philosopher Johannes Eichner, who was to be her companion until his death in 1958. She returned to Murnau in 1931, though continuing to live in Munich during the winters. Thanks to Eichner she did not suffer as badly as many artists during the Nazi period. She had a large exhibition in Bremen in 1933, and in 1934 was the subject of a touring retrospective, ending its run at the Galerie Valentien in Stuttgart in 1935. In 1937, she was the subject of a special showing at the Munich Kunstverein, which brought an angry protest from a Nazi minister, who visited on the last day. Despite this she was able to show again, later in the year, at the Galerie Valentien, and her work received a favourable press. This, however, was her last major exhibition for twelve years.

After the war ended, there was a revival of interest in Expressionist art, of which Münter possessed a considerable archive. A large Blaue Reiter exhibition, drawn in large part from these holdings, was held at the Haus der Kunst in Munich in 1949. Her work which, under pressure from the prudent Eichner, had swung in a conservative direction (though without ever losing its identity) in the Nazi epoch, now became bolder and more experimental again. She produced some wholly abstract paintings – her first since the early years of the century – in 1952. When she died at Murnau, ten years later, she had achieved international stature, and was rightly regarded as one of the pioneering figures in the history of German Modernism. Her own work, and the collection of work by others, notably Kandinsky, which had remained in her possession, was divided between the Lenbachhaus in Munich and the Gabriele Münter and Johannes Eichner Foundation in the same city.

ERNST LUDWIG KIRCHNER

One of the moving spirits in Die Brücke, the main group of Expressionist artists in northern Germany, Ernst Ludwig Kirchner is also one of the tragic figures in twentieth-century art, shattered and finally destroyed by the pressure of external events.

He was born in 1880 in Aschaffenburg – his father was a chemical engineer in the paper industry, while his mother came from a merchant family. During his childhood the family moved frequently, according to the demands of his father's career; they went to Frankfurt, to Switzerland and finally to Chemnitz in Saxony, where his father was appointed Professor of Paper Research in the Gewerbe Akademie. Kirchner was a nervous, over-imaginative child – he once described some of the terrors of his childhood in these words:

> In youth dreams prevailed, often faces at night when I was a boy. I would cry out, have to be brought to the light for hours. The nocturnal dreams continued into daytime life, fear of many people.

He started training as a draughtsman while still very young, and by the age of eighteen had decided to become an artist. His family opposed his ambitions, so when he left school in 1901 he acceded to his father's wishes and went to the Dresden Technische Hochschule to study architecture. He interrupted his course to study art in Munich, where he also copied works by Old Masters in the Alte Pinakothek and visited exhibitions of modern

ERNST LUDWIG KIRCHNER, *Self-Portrait as a Soldier*, 1915

art – he was particularly struck by a show of French Neo-Impressionist paintings. But after this hiatus he returned to Dresden and was awarded his diploma in 1905.

This was also the year which witnessed the formation of Die Brücke, a group of young artists with revolutionary ambitions. The founder members were Kirchner, his friend Fritz Bleyl, Erich Heckel and Karl Schmidt-Rottluff. Later Max Pechstein, Otto Müller and the Swiss painter Cuno Amiet were drawn in, together with the much older Emil Nolde. The climate was favourable for change; the main Dresden galleries specializing in modern art played host to a stream of exhibitions of new French painting, with the focus on Van Gogh and his successors, the Fauves. Kirchner and his friends absorbed all this, but did not win immediate recognition. Kirchner shared a studio with Heckel for a while – a former butcher's shop with furniture made out of boxes, and pictures painted on the walls, which were also ornamented with batik. He was often very poor during this period and earned money by painting stove-tiles, which he sold for 50 pfennigs each.

In 1911 Kirchner moved to Berlin, and here he began to win some recognition. He soon established a link with

the artists of the Blaue Reiter group, through Franz Marc, whom he met early in 1912. In the spring of that year artists from Die Brücke were included in the Blaue Reiter exhibition at the Fritz Gurlitt Gallery in Munich, and in April they were included in the huge and important Sonderbund exhibition in Cologne. One of Kirchner's paintings was chosen for the Armory Show to be held in America the following year. In a period of four months during 1913 and 1914, he had no less than three one-man shows, including one with the Jena Art Association whose Director recorded his impressions of Kirchner:

> He is an agreeably unprepossessing man with coarse hands from wood carving, which he practises with great skill. Aside from the artist's long hair, he is free of all pose; the *Berliner Luft* [Berlin air] stamps all these artists as big city people, but they consider life there to be a piece cut out of the universe, and they preserve their independence with great strength. If Heckel gives more the impression of being a tailor ... then Kirchner is the true shoemaker, headstrong and angular ... I would like to believe he is the most significant of the Brücke; a few of his pictures please me very much.

Kirchner was indeed producing some of his best work at this epoch, notably the hallucinatory Berlin street-scenes featuring prostitutes which give a strong impression of the feverish atmosphere of the German capital just before and just after the beginning of the war. His personal life was also reasonably happy: he had met and painted a dancer called Gerda Schilling, and through Gerda, met her younger sister Erna, who became his common-law wife and stayed with him through all his subsequent misfortunes. These began with the war. Kirchner became – to use his own phrase – 'an involuntary volunteer' and was posted to an artillery regiment as a driver. He said later:

> Military life was not for me. To be sure, I learned riding and the care of horses, but I had nothing left for the cannons. Service became too difficult for me and I thus became thinner and thinner.

In October 1915 he was declared unfit for duty after a physical and mental collapse. He suffered from morbid ears of persecution and was several times hospitalized. In 1916 he wrote:

> The pressure of the war and the increasingly prevailing superficiality weigh more heavily than everything else. I always have the impression of a bloody carnival. How is it all to end? One feels that crisis is in the air and that everything is mixed up.

In February 1917 he was struck by a car in Berlin, and developed paralysis which was probably largely psychological in origin. In May, dependent on pain-killing drugs and barely able to walk, he arrived in Switzerland, which was to be his home for the rest of his life. Here he made a slow recovery – the withdrawal from drugs was not complete until April 1921. In Switzerland his artistic style underwent a change. He now painted landscapes, often with mystical overtones, in response to something he had discovered in his own nature. In 1923 he said: 'I never had a means of being warm to people ... art is a good means to declare one's love to people, without inconveniencing them.' His prospects recovered, together with his health, and by 1924, when he paid an extended visit to the Germany he had abandoned, he could count himself as well-off. The German post-war art scene did not altogether please him, however – he found in it elements which contributed to his own sense of alienation:

> The great mistake in Germany in dealing with artists is that one never openly tells them anything bad to their face, that, in a way, one elevates them like gods on a pedestal and, by thus isolating them from the community and feelings of other human beings, withdraws from them the closeness and warmth of life.

Yet Germany did not intimidate him to the point where he refused to go there. In 1925–26 he made an extended visit to Frankfurt, Chemnitz, Dresden, where he visited his old haunts with much pleasure, and Berlin.

The late 1920s saw another less happy change in his style, as Kirchner belatedly began to experiment with

ERNST LUDWIG KIRCHNER, *Two Girls, c.* 1910

Cubism. This tendency first manifested itself around 1927, and reached a climax in 1930. In the 1930s his health began to deteriorate: in 1930–31 both he and Erna were seriously ill, and in 1935 he suffered from a recurrence of an earlier intestinal disturbance, followed by an attack of angina. The Nazi takeover distressed him deeply, and the assault on his own work as 'degenerate' revived all his latent feelings of persecution. By this point Kirchner was a somewhat eccentric personality. His friend Willi Grohmann reports:

> While he was talking to someone, he would often think of something quite different and conversations with him would take an unexpected turn. He might suddenly speak of a work he was planning, or reach far back into the past, or even disappear without a word to his studio in order to work, or go to fetch a zinc plate and start working with the needle on the metal while he continued the conversation.

A stream of young disciples continued to seek him out in his Swiss retreat, but when the Nazis came to power his financial situation once again deteriorated sharply, as his reputation was not an international one and Germany had always been the main market for his work. The accumulated strains of his position became too much for him, and in June 1938 Kirchner committed suicide by shooting himself through the heart.

MAX BECKMANN

Max Beckmann is now seen as one of the isolated geniuses of twentieth-century art. Though the great triptychs which form the core of his achievement have their roots in Expressionism, Beckmann pursued a course which was independent of that taken by his German contemporaries, and he became still more detached from them in the isolation of exile. His paintings are full of esoteric allusions which do not occur in other German art of the inter-war period.

He was born in February 1884, the third child of a flour merchant from Brunswick. His father died when he was ten, and when he was sixteen he overcame family objections and entered the Academy of Art at Weimar, having been refused at Dresden, studying there until 1903. In 1904 he spent a period in Paris thanks to the patronage of the art historian and critic Julius Meier-Graefe. Here he became acquainted with the work of the Impressionists and Van Gogh, and was greatly impressed

MAX BECKMANN, 1928.
Photographer unknown

by a major exhibition of French primitives (his art was to be full of allusions to the late Gothic period). He then went to Geneva and finally settled in Berlin.

Once he had launched himself as a professional artist, Beckmann made a rapid success. In 1906 a large painting was bought by Count Harry Kessler for the Weimar Museum; in the same year Beckmann was awarded the Villa Romana Prize, which enabled him to study for six months in Florence. He also married, and became a member of the Berlin Sezession. He was elected to the board of the Sezession in 1910, but resigned in 1911. During this period he exhibited frequently: his first one-man exhibition took place in Frankfurt in 1911, followed by a retrospective in Magdeburg the following year and a one-man show in Berlin with Paul Cassirer in 1913 – the first monograph on his work was published at this time. During the pre-war years the outward circumstances of Beckmann's life tell a story of immense energy and self-confidence; remaining diary fragments, on the other hand, suggest anxiety and doubt. His work at this period was not fully Modernist, and a dispute with Franz Marc, conducted in the pages of *Pan* in 1912, shows that he was out of sympathy with the German avant-garde of the time.

At the outbreak of war in 1914 Beckmann volunteered for the medical corps serving first on the East Prussian Front and later in Flanders and Strasbourg. In October 1915 he was invalided out of the army with a nervous breakdown. He was so badly shocked that he found it impossible to pick up the threads of his former life. He neither returned to Berlin nor attempted to rejoin his wife, who had taken up a career as an opera singer and was living in Graz, but instead settled with friends in Frankfurt and embarked on a struggle both to rebuild his life and reshape his style as a painter. By 1918 he had succeeded with the latter at least, and in the same year he wrote: 'So the war is reaching its unhappy end. It has done nothing to change my idea of life, only confirmed it.' In 1919 he endorsed this with the comment: 'My pictures are a reproach to God for all that he does wrong.' The harsh, hallucinatory style which he evolved to express his feelings of disillusionment forms a bridge between pre-war German Expressionism and the Neue Sachlichkeit (New Objectivity) which was to be dominant in the Weimar years, while conforming to neither.

Despite Beckmann's feelings of alienation from the post-war society that surrounded him, his reputation again increased rapidly as soon as his new work was shown. The year 1925 was significant for Beckmann: he had a retrospective exhibition with the Frankfurter Kunstverein, and there were other one-man exhibitions in Zurich and with Paul Cassirer in Berlin. He was appointed to a Professorship at the Stadtliches Kunstinstitut in Frankfurt, and he remarried. His new wife, Mathilde von Kaulbach, nicknamed 'Quappi', was henceforth to make frequent appearances in his art – but not as frequent as those made by Beckmann himself (he was one of the most prolific self-portraitists of the century). There were other major Beckmann exhibitions in 1928 (Mannheim, Berlin and Munich), and in 1930 (Basle and Zurich). But all this was abruptly brought to a halt by the accession of the Nazis to power in 1933, when he was promptly dismissed from his professorial post. He did not, however, decide to leave Germany for good until 1937, when ten of his paintings were included in the Degenerate Art Exhibition in Munich.

The transition to exile was eased by the fact that Beckmann had had a permanent studio in Paris since 1930, and was accustomed to spending several months there every year, though he seems to have had little contact with the Parisian art world. During the brief interval before the outbreak of the Second World War he divided his time between Paris and Amsterdam. He also paid a visit to London in 1938 for the exhibition *Twentieth-Century German Art*, intended as a retort to the show of Degenerate Art in Munich.

In 1939 Beckmann was awarded first prize in the Contemporary European Section at the Golden Gate International Exposition in San Francisco, and in 1940 he was invited to teach at the Chicago Art Institute. He accepted, but before he could obtain an exit visa he was trapped in Holland by the German invasion. He and Quappi lived throughout the war in the historic quarter of Amsterdam and suffered considerable privations. Yet it was also an exceptionally productive period for his painting. His diary shows a much more philosophical attitude with regard to this war than he had adopted to its predecessor. 'Many things are easier to bear,' he remarks, 'if one thinks of the war, or indeed the whole of life, as a mere scene in the theatre of infinity.' The image of the world as a stage, or alternatively as a circus ring, had always been one of his favourite pictorial metaphors.

In 1947 he was at last free to leave Holland, and travelled to Paris and the Riviera. Although he had many doubts as to whether he would now be equal to the task, he accepted an invitation to go and teach at Washington University, St Louis. He was well received in America. In 1948 he had a large touring retrospective which was seen in St Louis, Los Angeles, Detroit, Baltimore and Minneapolis. In 1949 he won first prize at the Carnegie International in Pittsburgh. When his contract at St Louis expired he moved to New York to take up an appointment at the Brooklyn Museum Art School. He had little time to make his mark in this post, as he was struck down by a heart attack on 27 December 1950, while taking his usual morning walk in Central Park. The evening before, he had added what he declared to be the final touches to his last triptych, *The Argonauts*.

MAX BECKMANN,
Carnival, 1920

FRANZ MARC

Franz Marc, whose career was cruelly cut short by the First World War, has in recent years been the most popular of all the German Expressionists. One reason for this is supplied by his eloquent and touching letters. Another may be the fact that his work is not very typical of Expressionism as it is generally understood. He found a way of giving the German Romantic painters – Runge, Friedrich, Kobell, Blechen, Rethel and Schwind (all of whom he warmly admired) – a new and modern guise.

Marc was born in Munich in February 1880. His father, Wilhelm Marc, was a professional landscape painter. His mother, a strict Calvinist, came from Alsace, but had been brought up in French-speaking Switzerland. Marc himself was a serious child, perhaps because of the repressive influence of his mother. In high school, his plan was to read theology, but he eventually enrolled at Munich University as a student of languages. In 1900, however, when his year of military service was over, he decided to follow in his father's footsteps and become a painter. He enrolled at the Munich Academy of Art.

In 1903, with the first stage in his training completed, Marc went to Paris, where he spent several months, also visiting Brittany. He was greatly excited by his discovery of the Impressionists at the Durand-Ruel Gallery and in letters home proclaimed them to be 'the only salvation for us artists', but they made little visible impact on his work. When he returned home he entered a state of deep depression with an 'anxiety that numbed the senses'. This was temporarily cured by a trip which he made to Salonika and Mount Athos in the spring of 1906, accompanying his brother, who was making a study of Byzantine manuscripts, but returned as soon as he got back to Paris. He tried to alleviate his condition by drowning himself in his work, but knew he was getting nowhere. He also got engaged to be married, which he regretted, and only disentangled himself by running away to Paris the day before the marriage ceremony, at Easter 1907.

Once back in Paris, he was again entranced by the Impressionists. In a prophetic metaphor he said that he walked among their paintings 'like a roe deer in an enchanted forest, for which it has always yearned'. He also discovered the work of Gauguin and Van Gogh, and was impressed by the latter in particular. He declared that his own 'wavering, anxiety-ridden spirit found peace at

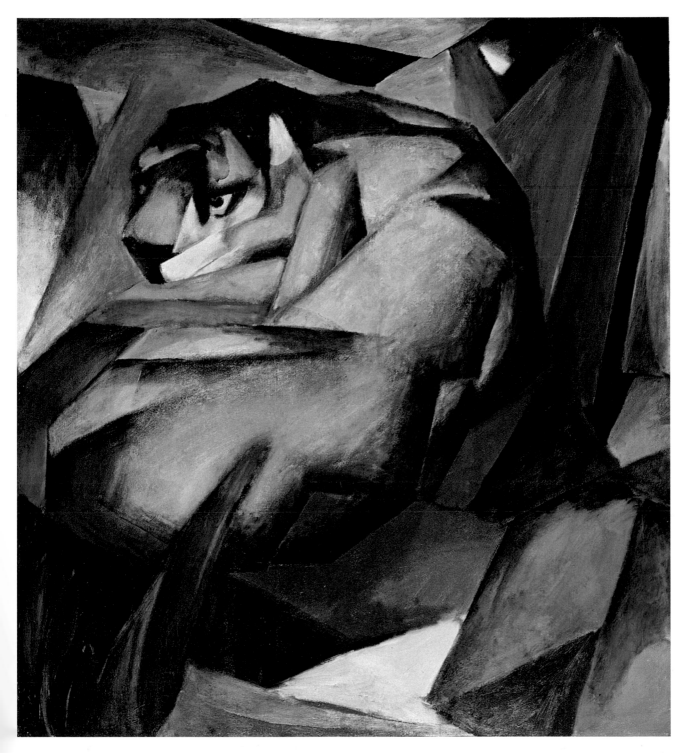

Franz Marc,
The Tiger, 1912

Franz Marc out walking, *c.* 1913–14. Photographer unknown

last in these marvellous paintings'. It was at this period that he began the intensive study of animals which was to lead to his mature style. He said that he wanted to recreate them 'from the inside', and made himself so complete a master of animal anatomy that he was able to give lessons in the subject, until 1910, in order to earn some money. Though he felt he was now making some progress, he destroyed his more ambitious works, as they continued to dissatisfy him. In December 1908 he wrote a letter to Reinhart Piper:

> I am trying to intensify my feeling for the organic rhythm of all things, to achieve pantheistic empathy with the throbbing and flowing of nature's bloodstream – in trees, in animals, in the air.

The year 1910 marked a significant turning point. In January he met August Macke, a painter seven years younger than him, but who seemed extremely sophisticated and well informed. Through Macke he learned something of the Fauves, and the following month was able to see what they were doing for himself, thanks to a Matisse exhibition in Munich. Macke also introduced him to the collector Bernard Koehler, who happened to be the uncle of Macke's wife. Koehler liked his work, and offered him a monthly allowance, which removed the worst of his financial worries. In September Marc defended the exhibition of the Neue Künstlervereinigung, which was being attacked by the local Munich critics, and was offered membership of the group as a result. He did not, however, meet Kandinsky, its leading spirit, until February 1911. By that time he had formed his own set of artistic principles, which were a mixture of Romanticism, Expressionism and Symbolism. In December 1910 he wrote a famous letter to Macke, assigning emotional values to colours:

> Blue is the male principle, astringent and spiritual. Yellow is the female principle, gentle, gay and spiritual. Red is matter, brutal and heavy and always the colour to be opposed and overcome by the other two.

In 1911 he found himself ready to embark on the series of paintings of animals which have since been the cornerstone of his reputation. And in December, after a split in the Neue Künstlervereinigung, organized the first Blaue Reiter (Blue Rider) exhibition. Formerly so ineffective and depressed, Marc had now become a most efficient organizer, and it was he who persuaded the publisher Reinhart Piper to bring out Kandinsky's fundamental text, *On the Spiritual in Art*, and he also played a leading part in the creation of the *Blaue Reiter Almanach* and the organization of a second and more ambitious Blaue Reiter show in 1912. In 1913 he took an important role in selecting and hanging *Der Sturm*'s First Autumn Salon in Berlin, and noted how many of the exhibitors were veering towards abstraction. This confirmed his feelings which had begun to emerge when he and Macke went to Paris to visit Delaunay in 1912, and saw some examples from the latter's *Window* series. By the spring of 1914 Marc's own work had become virtually abstract.

This promising career was cut short by the war. Marc was mobilized and wrote numerous letters home from the Front, expounding his aesthetic philosophy, and kept a notebook with drawings for the paintings he would create as soon as he was free to do so. But he was denied the opportunity he hoped for. In March 1916 he was killed instantly when he was struck in the head by a shell splinter.

T he pre-war Viennese milieu gave a flavour of its own to the art produced in the city – slightly behind the times in some respects, daring in others. The art of Klimt, Schiele and Kokoschka makes a transition from late Art Nouveau or Jugendstil to something closely allied to the Expressionism prevalent in Germany. One striking characteristic is its freedom of expression in sexual matters.

GUSTAV KLIMT

The undoubted leader of the Vienna Sezession, Gustav Klimt marks the transition from Symbolism to fully developed Modernism in Central Europe. He was born in 1862, the second of seven children. His father was an artisan – an engraver of precious metals – and came from peasant stock. His mother had apparently once nourished ambitions to be an opera singer; later in life she was mentally ill.

In 1874 Klimt was awarded a scholarship at the new School of Arts and Crafts attached to the Österreiches Museum für Kunst und Industrie. In due course he was followed into the School by two younger brothers, Ernst, who was also a painter, and Georg, who became a

Left: Artists at the Fourteenth Vienna
Sezession exhibition: (left to right)
Anton Stark, Gustav Klimt (in chair),
Kolo Moser, Adolf Böhm, Maximilian
Lenz, Ernst Stöhr, Wilhelm List, Emil
Orlik, Maximilian Kurzweil, Leopold
Stolba, Carl Moll, Rudolf Bacher,
1902. Photographer unknown
Above: GUSTAV KLIMT,
Portrait of Adele Bloch-Bauer I, 1907

Top: GUSTAV KLIMT, 1914.
Photo Anton Josef Trcka
Bottom: GUSTAV KLIMT,
caricatured self-portrait (detail),
c. 1902

sculptor and metalsmith. Gustav and Ernst formed a partnership with a fellow student, Frans Matsch, and before their training was fully complete they were already in demand as decorative painters. In 1886 this partnership undertook its most important commission, a series of paintings for the new Burgtheater in Vienna. The theatre was the centre of Viennese cultural and social life, and the site was therefore prestigious. The paintings were much admired, and on their completion in 1888 Klimt was awarded a gold cross of merit by the Emperor Franz-Joseph. Following this, the Klimt brothers and their partner were asked to continue the decorations on the staircase of the Kunsthistorisches Museum in Vienna which had been left unfinished by Hans Makart (1840–84), the best-known Austrian decorative painter of the time. The slightly archaizing style he adopted for this task marked Klimt's first departure from the academic norm. The decorations were, however, hugely successful, and the suggestion was now made that he and his two partners decorate the Aula (Great Hall) of Vienna University. Ernst Klimt died at the end of 1892, and the other two were asked to provide plans for the decorations which were accepted by the Ministry of Culture in 1894.

The slow and painful evolution of Klimt's part of the commission – three vast panels symbolic of *Philosophy, Medicine* and *Jurisprudence* – coincided with the rise of the Vienna Sezession. Klimt, like most leading Viennese artists, was a member of the Genossenschaftbildener Künstler Wiens, an exhibiting society founded in 1861. The Sezession was originally intended as a ginger group within this, with Klimt as President. But he and his followers were forced out by the ruling cabal, and in 1897 the Sezession became a separate entity. Its first year of full activity was 1898, and Klimt designed the poster for the opening exhibition – Theseus symbolically slaying the Minotaur.

Klimt was by this time having problems with his patrons at the Ministry over his University commission. He was asked to revise his designs, and threatened to withdraw. The real storm did not break until 1900, when he showed *Philosophy* in an unfinished state at the Seventh Sezession Exhibition. A group of university professors got up a petition against the work, accusing the artist of presenting 'unclear ideas in unclear forms'. His defenders responded vigorously. The following year *Medicine* was shown at the Tenth Sezession Exhibition, and the storm broke afresh. Twenty-two members of the

ustrian parliament addressed a petition attacking
he painting to the Ministry of Culture. Somewhat
ncomfortably the Minister replied:

It is altogether outside the power of the educational
authority to give any particular trend an official
character. First of all, as things are now, artistic trends
are not easily influenced, they can be neither encouraged nor suppressed artificially. They are the results
of a continual progressive development that lies deep
within the changes of all material and spiritual life.

One reason for the objections to Klimt's decorations
as not so much that they were innovative as that they
ere erotic. When *Ver Sacrum*, the official journal of the
ezession, published some preliminary drawings for
Medicine, the Public Prosecutor ordered the confiscation
f the issue on the grounds that it was an offence against
ublic morals. The President of the Sezession (the
residency rotated annually) had to take legal action
o raise the censor's ban.
   The final panel *Jurisprudence*, was the most daring of
l. The main group showed a miserable prisoner, nude,
owed and turned away from the spectator, attended by
iree Furies with abundant hair and about to be devoured
y a kind of nightmarish sea-creature, while Justice and
er attendants looked down from high above. It was
iown in Klimt's retrospective, organized by the
ezession at the end of 1903, and aroused very different
eactions. The critic Ludwig Hevesi saw it in Klimt's
udio just before the exhibition, and left a vivid account
 his visit:

I first saw *Jurisprudence* ... in the master's large studio,
right out in the Josephstadt ... A metal door, on which
were chalked the letters 'G.K.' and a notice 'Knock
loudly'. I hammered with my fists, but the master
himself was on the *qui vive*, and was at the door
straight away. It was afternoon, thirty-five degrees
centigrade. He had on only his usual dark smock, and
nothing underneath. His life is spent in front of the
great canvas, climbing up and down the ladder, pacing
up and down, looking, brooding, creating out of
nothing, trying, daring. He seems as if surrounded
by a mist, wrestling with this element of uncertainty,
kneading it, with both arms immersed up to the
shoulders. The floor covered in drawings, many

drawings for each figure, variants of every pose,
position, movement.

Karl Kraus, the radical satirist who cared more about
political liberty and personal freedom than anyone else
in the Vienna of his time, took the canvas as something
approaching a personal affront:

For Herr Klimt, the concept of Jurisprudence is
exhausted by the notions of crime and punishment.
To him 'the rule of law' means nothing more than
'hunt them down and wring their necks'. And to
those who are more than content to have 'nothing
to do with the law', he presents the terrifying image
of the transgressor.

The long saga of the university paintings ended in
1905 when Klimt renounced his contract, reclaimed his
work from the Ministry, and, with aid from friends,
repaid the money he had received. 'If my work, which has
already taken me years, is to be finished,' Klimt declared,
'I must first of all find pleasure in it, and I am completely
lacking in this as long as I must consider it in the present
situation as a state commission.' He went further, and
called for a 'clear-cut separation' between artists and the
State. Significantly, this was also the year in which Klimt
withdrew from the Sezession, which he had founded, to
lead a new and yet more radical group.
   In one sense he might now have become an 'outsider'
artist, but he was also acknowledged as the most important painter in Vienna. He kept to a strict routine. He
rose early, and walked from his flat on the Westbahn-
strasse to the Café Tivoli, where he ate a large breakfast.
This finished, he walked across Schönbrunn Park where
he spent the rest of his day in the studio. In the evenings
he returned once more to the Café to meet his friends –
very much *primus inter pares*, his nickname in this
intimate circle was *König* ('King'). A contemporary
described his appearance and manner at this time:

He is squat, somewhat heavy, athletic ... has the
cheerful rough ways of a country boy, the tanned
skin of a sailor, protruding cheekbones and lively
small eyes. He wears his hair brushed back from
his temples, perhaps to make his face appear longer.
He speaks in a loud voice and in heavy dialect. He
likes to tease and joke.

Klimt was interested in sports: he belonged to a rowing club, swam and trained with weights – and he also seems to have been blessed with a healthy sexual appetite. There were always one or two models in his studio, ready to pose (he made rapid life-studies as a break from larger projects), and he was notorious for sleeping with them. His real attachment was to the elegant Emilie Flöge, who kept a smart dress shop; Klimt sometimes designed clothes for her to sell. He invariably spent the fine summer months beside Lake Attersee, with Emilie and her sister Barbara, and it was during these breaks that he painted a series of beautiful landscapes, very different in their tranquillity from the rest of his work.

The final period of his life was less agitated than the stormy decade of the University commission. Summer 1908 saw the opening of the Kunstschau Wien, the first public exhibition of the group which had followed Klimt in withdrawing from the Sezession. The Österreiches Staatsgalerie acquired Klimt's *The Kiss* from the exhibition, despite its erotic theme. In 1910 he participated in the Ninth Venice Biennale. In 1917 the Academy of Fine Arts in Vienna and the Academy of Fine Arts in Munich elected him to honorary membership. Some dissentient voices were beginning to be heard from younger artists, however, as the new generation of Expressionists in Germany criticized his work.

Klimt's death was sudden. Immediately after Christmas 1917 he made a trip to Romania. On 11 January 1918, just after his return to Vienna, he had a stroke which paralysed his right side. He was taken to a clinic, where he died on 6 February of a lung infection.

OSKAR KOKOSCHKA, *The Tempest*, 1914

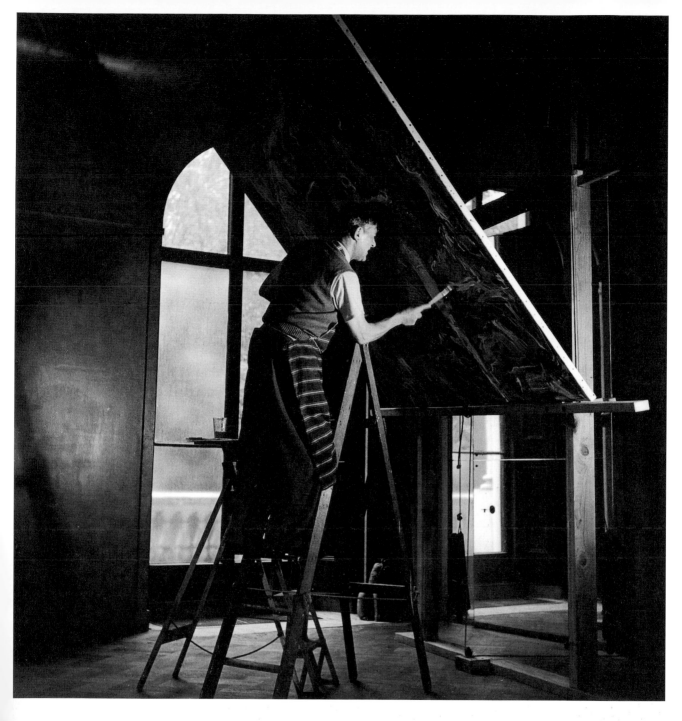

OSKAR KOKOSCHKA

Oskar Kokoschka is the third in the great trio of Viennese artists, and the one whose reputation is currently hardest to assess. He was born at Pöchlarn on the Danube in 1886. His father was Czech and came from a well known family of Prague goldsmiths. He was perhaps rather work-shy: Kokoschka later said of him, 'From him I learned to endure poverty rather than work slavishly at distasteful work.' His mother came from the mountain region of Styria, and claimed to have second sight. Oskar

was the second of their four sons; when he was still a child the family moved to Vienna where his elder brother died in 1891.

As a boy, Kokoschka was not particularly attracted to art. He wanted to study chemistry but was recommended for a scholarship at the Vienna School of Arts and Crafts by a teacher who had been impressed by his drawings. He entered the School in 1905, the year in which he started to paint in oils, and in 1907 he found work at the Wiener Werkstätte. Soon he began to expand his activities to literature. Asked to produce a children's book, he wrote his own text, *Die Träumenden Knaben* (The Dreaming Youths), which was scarcely suitable for the young, but made a good basis for his distinctive illustrations. He also wrote two plays, *Sphinx und Strohamann* (The Sphinx and the Scarecrow), and *Mörder, Hoffnung der Frauen* (Murderer, Hope of Women): these are now considered to mark the beginnings of Expressionist theatre in Germany.

In 1908 Kokoschka's work was shown in the Kunstschau exhibition in Vienna, which featured the avant-garde group around Klimt. His contributions were a centre of controversy because of their Expressionist violence, and he was dismissed from the School of Arts and Crafts as a result. In 1909 his work was shown at the second Kunstschau, and his two plays were performed in the little open-air theatre attached to the exhibition buildings. There was a tremendous scandal because of their violence, and their unconventional and apparently irrational structure, and even the Werkstätte would no longer employ him. At one time he managed to keep alive by betting on his own capacity to drink visitors to Vienna under the table. His chief protector was the pioneer Modernist architect Adolf Loos, who secured portrait commissions for him. One portrait was of the satirical writer Karl Kraus, editor of *Die Fackel* (The Torch). Kraus said of this: 'It is quite possible that those who know me will not recognize me. But it is certain that those who do not know me will recognize me.'

In 1910 Kokoschka's luck changed. He went to Berlin and was taken up by Herwarth Walden, the energetic owner-editor of *Der Sturm*, who commissioned him to do title-page drawings for the magazine and used one for almost every issue. He was also given a contract by the powerful dealer Paul Cassirer. In 1911 he returned to Vienna and was appointed as assistant teacher at the very school which had dismissed him. He had a show at the Hagenbund in Vienna, of which the opening reception was attended by Archduke Franz Ferdinand, the heir to the throne, who exclaimed indignantly: 'This fellow's bones ought to be broken in his body!' Most important of all, in 1911 he began a passionate affair with Alma Mahler, the widow of the great composer, an elegant society beauty considerably older than himself. The year 1912 was better still – he was able to give up teaching and showed at the Sonderbund exhibition in Cologne, which

united the whole German-speaking avant garde, and with the Blaue Reiter in Munich.

By 1913 his relationship with Alma Mahler was beginning to show signs of strain. They travelled to Italy together, and on one occasion visited the Naples aquarium. Kokoschka watched an insect sting and paralyse a fish, before devouring it, and at once associated the scene with the woman by his side.

He was still a controversial figure: when he began teaching art at a smart Viennese girls' school whose headmistress was known for her progressive views, some of the parents objected so strongly that the Austrian government actually banned him from teaching. War, when it broke out, seemed a release from an impossible relationship and in impossible situation. Adolf Loos used his influence to have him appointed Lieutenant in an exclusive regiment of dragoons with a particularly glamorous uniform. As soon as the appointment was gazetted Loos had a postcard made of Kokoschka in his finery which was sold in shops alongside those showing leading actresses.

At the beginning of 1915 Kokoschka was seriously wounded – and briefly taken prisoner – in Galicia: he suffered a head injury and a bayonet wound to the lung. He spent a period of convalescence in Vienna, but was then sent to the Isonzo Front, where his health soon broke down completely. He went to Stockholm to consult a brain specialist and then to Dresden to try and recover his health. His anguish was as much mental as physical, and was perhaps connected with his residual feelings for Alma Mahler. To exorcize his obsession he commissioned a life-sized doll, complete and life-like in all details, which he treated like a living companion – it has even been said that he escorted it to the opera.

After the end of the war the political situation in Dresden was very unstable, just as it was everywhere else in Germany, and Kokoschka formed part of a small, left-wing bohemian group. In the newly liberal climate of 1919 he was officially appointed Professor at the Dresden Academy, and this post brought with it a beautiful house and studio. Outside Dresden, his reputation continued to rise. The composer Paul Hindemith set *Murderer, Hope of Women* to music, and it received numerous performances, among them one at the Dresden State Opera. In 1922 Kokoschka was invited to exhibit at the Venice Biennale. His health had now improved and he was becoming restless. He resigned his post at the

Dresden Academy in 1924, simply giving a note to the porter and leaving the city before his intentions had been discovered. A period of travel followed, financed by the proceeds of his now lucrative Cassirer contract. Using Munich as his main base he went all over Europe, and also to North Africa, Egypt, Turkey and Palestine. The year 1931 brought great success for him, despite the darkening political horizon: he had a show at the Kunsthalle in Mannheim which Cassirer's successors brought to the Galerie Georges Petit in Paris, where it did well with the Parisian public. However, from this triumph there also came a conflict. Kokoschka demanded more independence from his dealers; they, in turn, were anxious to establish his work as a staple commodity in the art market. Kokoschka broke with them, and there was an acrimonious exchange of letters in the *Frankfurter Zeitung*.

In 1932 Kokoschka once again showed at the Venice Biennale, but now his reception was stormy. Mussolini made it plain that he disliked Kokoschka's art, and the pro-Nazi press in Germany seized the opportunity to attack him. By 1933 his finances were severely strained, and he left Paris for the provinces and then went to Vienna to be with his mother. He felt ill at ease in a city ruled by the fascist administration of Chancellor Dollfuss, and after his mother's death later that year he went to Prague and took Czech citizenship. The Austrian government tried to lure him back by offering him the Directorship of the School of Arts and Crafts, and in 1937 he was the subject of a major retrospective at the Österreiches Museum für Kunst und Industrie. This perhaps meant less to him than the fact that his work was also on show that year in the Degenerate Art Exhibition in Munich – at the same time more than four hundred of his works were removed from German museums. In Prague he had met Olda Pavlovska, who was later to become his wife, and he was busy expressing support for the Republic cause in Spain.

The Munich Agreement of 1938 indicated that Prague was no longer a safe refuge. In September Kokoschka left for England. This was the logical choice, but it was also the only place in Europe where his art was very little known. The Kokoschkas were desperately poor. In 1939 they moved to Polperro in Cornwall where Oskar made watercolours of the local scenery and Olda ran a pastry shop to help their finances. The next year, however, they returned to London, as Kokoschka was convinced that

their neighbours were suspicious of them. London bored and depressed him:

> What am I to do in this hole [their London flat]? I must invent new subjects for my paintings. I am quite starved for something to *see*. When the spring comes I feel how it stirs in me as in a migrant bird, and I become quite nervous: I must leave town and paint something real – a grasshopper or something. When I come back to town the landscapes turn into political pictures. My heart aches, but I cannot help it. I cannot just paint landscapes without taking any notice of what happens.

His fortunes began to look up as soon as the war was over. In 1945 he received a symbolic tribute in war-battered Vienna: an exhibition shared with Klimt and Schiele, both long dead. In 1947 there was a large Kokoschka retrospective at the Kunsthalle in Berne, and in 1952 a room was devoted to his work at the 26th Venice Biennale, Kokoschka had become a British citizen in 1947, but was not eager to remain in a country which he felt had slighted him. In 1953 he began to run his School of Seeing at the Internationale Sommerakademie für Bildende Kunst in Salzburg, thus re-establishing his ties with the Austrian milieu in which he began his career, and in the same year he settled permanently at Villeneuve on Lake Geneva. He was now once again an extremely celebrated artist, but he had drifted away from the post-war art world, and, though much respected, was a marginal figure by the time of his death in 1980.

EGON SCHIELE

Schiele was regarded by many of his contemporaries as the predestined successor to Gustav Klimt, but died before he could fulfil his promise. His fascinating but not wholly admirable character is accounted for, at least in part, by his family background and upbringing. His father Adolf worked for the Austrian State Railways, and was in charge of the important station at Tully where his son was born in June 1890. Since there was no suitable school at Tully, Schiele was sent away in 1901, first to Krems, then to Klosterneuberg on the northern outskirts of Vienna. In 1904 the whole family followed him there because of his father's deteriorating health. Adolf Schiele's condition soon degenerated into madness, and in the following year he died, aged fifty-four. Schiele afterwards felt that he had had a special relationship with his father. In 1913 he wrote to his brother-in-law:

I don't know whether there is anyone else at all who remembers my noble father with such sadness. I don't know who is able to understand why I visit those places where my father used to be and where I can feel the pain... . I believe in the immortality of all creatures ... why do I paint graves and many similar things? – because this continues to live in me.

He took a dislike to his mother because he felt she did not mourn for his father enough, or give her son the attention he craved:

My mother is a very strange woman ... She doesn't understand me in the least and doesn't love me much either. If she had either love or understanding she would be prepared to make sacrifices.

During his late adolescence Schiele's emotions were directed into an intense relationship with his younger sister, Gerti, which was not without its incestuous implications. When he was sixteen and she was twelve, he took her by train all the way to Trieste, where they spent the night in a double-room at a hotel. On another occasion, his father broke down the door of a locked room to see what the two children were doing in there together.

In 1906 Schiele overcame the opposition of his guardian, his mother's brother, and applied for a place at the School of Arts and Crafts in Vienna, where Klimt had once studied. Perhaps those in charge scented a troublesome pupil – in any case they sent him on to the more traditional Academy of Fine Arts. Schiele duly passed the entrance examination, and was admitted at the age of sixteen. The next year he sought out his idol, Klimt, to show him some of his drawings. Did they show talent? 'Yes,' Klimt replied. 'Much too much!' Klimt liked to encourage younger artists, and he continued to take an interest in this gifted young man, buying his drawings, or offering to exchange them for some of his own, arranging models for him and introducing him to potential patrons. He also introduced Schiele to the Wiener Werkstätte, the arts and crafts workshop connected with the Sezession. Schiele did odd jobs for them from 1908 onwards – he made designs for men's clothes, for women's shoes, and drawings for postcards. In 1908 he had his first exhibition, in Klosterneuberg.

Left: Egon Schiele,
Reclining Girl with Green Stockings, 1914
Above: Egon Schiele, 1914.
Photo by Anton Josef Trcka

In 1909 he left the Academy, after completing his third year. He found a flat and a studio and set up on his own. At this time he showed a strong interest in pubescent children, especially young girls, who were often the subjects of his drawings. Paris von Gütersloh, a young artist who was Schiele's contemporary, remembered that the establishment was overrun with them:

They slept, recovered from beatings administered by parents, lazily lounged about – something they were not allowed to do at home – combed their hair, pulled their dresses up or down, did up or undid their shoes ... like animals in a cage which suits them, they were left to their own devices, or at any rate believed themselves to be.

Already a superb draughtsman, Schiele made many drawings from these willing models, some of which were extremely erotic. He seems to have made part of his income by supplying collectors of pornography, who abounded in Vienna at that time.

Schiele was also fascinated by his own appearance, and made self-portraits in large numbers. He impressed not only himself, but others with whom he came into contact. The writer Arthur Roessler, one of his staunchest defenders and promoters, described him thus:

Even in the presence of well known men of imposing appearance, Schiele's unusual looks stood out ... He had a tall, slim, supple figure with narrow shoulders, long arms and long-fingered bony hands. His face was sunburned, beardless, and surrounded by long, dark, unruly hair. His broad, angular forehead was furrowed by horizontal lines. The features of his face were usually fixed in an earnest, almost sad expression, as though caused by pains which made him weep inwardly. ... His laconic, aphoristic way of speaking created, in keeping with the way he looked, the impression of an inner nobility that seemed the more convincing because it was obviously natural and in no way feigned.

During this period, and indeed afterwards, Schiele liked to give an impression of extreme poverty. But his claims that at this time he was virtually in rags are at odds not only with what his contemporaries have to say, but with the photographs taken of him. His letters make it plain that he suffered from a degree of persecution mania – for example, he wrote in a letter of 1910: 'How hideous it is here! Everyone envies me and conspires against me. Former colleagues regard me with malevolent eyes.'

In 1911 Schiele met the seventeen-year-old Wally Neuzil, who was to live with him for a while and serve as the model for some of his best paintings. Little is known of her, save that she had previously modelled for Klimt, and had perhaps been one of the older painter's mistresses. Schiele and Wally wanted to get out of the claustrophobic Viennese milieu, and went to the small town of Krumau, with which Schiele had family connections, but were drive out by the disapproval of the inhabitants. They then moved to the equally small town of Neulengbach, half an hour from Vienna by train. Just as it had been in Vienna, Schiele's studio became a gathering place for all the delinquent children of the neighbourhood. His way of life inevitably aroused animosity, and in April 1912 he was arrested. The police seized more than a hundred drawings which they considered pornographic, and Schiele was imprisoned, to await trial for seducing a young girl below the age of consent. When the case came before a judge the charges of abduction and seduction were dropped, but the artist

EGON SCHIELE,
Self-Portrait Pulling Cheek, 1910

was found guilty of exhibiting an erotic drawing in a place accessible to children. The twenty-one days he had already spent in custody were taken into account, and he was sentenced to only three days' imprisonment. Though the magistrate made a point of personally burning one of Schiele's drawings before the assembled crowd, he was very lucky to escape so lightly. While he was in prison, he produced a series of self-portrait drawings, inscribed with self-pitying phrases: 'I do not feel punished; rather purified'; 'To restrict the artist is a crime. It is to murder germinating life.'

The Neulengbach affair had no effect on his career, and apparently little on his character, apart from supplying him with tangible proof that he was indeed a victim. In 1912 he was invited to show at the Sonderbund exhibition in Cologne, and he was also taken on by the important dealer Hans Goltz of Munich. Their relationship was a constant struggle over money, Schiele always wanting the highest possible prices for his work. Meanwhile he was writing boastfully to his mother, in March 1913:

> All beautiful and noble qualities have been united in me ... I shall be the fruit which will leave eternal vitality behind even after its decay. How great must be your joy, therefore, to have given birth to me.

Schiele's narcissism, exhibitionism and persecution-mania can all be found united in the poster he produced for his first one-man exhibition in Vienna, held at the Galerie Arnot at the very beginning of 1915, in which he portrayed himself as St Sebastian.

The year 1915 marked a turning-point in Schiele's life. Some time in the previous year he had met two middle-class girls who lived opposite his studio. Edith and Adèle harms were the daughters of a master locksmith. Schiele was attracted to both of them, but eventually fixed his sights on Edith; by April 1915 he was engaged to her, and Wally Neuzil was rather cold-bloodedly dismissed. Schiele's last meeting with Wally took place at their 'local', the Café Eichberger, where he played billiards nearly every day. He handed her a letter in which he proposed that, despite their parting, they take a holiday together every summer – without Edith. Not surprisingly, Wally refused. She joined the Red Cross as a nurse and died of scarlet fever in a military hospital near Split in Dalmatia just before Christmas 1917. Schiele and Edith were married, despite her family's opposition, in June 1915. Schiele's mother was not present.

Four days after his marriage Schiele was called up. Compared with the majority of his contemporaries, he had an easy war. He was transferred to a detachment transporting Russian prisoners-of-war to and from Vienna, and later became a clerk in a prison camp for Russian officers in Lower Austria. Finally, in January 1917, he was moved to Vienna itself to work for the 'Imperial and Royal Commission for the Army in the Field' – a depot which supplied food, drink, tobacco and other comforts to the Austrian army. In a country where food was increasingly short, it was a privileged place to be.

Schiele's army service did not halt the growth of his reputation – he was now thought of as the leading Austrian artist of the younger generation, and was asked to take part in a government-sponsored exhibition in Stockholm and Copenhagen intended to improve Austria's image with the neutral Scandinavian powers. In 1918 he was invited to be a major participant in the Sezession's 49th exhibition. For this he produced a poster design strongly reminiscent of the Last Supper, with his own portrait in the place of Christ. Despite the war, the show was a triumph. Prices for Schiele's drawing trebled, and he was offered many portrait commissions. He and Edith moved to a new and grander house and studio. Their pleasure in it was brief. On 19 October 1918 Edith, who was pregnant, fell ill with Spanish influenza, then sweeping Europe. On 28 October she died. Schiele, who seems never to have written her a real love-letter, and who in the midst of her illness wrote his mother a very cool letter to say that she would probably not survive, was devastated by the loss. Almost immediately he came down with the same sickness, and died on 31 October, three days after his wife.

From the origins of Modernism until the outbreak of the Second World War Paris was a magnet and focus for artists of all kinds, from almost every corner of the world. Many of these, though important in themselves, do not fit easily into stylistic groupings, however loosely constructed. This is the case with the painters and sculptors whose lives are brought together here. Perhaps the most significant thing about the list taken as a whole is that only one of those named was actually born in France.

In other respects, they represent extremes. Rouault and Soutine can be regarded as French-based Expressionists, making work which exteriorizes turbulent feeling. Brancusi and Mondrian are numbered among the saints of art. Each of them pursued supreme refinement and simplicity – though simplicity of different kinds, since one derived his work from forms found in nature while the other, in maturity, rejected all sources of this type – and (not coincidentally) each created a studio environment which was almost as expressive of their ideas and standards as the work itself.

Modigliani, Brancusi's pupil in sculpture, lies somewhere between these two poles. His work has extreme refinement of line, often combined with simplicity of form, but it also reflects the bohemian wildness with which he lived.

GEORGES ROUAULT
with his wife Marthe and
their three eldest children
(left to right), Isabelle, Michel and
Geneviève, Versailles 1915.
Photographer unknown

GEORGES ROUAULT

Isolated among the artists of his time, George Rouault produced work which proved it was possible to be an independent yet wholly committed Modernist. He was born in 1871, in the cellar of a house in Belleville, a working-class quarter of Paris near the Père Lachaise cemetery. The city was at that moment being bombarded by government troops from Versailles, who were putting down the Paris Commune. His father was an artisan – a finisher and varnisher of pianos in the Pleyel factory. He was also a follower of the Catholic democrat Lammenais who sent his son to a Protestant school in disgust when Lammenais was condemned by the Pope. Rouault's grandfather was in his own way equally remarkable: he was an employee in the postal service and a modest collector – he bought Callot engravings, lithographs by Daumier and reproductions of paintings by Rembrandt.

The Protestant school was not a success, and in 1885 Rouault was taken away and apprenticed for two years to a maker of stained glass named Tamoni. He was then employed by another stained-glass maker, Georges Hirsch, who did some restoration work on medieval windows, which gave his young assistant a chance to examine them and to realize their superiority to modern work. From 1885 onwards Rouault also studied at evening classes at the Ecole des Arts Décoratifs, and in 1891 he was able to transfer himself to the Ecole des Beaux-Arts, where he entered Elie Delaunay's studio. Delaunay died the following year, and it was Rouault's good luck that his successor was Gustave Moreau, one of the leading Symbolists. Moreau immediately became a progressive influence in the school; his pupils included Matisse, Marquet, Evenepoel and Manguin, but it was Rouault who was his closest disciple.

During this period Rouault's ambitions were still conventional. He set himself to win the Prix de Rome, but failed on two occasions despite Moreau's encouragements. He did, however, manage to win some minor prizes, and he exhibited his work for the first time, sending it to the conservative Salon des Artistes Français. In 1898 Moreau died, and there was an immediate vendetta within the Ecole des Beaux-Arts against his more 'advanced' disciples. Rouault might have been put in a precarious position but was rescued by being offered a curatorship of the Gustave Moreau Museum which was set up under the terms of his teacher's will. He still endeavoured to maintain some links with the academic art world – for example, he exhibited at the Centennial Exhibition of French art held in connection with the Paris Exposition Universel of 1900, and was awarded a bronze medal. Nevertheless, the period was one of discouragement. In 1901 he spent some time at the Benedictine Abbey of Ligugé in Poitou, where the novelist J. K. Huysmans was endeavouring to form a religious community of artists. The experiment was brought to an end by the law against religious congregations introduced by the anti-clerical French government of the time.

It was at this point that Rouault claimed he had the good fortune to find himself as a painter, but to have been quite unconscious of what was happening to him:

It was not the influence of Lautrec, Degas or the moderns which made me experiment with a new style, but interior necessity, or the wish – maybe inconsistent – not to be trapped by conventional religious subjects.

In any case, he committed himself to the Modernist party, and in 1903 was one of the founders of the Salon d'Automne.

Equally significant was his meeting with the radical Catholic writer Léon Bloy. He was especially struck by Bloy's novel *La Femme Pauvre*, published in 1897, and in 1904, the author reported rather complacently in his diary: 'My book has touched him to the quick, and left a wound that will never heal. I tremble to think of the sufferings in store for the unfortunate man.' In fact their understanding was in many respect imperfect and required great tolerance on Rouault's part, as Bloy had no eye for modern art and detested Rouault's interpretations of his characters. Seeing the three works by Rouault in the Salon d'Automne of 1905, which used imagery drawn from his own creation, Bloy recorded sadly: 'Bourgeois foulness has wrought so violent and horrified a reaction in him that his art seems to have received the death blow.'

The phase immediately before the First World War was one of transition for Rouault. He experimented with glazed ceramics, a path he did not pursue; he travelled a little – he went to visit Bruges; and he married. His wife was Marthe Le Sidaner, sister of the painter Henri Le Sidaner, and she was to be a constant support for the rest of his life. Despite a successful one-man show at the Druet Gallery in 1910, Rouault was often very poor. In 1910 or 1911 (the sources differ) he moved to Versailles where he inhabited a miserable, rat-infested house in an old quarter of the town. On one occasion he went to tell his landlord, who was a veterinary surgeon, that he intended to complain to the local Committee for Public Health. 'It'll do you no good,' said the landlord complacently, 'I'm the chairman.' During the Versailles years Rouault did a series of watercolours of low-life subjects, including a series of paintings of prostitutes. These were apparently inspired by a single glimpse of a woman seen leaning out of a door, and Rouault was later careful to explain how the pictures came into being:

I am not a specialist in brothel subjects ... The woman I saw in the doorway is not the woman I painted. She

GEORGES ROUAULT, *Girl*, 1906

this direction. During the first decade of their association Rouault concentrated mainly on graphic work: during this period he produced the plates for *Misère*, which is generally considered his finest achievement. From 1918 onwards, he also returned to making paintings of sacred subjects. Some attention did come his way from outside: there was a scattering of exhibitions; in 1921 the first monograph on his work was published; in 1924 there was a retrospective at the Druet Gallery, where he had shown before; and he was awarded the Legion of Honour. In 1926 he published his book *Souvenirs intimes*, and in 1929 Diaghilev commissioned him to design his last major project, *The Prodigal Son*, with music by Prokofiev and choreography by Balanchine. It was not until 1937 that Rouault's reputation took a great stride forward: forty-two paintings, all in a style which was relatively 'new' for the critics and public but long established so far as the artist himself was concerned, were shown as part of the large 'Exposition des Artistes Indépendants', staged in connection with the Paris Exposition Universelle.

In 1939 Vollard was killed in an accident and the artist was thus released from his contract. It left behind it an important question: what was to happen to the great mass of unfinished work which was now in the possession of Vollard's heirs? In 1947 Rouault brought a suit against them to recover this material.

Rouault had always been very concerned with the artist's rights over his own creation. In 1943 he wrote:

> I sometimes dream, in these last years of my life, of upholding a thesis at the Sorbonne on the spiritual defence of works of art and the artist's rights before the law, and the ways and means of securing these rights, so that those who come after us may be better protected.

He succeeded perhaps better than he had hoped. He asked the courts for the return of 800 unfinished and unsigned paintings which had remained in Vollard's possession at the time of his death, and his right to them was eventually conceded. He only failed to recover those which had already been sold. In November 1948, to make his point quite clear, he ceremonially burned before witnesses 315 of the canvases he had recovered.

Rouault's reputation was not damaged by the war. He had already had a few exhibitions abroad in the 1930s, and in 1940–41 there were Rouault retrospectives in

and the rest corresponded to the emotional state I was in at the time.

In 1916 Rouault left Versailles and in 1917 he signed a contract with the famous dealer Ambroise Vollard which was to provide him with freedom to work for many years. Rouault agreed to give Vollard everything he produced in return for a salary; Vollard even went so far as to provide him with a studio on the top floor of his own house, where he could work undisturbed. As the artist was later to discover, there were certain drawbacks to this arrangement. Vollard was a jealous patron – he liked to monopolize the work of the artists he favoured and to keep it from prying eyes. The result was that for twenty years people judged Rouault by old work, rather than by what he was producing currently.

Vollard had a passion for fine illustrated books, and it was natural that he should encourage Rouault to turn in

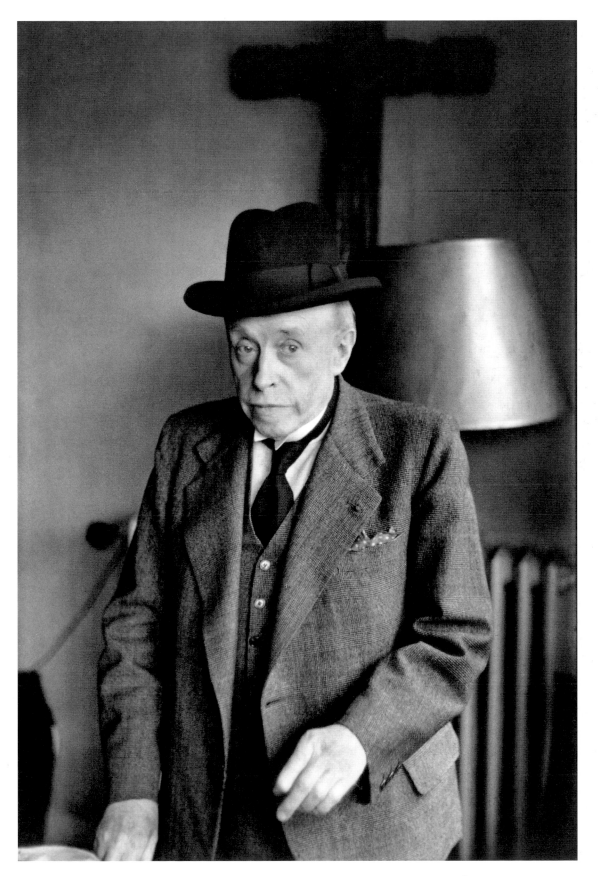

GEORGES ROUAULT, Paris 1944. Photo Henri Cartier-Bresson

Boston, Washington and San Francisco. In the immediately post-war period his sometimes sombre vision was in tune with the times. There was a retrospective at the Museum of Modern Art, New York, in 1945, and another, shared with Braque, at the Tate Gallery, London, in 1946. In 1948 he exhibited at the Venice Biennale and travelled to Italy for the first time.

When his eightieth birthday was celebrated at the Palais de Chaillot in Paris in 1951, the celebrations were organized by the Centre Catholique des Intellectuels Français. But the French state honoured him too: he was promoted to the rank of Commander of the Legion of Honour. In the 1950s, what had been a trickle of retrospective exhibitions became a flood, and when Rouault died in February 1958, he was given a state funeral.

PIET MONDRIAN

Piet Mondrian was one of the most important artists and art theorists of the first half of the twentieth century. His stringently controlled art carried the idea of abstraction to new extremes. He provided an example which other artists could imitate, but also one against which they could react.

He was born Pieter Cornelis Mondriaan in March 1872 at Amersfoort in the Netherlands, the second of five children and the eldest son. Mondrian's father was a strict Calvinist and a domineering personality – a friend who knew the family described Mondriaan senior as being 'frankly disagreeable'. The majority of Mondrian's biographers have seen the early part of his life as a long struggle to break free of parental influence.

In 1880 the Mondriaans moved from Amersfoort to Winterswijk, where Mondrian's father was head of the local Calvinist primary school. In 1886 Mondrian completed his basic schooling and started a period of self-education as an artist with some guidance both from his father, who was a gifted academic draughtsman, and from an uncle, Frits Mondriaan, who painted professionally. In 1889 Mondrian passed the state examination which permitted him to teach drawing in secondary schools, and his father, satisfied that he now had a means of earning a livelihood, allowed him to enter the Academy of Fine Art in Amsterdam. Here he studied for two years,

though he was still not quite sure of his vocation: at one time he thought of becoming a minister. In 1894 he returned to the Academy for evening classes in drawing, and he also attended a further series of classes in 1896. He was making exceedingly slow progress in making a name for himself, though he did exhibit a few pictures in Amsterdam. In 1901 he passed the preliminary examination for the Dutch Prix de Rome, but failed the next test, when candidates were required to draw from the figure, and was not admitted to the final examination. Henceforth he was to concentrate chiefly on landscape. In this year he made brief trips to Spain and to England, but they seem to have made no difference to his art.

In January 1904 Mondrian decided to break free of the Amsterdam environment. He rented half of a small house at Uden in Catholic Brabant, and spent a year painting in isolation. His choice of a Catholic area was significant in view of his father's bigoted Calvinism, but so too was the fact that he was still expected to visit the parental home as regularly as possible, and work there in the garden. During the second half of the decade he gradually became better known. From 1908 onwards he made yearly painting trips to Domburg on the Island of Walcheren, and these brought him into contact with a circle of moderately experimental artists around the Dutch Symbolist Jan Toorop. The year 1909 was significant for two reasons: he was given his first retrospective exhibition at the Stedelijk Museum in Amsterdam, and he joined the Dutch Theosophical Society. Theosophical ideas, particularly those of Madame Blavatsky, were to influence him for many years, and this was, in addition, a gesture of farewell to his Calvinist family background.

In 1910 he helped to found a progressive exhibition society called 'De Moderne Kunstkring', and at its first exhibition, held in October and November 1911, he saw works by Braque and Picasso for the first time. In 1912 Mondrian moved to Paris, and by 1913 was painting in a personal version of the Cubist style which attracted favourable notice from Guillaume Apollinaire, Cubism's most effective publicist.

He went to Holland in the summer of 1914, both for family reasons and because he had a one-man exhibition in the Hague, and was prevented by the outbreak of war from returning to France. He settled at the artists' colony of Laren, and in the isolation of wartime Holland began to move towards complete abstraction. His new artistic

PIET MONDRIAN,
c. 1942–43.
Photo Fritz Glarner

stance was summed up in a remark made to a friend in 1915: 'Yes, all in all, nature is a damned wretched affair. I can hardly stand it.' Mondrian was exhibiting regularly in the Netherlands throughout the war years, and soon found a group of kindred spirits, who came together to found the magazine *De Stijl*. Its first issue, which appeared in October 1917, contained his important essays on the nature and meaning of abstract art. He signed the De Stijl manifesto published in November the following year, but once the war was over could hardly wait to return to Paris. He arrived back in July 1919.

The Mondrian of the post-war Paris years is the one who is most familiar from the anecdotes of his friends. His studio in the rue du Départ was decorated with 'the same pure colours and geometric severity' which were now to be found in his paintings. It was immaculately tidy – Mondrian kept few personal possessions, even books, and destroyed all letters received as soon as they had been dealt with. He professed a horror of nature, and would even pick his seat in a restaurant so as not to have to gaze at the green outside; one eccentric object in his studio was a single artificial tulip which had been painted completely white. By this time Mondrian was a somewhat fussy middle-aged bachelor, very much preoccupied with his health. His great recreation was social dancing, and he took lessons in the fashionable dances of the time.

He admired the troupes of negro dancers who were then fashionable in Paris, and was a great fan of the black music-hall star Josephine Baker and of Mae West. He was also a devotee of the ballet companies directed by Diaghilev and by Diaghilev's rival, the Swede Rolf de Maré. He made a personal fetish of following French customs, rolling his cigarettes as French workers did, proclaiming the virtues of French cuisine (although he cooked in simple Dutch style when he entertained at home) and even insisting on pronouncing the names of Dutch friends with a French intonation. He was obsessed with the idea of preserving his anonymity – he would even change his grocer and greengrocer at frequent intervals so as not to become a familiar face.

In his early years in Paris Mondrian was very poor: until 1926 he was forced to paint watercolours of flowers as a sideline, in order to make a modest living. But he was gradually becoming known to an international circle of cognoscenti. In 1922 there was a retrospective exhibition in Amsterdam to celebrate his fiftieth birthday, and the next year a De Stijl group show at Léonce Rosenberg in Paris. This was followed by opportunities to exhibit in Germany and in the United States. Katherine Dreier, the founder of the Société Anonyme, became an enthusiastic and discerning patron from 1926 onwards.

PIET MONDRIAN meditating, 1909. Photographer unknown

In the early 1930s Mondrian was gradually drawn into the circle of abstract artists then forming itself in Paris. In 1930 he showed with the Cercle et Carré group founded by Joaquín Torres-García and Michel Seuphor, and in 1931 he joined the new and larger Abstraction-Création group put together by Georges Vantongerloo and Auguste Herbin. It was in this year that he finally reduced his compositions to simple oppositions of horizontal and vertical lines – he had already withdrawn from De Stijl because he found its principles insufficiently stringent. His notoriety, however, was always considerably greater with foreigners visiting and resident in Paris. Around 1934 he attracted the attention of the British artist Ben Nicholson and the young American Harry Holtzman, both of whom were to play an important part in his future.

Mondrian was one of the first artists to leave Paris under the threat of war. A group of English friends, headed by Nicholson, had been urging him to cross the Channel, and the threatening political situation in the summer of 1938 made up his mind for him. In particular he feared that Paris was likely to be a target for bombing. In September he settled in a studio in Hampstead, close to Nicholson and Naum Gabo. But the war did not spare London, and the house next to Mondrian's studio was bombed. He had always fantasized about New York, and he crossed the Atlantic in October 1940.

Despite his age, he settled well in his new environment, creating a studio which was almost a duplicate of the one in the rue du Départ. He continued to work on canvases he had brought with him from London. An American friend, Charmian von Weigand, wrote:

His ascetic bearing made one aware of an incredible self-discipline. This had been imposed on him partly through the extreme poverty he knew all his life and partly because he had a sole, unique goal, toward which he channelled all his energies.

In January 1942 Mondrian had a one-man exhibition at the Valentine Dudensing Gallery in New York, and a second one-man exhibition there in March 1943. This second show consisted of only six major paintings; one of them, considered to be Mondrian's final masterpiece, showed a marked shift in style. *Broadway Boogie-Woogie* eliminates the black lines which had been Mondrian's trademark for many years and concentrates on pure primary colours in an attempt to render the frenetically joyous quality the artist found in American life. He died of pneumonia in New York on 1 February 1944.

CONSTANTIN BRANCUSI

The sculptor Constantin Brancusi was an extraordinary combination of folk carver and highly sophisticated modern artist. He was born in 1876 at Hobitza in Oltenia, southern Romania, of poor peasant stock. In 1883 he was put to work as an apprentice shepherd in the Carpathian mountains. It was at this time that he first learned wood carving. He was to prefer carving to modelling all his life. 'The work of art,' he said later, 'requires great patience, and above all a determined struggle against the medium.' Later Brancusi worked as a dyer, as an assistant in a grocer's shop, and then as a servant at an inn. While working at the inn he was challenged to make a violin as a bet. He succeeded so well that he came to the attention of a rich manufacturer who sent him to the local school of Arts and Crafts. It was only then that he taught himself to read and write. In 1896 he won a scholarship to the Fine Arts School in Bucharest – his first contact with the world of high art.

At this time he was producing academic work, in the standard fashion of the day. On the proceeds of a couple of sales, he was able to leave Bucharest for Munich in 1903. But he found Munich unsympathetic and decided to set out for Paris, travelling on foot because he had no money left. He arrived after a journey during which he received much help from peasants and country people who (he said) immediately recognized him as one of themselves. Paris became his home for the rest of his life. Supporting himself by doing odd jobs – he worked first as a dishwasher, then sang in the choir at the Romanian Orthodox Chapel – he continued his studies at the Ecole des Beaux-Arts, under an academic sculptor called Antonin Mercié. On the walls of his makeshift studio, up many flights of stairs, he pasted strips of paper which carried admonitions in red letters: 'Don't forget you're an artist', 'Don't be discouraged', 'Don't be afraid, you'll make it!', 'Create like a God, order like a King, work like a Slave!' Proudly, he refused an offer to study with Rodin, whom he admired enormously. 'Nothing,' Brancusi said, 'ever grows well in the shade of a big tree.'

In 1906 Brancusi exhibited his work in public for the first time since leaving Romania, and in 1907 he received his first commission – a statue for the tomb of a compatriot. Another tombstone followed the next year. This was *The Kiss*, with two embracing figures locked together in the same block. In style this announced

Aerial view of Brancusi's studio,
Paris, *c.* 1925.
Photo Constantin Brancusi

Brancusi's mature work; the theme itself was one which he was to use repeatedly for the rest of his career.

By this time Brancusi had made many friends in the Paris art world. Among those to whom he was closest were Modigliani, whom he taught to carve, and 'Le Douanier' Rousseau, who once said to him jovially: 'Well, old boy, you've made the ancients modern.' No more perceptive remark has ever been made about Brancusi's work. Another friend was the difficult Chaïm Soutine. The two men used to go to the Bobino Music Hall and the Théâtre de Montparnasse together. They relished the bedroom farces presented there, and sometimes made such a noise that they were thrown out.

In 1914 Brancusi's reputation was established in the United States, thanks to a group of five pieces included in the New York Armory Show. The patronage he found there considerably eased his financial situation, and the charm and simplicity of his nature won him yet more friends, though he could be secretive and sometimes touchy. Part of his secretiveness may have been due to a desire to conceal homosexuality. He had no known close relationships with women, and once made an improvised trip to Corsica with the young writer Raymond Radiguet, notoriously Cocteau's lover. But Brancusi was not reclusive; he would entertain in his studio, cooking superb meals in his kiln. It was noticeable that he retained many basic peasant qualities, among them an obsessive fear of the devil and of magic spells. Max Ernst, who was his neighbour, once made the mistake of giving him a carved hand from Africa. Brancusi soon became so afraid of it that one night he threw it over the fence, and ever afterwards harboured a grudge against the donor.

During the inter-war period Brancusi unwillingly played a starring role in two major artistic scandals. In 1920, after a period during which he had submitted no work to any of the major Paris exhibitions, he sent his sculpture *Princess X* to the Salon des Indépendants. It was denounced by a die-hard faction as indecent (they thought it resembled a phallus) and the police were summoned to remove it from the show. The poet Blaise

Above: Constantin Brancusi, *Mademoiselle Pogany*, 1925
Right: Constantin Brancusi, *The Kiss*, 1925

Constantin Brancusi 97

Cendrars and the painter Fernand Léger immediately brought it back, but the incident left Brancusi permanently disgusted with the Paris art world, and he refused ever to exhibit in Paris for the rest of his life.

In 1926, when he arrived in the United States for an exhibition of his sculptures at the Brummer Gallery, the Customs Office refused to admit one of his most abstract pieces as a duty-free work of art. Brancusi was forced to pay duty to get the sculpture released, and sued the Customs Office for the return of the money. He won the case, though the verdict was not published until 1928. Meanwhile, the uproar had ensured the success of his show.

Brancusi travelled quite widely at this time: to the United States; to India in 1937, at the invitation of the Maharajah of Indore (the temple he designed for this patron was never built); and back to Romania, where he had been invited to make a series of monuments for the public part at Tîrgu Jiu in his native Oltenia. Completed in 1938, this work was attacked by the local press, already very fascist in its sympathies, but Brancusi was satisfied to have seen some of his ideas carried out on a large scale. 'Simplicity', he said, 'is at bottom complexity, and one must be weaned on its essence to understand its significance.'

Brancusi moved to his last studio, at 8 impasse Ronsin, in 1918. The building had formerly been occupied by Mme Steinheil, the central figure in a notorious murder case. Brancusi furnished the studio with his own hands, in a style of peasant simplicity. With the coming of the Second World War he withdrew more and more into this private world. He made little entirely new sculpture, though he continued to recast old ideas. In 1948 two young Romanian painters, Alexander Istrati and his wife Natalia Dumitresco, settled next door in a deserted building and henceforth kept him company. His health began to deteriorate, especially after a fall in 1954 in which he broke his thigh, but he was determined not to leave his own surroundings. He died in his studio on 16 March 1957.

AMEDEO MODIGLIANI

Amedeo Modigliani was the bohemian artist *par excellence* – his posthumous legend is almost as famous as Van Gogh's. In stylistic terms he was an oddity: contemporary with the Cubists, but not part of their movement, he forms a bridge between the generation of Toulouse-Lautrec and the Art Deco painters of the 1920s.

He was born in Livorno in July 1884. Both sides of his family were Sephardic Jews. His father Flaminio was an unsuccessful entrepreneur who had a small money-changing business, and his mother, Eugenia, by far the stronger personality of the two, ran an experimental school. Amedeo, in childhood nicknamed Dedo, was their fourth and youngest child. Thanks largely to Eugenia Modigliani, the atmosphere of the household was always unconventional; in 1898 the eldest son, Emmanuele, then aged twenty-six, was sentenced to six months imprisonment as an anarchist.

In 1898 Modigliani began formal art training under Guglielmo Micheli, a pupil of Giovanni Fattori, the leader

AMEDEO MODIGLIANI
as an adolescent, *c.* 1900.
Photographer unknown

Right: Modigliani (centre right)
and Adolphe Basler (right)
at the Café du Dome,
Montparnasse, Paris *c.* 1918.
Photographer unknown

of the Macchiaioli – the Italian equivalent of the Impressionist movement. To begin with, Modigliani's literary tastes were more advanced than his artistic ones: his favourite poet was Lautréamont, author of *Maldoror*, who was later to have immense significance for the Surrealists. He left home and went to Florence, where in May 1902 he registered under Fattori at the Scuola Libera di Nudo (Free School of the Nude). In March 1903 he transferred himself to Venice, where he registered at a similar academy. There he met two of the artists who were to be among the leaders of Futurism – Umberto Boccioni and Ardengo Soffici. More important, he had his first real introduction to the pleasures of drugs and drink.

In the winter of 1906 he decided to go to Paris, and his mother agreed to give him a small allowance. The Paris which attracted him was already fading into the past, and he seems to have been rather wary of the new generation of experimentalists which gathered round Apollinaire, though he did go to live in Montmartre, which was at that time undoubtedly the focal point of the avant-garde. Thanks to French anti-semitism (of a sort which at that time was almost unknown in his native Italy) he discovered a much stronger sense of Jewish identity, and his friends in the Paris art world were mainly Jewish. They included Soutine, Kisling, the sculptor Lipchitz and the poet Max Jacob – his one real link with the circle around Picasso. He rapidly made a reputation for his excesses (he had a habit of stripping stark naked when drunk), and his nickname changed from the childish Dedo to Modi (a pun on the French *maudit*, or 'accursed'). In 1909 he retired for a while to Livorno, sick and exhausted.

When he returned, now settling in Montparnasse, the new artists' quarter, he decided to change direction, and became a sculptor. The master he chose was Brancusi, and there is a definite link between his work and Brancusi's in this medium. There are also clear signs

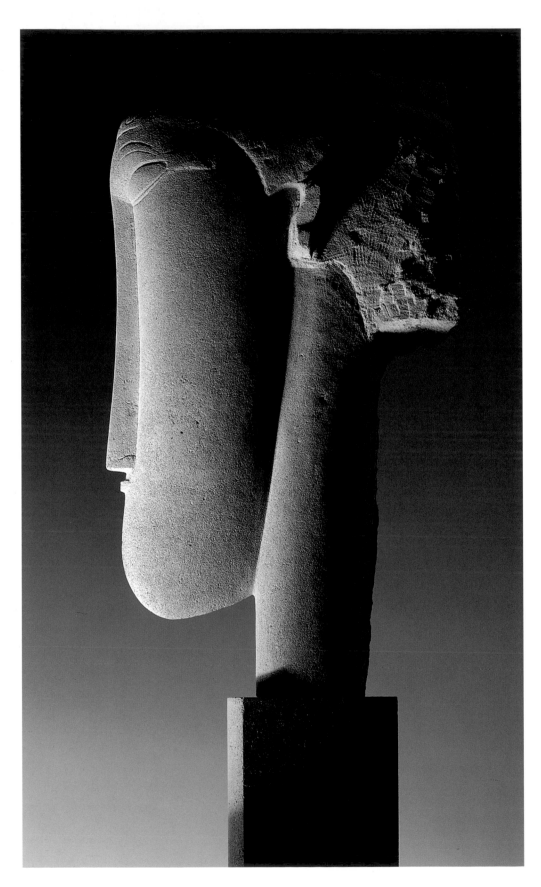

AMEDEO MODIGLIANI, *Head, c.* 1913

of influence from the art from Africa and Oceania which Modigliani saw in the Musée de l'Homme. Though he was closer to finding his artistic direction, he was still miserably poor – his sculpture was made mostly from stone stolen from building sites, easy to find as Paris was then in the grip of a building boom. In 1912 he once again fell ill, and was forced to go home for a rest. But it never seems to have occurred to him to remain in Italy; he returned to Paris as soon as he could.

What stopped him carving, and led to the final phase in his work, was the outbreak of the First World War. This brought the building boom to an abrupt halt; Modigliani in any case was no longer feeling strong enough for the hard physical labour of shaping blocks of stone. When he painted it had always been directly from the motif, and now he became a specialist in portraits whose delicate stylization showed the influence of his period as a sculptor, and whose elegance and wit belied his reputation for uncouth behaviour. Some of his acquaintances thought that the uncouthness was a little cultivated – Picasso said sarcastically: 'It's odd but you never see Modigliani drunk anywhere but at the corners of the boulevard Montmartre and the boulevard Raspail.'

In the early years of the war Modigliani embarked on an affair with the South African writer Beatrice Hastings. She was some five years older than he was (he was now thirty), and had had a picturesque career. One of her previous conquests had been Katherine Mansfield. She had a little money, and Modigliani was able to live in more comfortable circumstances. But the relationship was marked by heavy drinking and Modigliani and Beatrice often came to blows – on one occasion he threw her out of a window.

From a professional point of view he was doing a little better – the ambitious young dealer Paul Guillaume was starting to take an interest in his work. But, as a portrait shows very clearly, Modigliani found Guillaume's personality unsympathetic, and in 1916 he transferred his allegiance to the Polish dealer Zborowski.

Modigliani's affair with Beatrice Hastings was now over. He had been doing some drawing at the Académie Colarossi, and here, in July 1917, he met Jeanne Hébuterne, who was then aged nineteen. Soon they were living together. Their public scenes became even more famous in Montmartre than Modigliani's rows with Beatrice. One eye-witness, André Salmon, reports:

Amedeo Modigliani, *Portrait of Jeanne Hébuterne*, 1918

He was dragging her along by an arm, gripping her frail wrist, tugging at one or another of her long braids of hair, and only letting go of her for a moment to send her crashing against the railings of the Luxembourg. He was like a madman, crazy with savage hatred.

Yet some – though not all – of Modigliani's many portraits of Jeanne show real tenderness; others show her as impassive and curiously graceless.

By early 1918 conditions in Paris had become so difficult that Zborowski decided to move his whole stable to the South of France – he now represented Soutine, Kisling and the Japanese artist Foujita, as well as Modigliani. Modigliani settled obediently in Nice, but the Mediterranean climate and landscape had no real appeal for him. He continued to paint portraits indoors, often of local shopkeepers and their children. In February 1918 Jeanne became pregnant, and soon afterwards she and Modigliani separated for a while, probably because he loathed her disapproving and overbearing mother who had also moved South. They were reunited before the baby, a daughter, was born. Modigliani got drunk on the way to register the child as his own, and she remained officially fatherless, though she was later adopted by his family in Italy. In May 1919 he returned joyfully to Paris, the only environment he really liked. Jeanne, for the moment, was left behind, pregnant for a second time.

Thanks to Zborowski's efforts, Modigliani's paintings were at last starting to fetch respectable prices. In the summer of 1919, with the help of Osbert Sitwell, Zborowski arranged a show of French art at the Mansard Gallery in London. It was a success, and it was one of Modigliani's works which fetched the highest price. The purchaser was the writer Arnold Bennett, who said that the painting reminded him of his own heroines. In June 1919 Modigliani and Jeanne were able to move into their first real home, an apartment in the rue de la Grande Chaumière, immediately above one which had once been occupied by Gauguin. But Modigliani's health was steadily deteriorating and his alcoholic collapses were becoming more frequent. He celebrated the New Year of 1920 in fine style, but about a fortnight later was stricken with pains in his kidneys and took to his bed. After some days his neighbour downstairs, another painter called Ortiz de Zárate, called in to see if anything was the matter. He found Modigliani delirious, complaining of a violent headache. The bed was strewn with empty bottles and half-opened cans of sardines which were dripping their oil on to the coverlet. Beside him sat Jeanne, who was nearly nine months pregnant; she had not thought of sending for a doctor. Ortiz de Zárate summoned one immediately. He came, and declared the case was hopeless: Modigliani was suffering from tubercular meningitis. He died on 24 January 1920, without regaining consciousness. There was an enormous funeral, attended by the whole of Montmartre. Jeanne, who had been taken to her parents' house, threw herself out of a fifth floor window two days after Modigliani's death, killing both herself and her unborn child.

CHAÏM SOUTINE

Chaïm Soutine was typical of the exiled, spiritually and culturally isolated modern artist. He was born in 1893, the tenth of eleven children, in Smilovich, a small, almost entirely Jewish town in the Lithuanian part of Russia. His father was a mender of clothes – the bottom rung of the social ladder. Soutine very early showed an interest in art, which was actively discouraged both by his family (two of his elder brothers used it as an excuse to bully him) and by the community that surrounded him which observed the strict orthodox Jewish prohibition against the making of images. When Soutine had the temerity to ask a local rabbi to pose for him, he was severely beaten by the man's son. As a result, the rabbi was forced to pay damages to Soutine's mother, and with this money he was at last sent to study art.

He went first to Minsk in 1909 with his friend Michel Kikoïne, who also wished to become an artist; here they studied privately. A year later, in 1910, they went to Vilna to sit the entrance examination at the School of Fine Arts. Soutine was so nervous that he blundered over his perspective and failed. He flung himself, weeping, at the feet of the Director, who out of pity allowed him to try again. This time he was successful.

In 1913 Soutine and Kikoïne completed their course at Vilna and left as soon as they could for Paris. Here they met another painter who had studied with them at Vilna, Pincus Kremègne, and who was living in La Ruche (The Beehive) in Montparnasse. This was a rotunda built for the Paris Exposition Universelle of 1900 which had been converted into artists' studios. At various times Léger, Chagall, Lipchitz and Modigliani all worked there.

At this time Soutine was desperately poor. He did any work he could to keep alive, loading railway vans at the Gare Montparnasse at night, working for Renault (he was sacked after one day for hopeless clumsiness) and digging ditches during the War. He was always ragingly hungry – he claimed half-jokingly to have a tapeworm, and would later tell stories of how he stood for hours at a café counter, hoping against hope that someone would buy him something to eat. Among the artists he lived with he was celebrated not only for his poverty but for extreme dirtiness, which often lost him their sympathy. The poet André Salmon said:

His art deserved the closest attention, but I confess there was too much about the physical presence of the man himself which revolted me. Not only the filthy state in which he stumbled through life, but above all his slobbering speech ... I just couldn't come to terms with the poor fellow, who incidentally gave the ear-specialist quite a surprise when he finally decided to consult him about his terrible earache. In the canal of the painter's ear the doctor discovered, not an abscess, but a nest of bed bugs ...

In Paris, Soutine continued his studies with the academic artist Cormon at the Ecole des Beaux-Arts, and also worked in the Louvre. One observer who saw him in the museum said: 'He looked at the old masters the way a believer looks at holy images.' Throughout his life he could only paint from the motif, and he developed an acute feeling for what was for him the 'right' model, whether this was a person or a landscape. When his eye fell on such a person he would plead, threaten, even bribe, to persuade them to pose. His tenacity before the subject was notorious: when he installed a whole ox carcass in his studio (this was when he at last had some money) he went on painting it until the stench brought the police and the health authorities. Even then, he begged them to allow him to keep it a little longer, insisting that art was more important than sanitation. During the 1920s, he would search the poultry shops of Paris for exactly the right chicken – 'one with a long neck and a blue skin' – to the dismay of poulterers, who could not understand why he wanted something so miserably scrawny.

He was also famous for the manic intensity with which he painted. One eye-witness said that he 'flung the colours on the canvas like poisonous butterflies', another that he 'threw himself from a distance *bang bang bang* at the canvas'.

In 1923 his fortunes underwent a dramatic change for the better. He was discovered by the wealthy American collector Albert C. Barnes who bought a large number of his canvases. This established his reputation with other collectors, and Soutine became prosperous. His first one-man show was held in 1927 at the gallery of Henri Bing, and through this he made contact with the wealthy collectors Madeleine and Marcellin Castaing, who became steady patrons and often had him to stay at their country retreat. Madeleine Castaing describes him as

CHAÏM SOUTINE,
c. 1918.
Photographer unknown

CHAÏM SOUTINE, *Carcass of Beef*, c. 1925

looking 'like a Dostoevsky hero, creeping about with his hat pulled down over his face and his eyes wet with tears.' In prosperity, Soutine had developed a passion for hats, buying dozens of grey ones, all of exactly the same size and shade. He had other quirks as well. He was, for example, afraid to deposit money in a bank because he was convinced that the uniformed guard would creep up from behind and strangle him as he stood at the teller's window.

In the 1930s Soutine's occasional fits of depression increased, and his productivity dropped. He had fallen out with many of his friends of less prosperous days, and some felt bitter about his ingratitude to them. He was, however, reaching new heights of reputation. In 1937 a large group of his paintings were included in the big official exhibition at the Petit-Palais, 'Exposition des Artistes Indépendants' – this was an honour of a kind then rarely given to a foreigner in France.

The outbreak of war brought a catastrophic change in his situation. He was working in the countryside, at Civry, when hostilities began, and he and his German mistress, Gerda Groth, nicknamed 'Mademoiselle Garde', were forbidden to return to Paris because they were aliens. Soutine was afterwards allowed to return for medical reasons: Groth followed him early in 1940 but was interned with other Germans, then deported to a concentration camp in the Pyrenees. They never saw one another again. Soutine was invited to go to the United States, but failed to take up the invitation, perhaps because he had long ago lost any papers he may have possessed.

Under the German Occupation life became very dangerous for Soutine since he was now a registered Jew. He was forced to leave Paris and took refuge in the hamlet of Champigny-sur-Veuldre near Tours. Friends provided him and Marie-Berthe Aurenche, the ex-wife of Max Ernst with whom he was now living, with hiding places and false identity cards. Nevertheless, their presence in the countryside aroused suspicion and they were threatened with denunciation. Anxiety aggravated Soutine's long-standing stomach problems and in August 1943 he suffered a severe ulcer attack. He was taken first to Chinon and then, by a circuitous route that took twenty-four hours, to Paris, where he was immediately operated on for perforated ulcers and internal bleeding. The operation was too late, and on 9 August he died on the operating table.

CHAÏM SOUTINE,
Chartres Cathedral,
1933

Pre-Revolutionary Russia very readily accepted Modernist ideas. It produced a group of major collectors, notably Shchukin and Morosov; and it spawned a substantial number of modern artists and a plethora of experimental art-styles – Primitivism, Cubo-Futurism, Rayonnism, Suprematism and Constructivism.

The artists whose lives are recounted here may be divided into those who left Russia and those who stayed. Larionov, Goncharova, Gabo and Chagall all exiled themselves shortly after the Revolution, though all had supported it; Malevich, Tatlin and others remained. Both Malevich and Tatlin became unproductive, not merely because of the Stalinist clampdown in the 1930s, but because of the inexorable logic of their own development. Others, such as Liubov Popova, died young. Others still – El Lissitzky, and the husband-and-wife team of Alexander Rodchenko and Varvara Stepanova – moved away from easel painting, and into more utilitarian fields of activity, such as book design. This was in keeping with the doctrines of Constructivism, a style, which, as it developed, laid increasing emphasis on the utilitarian, and on the creation of objects of practical use.

KASIMIR MALEVICH

Kasimir Malevich was born near Kiev in 1878. His father was a foreman in a sugar factory and his mother was of Polish peasant stock. The family was not cultured, but Kasimir very early showed signs of an artistic vocation, notably with a *Moonlight Landscape* which was much admired when it was displayed in a shop window. In 1895 he entered the Kiev School of Fine Art where his work was influenced by that of the Russian Symbolist, Victor Borisov-Mussatov (1870–1905). Malevich married young, in 1901 (this was the first of three marriages), and his father died in 1902. He was then forced to work for the local railway company to raise money for his studies in Moscow, where he arrived in 1905.

Malevich's arrival in Moscow coincided with the December Revolution of that year, and he became involved in underground politics, distributing illegal literature. He worked privately in the studio of an artist called Roerburg, which was considered most avant-garde, and through Roerburg he met Mikhail Larionov and the rest of the progressive artists in Moscow. At this period Malevich was absorbing the influence of contemporary French art, which he studied in periodicals and in the houses of the great Moscow collectors Shchukin and Morosov. His first truly independent works were large gouaches on peasant themes, with subjects inspired by the work of Larionov and his wife, Natalia Goncharova. His actual style owed more to the Matisses which Shchukin was then acquiring.

Malevich, Larionov and Goncharova were the central figures in the all-Russian group show, *The Donkey's Tail*, organized by Larionov in 1912, and in its successor, *The Target*, a year later. Malevich had by this time become

Right: 'Unovis' group at Vitebsk station in 1920. KASIMIR MALEVICH is in the centre holding a round plate with black square and circle. Photographer unknown
Far right: KASIMIR MALEVICH, Leningrad *c.* 1925. Photographer unknown

Top: Kasimir Malevich,
costume designs for the opera
Victory Over the Sun, 1913
Bottom: Kasimir Malevich,
Supremus No. 50, 1916

fully identified with the Russian Futurist movement. In 1913 he designed the scenery and costumes for *Victory over the Sun*, a Futurist opera with music by Matyushin and a nonsense libretto by Alexei Kruchenikh. To this project he was later to trace the beginnings of his own system of art, Suprematism. One of the backdrops he

created was a totally abstract design of a black square on a white ground, which marked a break with everything he had so far produced.

His first Suprematist works were not shown until an exhibition held in Petrograd (now St Petersburg) in December 1915. These were completely and radically abstract – combinations of simple geometrical elements to which Malevich attached a mystical meaning. 'At the present moment man's path lies through space,' he wrote in 1919. 'Suprematism is the semaphore of colour in his endlessness.'

Malevich began to gather a band of followers around himself. He also entered into an enduring rivalry with Vladimir Tatlin, the founder of Constructivism. In 1917, when the October Revolution took place, Malevich automatically supported the Bolsheviks. Like most of the Russian artists of the avant-garde, he considered political revolution to be a logical continuation of what had already been accomplished in the aesthetic sphere. He became an active member of various revolutionary committees, but his mystical aspirations were not well adapted to the 'dialectical materialism' of Marxism, and by 1919 he was at odds with the Constructivists, whom he had already offended by his quarrels with Tatlin. Alexander Rodchenko, remembering an incident in 1916, described him as 'not sincere, with disagreeably shifty eyes; he was most infatuated with himself and seemed particularly biased in his judgments.'

In 1918 Marc Chagall invited Malevich to teach at the Vitebsk School of Art. The two men soon fell out, as Malevich attempted to take over the running of the School. Profiting from Chagall's frequent absences in Moscow, he extended his influence over the staff and pupils. One day Chagall returned to discover that the sign which read 'Free School' had been replaced by one which read 'Suprematist School'. Disgusted with the situation, Chagall gave up his post, and Malevich, now fully in charge, renamed the college 'Unovis' ('College of the New Art'). His followers sewed a black square, the first Suprematist design, on to their sleeves, and in 1920, for the third anniversary of the Revolution, they decorated the walls of Vitebsk with squares, triangles and circles. But Malevich was unpopular with the local authorities, and at the end of 1921 he and his followers were forced to quit the town.

After an unsuccessful attempt to obtain a post in Moscow, he was given a studio and living quarters at

the Museum of Artistic Culture in Leningrad, the first
museum of modern art in the world. Here he remained
until the Museum itself was dissolved in 1928. During
this period he was able to maintain contacts with artists
and institutions abroad. He exhibited three Suprematist
paintings in the Venice Biennale of 1924, and in 1927
he was allowed to go to Poland and Berlin to exhibit
his work.

In Berlin he was well received, and was given
an entire room for his work in the 'Grosse Berlin
Kunstausstellung'. He took the opportunity to go to
Dessau to visit the Bauhaus, but most of the staff and
students were on vacation and to his great disappoint-
ment he was only able to meet its founder, Walter
Gropius. He was, however, able to meet a number of
important modern artists during his trip: Hans Arp,
Kurt Schwitters, Hans Richter and László Moholy-Nagy.
Moholy-Nagy arranged for the publication of some of
Malevich's manuscripts in the Bauhausbücher series.

Early in June 1927 Malevich was recalled urgently
to Russia, probably because the authorities had become
suspicious of his conduct, and left both his paintings
and his manuscripts behind in the hands of friends in
Germany; these now form the basis of our knowledge
of his work.

In 1928 he found another post at the Zubovsky Art
Historical Institute in Leningrad, and in the same year he
was given a retrospective exhibition at the Tretyakov Art
Gallery in Moscow. This was his last moment of official
favour. In 1930, as a result of an invitation to exhibit in
Germany for a second time, he was arrested. He was
soon released, but his friends prudently destroyed a
number of documents and manuscripts. He continued
to write and paint after his release, and to make
architectural maquettes, but the chronology of his later
work is confused by the fact that he now antedated some
of his paintings for fear of further trouble. Essentially
his final years witnessed a return to figuration – most
of his paintings were now portraits of members of his
immediate family.

In 1934 Malevich fell ill. Cancer was diagnosed, and
he died in 1935. He was buried in a coffin decorated with
Suprematist designs he had painted himself.

NATALIA GONCHAROVA,
curtain design for the ballet
Le Coq d'Or, 1914

MIKHAIL LARIONOV AND NATALIA GONCHAROVA

Mikhail Larionov and his lifelong companion Natalia
Goncharova were the chief apostles sent by the nascent
Russian avant-garde to the outside world, and the main
organizers of the pre-revolutionary phase of avant-garde
activity within Russia itself. They left Russia just before
the Revolution, and were for many years virtually
forgotten. Their reputations were revived shortly before
their deaths thanks to a retrospective exhibition put on
by the Arts Council of Great Britain.

Larionov was born in 1881 in Teraspol, the son of an
army doctor. Though he was sent to a private school in
Moscow in 1891, he continued to visit the family estate,
which belonged to his grandfather, throughout his years
in Russia, and much of his best work was done there. He
entered the Moscow School of Painting, Sculpture and
Architecture in 1898 – he was fortunate to get in, as
there were thirty places available and after the entrance
examination he was placed thirty-third on the list;
three candidates ahead of him were rejected for lack
of appropriate academic qualifications.

Goncharova, who was also born in 1881, entered the
College in the same year as Larionov, and within two
years they became inseparable. She came from a slightly
more elevated social background than her partner – she
belonged to an impoverished noble family and was
related by marriage to the great Russian poet Pushkin.
Her father was a professional architect.

Larionov signed the usual ten-year contract on
entering the College, but part-way through his course he

ran into trouble. Students were expected to send in work every month for display and criticism; Larionov, who was very prolific, submitted so many paintings in 1902 that he took up all the space allotted to students of his year. He was asked to remove some, refused, and was expelled. The authorities relented in the following year, and allowed him to complete his course. Before they had graduated he and Goncharova were already making a reputation for themselves. In 1906 they exhibited their work in the *World of Art* exhibition in St Petersburg. This brought them into contact with the circle dominated by Sergei Diaghilev, later to be the impresario of the Ballets Russes. Diaghilev invited them to show in the great exhibition of paintings by Russian artists which he arranged that year for the Salon d'Automne in Paris. Larionov travelled to Paris in connection with the show, and then went on to London.

Up to this point Larionov had been painting in a style which combined Symbolism and Impressionism. Now, after making friends with David Burliuk (1882–1967) and the latter's brother Vladimir, he abandoned this and painted his first Primitivist works. Larionov's Primitivism combined a number of different influences, among them child art; folk imagery and motifs and their derivations in

Russian *lubok* (popular prints); and the use of words and letters. The images and their accompanying inscriptions were often erotic or even scatological.

In 1908–9, after leaving art school, Larionov did his compulsory military service, being stationed partly in the Kremlin and partly in a tent camp just outside Moscow. This provided the inspiration for a series of works showing soldiers. He continued to paint and exhibit prolifically after his discharge. He and Goncharova became associated with the Union of Youth, founded in March 1910, which sponsored not only exhibitions, but also public discussions which were as much performances as debates. The choreographer Mikhail Fokine, who was to collaborate with Goncharova on the ballet *Coq d'Or*, described the apprehensions which these antics aroused in him:

I had heard that she and Larionov, who worked with her, belonged to a set of 'Moscow Futurists' who painted their faces, organized violent lectures on 'new art' and 'the art of the future', and that at these lectures, as the strongest argument, pitchers full of water were tossed into the audience. ...

After all the horrors I had heard, I found myself in the company of the most charming people, modest and serious. I recall the degree of admiration with which Larionov described the beauty of Japanese art ... And the thoroughness with which Goncharova discussed each detail of the forthcoming production.

The years 1911 to 1913 were the highpoint of their joint careers in Russia. In 1911 Larionov produced his first Rayonnist works, followed by completely abstract Rayonnist paintings in the following year. In 1912 they were both invited to show with the Blaue Reiter in Munich and in Roger Fry's second Post-Impressionist exhibition at the Grafton Gallery in London. This was also the year in which they organized *The Donkey's Tail*, an exhibition which represented a conscious breach with the art of Europe. In 1913 Larionov published his *Rayonnist Manifesto* which mingled Futurism with Russian nationalism. It read in part:

We declare the genius of our days to be trousers, jackets, shoes, tramways, buses, aeroplanes, railways, magnificent ships – what an enchantment – what a great epoch unrivalled in world history. ...

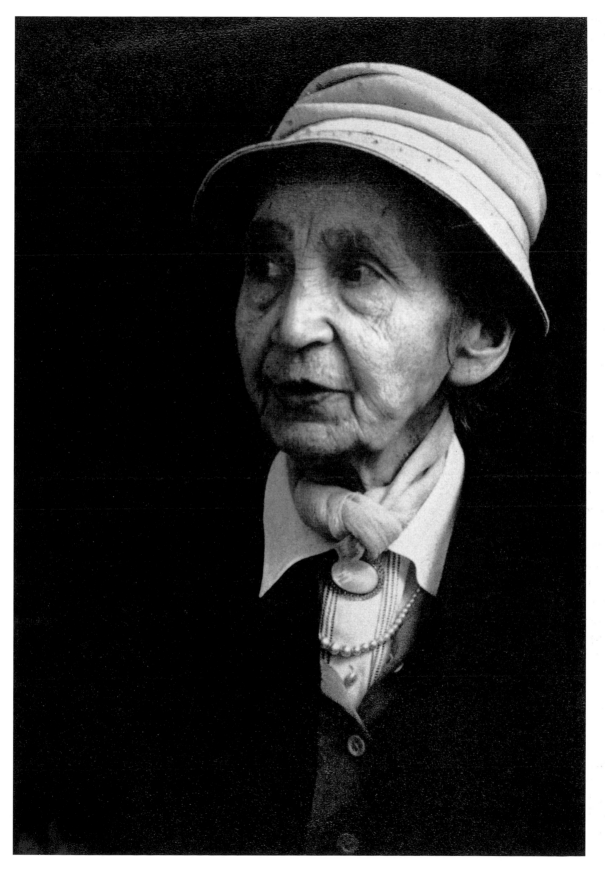

NATALIA GONCHAROVA. Photo Charles Gimpel

MIKHAIL LARIONOV,
Portrait of Vladimir Tatlin,
1911

Opposite top: VLADIMIR TATLIN and
students constructing model of
his Monument to the Third
International, Petrograd, 1920.
Photographer unknown
Opposite bottom: VLADIMIR TATLIN,
Paris, March or April 1913.
Photographer unknown

Hail beautiful Orient! We unite ourselves with
contemporary Oriental artists for communal work. ...

Hail nationalism! – we go hand in hand with
house-painters. ...

We are against the West, vulgarizing our Oriental
forms, and rendering everything valueless. We
demand technical mastery. We are against artistic
societies which lead to stagnation. We do not demand
attention from the public, but ask it not to demand
attention from us.

The commission for *Coq d'Or*, which Diaghilev offered
to Goncharova in 1914, drew the couple into the hothouse
world of the Ballets Russes. They went to Paris to work
with the company, and Goncharova had a show at
the fashionable Galerie Paul Guillaume, for which
Apollinaire wrote the catalogue introduction. But the
outbreak of war forced them to return to Russia. Larionov
was mobilized, wounded in the fighting, hospitalized and
finally invalided out of the army in 1915. The couple then
left Russia to rejoin Diaghilev in Lausanne. They may not
have known it at the time, but this represented a final
break with their native country.

They continued to work for the Ballets Russes as long
as Diaghilev was alive, and indeed became part of the
impresario's unofficial family of friends and advisers.
Larionov's witty caricatures give many glimpses of this
peripatetic Russian world in exile. Goncharova prepared
designs for the never produced project *Liturgie*, which
was to have been Massine's début as a choreographer, and
Larionov, who had no dance training, advised on dance
movements. Goncharova also designed costumes for
Stravinsky's *Les Noces*, with choreography by Bronislava
Nijinska – the masterpiece of the whole post-war
repertory. But two complete sets of designs were rejected
as too elaborate, and in the end the dancers wore what
were really practice costumes with the simplest decoration. Larionov designed the settings for Prokofiev's *Chout*
and Stravinsky's *Le Renard*, in both cases very much
under instruction from his patron. Diaghilev valued
the couple for their loyalty and he found Larionov in
particular a useful dogsbody, but he soon felt that there
were newer and more fashionable talents available to him.

From the mid-1920s Larionov and Goncharova sank
gradually into obscurity. Goncharova died in 1962, shortly
after their joint retrospective in London, and Larionov
died two years later.

VLADIMIR TATLIN

The leader of the Constructivists, Vladimir Tatlin was probably, together with Kasimir Malevich, one of the most important figures in the Russian avant-garde. Unfortunately his achievement is less well documented than that of Malevich because no substantial group of his work survives in the West, in contrast to the Malevich collection now in the Stedelijk Museum, Amsterdam.

Tatlin was born in 1885 in Kharkov, the son of a railway engineer. His mother, a poet, died two years after her son's birth. Tatlin's father soon married again; the boy detested his stepmother, and he disliked his father, who was a stern disciplinarian, almost as much. Tatlin had a difficult and unhappy childhood in consequence, and the circumstances of his youth left him with a morbidly suspicious and distrustful nature, well described by Alexander Rodchenko, who was to become one of his closest disciples:

> I learned everything from Tatlin – my attitude to the profession, to objects, to material, to food, to life itself – and this left an imprint on my entire life. He was, however, suspicious of everyone since he thought that people wished him evil, were betraying him. He thought that his enemies such as Malevich were sending certain persons round to him to find out his artistic plans. Consequently, he revealed himself to me only very gradually, for he was constantly on the *qui vive*.

At the age of eighteen Tatlin ran away to sea. The ship he joined was on its way to Egypt. He continued to earn a living on occasional voyages to the Eastern Mediterranean until after the outbreak of the First World War, though in 1904, the year in which his father died, he also enrolled himself at Penza Art School. In 1909, prompted by Mikhail Larionov, whom he had known during his boyhood, he entered the Moscow School of Painting, Sculpture and Architecture, where he studied under leading Russian masters of the older generation such as Konstantin Korovin (1861–1939) and Valentin Serov (1869–1911).

Meanwhile, he had to struggle to earn a living: in addition to his spells as a sailor he did numerous odd jobs. One was working as a wrestler in a circus, but he was so inexpert that he was injured, and lost the hearing

VLADIMIR TATLIN, *Sailor (Self-Portrait)*, 1911

in his left ear. However, thanks to his connection with Larionov and Natalia Goncharova, with whom he remained closely linked until a quarrel separated him from them in 1913, Tatlin had a number of opportunities to exhibit his work with the emergent Russian avant-garde. One of the important shows in which he participated was *The Donkey's Tail* of 1912. The work he was then producing showed his interest in primitive art and Russian icons. His interest in icons, which was to endure throughout his life, was probably originally kindled by Goncharova, who had access to many important private collections. Goncharova remembered Tatlin at this period as tall and thin, looking 'rather like a fish', with a long upper lip, upturned nose and prominent eyes.

More than most of his Russian contemporaries, Tatlin was keenly aware of what was going on abroad and wished to experience the new European art at first hand. His chance came in 1913, when he travelled to Berlin with a group of Ukrainian musicians for a 'Russian Exhibition of Folk Art'. Tatlin played the accordion in the group, and pretended to be blind. Somehow he attracted the attention of Kaiser Wilhelm II, who presented him with a gold watch which Tatlin promptly sold to pay for a ticket to Paris. He made straight for Picasso's studio, which he haunted for as long as his funds lasted – about a month –

absorbing everything he could. Picasso rather enjoyed the young Russian's accordion playing, but refused his offer to stay on and act as studio dogsbody. Tatlin was forced to return to Russia.

He had been hugely impressed by the Cubist reliefs Picasso was then making, and when he got back began to attempt something similar of his own, though in his case they were purely abstract. This line of experiment produced what is now considered Tatlin's most important group of works, despite the fact that they are known only from descriptions, poor photographs, and the modern reconstructions based on them. The culmination of this phase was the Corner Counter-Reliefs of 1916 which exemplified Tatlin's new dictum, 'Real materials in real space'. He had come to believe that each material generated its own precise repertory of forms.

In 1916 Tatlin organized an exhibition for himself and his associates in a vacant Moscow shop. This provided the occasion for a major quarrel with Malevich, which led to an enduring rivalry. Tatlin, though jealous of Malevich to the point where he said he could not bear to be in the same town as him, still retained a wary respect for the quality of Malevich's work. He even made a point of attending Malevich's funeral in 1935, though by then they had not met for many years.

Tatlin, like most of the other members of the Russian avant-garde, sided wholeheartedly with the Bolshevik Revolution, and in 1918 he was appointed head of the Moscow section of the Department of Fine Arts of the Commissariat for the People's Education (IZO Narkompos). He was commissioned by IZO to design a monument to the Third International to be erected in the centre of Moscow. Tatlin planned a vast Utopian structure which was to be twice the height of the Empire State Building. It was to be constructed of glass and iron and was to contain four thermal glass enclosures – a cylinder, a hemisphere, a pyramid and a cube – each of which would revolve on its axis at a different rate, once a year, once a month or once a day. Among other things it was to contain a propaganda centre equipped with telegraph, telephone and radio, and a vast open-air screen. He continued to work on this project after he was transferred to Petrograd in 1920, but it never got past the model stage, as it was well beyond the technological capacities of the time.

In 1921 Tatlin was appointed head of the Department of Sculpture at the restructured Academy of Arts in

Petrograd. Like Rodchenko, he became more and more interested in practical design, as he felt that conventional painting and sculpture were finished. He was sent to the Kiev Art Institute in 1925 to run the Theatre and Film Department, but in 1927 he succeeded in returning to Moscow as the head of the Wood and Metalwork faculties in the reorganized Vkhutemas (the Higher State Art Technical Studio), later to be reorganized yet again under the name Vkhutein (Higher Technical Institute). Tatlin was later put in charge of the Ceramics faculty, which in 1931–32 became the Institute of Silicates. Whatever his designated responsibility, Tatlin continued to teach with his customary intensity; pupils of the inter-war epoch remembered him as dedicated but very narrow.

In the 1930s Tatlin was given a laboratory at the former Novedeichi Monastery on the outskirts of Moscow. Here he worked on a project for a manpowered glider, the *Letatlin* – the name was a combination of the Russian verb 'to fly' and Tatlin's own name. The glider was based on Tatlin's study of insects: he bred certain species in boxes and liberated them when adult to see how they flew and responded to the wind. He declared:

> My machine is built on the principle of life, organic forms. Through the observation of these forms I came to the conclusion that the most aesthetic forms are the most economical. Work on the formation of material is art.

Nevertheless, like the earlier monument to the Third International Exhibition, the project never took on fully practical form, and the *Letatlin* never left the ground.

Despite the Stalinist freeze, Tatlin was given a retrospective exhibition at the Museum of Decorative Arts in Moscow (now the Pushkin Museum) in 1933. Among the items exhibited were models and drawings for his glider. Between 1933 and 1952 he worked chiefly as a theatrical designer and was responsible for more than twenty productions. Like Rodchenko at the same epoch, he began to paint again, producing mostly nudes and still lifes. Many of these late paintings were on wood, using various experimental techniques derived from icon painting. Tatlin died in 1953.

MARC CHAGALL,
*Double Portrait with
a Glass of Wine*, 1917

MARC CHAGALL

The details of Chagall's life, especially his early life, are often vague, despite the fact that he wrote an enchanting poetic autobiography covering his childhood and youth entitled *My Life*. This vagueness and imprecision are perhaps not surprising, since in his art he is an unclassifiable master of fantasy, who belongs to no school.

He was born in 1887, the eldest of eight children, into a poor Jewish family in Vitebsk, a bustling town in the Russian part of the Pale of Settlement (the area where Jews were allowed to reside). His father worked as a labourer for a herring merchant; his mother, by far the more positive personality of the two, ran a little grocery store. He often visited his maternal grandfather, a ritual butcher, who lived nearby in the countryside. At first he was educated at the local *cheder*, the Jewish religious school; then at the age of thirteen he entered a Russian communal school. He was first seized with a desire to draw when he saw another boy in the school copying an illustration in a magazine – up to that point he had never seen either drawings or paintings. He copied his schoolmate's example, and his drawings were pinned up at home, despite the Jewish religious prohibition against the making of images.

When he was seventeen he persuaded his parents to send him to study with a minor Jewish academic painter, Jehuda Pen, who lived in Vitebsk. Chagall worked with him for several months, and then briefly took a job as a photographic retoucher; but by this time he was determined to go and study in St Petersburg, despite the difficulty of obtaining a residence permit. At first he was lucky – he found a patron, a rich Jewish baron with a celebrated library, who supported him for four or five months. But after this his subsidy was cut off, and he was forced to live as best he could, sharing rooms with near-strangers, and sometimes even forced to share a bed. At one point, in order to solve the perpetual problem of his residence permit, he took a job as a footman; at another he was a sign-painter.

Chagall did not live continuously in St Petersburg; he made frequent returns home to his family. On one of these visits, around 1908 or 1909, he met Bella Rosenfeld, the daughter of a Jewish family of much higher social status than his own, who was later to become his wife. Meanwhile, he was shifting from teacher to teacher in St Petersburg, trying to find one who suited him. Eventually he studied with Léon Bakst, who had just achieved major international acclaim for his designs for the Ballets Russes for their first season in Paris. From Bakst and those who surrounded him Chagall learned of the world outside Russia, and he was soon filled with a desire to follow in their footsteps and make his way to Paris.

The trip was made possible by a magazine editor called Maxim Vinaver, who was also a deputy to the Russian Parliament. In 1910 he purchased two of Chagall's paintings to provide him with his fare, and promised to give him an allowance of forty roubles a month. Chagall quickly settled in after he arrived in France. He took a studio in La Ruche, where he was surrounded by a polyglot circle of artists and would-be artists. He exhibited at the Salon des Indépendants of 1912, and then at the Salon d'Automne of the same year. Robert Delaunay was one of his sponsors for the Salon d'Automne, and he was soon familiar with other important members of the avant-garde. In March 1913 Apollinaire introduced Chagall to Herwarth Walden, editor of *Der Sturm*, who invited him to exhibit at the First German Autumn Salon planned for the following September. Chagall's reputation continued to grow, and in 1914 Walden gave him his own one-man exhibition at the *Der Sturm* Gallery. It was an outstanding success. After visiting Berlin for the opening of the show, and then returning to Paris, Chagall decided to make a three-month visit to Russia. While he was there war broke out, and he found himself trapped for the duration.

An early priority, once he was home, was to continue his courtship of Bella. It took him some time to overcome the opposition of her family, but finally he succeeded and the wedding took place in July 1915. An unwise application for an exit visa to return to France brought him to the attention of the authorities, and he was conscripted, but through family influence he managed to get a job as a clerk under Bella's brother, recently appointed Director of the Office of War Economy in St Petersburg (which had now become Petrograd).

With the coming of the Revolution, Chagall sided with the Bolsheviks. He was now known in avant-garde circles, and was also known personally to Anatoly Lunacharsky, Minister for Culture in the new government, who had once paid a visit to his Paris studio. In September 1918 Chagall was appointed Commissar for Art in Vitebsk, one of his duties being to set up a new school. His tenure of office was stormy, as he was soon confronted by a faction led by Kasimir Malevich, whom he had invited to come and teach at the new institution. During one of Chagall's absences to seek support in Moscow, Malevich and his following took control of the school, renaming it a 'Suprematist School'. Chagall succeeded in reinstating himself with difficulty, but in May 1920 he departed for Moscow, where living conditions were very hard but there was less psychological pressure. He was given a commission to paint a series of huge canvases for the State Kamerny Jewish Theatre, and then, in search of a more tolerable environment, moved to a small town near Moscow where he taught in a colony for homeless children. But he had become disillusioned with the

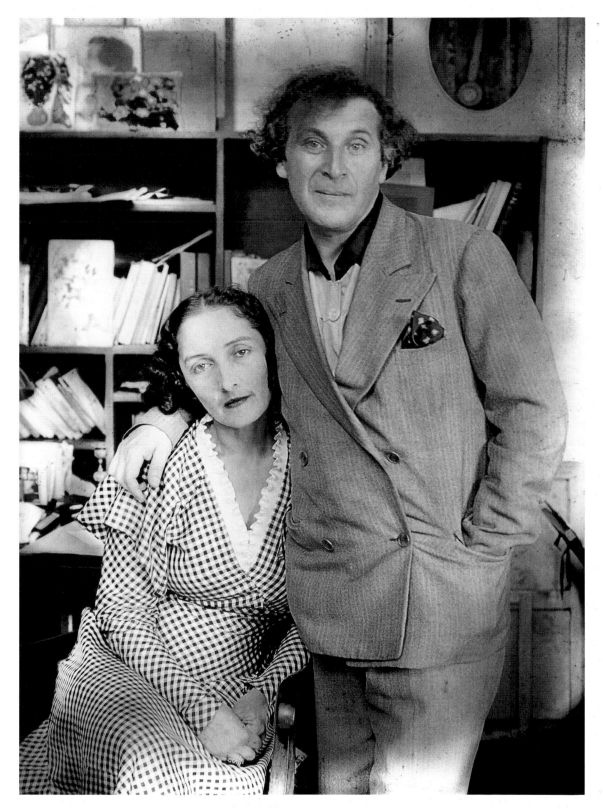

Marc and Bella Chagall, Paris 1933. Photo André Kertész

Revolution, and perhaps even more so by the dictatorial attitudes of the Russian Constructivists. He obtained an exit visa in 1922, and left Russia via Kaunas on the Lithuanian frontier. From here he went to Berlin, where he became involved in a lawsuit against Herwarth Walden, who had shown his pictures at the *Der Sturm* Gallery during the war years and had sold many of them.

In 1923 the way was paved for Chagall's return to France by an approach from the dealer Ambroise Vollard, who wanted to discuss a series of book illustrations. Chagall was back in Paris early in 1924. Vollard commissioned him to illustrate a work of his own choice; the artist chose Gogol's *Dead Souls*. He also started to paint replicas and versions of old work, motivated by a desire to reconstruct his *oeuvre*, much of which had been scattered and lost during the war. Chagall's subject-matter had from the beginning been rooted in his own life – in recollections of his youth in Vitebsk and in celebrations of his love for Bella. Cut off from his Russian roots, he now began to recycle these themes, often sentimentalizing them in the process. During this period he rejected a formal offer to join the new Surrealist group.

In 1930 he received a contract from Vollard to illustrate the Bible, which led to a visit to Palestine in 1931 – he was present at the laying of the foundation stone for the new Tel-Aviv Museum. The trip gave Chagall a new sense of his Jewish identity. In 1935 he was invited to Vilna, for the opening of the Yiddish Institute there. He accepted, because it meant a return to the Pale of Settlement, though to an area safely on the other side of the Russo–Polish border. During his visit to Poland Chagall saw the Warsaw ghetto, and became aware of the rising tide of anti-semitism in the country. These experiences duly found their place in one of his most impressive canvases, the *White Crucifixion* of 1937.

In 1937 Chagall became a French citizen. He was not to enjoy the benefits of his new passport for long, as he was stripped of his French nationality under the new anti-Jewish laws brought in by the Vichy Government in 1940. He lingered dangerously long in France: it was only in April 1941 that he and his wife and daughter moved to Marseilles, hoping to take passage for America. Here they were arrested in a raid on the hotel where they were staying, and only freed through the urgent intervention of Varian Frey, head of the Emergency Rescue Committee, and of the American Consul General. Early in May they crossed the border into Spain.

On 23 June 1941 they arrived in New York, and they lived in the United States until 1948. Chagall was honoured as an artist, but the epoch was marked by personal traumas. In 1944 Bella died suddenly from a viral infection. Chagall, who had never learned English, was lost without her and felt extremely isolated. Shortly after his wife's death he began an affair with a young Englishwoman living in New York who happened to speak excellent French. In due course the couple had a son. In May 1946, just when the child was due, Chagall paid his first visit to France since the war. In the same year he had a major retrospective exhibition at the Museum of Modern Art in New York, and then, in 1947, a somewhat reduced version was shown at the Musée National d'Art Moderne in Paris. His reputation was now rising rapidly, and he found himself recognized as one of the Old Masters of the Modern movement. There were further exhibitions in Chicago in 1946–47, at the Stedelijk Museum in Amsterdam in 1946, and at the Tate Gallery, London, in 1948.

He then made up his mind to return to France, and in 1948 settled permanently on the Côte d'Azur. In 1952, his English mistress, who had accompanied him, left him for another man, and in the same year Chagall married Valentina Brodsky, a friend of his daughter, Ida. Valentina became his indispensable helpmate in old age.

Throughout the post-war epoch Chagall experimented with new media. In particular, some of his most impressive late work is in stained glass. In 1972 he set up his Musée National Message Biblique in Nice, which is as much a personal monument as Matisse's chapel in Vence. He continued to paint until the end of his life, which came very suddenly at the beginning of 1985, just before the closure at the Royal Academy in London of his last major exhibition which then transferred to the Philadelphia Museum of Art, USA. Chagall was the last representative of the first generation of Modernists.

LIUBOV POPOVA,
stage design for Meyerhold's
production of Crommelynck's play
The Magnanimous Cuckold, 1922

LIUBOV POPOVA

Liubov Popova is one of the galaxy of talented women artists associated with the revolutionary years in Russia. She was born near Moscow in 1889, the daughter of a wealthy and cultivated textile merchant. Her mother, however, was the daughter of a serf. In 1902, the family moved briefly to the Crimea, but returned to live in Moscow in 1907. She began her formal study of art in 1907, in the studio of the Russian Impressionist Stanislas Zhukovsky. In 1909 she travelled to Kiev, where she saw the work of the leading Symbolist Mikhail Vrubel in the Church of St. Cyril – these had an enormous impact on her. Over the next few years she travelled widely both in Russia and in Italy. In Italy she greatly admired the painters of the early Renaissance, notably Giotto; in Russia she visited the ancient cities of Novgorod, Pskov, Rostov and Suzdal, and was impressed by the strength of Russian medieval church art and architecture.

Popova became acquainted with the French Cubist painting in 1912, through visits to the collection of Sergei Shchukin in Moscow, which was open to the public. In the autumn and winter of 1912–13 she spent some months in Paris, visiting the studios of the Russian artists then living in the city, among them the sculptors Zadkine and Archipenko, and studying under the French Cubist painters Jean Metzinger and Robert Le Fauconnier. On her return to Russia, she worked for a time in Vladimir Tatlin's studio, and her commitment to the experimental art being made in Russia became complete. In January 1914 she exhibited for the first time, with the Jack of Diamonds group. Among the other exhibitors were Malevich, Braque, Picasso, Vlaminck and Derain.

In March 1914 she returned to Paris with Vera Mukhina, later a well known Socialist Realist sculptor. The two women toured extensively in Italy during the spring and early summer, but were forced to return to Russia on the outbreak of the First World War. She continued to work in Tatlin's studio, and now became an active organizer of artists whose own sympathies lay on the political left. Her own work done at this time shows a mixture of Cubist and Italian Futurist influences. In March 1915 she was a participant in *Tramway V*, an exhibition in Petrograd (now St Petersburg), which proclaimed itself to be 'The First Futurist Exhibition of Paintings'. She was now involved with the Cubo-Futurist group surrounding Malevich. By 1916, her work had become completely non-objective. One influence seems to have been Islamic architecture

LIUBOV POPOVA, *c.* 1920. Photo Alexander Rodchenko

and decoration, which she saw on a visit to Samarkand.

With the outbreak of revolution in Russia, Popova, like many colleagues in the Russian avant-garde, threw herself into work on its behalf, painting public buildings and designing posters. In 1918, she became a faculty member of Svomas (Free State Art Studios), the post-revolutionary art school in Moscow, and in March of that year she married Boris von Eding, an art historian specializing in ancient Russian architecture. Their son was born in November; but during a journey they both made to Rostov in the summer of 1919, her husband died from typhus. Popova was also seriously ill but recovered. She only began to paint again a full year after the birth of her son.

In 1920, she began working for the theatre, and became a member of Inkhuk (the Institute of Artistic Culture), established under the leadership of Vasily Kandinsky. Dissatisfied with conditions in Russia, he resigned in 1920, and returned to Germany. Popova continued to be an active member, participating in debates which led to the formulation of an agreed theory of Constructivism. Svomas, meanwhile, was reorganized as Vkhutemas (Higher State Artistic and Technical Studios), now with the aim of training artists for industrial production, and Popova became director of the section dealing with the use of colour. Her own work was now rigorously abstract, and in 1921–22 she produced her last easel paintings, a series of 'Space-Force Constructions'. In November 1921, she and twenty-five other artists signed an Inkhuk proclamation rejecting easel painting in favour of utilitarian art.

She continued to work for the theatre, collaborating with the great director Vselvod Meyerhold, and scoring a particular success with her Constructivist designs for his production of Fernand Crommelynck's play *The Magnanimous Cuckold* in April 1922. Despite her renunciation of painting, some of her work was shown in Berlin in 1921, at the 'First Russian Art Exhibition' organized by Lissitzky at the Galerie van Diemen.

In 1923 and 1924 she worked at the First State Print Textile Factory in Moscow with her fellow artist Varvara Stepanova, producing designs for dress fabrics. She said that seeing these actually being worn gave her more satisfaction than her work as a painter. She also made designs for posters, book covers and ceramics, in keeping with the new 'productivist' ethos.

In May 1924 her son caught scarlet fever and died. Popova contracted the disease from him, and died on 25 May.

EL LISSITZKY

El (Lazar Markovich) Lissitzky was born in 1890 to a Jewish family living near Smolensk. Shortly after his birth, his father, like so many Russian Jews of that period, emigrated to the United States, but when he sent for his wife, she took the advice of her Rabbi and refused to go. His father was forced to return, and Lissitzky grew up in the almost wholly Jewish town of Vitebsk, later going to secondary school in Smolensk. He had already shown signs of artistic talent, and when he graduated he took the entrance exam for the St Petersburg Academy of Arts, but was rejected, because he was Jewish. His family therefore scraped together the money to send him to study abroad. In 1909 he left Russia to enrol at the Technische Hochschule (technological university) in Darmstadt. His course of studies was not in art but architecture, and Lissitzky earned extra money making architectural and technical drawings for fellow students less gifted or industrious than himself.

Darmstadt, though only a small grand-ducal capital, was at this time a centre of innovation in the decorative arts, with a particular penchant for Jugendstil – the German term for Art Nouveau. Lissitzky made the most of his opportunities there, then in 1911 managed to visit Paris. On his way back to Darmstadt he visited the Belgian architect Henri van de Velde, whose work was known in Russia from the interior decor he had designed for the great Russian collector of avant-garde art, Sergei Shchukin. In 1912 he went to Italy, where he was particularly impressed by the Byzantine mosaics in Ravenna.

The outbreak of war took Lissitzky by surprise while he was still in Darmstadt, and he had to make a hasty and circuitous return home. He finally received his diploma in engineering and architecture from Riga technological university which, because of the war, had been evacuated to Moscow. In 1916, he went to work in a Moscow architect's office, where one of his tasks was to help redesign the displays in the Ancient Egyptian section of the Pushkin Museum.

Lissitzky still had artistic ambitions, but in wartime found it easier to work as an illustrator, designing a series of innovative Yiddish picture books. The illustrations for these were heavily influenced by *lubok* – the traditional popular prints which then appealed to many members of the Russian avant-garde. Lissitzky was somewhat late in discovering them – they had already influenced artists otherwise as different from one another as Malevich and Goncharova.

Like most of the young Russian artists of the period, Lissitzky was an eager partisan of the October Revolution. In 1918, it was he who designed the first flag for the Central Committee of the Communist Party of the Soviet Union, which was solemnly paraded on May Day in Red Square. In 1919, Marc Chagall, now in charge of the art school at Vitebsk, invited Lissitzky to return there as professor of architecture and applied arts. One of his colleagues was Malevich, ten years older and far more mature as an artist. Though Lissitzky was unsympathetic to the transcendental side of Malevich's art, the latter's experiments with radical abstraction led him towards a new style, and in particular to the invention of what he called 'Prouns', works which, as Lissitzky himself said were 'an interchange station between painting and architecture'. Lissitzky put his new feeling for abstract forms to work in a series of propaganda posters, the most famous of which is the civil war image 'Beat the Whites with the Red Wedge'.

The radical regime at the Vitebsk art school soon fell victim to warring factions. Malevich staged a coup against Chagall, who then left Russia. Malevich himself became unpopular with the local authorities, and he and his followers were forced to quit the town. More fortunate than Malevich, Lissitzky obtained a post in Moscow, as head of the faculty of architecture in the new Vkhutemas art school (the Higher State Artistic and Technical Studio). Like his colleagues Tatlin and Rodchenko, both also heads of departments of Vkhutemas (though Tatlin did not arrive there until 1927), Lissitzky now became more interested in what was called 'productivist art' – art applied for practical purposes, rather than existing for its own sake. Together they formed the core of a new Constructivist grouping which was momentarily dominant in Soviet art.

Lissitzky, because of the period he had spent in Germany, was ideally qualified to serve as artistic ambassador for the new regime. In 1921 he was sent to Berlin, to set up an exhibition of the new Russian art and establish contacts with avant-garde groupings in Germany. One of his most useful contacts was the Dadaist George Grosz. He also accompanied the exhibition of Russian art to Amsterdam, and there made

EL LISSITZKY
in his studio at Vitebsk, 1919
Photographer unknown

El Lissitzky, *Beat the Whites with the Red Wedge* (poster), 1919

In the 1930s his health grew increasingly worse, and he had to spend longer and longer periods in various sanatoria. He was still, however, fully employed as a designer of exhibitions as well as of books and photographic albums. He remained an enthusiastic supporter of the Soviet way of life and, in his widow's account at least, was untouched by the great political purges of the period. He died of tuberculosis at the end of December 1941, a few months after the German invasion of Russia.

contact with various members of the Dutch avant-garde group De Stijl, which had much in common with the Constructivists. Another important friendship was with the German Dadaist Kurt Schwitters, who lived in the conservative provincial city of Hanover. Through Schwitters, Lissitzky attracted the patronage of the Kestner-Gesellschaft, a society formed to promote radical new art in this slightly unpromising environment. In particular he formed a warm friendship, soon ripening into love, with the widow of its first artistic director, Sophie Küppers, whose husband was one of the last victims of the post-war Spanish influenza epidemic.

Lissitzky was offered a studio in the Kestner-Gesellschaft's premises, but soon fell ill with a lung infection, and had to be sent to Switzerland to recuperate. He was to be dogged by ill health for the rest of his life. In 1925 he returned Moscow; in 1926, after many delays in getting a passport, he returned to Germany. The following year he took Sophie back with him to Russia, where they married. Though the tide had already begun to turn against the Constructivist avant-garde, Lissitzky was still much in demand as a designer of exhibitions, particularly in Germany. His talents for this kind of work enabled him to travel in and out of Russia fairly easily until the period of Nazi government. His artistic reputation, at this period, rested largely on his experiments as a typographer, and as a creator of radically novel exhibition spaces, where both enlarged type and blown-up photographs played an important part.

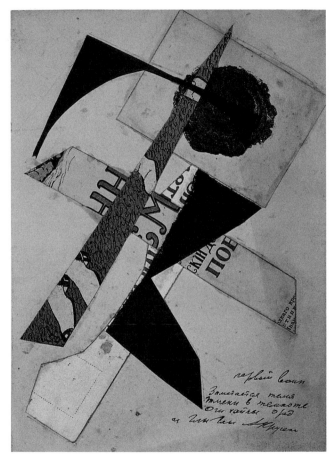

ALEXANDER RODCHENKO AND VARVARA STEPANOVA

Alexander Rodchenko and his wife Varvara Stepanova formed one of the husband-and-wife partnerships not uncommon in the history of the Russian avant-garde. Rodchenko was born in St Petersburg in November 1891. His father made props for a theatre and his mother was a laundress: both parents were of peasant stock. He studied

Above: Varvara Stepanova, cover design for *Zigra ar*, 1918

ЧЕМПИОНЫ
Англіи и Франціи

ALEXANDER RODCHENKO, *France and England*, 1920

VARVARA STEPANOVA, 1928. Photo Alexander Rodchenko

at the Kazan School of Art from 1910 to 1913, as an external student. Here he met Varvara Stepanova, the daughter of a petty official, who had been born in 1894 in Kaunas, in Lithuania. Stepanova was already married – she had entered a marriage of convenience with an architect called Fedorov (later killed in World War I) to be allowed to stay in Kazan.

In February 1914 the poet Vladimir Mayakovsky, together with the poet-painter David Burliuk and Vasily Kamensky, gave a Futurist performance in Kazan. This was the Rodchenkos first meeting with the new avant-garde. They were entranced, and Rodchenko later described the meeting as 'one of the most important of my life'.

Stepanova left Kazan without completing her studies, and went to Moscow, where she made contact with other members of the burgeoning avant-garde, among them

Liubov Popova and Vladimir Tatlin. To make a living, she worked as a book-keeper in a factory and also learned to type. The couple kept in touch by letter until Rodchenko too could come to Moscow. He left Kazan without a diploma, since he lacked the necessary educational qualifications to obtain one, and continued his studies at the Stroganov School of Decorative Arts, where he soon found himself in conflict with the academic nature of its curriculum. He met Tatlin, and was immediately invited by him to participate in a co-operative exhibition to be held in a Moscow shop in 1916. Rodchenko, who had no money, made his contribution by hanging and invigilating the exhibition. During its run a row erupted between Tatlin and Malevich, who was also one of the exhibitors. Rodchenko, who sided with Tatlin, withdrew his work in protest.

The following year, after the fall of the Tsar and the setting up of the Kerensky Government, a Union of Painters was formed in Moscow and Petrograd. Stepanova and Rodchenko immediately joined – they were members of the most avant-garde of its three divisions, the Left Federation, which drew support mainly from the Futurists. Rodchenko became secretary of the Federation's Moscow branch. At this time they were attracted by nihilist and anarchist ideas, but after the October Revolution they threw in their lot with the Bolsheviks. Rodchenko became the first Director of the Museum of Artistic Culture, the earliest museum of modern art in the world. Ironically, considering their dislike of one another, Malevich was to succeed him in this post. While he was still Director, Rodchenko made a series of *Black on Black* paintings intended as a direct criticism of Malevich's contemporary *White on White* canvases. Stepanova, meanwhile, was continuing the experiments with 'visual poetry' which she had already begun to make before the Revolution. 'By turning the monotony of printed letters upside-down and fusing them with painterly graphics,' she said, 'I am approaching a new type of creativity.'

In 1918 Rodchenko became co-director of the Industrial Art Faculty in Moscow with Olga Rozanova (who died almost immediately after her appointment). At the same time he was making photomontages which paralleled those being created by the German Dadaists. In 1919 Rodchenko's work became more fully Constructivist, asserting the importance of the concrete

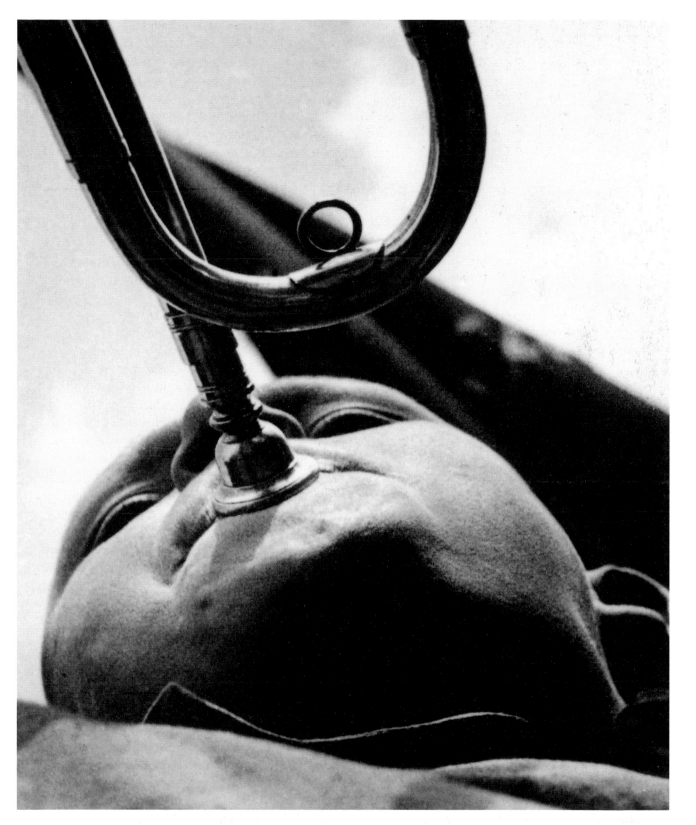

ALEXANDER RODCHENKO, *The Pioneer Trumpeter*, 1930

(the nature of materials, of light and of colour) as opposed to mysticism and symbolism.

Stepanova, meanwhile, was reluctant to abandon figurative painting, and produced a rich new series of paintings and graphic works showing stylized figures. These scored a great success for her at the 19th State Exhibition held in Moscow in October 1920. Rodchenko and Stepanova were the dominant personalities at this exhibition, and Marc Chagall, then still in Russia, noted the difference in their personalities. Echoing Chagall's remarks, Stepanova wrote in her diary: 'I have an ungovernable, unbalanced temperament with a good measure of chaos. Anti's [Rodchenko's] is cold, calm, analytic, with a tendency to abstraction. Chagall doubted whether Anti could ever have painted the world of objects.'

In 1920, Rodchenko was put in charge of the metalwork faculty at Vkhutemas (the Higher State Artistic and Technical Studio), where he was to remain for a decade. He also renewed his contacts with Mayakovsky, with whom he collaborated closely until the poet's suicide in 1930. Rodchenko was now an advocate not merely of Constructivism, but of what was called 'Productivism' – the mass production of art by industrial means. Its ideals were summed up in a statement Rodchenko pinned up in an exhibition where his work was displayed:

The art of the future will not be the cosy decoration of family homes. It will be just as indispensable as 48-storey skyscrapers, mighty bridges, wireless aeroplanes and submarines which will be transformed into art.

Stepanova was also moving in the same direction, but perhaps with less conviction. In March 1922 she noted in her diary: 'It's not easy to agitate for Constructivism, but it's even harder to really reject art and begin work in production.' Her way out of this dilemma was to throw herself into theatre-design, where she followed the example already given by Liubov Popova, creating elaborate mechanical stage-settings which recall Rodchenko's constructions of the same epoch. She also, in conjunction with Popova, began to work on textile and clothing design. In addition, and this was a more lasting interest, she began to specialize in book design, an activity in which she and her husband were to become close collaborators.

Rodchenko meanwhile had become completely disillusioned with easel painting. His attitudes were expressed in a note written a few years later, in 1927:

When I look at the mountains of my paintings from previous years I sometimes wonder what to do with them all. It's a pity to burn them all. I worked for ten years on them. It's all an empty business, like a church building.

He found substitute activities. In 1925, for example, he made his first and only trip out of Russia, having been asked to design furniture and fittings for a Workers' Club as part of the Soviet contribution to the great International Exhibition of Decorative Art in Paris. He produced a remarkably original plan, and left an amusing account of the way in which he was forced to improvise, using the cheapest materials because of lack of funds. One improvisation was not wholly successful: he had the floor covered in a mixture of soot and glue. Visitors trailed this into the rooms used by the other exhibitors, who eventually paid for a carpet to be laid down in the Soviet room.

In 1928 Rodchenko began to come into conflict with the Soviet authorities, though never as acutely as other Russian writers and artists. The journal *Sovetskoye Foto* criticized the photographic work with which he was now increasingly involved, and accused him of plagiarizing Western models and of formalism (the latter because of his use of extreme close-ups and of tilted angles). It was still possible for him to make a vigorous reply, but *Sovetskoye Foto* returned to the attack in 1930, and the following year Rodchenko was expelled from the October Group of artists, which he had joined in 1928.

Despite these problems, he was still employed on official projects. In 1930 he made the first of a number of trips to document the building of the White Sea Canal, largely the work of political prisoners who were being 're-educated' by forced labour. His photographs eventually filled a special issue of the quadrilingual propaganda magazine *USSR in Construction* with which he was associated almost throughout the 1930s. Though he did not travel abroad again, his typographical work was exhibited in the Soviet Pavilion at the Paris Exposition Universelle of 1937, and his publications were also shown at the New York World's Fair of 1939. Stepanova was Rodchenko's regular collaborator on book and magazine projects at this period, and did much of the administrative work, seeing the finished designs through the press.

In 1935, the year after Socialist Realism was proclaimed the official art-style of the Soviet Union, Rodchenko began to paint once more. At first he produced figurative circus scenes, but in 1943, in an amazing reversal of all his previous attitudes, he began work on a series of 'drip-paintings'. These paralleled, and were perhaps somewhat in advance of, Pollock's similar paintings of the middle and late 1940s, although it is probable that Rodchenko, in wartime Russia, was quite unaware of Pollock's activities. The drip-paintings made strange successors not only to the circus scenes which preceded them but to the three monochrome paintings, in pure red, pure yellow and pure blue, which Rodchenko had exhibited as long ago as 1921 – at that point describing them as 'the last paintings'.

Stepanova also returned to easel painting in the late 1930s, but her work, unlike that of her husband, was done directly from the motif – small landscapes and still lifes, in thickly encrusted paint. Both continued working actively on photomontages and other projects for print until the end of their lives. Rodchenko died in 1956, and Stepanova in 1958.

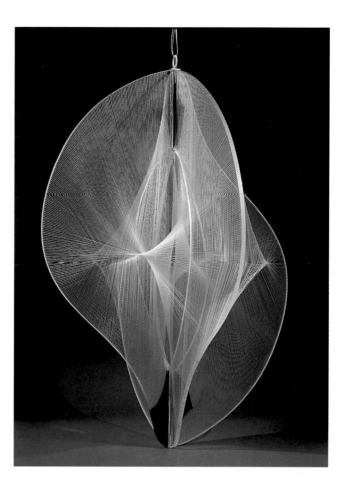

Naum Gabo, Linear Construction in Space No. 2, 1972–73

NAUM GABO

Naum Gabo's sculpture is a prime example of the application of scientific ideas and principles in art. Though he is labelled a 'Russian' Constructivist, he did very little work in Russia, and represents the modern spirit at its most international.

He was born Naum Neemia Pevsner in 1890 in Briansk, the fourth of five sons. As his brother Alexei later described it, this was 'a remote, quiet part of Russia ... a small town surrounded by fields, meadows and woods'. His father was a prosperous engineer and an important figure in the town, and his mother was of peasant stock. His youth was somewhat turbulent: he was expelled from primary school for writing a rude poem about his headmaster; he was then taken to Tomsk in Siberia by his eldest brother, Mark, for coaching by himself and his fellow students. But he was sent back home thanks to the unrest caused in Tomsk by the abortive revolution of 1905. Soon after he returned home he was arrested by the local police for his involvement in an illegal group, but was released after only two hours when his father intervened. It was thought wise, however, to send him away again and he was packed off to secondary school at Kursk, where he spent most of his time writing poetry.

After graduating from the Gymnasium at Kursk he enrolled to read medicine at Munich University, and then in 1911 transferred to study natural sciences. At this time he started to take an interest in art. In 1912 he moved to the polytechnic school in Munich to study engineering, and at the same time attended Heinrich Wölfflin's lectures on the history of art. This year saw his first visit to Paris. In 1913, at the urging of Wölfflin, he went to Florence and Venice, travelling on foot from Munich since he was short of funds. In 1913–14 he was again in Paris, visiting his second brother, Antoine, who was there to study painting. He returned to Russia, and then in April 1914 accompanied his mother on a trip abroad. In July he found himself in Munich once more, in the company of his brother, Alexei.

When it became clear that war was imminent, they left hastily for Scandinavia, going first to Copenhagen, then to Stockholm and finally to Christiania (now Oslo). Their parents sent them instructions to remain abroad and continue their education as best they could. In the isolation of Norway Gabo held many discussions with Alexei, and later with Antoine, who was able to join them from Paris in 1915. It was here, though he had had little practical art training, that he decided finally to become an artist, and more specifically a sculptor, applying to art what he had already learned from his scientific studies. His first sculptures were made in the winter of 1915–16, notably a girl's head constructed from joined planes of plywood. From the beginning he signed his work 'Gabo', so as to distinguish himself from Antoine, who had also opted for a career in art.

In April 1917 the brothers returned to Russia, following the abdication of the Tsar in mid-March. Gabo was soon caught up in the revolutionary ferment of the time – in 1919–20 he was busy designing a radio station which had certain similarities to Tatlin's more famous and equally abortive project for a monument to the Third International. But Gabo was opposed to the Productivist philosophy of Tatlin and his supporters, and in August

NAUM GABO with his wife Miriam,
South of France, c. 1936.
Photographer unknown

1920 published a Realist manifesto in poster form, in which he proclaimed that 'The realization of our perceptions of the world in the forms of space and time is the only aim of our pictorial and plastic art.' Since the poster was pasted up on street-corners, in places where people had become accustomed to reading government decrees, it caused a certain stir. In 1920 Gabo made some of his most prophetic work, notably a small motor-powered construction with a vibrating rod, which foreshadowed Kinetic Art.

Gabo felt that the tide was running against him in Russia, and in 1922 he left for Berlin, though he did not wholly sever his connection with the Soviet government: he exhibited in the First Russian Art Exhibition organized, with Soviet backing, at the Galerie van Diemen, and in 1931 he was busy with a project for a Palace of the Soviets. In 1924 he had a joint exhibition in Paris with his brother, and it may have been this which led to a commission from Diaghilev to design the décor and costumes for the ballet *La Chatte*, with music by Sauguet. One of the most successful of Diaghilev's late productions, this had crystalline plastic structures against a backdrop and floorcloth of black American cloth. The first performance took place in Monte Carlo, in April 1927. Gabo had a certain amount of trouble with the prima ballerina, the distinguished classical specialist Olga Spessivtseva. Diaghilev made the mistake of telling her that Gabo was trying to turn her into a work of art, and the woman (who in any case had little sense of humour and was famous for never smiling on stage) was not pleased, as she thought she was one already.

From this point onwards Gabo's career consisted of exhibitions in various parts of the world and occasional commissions for monumental sculpture. He based himself in Germany until 1932, when he left for Paris. In 1935 he decided to settle in London, where he formed part of the circle which included Ben Nicholson and Barbara Hepworth. During his stay in England he was one of the editors of a book appropriately entitled *Circle*, concerned with Constructivist art.

In 1936 Gabo married Miriam Israels, and in 1939, on the outbreak of war, they moved to Carbis Bay in Cornwall. During the war he did some broadcasting for the BBC, and had a productive exchange of ideas with Hepworth, who was living nearby. In 1946 the Gabos emigrated to America.

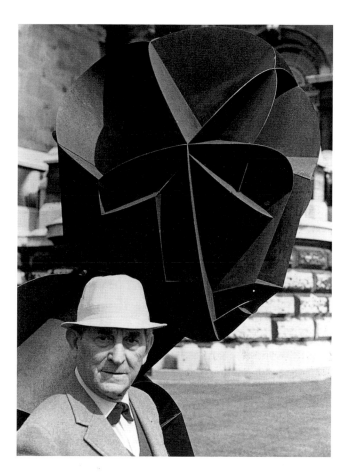

NAUM GABO with *Head*, 1968. Photo Herbert Reid

Two years later Gabo and his brother, Antoine Pevsner, were the subject of a joint exhibition at the Museum of Modern Art, New York, and in 1952 Gabo became an American citizen. In 1953 he won second prize in the 'Unknown Political Prisoner' sculpture competition and from 1953–54 he was Professor at the Harvard University Graduate School of Architecture. In 1962 he was able to visit his three brothers who had remained behind in Russia at their homes in Moscow and Leningrad. There were major travelling retrospectives of his work, which showed his continuing formal inventiveness and his interest in new materials, in 1965–66 and again in 1970–72. Gabo died in 1977 at the age of eighty-seven.

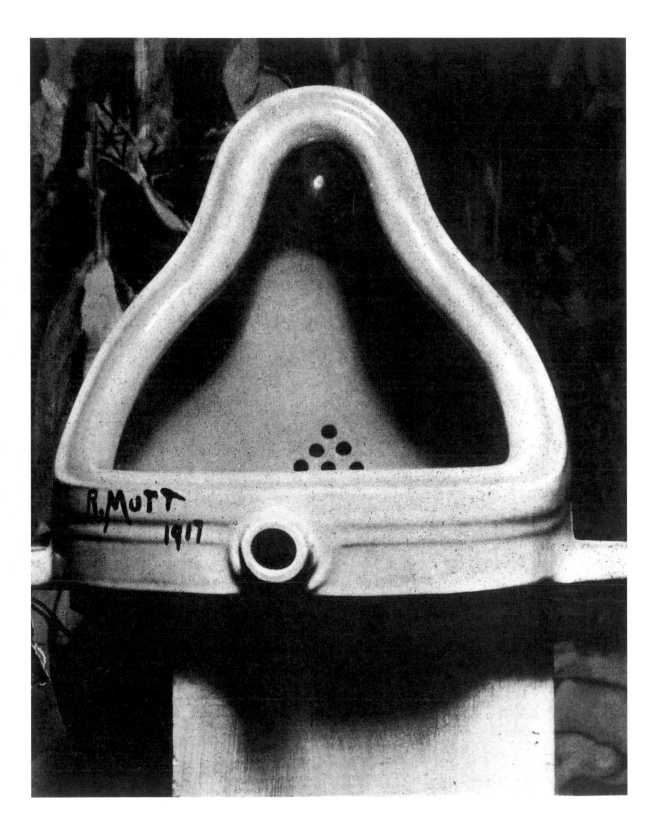

The essence of Dada was that it was against rather than for the status quo. Sometimes this opposition was of an esoteric and intellectual kind, as was the case with Duchamp; sometimes it was largely the product of circumstances – these played a large part in inspiring the activities of Arp and the other Dadaists who took refuge in Zurich during the First World War. And sometimes it was almost purely temperamental – here one can cite the otherwise very different personalities of Francis Picabia and Kurt Schwitters, each of them incurably individualistic. In the special circumstances of post-1918 Berlin, Dada became a political weapon.

Dada had an explosive effect both on art forms and people's expectations of art. Duchamp, as the inventor of the 'ready-made', has probably exercized an influence over Modernism second only to that of Cézanne.

Left: Marcel Duchamp,
Fountain,
New York 1917
Right: Hans Arp's navel,
Brittany *c.* 1928.
Photographer unknown

PARADE AMOUREUSE

Francis Picabia 1917

Francis Picabia, *Parade Amoureuse*, 1917

FRANCIS PICABIA

Picabia occupies a strangely unsettled position in the history of Modernism, universally acknowledged as an important influence and connecting link, but receiving little support for his own achievements as an artist, more especially for work done either before 1912 or after 1922.

He was born in January 1879 in Paris into a wealthy family – his father was a Cuban-born Spaniard and his mother came from a French *haut bourgeois* background. She died in 1886 and the young Francis was raised by his father, uncle and grandfather, and became thoroughly spoilt in the process. He passed a rebellious boyhood at the Lycée Monge and Collège Stanislas in Paris, and in 1895 entered the Ecole des Arts Décoratifs. He very early showed a penchant for love affairs, and in 1897 ran away to Switzerland with another man's mistress. But he was a surprisingly committed artist. He showed at the conservative Salon des Artistes Français in 1899, but

was sufficiently dissatisfied with his own work to go on studying for another six years. In 1902 he met two of the sons of Camille Pissarro, who introduced him to their father. Pissarro's influence had a decisive impact on the development of Picabia's work, and he became a belated and rather unadventurous Impressionist.

In 1905 he had his first one-man exhibition. It took place at the fashionable Galerie Haussmann, and was greeted with overwhelming critical acclaim – *Le Figaro* went so far as to say that the show 'was taking on the importance of a major event'. Not content to rest on these laurels, Picabia evolved rather uncertainly through Neo-Impressionism towards Fauvism, a process accelerated by his meeting with a young musical student called Gabrielle Buffet, who was soon to become his first wife. Eventually he made the flamboyant gesture of auctioning off his old work at the Hôtel Druot (the auction was very successful, though the dealers boycotted it because Picabia had broken his contract with the gallery which launched him), and took the plunge into Cubism. He had become friendly with Marcel Duchamp by the autumn of 1911, and with Apollinaire by 1912. He also formed links with the artists of the Section d'Or group. By the end of 1912 he had produced his first totally abstract paintings.

In 1913 Picabia took a decisive step. He went to New York for the Armory Show, and once in America seized the opportunity to present himself as a spokesman for 'Extremist' art. He became friendly with the circle round Alfred Stieglitz and was given a one-man show at Stieglitz's 291 Gallery. At first the war looked as if it might interrupt his triumphant career as a leader of the avant-garde. He was drafted in 1914, but was rescued before he was sent to the front line by his father-in-law, who managed to find him an appointment as a chauffeur to a general – Picabia always had a passion for fast cars. In 1915, thanks to further leverage exercized on his behalf, he was given a military supply mission in the Caribbean. But once he reached New York he simply abandoned his task in order to join in the activities round 291, which were now influenced by the presence of Duchamp. His wife Gabrielle found him in poor shape thanks to his consumption of drink and drugs. The couple eventually found their way to the Caribbean, but Picabia's position *vis-à-vis* the French authorities was now ambiguous because of his dereliction of duty, so they thought it wiser not to return directly to France and went instead to Barcelona. Picabia had already started producing 'mechano-morphic' drawings, often portraits of friends constructed from blueprint-like diagrams of machine parts – these are recognizably Dadaist in style, and in Barcelona he founded the Dada magazine *391*. In characteristic fashion it spared no one – not Picasso (of whom Picabia was always jealous), not the recently wounded Apollinaire (now lauded as a war hero), nor even the poet Max Jacob (recently a Catholic convert). In April 1917 Picabia, still restless, returned to New York, where he had a brief affair with Isadora Duncan, whom he had also attacked in *391*, then in September he once more crossed the Atlantic to find refuge in Barcelona. In November Gabrielle, who had gone to Switzerland to look after their children, at last managed to get him a passport, and he was free to return to Paris. Asked on one occasion what he had done in the war, he made a typical response: 'I got bored as hell'.

His life was soon as full of complications as ever. He met a young woman called Germaine Everling, soon to be his mistress, though without abandoning Gabrielle. In 1918 they all took refuge in Switzerland to unravel the chaos into which Picabia's personal affairs had now fallen, but to little effect – the one major consequence of the trip was that he established contact with the Zurich Dadaists. By March 1919 they were all back in Paris, and by August both women were pregnant by him. Picabia officially announced his return to Paris by creating a splendid scandal at the Salon d'Automne, showing a major Dada painting. During the next two years, while Dada established itself in Paris, he was at the height of his influence with the avant-garde, alternately allying himself with André Breton and then denouncing him. He first denounced Dada itself in 1921, but did not move decisively away until 1923 when he held an exhibition of figurative paintings at the Galerie Haussmann, which he had abandoned amid a certain amount of ill feeling nearly fifteen years previously. He did not, however, completely sever his links with the avant-garde. In 1924 he collaborated with Erik Satie on the ballet *Relâche*, for Rolf de Maré's Ballets Suédois.

In 1925 he came into a large inheritance, and he and Germaine, with whom he was now living, moved south to Mougins, where he built a luxurious new house called the Château de Mai. This became the centre of an ideal, lotus-eating existence. He soon began an affair with Olga Mohler, who had been engaged to look after his son by Germaine. Soon the Château de Mai was amicably abandoned to Germaine (Picabia still kept his studio there), while he and Olga lived on one or other of a series of yachts. Olga later wrote tolerantly:

He has had seven yachts, 127 automobiles; that is little compared to his women. And what is rather curious is that he remains a friend with all of them except, as he tells me, 'those who are too tart'.

This was a prosperous and successful period – the eminent Léonce Rosenberg became Picabia's dealer; he held frequent shows on the Riviera; and in 1931 was even awarded the Legion of Honour by the French government. He painted figuratively, in a wide variety of styles, though all the paintings have in common a certain heaviness and coarseness of handling. Like de Chirico's later work, they have been generally regarded as a sad falling off, although there has more recently been a tendency to revalue them as ancestors of the 'bad painting' of the 1970s and 1980s.

Picabia continued to live in the south during the war, though his lifestyle was severely restricted. He married Olga in the 1940s, in order to solve the difficulties caused by her Swiss–German nationality, and they managed to offend both the patriotic French and the German occupiers. Picabia would in all likelihood have been prosecuted for suspected collaboration, but he suffered a stroke in 1945 and was in hospital for five months. During this period all charges were dropped. After he recovered he and Olga returned to Paris and settled in a comfortable apartment on the top storey of the old family home. Picabia was now producing abstract pictures once again, and in 1949 he had a large retrospective show at the Galerie René Drouin – the most progressive establishment of the period, which handled all the 'new' post-war names, such as Wols, Dubuffet and Fautrier. It was well received, but the triumph was spoilt by a burglary at Picabia's apartment three days before the exhibition opened, in which a collection of jewels, on which Picabia had been relying for security in his old age, was stolen.

In 1950 he received an indication that his suspected wartime collaboration had been forgiven: he was promoted to Officer of the Legion of Honour. His last years, however, were cruel. In 1951 he had another and severely disabling stroke. Unable to work and increasingly miserable and enfeebled, he lingered on until 1953.

MARCEL DUCHAMP

Marcel Duchamp was perhaps the most important art-theorist and avant-garde *provocateur* of the twentieth century. He directed attention away from the work of art as a material object, and instead presented it as something which was essentially an idea: he shifted the emphasis from making to thinking.

He was born in 1887, near the small town of Blainville in Normandy, the son of a successful notary. He was one of six children – three brothers and three sisters. His two brothers, who were older than he was, both became artists and adopted the surname Villon because of their father's disapproval of their choice of profession. Duchamp himself never seems to have had any difficulties with his parents when he decided to be an artist. He began his painting career as a follower of Cézanne, and then transferred his allegiance to the Cubists. In 1912 he produced *Nude Descending a Staircase*, a combination of Cubism and Futurism and his most important early work. It was considered so disturbing by the hanging committee of the Salon des Indépendants (themselves mostly Cubists) that Duchamp withdrew it. But the painting was to change the pattern of his life. In 1913 it was included in the Armory Show (from 17 February to 15 March), which introduced the Modern movement in art to New York. It became the focus of attention and controversy, and made Duchamp a celebrity in America, if not in his own country.

In 1915 Duchamp, who was exempt from war service because of his poor health, paid his first visit to the United States. He had already begun to stretch the accepted boundaries of art. The previous year he had selected (or created) the first of his 'ready-mades' – everyday objects isolated from their normal environment and presented by the artist as fully-fledged works of art. In New York Duchamp became the focus of a lively group of avant-garde artists, followers of the doctrines of Dada, the new group that used nonsense and provocation to protest against the lofty pretensions of Western civilization, which had all been called into question by the war. He began work on the *Large Glass (The Bride Stripped Bare by Her Bachelors, Even)* for which he had already made studies several years before. This was finally abandoned in 1923. Its complex imagery, full of erotic overtones, and its use of chance procedures, such as dropping pieces of string and marking the curves into which they fell, helped to cement Duchamp's reputation, as did his own subsequent elaborate commentaries on the work.

From New York Duchamp travelled to Rio de Janeiro, where he indulged his lifelong passion for chess. He then returned to France in 1919, where he forged links with the newly established Dada group in post-war Paris. During the inter-war years he divided his time between France and the United States, playing chess, working out a roulette system which neither won nor lost, publishing two books of puns and occasionally dealing in art (an occupation which, in theory at least, he despised). He played a major part in establishing Brancusi's reputation in America. His first marriage in 1925, to the daughter of a French automobile manufacturer, ended in divorce after only six months, but Duchamp was always sympathetic to

MARCEL DUCHAMP. Photo Eliot Elisofon

women and they to him. He established a close relation-ship with the wealthy American collector Katherine Dreier, and with Man Ray they founded the Société Anonyme – the first American Museum of Modern Art – in 1920. He also advised Peggy Guggenheim, first in connection with her London gallery, which opened in 1927, and then with her New York one, which launched Abstract Expressionism. Occasionally Duchamp himself would jestingly adopt a female *alter ego*, Rrose Sélavy. This invented name is typical of the puns which delighted him: Rrose Sélavy – *Rrose, c'est la vie* (Rrose, that's life). Man Ray made a superb portrait photograph of Duchamp in this guise, which the subject duly signed.

From 1924 onwards Duchamp half-heartedly tried to give the impression that he was no longer making new works of art. He made some kinetic experiments, culmin-ating in a set of six *Rotoreliefs* in 1935, but he was careful to exhibit these at the Concours Lépine, the Paris Inventors' Salon, and not at an art gallery. Nevertheless, he maintained his contacts with the avant-garde art world, particularly with the Surrealists, who had succeeded the Dadaists, and participated in a number of exhibitions, among them the International Surrealist Exhibition in Paris in 1938, for which he acted as 'generator-arbitrator'.

In 1941 Duchamp published *Box in a Valise*, a portable museum of miniature replicas, photographs and colour reproductions which summarized his career. In 1942 he returned to the United States where he lived for the rest of his life. Four years later he began working in secret on a tableau-assemblage called *Etant donnés: 1° La chute d'eau, 2° le gaz d'éclairage*. This was his last major work, and it occupied him for the next two decades. Its existence was only revealed at the end of his life, when he started to make arrangements for its transfer to the Philadelphia Museum of Art.

In 1954 Duchamp married, very happily, for a second time. His new wife was Alexina (Teeny) Sattler, who had previously been married to the dealer Pierre Matisse, son of the painter. The following year Duchamp became a naturalized United States citizen.

During the 1960s his reputation grew rapidly, thanks to the rise of Neo-Dada, and then of Pop Art. He did not wholly approve of his disciples, writing to Hans Richter, the one-time Zurich Dadaist:

This Neo-Data, which they call New Realism, Pop Art, assemblage etc., is an easy way out and lives on what

Dada did. When I discovered ready-mades I thought to discourage aesthetics. In Neo-Dada they have taken my ready-mades and found aesthetic beauty in them.

Despite his dislike of this new direction, Duchamp granted an increasing number of interviews to critics and journalists. His first major European retrospective took place at the Tate Gallery in London in 1966, the year in which *Etant donnés* was completed.

Duchamp died on 2 October 1968, during his annual visit to France. He is buried with the rest of the Duchamp family in the Cimetière Monumental in Rouen. His gravestone is inscribed: '*D'ailleurs c'est toujours les autres qui meurent*' – 'All the same, it is always others who die.'

MARCEL DUCHAMP, 1966.
Photo Jorge Lewinski

KURT SCHWITTERS

Not all the leading German Dadaists were concerned with politics, and Kurt Schwitters, who based his activities on his home town of Hanover, represents the more playful side of the Dada movement in Germany.

He was born in 1887 and began professional studies as an artist in 1908 at the Hanover School of Arts and Crafts, then, between 1909 and 1914, at the Dresden and Berlin Academies. He married Helma Fischer in 1915 and returned to his native town. In 1917 he was called up, and put to work in a local regimental office. He later said that he 'fought gallantly on all fronts of the Waterloo Square' (Hanover's parade ground). He was then transferred to work as a draughtsman in the Wülfel Ironworks, where he remained until the end of the war.

The year 1917 marked a turning-point for Schwitters in a number of respects. He broke away from academic art and began experimenting with Expressionism and Cubism, and he also began writing experimental poetry, with the emphasis on sound rather than sense. In 1918 he made his first purely abstract oil paintings, a number of which were shown in June at the *Der Sturm* Gallery in Berlin. In the following year he started making collages, the so-called 'MERZ-paintings'. The name was taken from the word *kommerz* (commerce) which appeared on one of

the scraps of paper he used. *Der Sturm* published an article on his new technique, and also Schwitters's most famous poetic text – the nonsense poem 'An Anna Blume – Merzgedicht 1'. This was followed by the publication of a book of his poems, *Anna Blume*. The Zurich Dadaists had by this time heard of Schwitters's work and had recognized its kinship to their own activities, though his association with *Der Sturm* later caused the Berlin branch of the movement to reject him temporarily – they despised the pre-war Expressionists for being too subjective. The Berlin Dadaists continued to be suspicious of his lack of political affiliations.

In 1920 Schwitters applied the MERZ technique to three-dimensional experiments, perhaps inspired by an architectural course he had taken the previous year, the principal experiment being the transformation of the interior of his own house in Hanover into MERZ-*bau* (MERZ-building). By the early 1920s he had become one of the busiest and most widely publicized members of the new German avant-garde, though more for his activities as a poet, performer and lecturer than as a visual artist. Kate Frauman Steinitz, a friend from that time, remembered that:

> Schwitters was always talking business, sales deals, lecture arrangements, whatever. He was always starting something – projects or enterprises to benefit himself or his friends. He travelled a lot, always with a second suitcase filled with Hanover potatoes and carrots. These he cooked over a portable oil burner so as not to spend any money in restaurants. . . . Sticking out of his pants pocket was a much used notebook containing addresses of all progressive publishers, artists, dealers and collectors everywhere.

In 1923 he started his occasional publication, MERZ, which achieved a considerable circulation. In addition to publishing the work of artists connected with the Dada movement it documented that of the Dutch De Stijl group, notably Van Doesburg and Mondrian, and of Constructivists such as Lissitzky. Schwitters began to build a reputation as a typographer; he redesigned all the municipal forms used by the City of Hanover and worked on the typography used in the Dammerstock Exhibition in Karlsruhe (an exhibition of municipal housing organized by Walter Gropius in 1929).

KURT SCHWITTERS, 1924.
Photo El Lissitzky

KURT SCHWITTERS, MERZ-*bau*, *c.* 1930

In 1929 Schwitters paid his first visit to Norway; thereafter he spent at least a month there every year, and after the Nazis came to power the length of these visits steadily increased. In 1936 his son Ernst, who was threatened with compulsory military service, moved to Norway permanently, and on 1 January 1937 Schwitters himself left Germany for good and went to live at Lysaker on the outskirts of Oslo. Here he almost immediately started work on a second MERZ-*bau* . While in Norway he tried to make a living by painting comparatively conventional landscapes and portraits. Meanwhile four of his earlier works were included in the Nazis' Degenerate Art Exhibition in Munich, while others were confiscated from various German museums.

When the Germans invaded Norway in 1940 Schwitters and his son made a difficult escape (his wife had remained behind in Germany). On their arrival in Scotland he was interned, first in Edinburgh and then in various other camps. He continued to work on abstract and figurative paintings throughout this period, and also lectured in the camp theatre. After seventeen months he was released and moved south to join his son in London. He tried to earn money as a portrait painter, but his life in Britain was extremely impoverished and he felt rejected by the British arts establishment:

Life is sad. Why did the director of the National Gallery not even want to see me? He does not know that I belong to the *avant-garde* in art. That is my tragedy. Why did Mr A. tell me that not even the really famous painter, Lieutenant F., could get portrait commissions, and so I should be quite satisfied? Why did people tell me I should wait till after the war? I have already been waiting seven months for work, and cannot wait without eating.

In 1943 Schwitters's house in Hanover containing his first MERZ-*bau* was destroyed during an Allied air-raid, and many of his accumulated papers and notes perished at the same time. In 1944 he suffered from the first of several minor strokes. In 1945, at the end of the war, his son returned to Norway, and the artist, with a devoted female companion whom he nicknamed 'Wantee', moved to Little Langdale, near Ambleside in the Lake District. Here he again tried to make a living by painting portraits and landscapes, as he had done during his Norwegian years. He was given financial help through a Fellowship

Award from the Museum of Modern Art in New York, which enabled him to embark on a third MERZ-*bau* in a barn made available to him by a local farmer. The journey between the place where he and Wantee lived and the barn itself was tiring, but Schwitters pushed himself hard because he felt he had little time left.

In 1947 work on the barn was temporarily halted when he was confined to bed with a fractured hip, but he was able to resume later in the year. The third MERZ-*bau* was nevertheless still incomplete when Schwitters died of heart failure on 8 January 1948, the day after he became a British citizen. None of the three MERZ-*baus* – considered by Schwitters to be his major works – survives in its original form. The earliest and most ambitious, in Hanover, perished as a result of allied bombing in the Second World War. It has been reconstructed in Hanover, and another reconstruction was made for the Lyons Biennial of Contemporary Art in 1992. The Norwegian MERZ-*bau* perished in a blaze started by playing children in 1951. The unfinished one at Ambleside, which occupies a single wall rather than offering a complete environment, has now been transported from its original setting to a local museum.

Above: SOPHIE TAEUBER-ARP, Munich 1913. Photographer unknown Below: SOPHIE TAEUBER-ARP, *Composition with Bird Motifs*, 1927

HANS ARP AND SOPHIE TAEUBER-ARP

Hans Arp was one of the most important sculptors of the twentieth century. He had connections with many art movements, but the closest were probably with Dada and Surrealism. His wife, Sophie Taeuber, on the other hand, was closer to the Constructivists.

Arp was born in Strasbourg in 1887 when the city was part of Germany, following the French defeat in the Franco-Prussian War of 1870–71. Arp's father came from Schleswig-Holstein, and the boy was brought up speaking three languages: German, French and the local Alsatian dialect. He was obsessed with art from an early age. In an autobiographical sketch he said:

> I can remember, when I was eight years old, that I passionately made drawings in a book that resembled a ledger. I used coloured crayons. No other means of expression, no other vocation interested me; and those childhood games, the exploitation of unknown dreamlands, already foretold that my aim should be a conquest of the limitless boundaries of art.

At the age of sixteen he left the local school in order to attend the School of Arts and Crafts in Strasbourg. But here he quickly tired of the 'everlasting copying of stuffed birds and withered flowers' which 'not only poisoned drawing for me but destroyed my taste for all artistic activity. I took refuge in poetry.' His reading included the writings of the German Romantic Clemens Brentano, the German poets of the Sturmer Group, Rimbaud's *Illuminations* and Maeterlinck's *Serres Chaudes*. He was later to write much experimental verse himself.

Between 1904 and 1907, Arp continued his academic training under Ludwig Hoffman in Weimar. There followed a period when he worked in isolation at Weggis on Lake Lucerne in Switzerland. (His father owned a cigar and cigarette factory and had moved to Switzerland.) At intervals, however, Arp was able to visit Paris where he studied at the Académie Julian and discovered Kahnweiler's small avant-garde gallery. In 1911 he organized an exhibition in Lucerne with work by Hodler, Matisse, Picasso and himself. In the same year he visited Munich, where he made friends with Kandinsky and was invited to exhibit with the Blaue Reiter group.

In August 1914 Arp arrived by train in Paris from Strasbourg just as war was declared. He was almost penniless (especially as he could not change his German money) but managed to exist for a while, living in the group of studios in Montmartre called the Bateau-Lavoir. During this period he was in contact with Apollinaire, Max Jacob, Picasso and Delaunay. He had already begun to experiment with collage, in collaboration with an occultist friend. In 1915 he was forced by lack of money to go to Zurich. He was summoned by the German consulate to be drafted into the army (he still held a German passport) but managed to gain exemption by

convincing the officials there that he was insane. The tricks he used in order to do so were probably suggested by his association with the Zurich Dadaist group, of which he was one of the founder members. The headquarters of the group was the Café Voltaire, and although some Dadaists claimed that Arp hardly, if ever, showed himself there, he left a lively description of its atmosphere:

On the stage of a gaudy, motley, overcrowded tavern there are several weird and peculiar figures representing Tzara, Janco, Ball, Huelsenbeck and your

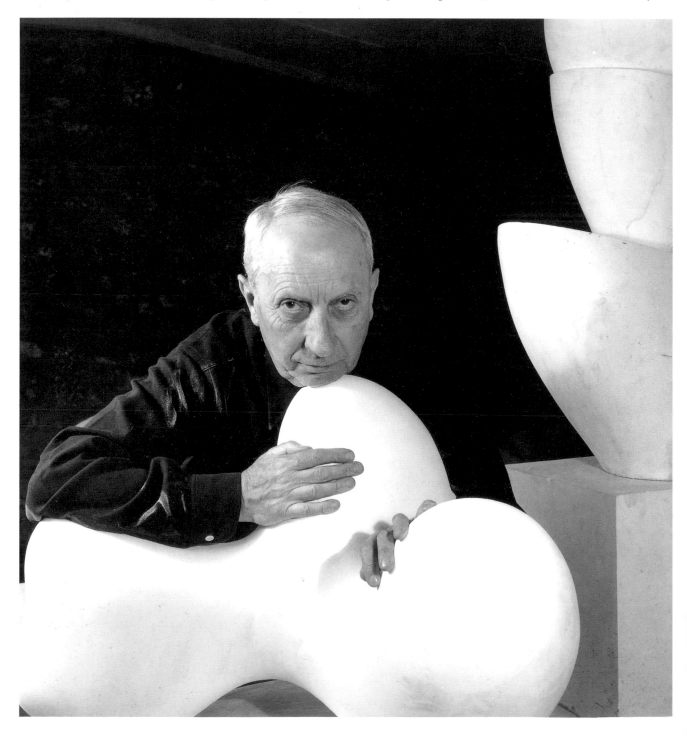

humble servant. Total pandemonium. The people round us were shouting, laughing and gesticulating. Our replies are sighs of love. Volleys of hiccups, poems, moos and miaowings of medieval Bruitistes. Tzara is wiggling his behind like the belly of an Oriental dancer. Janco is playing an invisible violin and bowing and scraping. Madame Hennings, with a Madonna face, is doing the splits. Huelsenbeck is banging away non-stop on the great drum, with Ball accompanying him on the piano, pale as a chalky ghost.

In fact Dada was just as much a release for Arp as it was for the others who made up the group. Later he wrote gratefully to Huelsenbeck:

> It was like having waited a long time in the dark and then having been aroused by a loud signal. I stepped forward and I thought there would be nothing but catcalls. But there were all of you, friends, interested, and full of praise.

Arp formed one special relationship when he joined the Dada group. He met Sophie Taeuber, who was to become his wife in 1922. Sophie had been born in 1889 in Davos-Platz, Switzerland, the fifth child of a pharmacist. She had studied art and textile design in Switzerland, then in Germany. She was also, just at the time she met Arp, becoming involved with the experimental dance group of Rudolph von Laban. Arp wrote later: 'In the motley crowd of people that I have met throughout my life Sophie Taeuber was the most graceful and the most serene. She moved like a figure in a prayer-book, studious in her work and studious in her dreaming'.

Other members of the Dada group remembered Sophie's serenity and the grace of her dancing. The poet Hugo Ball commented: 'All around her is the radiance of the sun and the miracle that replaces tradition.' He also called her 'a bird, a beautiful swallow – so astonishing were the lightness of her movements which made one almost forget that she touched the ground.'

Shortly after she met Arp, Taeuber was appointed to run the textile department at the Zurich School of Arts and Crafts. Her background in crafts and design was to have a strong effect both on her own work and on that of her future husband, though it seems that she was never

HANS ARP, *The Dancer*, 1925

very interested in theoretical discussion. Where Arp wrote prolifically, she left very few texts. But Arp himself was convinced of the importance of her influence. 'It was Sophie Taeuber,' he said later, 'who, through the example of her clear work and her clear life, showed me the right way.'

In the early years, and particularly from 1916 to 1918, Arp and Taeuber often worked collaboratively. What they did was different from the output of the other Dadaists – deliberately impersonal abstract objects with a Constructivist orientation. After the war, when international communications eased, Arp and Taeuber were both amused and amazed to discover how similar some of these experiments were to those made by the artists of De Stijl, working in Holland.

Arp's own, independent work also progressed rapidly. In 1915 he painted what he later considered to be his first successful picture: it was inspired by a set of child's building blocks. In 1916–17 he created his first painted wooden reliefs, his first venture into sculpture. He also experimented with chance procedures which paralleled those of Duchamp.

The coming of peace ended the isolation of the Zurich Dadaists and set Arp and Taeuber free to travel. They went to Italy and Germany. Meanwhile Arp attempted unsuccessfully to obtain Swiss citizenship. He then managed to obtain a French passport through a period of residence in his native Strasbourg. The couple's thoughts were in any case beginning to turn towards Paris, the established capital of modern art. In 1925 they rented a studio there, and in 1927 they bought a piece of land at Meudon, just outside the city. Here they built a house, designed by Taeuber, and paid for from the proceeds of a large decorative and architectural commission she had carried out during their period in Strasbourg.

It is clear that, during the early post-war years, Arp and Taeuber had somewhat different attitudes towards art. In the early 1920s Arp was active in the Dada movements which had now sprung up in Cologne and in Berlin. He became friendly with Kurt Schwitters and collaborated with Max Ernst on what they called 'Fatagaga' pictures – 'guaranteed to be gasometric'. He also came into contact with the Surrealists, and was invited to take part in the First Surrealist Exhibition in 1925, at the Galerie Pierre in Paris:

[The Surrealists] encouraged me to ferret out the dream, the idea behind my plastic work, and to give it a name. For many years, roughly from the end of 1919 to 1931, I interpreted most of my works. Often the interpretation was more important than the work itself ... Suddenly my need for interpretation vanished, and the body, the form, the supremely perfected work became everything to me.

Taeuber, who retained her job in Zurich until as late as 1929, was more interested in experimenting with geometrical forms, which suggested the presence of a universal, impersonal order. At the beginning of the 1930s, it was again her influence which seemed to prevail. In 1930 both she and Arp were founder members of Cercle et Carré, the group which represented the Constructivist opposition to Surrealism, and later they were both members of the successor group, Abstraction Création, which they left in 1934. Their work continued to evolve in ways which took them both away from all

groupings. In 1929 they paid a visit to Carnac in Brittany, and Arp was enormously impressed by the primitive monuments he saw there. The next year he made his first free-standing sculpture, *Hand Fruit*, and in 1932 he started to work in bronze and stone rather than in wood. These 'perfected' works contrasted with the deliberately rough torn-paper collages he began to make at about the same time and which were first exhibited in 1933. Of these he said: 'I had accepted the transience, the fading, the withering, the spookishness of our existence.' Taeuber changed as well. In 1935 she began to transform her hitherto flat geometric forms into three-dimensional reliefs and to re-introduce organic elements based on shells, leaves and flowers. In 1939, a quarter of a century after they first met, they held their first joint exhibition.

In 1941 the Second World War forced them to flee from Paris to the South of France. They planned to leave for the United States, but had difficulty in obtaining visas, and remained in Grasse for nearly two years, leading an existence which Arp afterwards recalled as being idyllic in spite of the war. There were, nevertheless, elements of foreboding about it. '[Sophie] had dreams she never wanted to tell me about,' Arp later recalled. 'She hid them from me behind exaggerated boisterous jokes.'

In 1942 they left Grasse, to pay a clandestine visit to Switzerland, still in the hope of obtaining American visas, and here, in 1943, Taeuber died in an accident – asphyxiated in her sleep by a defective charcoal stove. Arp was shattered. He recalled dreaming about her immediately after her death – they met, and Arp said to her that they would meet again. 'Yes,' said Taeuber, 'in Cairo'. Arp immediately understood that she meant not Cairo in Egypt, nor some New Cairo in America, 'but a Cairo situated in some infinitely remote heavenly realm, on some infinitely remote star.'

The wound was at least partially healed by his remarriage in 1945 to Marguerite Hagenbach, another Swiss woman and a long-time collector and admirer of both his and Taeuber's work. In 1949 and 1950 he visited America at long last, and in 1954 he was awarded the major prize for sculpture at the Venice Biennale. Until this point, Arp, though well known and respected in the world of modern art, had been comparatively poor. Now the commissions poured in and he was offered many opportunities to work on a large scale. He died in Basle in 1966.

JOHN HEARTFIELD

John Heartfield is the outstanding example of a twentieth-century artist who dedicated his art almost entirely to politics. In his search for new weapons he invented a form of photocollage which has had an immense effect on the graphic design of our own day.

He was born in Berlin in 1891, the first of four children. His father, Franz Herzfeld, was a socialist poet and dramatist, and his mother, Alice, had been a worker in a textile factory: his parents met at a strikers' meeting, where Alice was one of the speakers. In 1895 Franz Herzfeld was sentenced to a year's imprisonment for blasphemy, and the family fled to Weggis in Switzerland, where their last child, Wieland, was born. They were promptly turned out of the country, for fear that the baby would become a charge upon the state. They moved to Austria, and settled in an isolated mountain hut on the outskirts of the village of Aigen, near Salzburg. But in 1898 the children were abandoned by their parents, who vanished without trace, and were taken in by the village burgomaster. In 1905 Heartfield left school and moved to Wiesbaden, taking his brother Wieland with him; he worked as an apprentice to a bookseller and then studied for two years with a local painter. In 1908 he transferred to the School of Applied Arts in Munich, remaining there until 1912, when he moved to Mannheim and took a job as a designer in a paper plant. At about this time he learned that his father had died in an asylum some four years earlier.

Heartfield went to Berlin in 1913, and was followed there by the daughter of his landlord in Mannheim. She became the first of his three wives and the mother of his two children. He enrolled in the Berlin School of Arts and Crafts, and in July 1914 he won first prize at the Werkbund Exhibition in Cologne for a design for a mural. He was mobilized in November 1914 but was from the beginning opposed to the war, and would desert from time to time to go back to Berlin and engage in anti-militarist activity. Though posted to the infantry in 1915, he managed to avoid being sent to the Front.

It was at this period that he met George Grosz, who had similar views to his own. Heartfield admired Grosz enormously and destroyed all his own work as being insignificant. In 1916 he decided to anglicize his name to John Heartfield as a protest against the violent anti-

JOHN HEARTFIELD, *John Heartfield with Chief of Police Zörgiebel*, from *AIZ*, 8, no. 37, 1929

English campaign of the German propaganda machine, but he was refused permission by the authorities to register the change legally. It was at this period that he and Grosz evolved the kind of photomontage which became associated with the German Dada movement.

In 1917 his brother Wieland, who had become his inseparable ally and who shared all his political and social views, bought a defunct school magazine called *Neue Jugend* (thus evading a ban on new publications) and turned it into a scurrilous anti-establishment rag and a foyer for typographical experiments which were later to influence the Bauhaus. In the same year the brothers also formed a publishing house called Malik Verlag. This was to publish all the early Grosz albums, and books by many other left-wing authors, and it enabled Heartfield, who was responsible for the book jackets, to extend and polish his skills as a designer. He, Wieland and Grosz were all founder-members of the German Communist

Hurrah, die Butter ist alle!

Goering in seiner Hamburger Rede: „Erz hat stets ein Reich stark gemacht, Butter und Schmalz haben höchstens ein Volk fett gemacht".

JOHN HEARTFIELD, *Hurrah, the Butter is Finished!*, 19 December 1935

Party in 1918, and of the Berlin Dada Group the following year. At this time Heartfield's nickname was 'Dada-monteur' because of his predilection for wearing blue workmen's overalls (in German *Monteur* means 'mechanic' or 'fitter').

In 1924, Heartfield's graphic style changed. The jazzy, rather bitty photomontages of the Dada epoch were replaced by photocollages so beautifully fitted together that it is often hard to believe that the astonishing, immensely hard-hitting images were not originally one piece. He combined borrowed images – the heads of his figures, for example, might be taken from news photographs – with other images photographed specifically for the purpose by a painstaking process of retouching. The first of these, a parade of skeletons, was hung in the window of the Malik bookshop on the tenth anniversary of the outbreak of the First World War.

From this time onwards Heartfield was a well known figure in Weimar Germany: he designed stage sets for Max Reinhardt and Erwin Piscator: he made a hugely successful series of illustrations for a book by the satirical poet Kurt Tucholsky: and he produced a stream of photo-collages satirizing the emergent Nazi party. He became one of the artists whom the Nazi leadership hated most personally, because of the directness and vigour of his attacks upon them. He was in mortal danger as soon as the party came to power and little time was wasted in moving against him. In mid-April 1933 a detachment of the SA (Nazi police) raided his flat; Heartfield fled to Prague, where he continued his attacks. In 1934 he was deprived of his German citizenship, and the German Ambassador to Czechoslovakia protested at his participation in the International Caricature Exhibition held at the Mánes Gallery in Prague. The protests were repeated on subsequent occasions with increasing success, until in 1938 the Nazis actually demanded Heartfield's extradition. In December of that year he fled again, this time to London.

In the brief period that remained before the outbreak of war Heartfield participated in various anti-Nazi activities in England, notably in the programme of the Freier Deutsche Kulturbund. He also had shows in London at the ACA Galleries and at the Arcade Gallery. But soon after the outbreak of war he was interned, with many other anti-Nazi exiles from Germany, in three camps in rapid succession. He then fell seriously ill and was taken to hospital; his health was poor for the rest of the war years and for some time afterwards, and his political activities were pushed somewhat to the side. He made a living designing book covers for Penguin and other British publishers.

By 1950 his health had improved, and he and his third wife, Gertrude, decided to leave England and settle in East Germany, which had already welcomed many other exiles with the same political convictions. Heartfield was a long-time friend and admirer of Bertolt Brecht, who invited him to design scenery and posters for the Berliner Ensemble and the Deutsche Theater in Berlin. His photo-collages, however, were viewed with some suspicion by the bureaucrats of a regime then heavily committed to Socialist Realism. The situation changed for the better after 1956, when Brecht nominated Heartfield for membership of the German Academy of Art – the following year the Academy gave its new member a retrospective exhibition, and he was awarded the German National Prize for Art and Literature, followed in 1961 by the Peace Prize of the German Democratic Republic. He had exhibitions not only within East Germany, but in Moscow, Peking, Shanghai and Tientsin, and later in Western Europe – in Italy, where the Communist party had strong cultural aspirations. But his new work was seldom as pungent as his pre-war work – the exception is a paradoxically savage peace poster showing a dove impaled upon a bayonet – and it clearly did not suit his temperament to be an official artist. He was nevertheless honoured by the East German regime after his death in 1968, when the German Academy of Art promptly established an archive devoted to him, under the direction of his widow.

Pittura Metafisica (Metaphysical Painting) was an extremely ephemeral art movement. It resulted from the meeting of Giorgio de Chirico and Carlo Carrà in 1917, when both were in a military hospital in Ferrara. De Chirico was the stronger personality of the two, and Carrà, who had originally been a Futurist, took over the paraphernalia which De Chirico had already evolved, to express his sense of an alienated and alienating world. In 1919 Carrà published a book entitled *Pittura Metafisica*, and his erstwhile colleague promptly attacked it – this was more or less the end of the movement as such. The still immature Morandi joined in 1918, but remained in the fold for only a short time. Metaphysical ideas did, however, leave a permanent legacy in his painting as he modified them to produce his own characteristic brand of hushed quietism.

In a broader historical context, the real importance of Pittura Metafisica is the influence which De Chirico's work exercized over the Surrealists. They were particularly struck by its most prominent characteristic, the power to suggest a mysterious, more powerful and authentic reality beyond the reality of what was actually depicted.

Left: GIORGIO DE CHIRICO,
Large Metaphysical Interior, 1917
Above: GIORGIO DE CHIRICO, 1929.
Photographer unknown

GIORGIO DE CHIRICO

Giorgio de Chirico is probably the strangest 'case' in modern art – his career has been described as 'a tragedy which turned into a farce'. While his importance is universally acknowledged, his exact place in the Modernist hierarchy remains very uncertain.

He was born in 1888 in Volos, Greece, where his father, who came from an aristocratic Sicilian family, was a railway engineer. His childhood and most of his adolescence were divided between Volos and Athens. This early period of the artist's life seems to have been somewhat melancholy: his father suffered from constant ill health and an atmosphere of 'puritanism and Jesuitism' pervaded the family.

De Chirico learned to draw early, receiving some basic instruction first from his father, then from one of the railway employees. When his family moved permanently to Athens in 1899 he was sent to the Polytechnic Institute there where he followed an old-fashioned course of instruction in art. He was not considered particularly gifted and failed the final examination. In 1906 his father died, and his mother, who was also Italian, decided to move to Munich for the sake of her sons' education (Giorgio had a younger brother who was a musician). In Munich he attended the Academy of Fine Arts, but found the instruction boring and sterile. Nevertheless, he was not attracted to the main anti-academic alternative, the Munich Sezession. But he did develop a taste for the work of two German late Romantics, Böcklin and Klinger, and he discovered the writings of Schopenhauer and Nietzsche. With inspiration from these sources he started to evolve his own style.

The years 1909–10 were spent in Italy, which De Chirico was now seeing in some depth for the first time. His time was divided between Milan, Turin and Florence. It is generally the arcaded streets of Turin which are said to have provided inspiration for the 'metaphysical' pictures which he now started to paint. His own earliest account, written in 1912, is rather different:

One clear autumn afternoon I was sitting on a bench in the middle of the Piazza Santa Croce in Florence. Of course it was not the first time I had been in this square. I had barely recovered from a long and painful intestinal illness and was in a state of almost morbid sensitivity. The whole world around me, including the marble of the buildings and the fountains, seemed to me to be convalescing. At the centre of the square stands a statue of Dante, wearing a long tunic and clasping his works to his body, his head crowned with laurel and bent slightly forward. ... The hot, strong, autumn sun brightened the statue and the façade of the church. Then I had the strange impression that I was looking at these things for the first time, and the composition of the painting [*Enigma of an Autumn Afternoon*] revealed itself to my mind's eye. Now every time I look at this picture, I see that moment once again. Nevertheless the moment is an enigma for me, in that it is inexplicable. I also like to call the work derived from it an enigma.

In July 1911 De Chirico left Florence for Paris, summoned by his brother, who was already settled in France. The young artist was soon in touch with the leaders of the Paris avant-garde, among the Picasso, Max Jacob, Derain and Apollinaire (who was to become his particular champion). De Chirico afterwards claimed to have been less impressed with these new friends than they were with him. He gives an ironic description of Apollinaire's famous 'Saturdays' in his autobiography:

Apollinaire pontificated from the chair at his worktable. Taciturn and consciously thoughtful individuals sat on the armchairs and divans; most of them, in line with the fashion of that time and that circle, smoked the clay pipes which can be seen in the shooting-booths at fairs.

The poet provided De Chirico with what practical help he could, publishing two articles on him in the magazine he edited, *Les Soirées de Paris*. He also seems to have been responsible for finding De Chirico a dealer – the young and able Paul Guillaume.

In 1915, when Italy entered the war, De Chirico and his brother Andrea, who now used the professional name Albert Savinio, returned to their native country. They joined up and were stationed at Ferrara, where they developed further the concept of 'metaphysical painting' through their conversations. The intestinal troubles from which De Chirico had suffered in the years before the war now returned and prevented him from seeing active service; he also seems to have suffered a mental breakdown. It was while he was in hospital that De Chirico met Carlo Carrà, who was promptly caught up in the enthusiasm for the new style. In 1918 he was discharged from the Italian Army and enjoyed a limited success with an exhibition held in Rome. Meanwhile, a profound change was taking place in his own attitudes towards art. This was heralded by another epiphany, rather like the one he had had nearly ten years previously in Florence:

It was one morning at the Villa Borghese, in front of a painting by Titian, that I had a revelation of what great painting was: I saw tongues of fire appear in the gallery, while outside beneath the clear sky over the city, rang out a solemn clangour as of weapons beaten in salute, and together with a great cry of righteous spirits there echoed the sound of a trumpet heralding a resurrection.

This revelation took place in the summer of 1919, the year in which De Chirico published an article in the

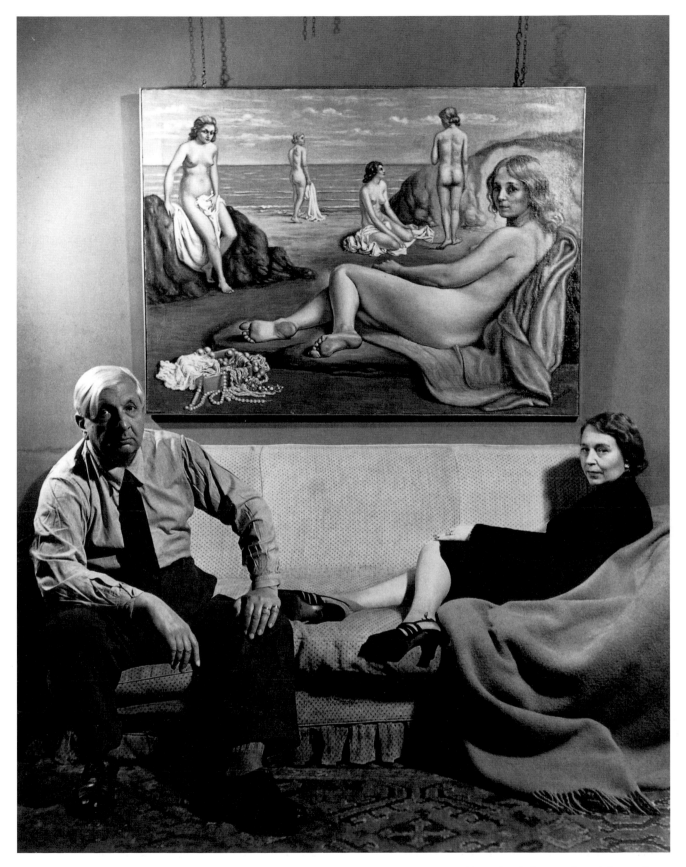

GIORGIO DE CHIRICO and his wife Isabella, 1951. Photo Philippe Halsman influential magazine *Valori Plastici*, proclaiming that there should be a return to tradition.

He was now obsessed by what he considered to be the 'inadequacy' of his own technique as a painter, and began a laborious investigation of traditional techniques and materials, particularly tempera. He made frequent trips between Paris and Italy – in Paris he was in touch with the nascent group of Surrealists under the leadership of André Breton, who revered his early metaphysical work as a foreshadowing of their own investigations. Later, De Chirico was to denounce the Surrealists with his habitual vehemence, but for a while he was close to them. The real break only came in 1926, when he had a one-man show with Paul Guillaume with whom he had maintained his connection. Even after this, several paintings of his were included in the first group exhibition held by the Surrealists in 1925 at the Galerie Pierre. This was the period in which he met and married his first wife, Raïssa Calza. In 1933 he remarried – his second wife was Isabella Packswer, who wrote (mostly about her husband and perhaps at his direct dictation) under the name Isabella Far.

Throughout the 1920s and early 1930s De Chirico continued to flirt with avant-gardism: in 1929 he published his fantastic novel, *Hebdomeros*, which contains some of his most interesting writings; he also provided designs for the ballet *Le Bal*, a late production of Diaghilev's Ballets Russes; and in 1931 he produced

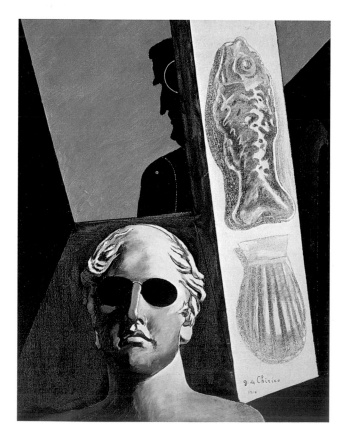

a suite of lithographs to illustrate Apollinaire's collection of poems *Calligrammes*.

The Fascist regime had now established itself in Italy, and De Chirico's attitudes were somewhat ambiguous. He recognized, for example, that the artistic policies of Mussolini's regime were on the whole extremely tolerant – which, in one mood, did not entirely please him:

> For the sake of truth it must be said that the Fascists never forbade people to paint as they wished. The majority of the Fascist hierarchy were in fact modernists enamoured of Paris, just as the democratic and republican Italians are today ...

He was pleased when the regime offered him recognition, for example when a whole room was devoted to his work in the Rome Quadriennale of 1935, but he felt a characteristic paranoia and resentment at imagined slights:

> In Rome they had created the impression that I was anti-Italian and as a result I was never given any prizes at the official exhibitions, while in general I was not able to benefit from even a minute share of all the money that the fascist government distributed so generously to painters and sculptors.

De Chirico unequivocally condemned Mussolini and his regime for anti-semitism – his second wife (though he does not mention this fact in his autobiography) was Jewish. Despite this, he lived unmolested in Italy throughout the war, and was even invited to exhibit at the Venice Biennale of 1942.

In 1946 De Chirico, who had now settled permanently in Rome, published the first volume of his autobiography. This was also the year in which he was involved in a sensational lawsuit. The powerful Galleria del Milione in Milan, which had long been on his list of *bêtes noires*, sued him for denouncing as a forgery a painting of the metaphysical period brought to him for authentication, and for having it seized as such by the police. After a long legal wrangle De Chirico emerged victorious.

In 1948 there was another and even more resounding scandal, when a retrospective of metaphysical painting was held as part of the Venice Biennale, and the artist denounced some of the paintings attributed to him which were included. The situation was complicated by the fact

GIORGIO DE CHIRICO,
Portrait of Guillaume Apollinaire,
1914

that De Chirico had now taken to producing numerous replicas of his own early compositions. Between 1945 and 1962 he turned out no less than eighteen more versions of *The Disquieting Muses*, and in his later years he was unscrupulous about passing off these autograph copies as much earlier originals.

From the mid-1920s onwards he produced a great flood of new work. Some paintings were pastiches of Baroque and Renaissance art. Especially characteristic are a series of opulent still lifes, and an equally extensive series of self-portraits, some of the latter boastfully signed 'G. de Chirico, Pictor Optimus' – 'G. de Chirico, the best painter'. There was also an intermediary category of works related to the metaphysical paintings in style and subject-matter, but which replaced their intensity with a kind of easy decorativeness. This group includes the well known series showing horses by the shore, pictures of gladiators, the 'mysterious baths', and pictures which are echoes of Pompeian frescoes. For many years De Chirico was treated as a superannuated artist. Just before his death in 1978, however, the attitude of part of the avant-garde began to change, and there was a tendency to celebrate him as a premature Post-Modernist and to discover hidden ironies in work which had previously been dismissed as vulgar and shameless. If he intended the late paintings to be ironic, De Chirico never admitted it. The claims he made for himself in his second volume of memoirs, published in 1960, were more self-applauding than ever:

> If you think of all of my exhibitions from 1918 until today you will see consistent progress, a regular and persistent march towards those summits of mastery which were achieved by a few consummate artists of the past. Naturally, in order to see and say all this, in addition to my exceptional intelligence so far as true painting is concerned, one must also have my mighty personality, my courage and my ardent desire for truth.

GIORGIO MORANDI,
Still Life, 1946

GIORGIO MORANDI

Giorgio Morandi, who is arguably the greatest artist Italy has produced in the twentieth century, was as much a quietist in his life as in his painting. His attachment to the two of the three groups with whom he exhibited, the Futurists and the Novecento Italiano, seems to have been an accident, since he had little in common with either. He did owe a little more to Pittura Metafisica, but his true master, in his landscapes and still lifes, was always Cézanne.

He was born in Bologna in July 1890, the eldest of a family of five sons and three daughters. In 1906 he worked for a year at the import-export agency where his father was employed, and after that set his sights on a career as an artist. In 1907 he began his studies at the Academy of Fine Arts in Bologna, and in 1909 saw reproductions of Cézanne's work for the first time. The following year he saw a group of Renoirs at the Venice Biennale, which was always to be his chief direct source of information about new art. He also went to Florence and was particularly struck by Giotto, Masaccio and Uccello, whom he seems to have interpreted in the light of what he had already learned from Cézanne. His earliest surviving painting, a landscape, dates from 1911, and his first etching from 1912. He left the Academy of Fine Arts in 1913.

In 1914 Morandi came into contact with the Futurists. He saw a show of Futurist painting in Florence and attended a Futurist evening staged at the Teatro del Corso in Bologna. Here he met Boccioni and Carrà. He was then

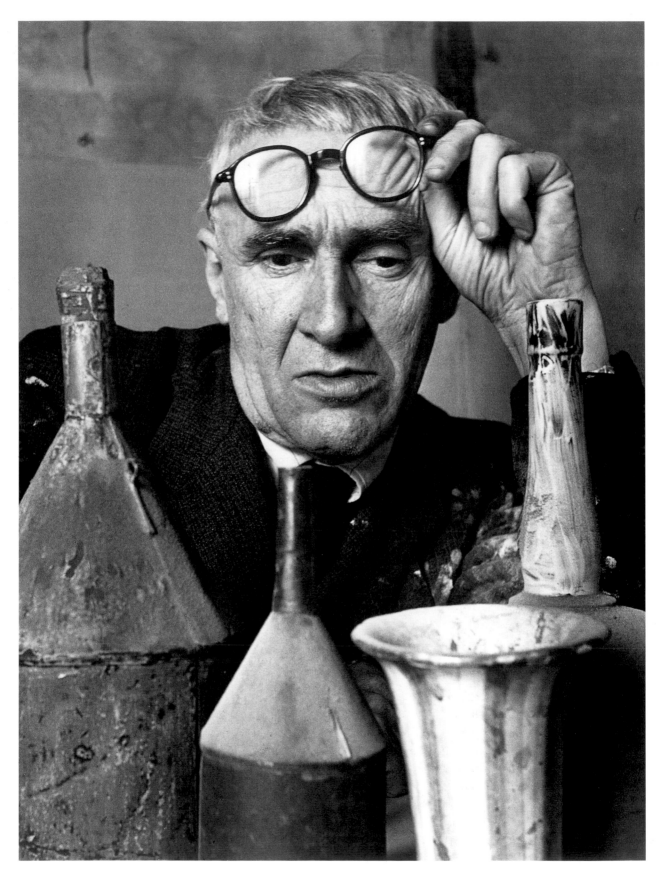

GIORGIO MORANDI, Bologna 1953. Photo Herbert List

invited to take part in the Futurist exhibition held in the Palazzo Baglioni in Bologna, and in the Libera Futurista show in Rome. He also secured a post as teacher of drawing in a Bologna primary school. He was to remain in this job – with two breaks – until 1930. He joined the army in 1915, but fell seriously ill and was discharged after serving for only six weeks. On his recovery he destroyed a number of his early paintings. He was seriously ill again in the winter of 1916–17.

After 1918 his reputation began to grow, but at first only slowly. He was still in touch with Carrà, and now went to Rome and met Giorgio de Chirico. During the early 1920s his work had something in common with De Chirico's: he made use, for example, of the blank mannequin heads which are such a feature of de Chirico's imagery. Morandi, De Chirico and Carrà exhibited together in a show organized by the magazine *Valori Plastici* at the Museum of Modern Art in Berlin in 1921 and again at the Primaverile in Florence in 1922. On the second occasion De Chirico, so often jealous of other artists, wrote a flattering text about Morandi's work. In 1926–27 Morandi was made Director of Art in primary schools in the provinces of Reggio Emilia and Calabria, but the task did not suit him, and he soon returned to his old job. In the same year he was included in the first Novecento Italiano exhibition in Milan. The Novecento was an attempt to create a 'classic' Italian art in keeping with the ambitions of Mussolini's regime, and the Duce himself for a while took a great interest in the group. In 1928, Morandi showed his prints at the Venice Biennale, and he was represented in various official exhibitions of the early 1930s, notably the Rome Quadriennali of 1931 and 1935. He never at any time clashed with the Fascists, and in 1930 was made professor of printmaking at the Academy in Bologna, a post he retained until he retired in 1956.

By the 1930s Morandi was a man of extremely regular habits. He spent the summer months in Grizzana, just outside Bologna, and the rest of the time at a blandly bourgeois apartment in the city, where his sisters kept house for him. During the Second World War more and more time was spent at Grizzana, his country retreat, until this was caught up in front-line fighting in July 1944.

The post-war years brought Morandi increased celebrity, but no alteration in a style which by this time had long shaken off all traces of De Chirico's influence.

Giorgio Morandi, *Mannequins on a Round Table*, 1918

He painted small still lifes of bottles, vases and other objects, grouping and regrouping the same restricted repertoire of beloved shapes, and during the summer months he painted modest landscapes. He had his first one-man show at the Fiore Gallery, a commercial gallery in Florence, in 1945; in 1948 he became a member of the Academy of Saint Luke in Rome and was awarded the first prize for an Italian artist at the Venice Biennale. In the 1950s his fame began to spread abroad – he was given the Grand Prix for prints at the São Paulo Biennale of 1953 and the Grand Prix for Painting at São Paulo in 1957.

By 1958 he had retired almost completely to Grizzana, where he continued to paint, just as he had always done. He died in Bologna in June 1964.

The Surrealist Movement was founded in 1924 under the leadership of André Breton (1896–1966), and was one of the major forces in art between the two world wars. The term itself was taken over from the poet and critic Guillaume Apollinaire (1880–1918), who first employed it in 1917. Breton defined it as follows in the First Manifesto of Surrealism: 'Pure psychic automatism, by which it is intended to express, verbally, in writing, or by other means, the real process of thought. Thought's dictation, in the absence of all control exercized by the reason and outside aesthetic or moral preoccupations.'

The chief sources for Surrealist painting were Dada, Pittura Metafisica, and the doctrines of Freud. The Surrealist painters are usually split for convenience into two groups: the Veristic Surrealists – such as Dalí and Magritte – who paint dream-images in a literal, highly detailed, unspontaneous way; and the Calligraphic Surrealists, where the design evolves on the surface by means of a process akin to automatic writing. This latter description is generally applied to the work of Miró. Ernst lies somewhere between the two extremes – he evolved images which are sometimes very detailed through the use of procedures which exploit chance, such as *frottage*, in an attempt to eliminate the conscious control of the artist.

Above: MAX ERNST,
The Robing of the Bride, 1940
Right: MAX ERNST,
Sedona, Arizona 1946.
Photo Lee Miller

MAX ERNST

Max Ernst's work links Surrealism to the heritage of German Romanticism. Ernst was also the most important technical innovator amongst the Surrealists.

He was born in April 1891 in Brühl, between Cologne and Bonn, the second of six children. His father was a strict Catholic, a teacher in a school for deaf-mutes and an enthusiastic Sunday painter. Max was a gifted child with a strong imagination. In 1906 he was deeply affected by the simultaneous death of a favourite pink cockatoo and birth of his youngest sister. From this moment, he said, he felt a confusion between birds and men, and Loplop, the bird-like creature which appears in so many of his paintings and drawings, was ready to take the stage.

Ernst was well educated. He studied from 1908 until 1914 at the University of Bonn, avoiding formal lectures and classes but using the University as a source of material. When still a student at Bonn he met August Macke, who lived in that city while at the same time frequenting the Blaue Reiter circle in Munich. This was Ernst's first contact with the avant-garde. In 1912 he joined Das Junge Rheinland, a group of poets and painters largely inspired by Macke, and the following year, also thanks to Macke, he showed his own work at the Autumn Salon organized by *Der Sturm* in Berlin.

In August 1913 he made a trip to Paris, paid for by painting a Crucifixion for a friend who wanted a respectable male nude. He was too shy to use the introductions Macke had given him, but nevertheless fell in love with the city. In 1914, before the outbreak of war, he met Hans Arp in a Cologne art gallery, and formed an immediate friendship with him; Arp was the only one of his pre-war comrades whom he was to see again.

During the war Ernst served as an artillery engineer. He was twice wounded, once by the recoil of a gun, once by the kick of a mule, and was nicknamed 'Ironhead' by his comrades as a result. In the summer of 1915 he was picked out of the ranks by an officer who was an art-lover and was given an easy job on the staff; this allowed him to paint enough work to have an exhibition at the *Der Sturm* Gallery in Berlin in early 1916. But an outraged commanding officer put a stop to this pleasant situation and returned Ernst to the Front. He finished the war on marriage-leave in Brussels: Louise Strauss, the first of his wives, was assistant to the Director of the Wallraf-Richartz Museum in Cologne. The marriage broke up in 1921; subsequent marriages and love affairs were to play a much larger part in Ernst's career.

Ernst was hungry for information about the way art was now developing. In 1919 he visited Paul Klee in Munich, and he first encountered the work of Giorgio de Chirico in the pages of the magazine *Valori Plastici*. He also got hold of a series of Dada publications from Zurich, which spurred him into immediate action: he formed a Rhineland Dada Centre and arranged the first Dada Exhibition in Cologne. This was held in a back courtyard approached through a public urinal, and axes were supplied in case anyone felt like attacking the exhibits. The local police tried to close it on grounds of obscenity, but it was soon opened again when the charge could not be supported. The local police chief was reduced to begging the organizers to tone down their posters.

Ernst was longing to go to Paris, but the post-war situation made this almost impossible. As a substitute for going in person, he sent a collection of his collages which were shown in May 1920 and caused a sensation amongst the Parisian avant-garde. They particularly attracted the poet Paul Eluard, and eventually the two men met in Germany. This made Ernst more than ever determined to leave, and in 1922 he slipped away to France without papers or money. At first he was forced to work in a factory which manufactured cheap plastic souvenirs for tourists.

Eluard and Ernst immediately began to collaborate on literary projects, and both participated in the so-called *saison des sommeils*, the hallucinatory self-induced trances which preceded the official foundation of Surrealism. But they nevertheless missed the crucial moment: on impulse Eluard absconded with a sum of money his father had

given him to take to the bank, and fled to Saigon. Ernst and Eluard's wife Gala (later to marry Dalí) were summoned to join him. The trip was not a success and the trio returned to find that Surrealism had achieved official recognition.

In 1925 Ernst made one of his most significant technical innovations – the rediscovery of *frottage*, the process of rubbing a pencil across a piece of paper laid against grained wood or some other textured surface, with the result that various images magically appeared. Ernst used this technique to generate the designs for his *Histoire Naturelle* published in 1926, the year in which Diaghilev commissioned him, together with Miró, to make décors for the new ballet *Roméo et Juliette*.

In 1927 Ernst married his second wife, Marie-Berthe Aurenche, without the consent of her parents. He was now very much at the centre of the whole Paris art-scene. He met Giacometti in 1929, and formed a lifelong friendship with him; and in 1930 he was one of the actors who appeared in the notorious Surrealist film *L'Age d'Or* by Dalí and Buñuel, which took much of its inspiration from Ernst's imagery. In 1931 he had his first American exhibition at the Julian Levy Gallery in New York, and in 1936, ignoring Breton's attempted veto, he took a major part in the 'Fantastic Art, Dada and Surrealism' exhibition organized by the Museum of Modern Art in New York. In 1936 he met Leonor Fini, and in 1937 the aristocratic Englishwoman Leonora Carrington. Ernst at this time undoubtedly saw himself as something of a Don Juan. Part of his written self-portrait of 1936 reads:

> Women find it difficult to reconcile the gentleness and moderation of what he says with the tranquil violence of his ideas. They liken him to an earthquake: but an earthquake so well behaved that it hardly moves the furniture around and intends, unhurriedly, to 'put things in order'. What is particularly disagreeable to them – what they can't bear in fact – is that they cannot put their fingers on WHAT HE IS, so flagrant is the (apparent) contradiction between his spontaneous behaviour and the behaviour which is dictated to him by processes of conscious thought.

His growing disillusionment with the Surrealist Group culminated in 1938, when Breton demanded that its membership should 'sabotage in every possible way the poetry of Paul Eluard'. Ernst was not prepared to abandon one of his oldest and closest friends in this way, and left the Group. In the same year, 1938, he and Leonora Carrington settled in a remote house at Saint Martin d'Ardèche, about thirty miles north of Avignon. They were not to live there in tranquillity for long: when war broke out Ernst was interned as an enemy alien, but was soon liberated thanks to an official petition made by Eluard. He was just able to survive on subsidies sent by another French writer, Joë Bousquet. In May 1940, after the German advance, he was interned for a second time, but escaped from a camp near Nîmes and returned to Leonora at Saint Martin. Once there, he was immediately denounced and recaptured. He escaped again, just as the papers for his release arrived, and this time was allowed to remain at liberty. He returned once more to Saint Martin, to discover that his companion had had a nervous breakdown, and had sold the house for a bottle of brandy and then vanished – it later transpired that she was in a mental institution in Spain. There were rumours that the Gestapo were on his trail, and Ernst decided to leave Europe, especially as he had received offers of shelter in the United States.

In 1941 Ernst met Breton and the American collector Peggy Guggenheim. Because of his uncertain status, Ernst could not take the obvious route and leave by sea, but decided instead to cross the Spanish border. He eventually reached Madrid and finally, in the company of Peggy Guggenheim, left by air from Lisbon. His adventures were not quite over: when he arrived at La Guardia Airport he was arrested and detained for three days on Ellis Island by the US immigration authorities.

Ernst celebrated his release by journeying across the United States, and then married Peggy Guggenheim in 1941. His friends worked hard to create a position for him in the American art world, and in 1942 he had exhibitions in New York, Chicago and New Orleans; but in the wartime climate they were poorly received. He was, however, able to co-operate with Breton and Duchamp on a new periodical called *VVV*. His marriage to Peggy Guggenheim was increasingly unhappy; in 1943 he met a young painter named Dorothea Tanning and separated from his wife. The affair caused a scandal in the New York art world, and Ernst and Dorothea retired to Sedona, Arizona.

Unlike Masson, Ernst did not hurry back to Europe as soon as the war was over but remained in the United States, becoming an American citizen in 1948.

Meanwhile, his reputation in France was kept alive by a retrospective exhibition held at the Galerie Denise René in Paris which Eluard organized for him. He returned to Paris in 1949 and there was a second retrospective exhibition in 1950, organized by the Galerie René Drouin. This was followed by a larger retrospective the following year at Brühl, his birthplace, organized by his sister and brother-in-law. Post-war Germany was not yet ready for Ernst, and the show was a financial disaster and aroused considerable local controversy. The tide only turned when he was unexpectedly awarded the Grand Prix for painting at the Venice Biennale of 1954. Though Ernst was still an American citizen, the American contingent in Venice were backing the candidacy of Ben Shahn, and Ernst's success came as a considerable shock to them. In 1955 he decided to settle permanently in France, and bought a property at Huismes in Touraine; in 1958 he once again changed citizenship and became French. The final twenty years of Ernst's life were marked by a series of major retrospective exhibitions, including those at the Musée National d'Art Moderne, Paris (1959), at the Museum of Modern Art, New York (1961), at the Wallraf-Richartz Museum, Cologne (1963), and at the Grand Palais, Paris (1974). He died in 1976.

JOAN MIRÓ

Joan Miró, now recognized as one of the most influential artists of the century, never committed himself fully to the Surrealist movement, but nevertheless remains associated with it. A quiet and private man, some of the other Surrealists unjustly mocked him for what they considered a constitutional timidity.

He was born in April 1893 in Barcelona, the eldest child of a prosperous goldsmith and locksmith. His mother came from the island of Majorca. At school he was, as he afterward declared, 'an extremely poor pupil, silent, or rather taciturn and dreamy.' The only occupations he enjoyed as a child were the drawing lessons he took after regular school hours:

This class was for me like a religious ceremony. I washed my hands carefully before touching the paper and crayons. The artist's tools were sacred objects for me, and I worked as if I was participating in a rite.

Joan Miró, *Women Encircled by the Flight of a Bird,* from the *Constellations* series, 1941

JoAN Miró at the Maritime Museum, Barcelona 1955. Photo Brassaï

In 1907, because of his poor results at school, his father enrolled Miró at a commercial college, though, while studying there he was also allowed to attend classes at a local art school. In 1910, at the behest of his family, who now felt he had no artistic talent, he took up a position as a clerk, and for the time being abandoned painting. His business career did not last long: within a year he fell seriously ill, with severe depression followed by typhoid fever. As a result of his illness, he at last won permission to follow his own bent, and after a period of convalescence at Montroig in Catalonia, where his family had a holiday house, he enrolled at another art school in Barcelona directed by Francisco Galí, which offered an

extremely liberal curriculum for the period. In 1913 he rented his own studio and started painting his first independent works – still lifes and portraits in a style derived from Fauvism. During this period he was reading the work of the French avant-garde poets of the day, notably Pierre Reverdy and Guillaume Apollinaire.

In 1916 the Paris dealer Ambroise Vollard sent an important loan exhibition of recent French paintings to Barcelona, and Miró was dazzled by his first sight of originals by Cézanne, Monet and Matisse. The following year he was subjected to a different influence, that of Francis Picabia, who was publishing the Dadaist review 391. In 1918 Miró had his own first exhibition, at the

Dalmau Gallery, which was then the best in Barcelona. The show was a total failure, and the artist once again retired to Montroig to lick his wounds. Here he began to paint in a new, ultra-precious, semi-primitive manner. He decided it was absolutely necessary to go to Paris, and when he arrived there in 1919 made straight for the studio of Picasso, though he had been too shy to accost his famous compatriot when the latter had visited Spain only a few years previously.

From this time onwards Miró spent winter in Paris and summer in Montroig. His studio in Paris was in the crumbling and insanitary building at 45 rue Blomet, which was also occupied by Masson. Miró remembered the persistent lice, the beautiful lilac in the courtyard and the 'horrible concierge, a big blonde, a real witch, very nasty.' In his early years in Paris he was extremely poor, as he would not ask his unsympathetic family for help. But the circle around him was immensely stimulating and included not only Masson, but also many writers – Robert Desnos, Georges Limbour, Michel Leiris, Antonin Artaud, and a little later the Americans Henry Miller, Ernest Hemingway and Ezra Pound. In 1923 Miró's style began to shift again; an important influence was the work of Paul Klee, which was just becoming known in Paris.

By 1924 the group which met at the rue Blomet had begun to amalgamate with one around André Breton, and Miró attended Surrealist meetings while still abstaining from full commitment. The next year some of his work was reproduced in *La Revolution Surréaliste* and in June he had an exhibition, his second in Paris, at the Galerie Pierre. The catalogue preface was written by the poet Benjamin Péret and the opening was attended by 'le Tout-Paris ... avec le Tout-Montmartre'. Sales were poor, but the show, and especially the 'picture-poems', with their defiant emphasis on words rather than images, caused a considerable scandal. In November Miró was asked to participate in the First Surrealist Exhibition in the same gallery. By 1926 he had become sufficiently well known to attract the attention of Diaghilev and, on Picasso's recommendation, Miró and Max Ernst were jointly commissioned to provide décors for the new ballet *Roméo et Juliette*, with music by the young English composer Constant Lambert. It was not a happy enterprise. Lambert was outraged that the commission had not been given to his friend Christopher Wood, to whom it had originally been promised. The other Surrealists were jealous and, egged on by a mischievous

Picasso, staged a protest on the opening night. Miró's suspicions of Surrealist dogmatism were thus confirmed.

In 1928 he travelled to Holland, and painted a series of *Dutch Interiors* which were fantastic paraphrases of the seventeenth-century genre-scenes he found reproduced on postcards. This trip was followed by a show at the Galerie Georges Bernheim in which he showed his first collages and collage-objects.

In 1929 he married Pilar Junicosa, who came from an old Majorcan family. The marriage was solid and enduring: Pilar organized Miró's life for him, but took little interest in his art – an arrangement which precisely suited him. Though he was still not rich he was becoming better known, and in 1930 he had his first show in America. He was constantly experimenting with new techniques – in 1934 he made his first paintings on sandpaper. The political situation in Spain was deteriorating, and Miró's images, though they did not allude directly to political events, became more and more monstrous as his technical experiments became rougher and wilder. He was at Montroig in 1936, when the Civil War broke out, and he and his wife and small daughter Dolores had to leave the country in a hurry because his sister had just married 'an imbecile of the far right', and Miró had been listed in the local paper among the wedding guests.

He settled again in Montparnasse and tried to regain his equilibrium by doing something he had not attempted since his student days: he went back to drawing nudes at one of his Paris *ateliers libres*, the Grande Chaumière. He also became more politically involved than before – he produced an effective poster, *Aidez l'Espagne*, to be sold in aid of the Republican cause, and he designed a large mural painting for the Spanish Pavilion at the Paris Universal Exhibition of 1937, the building which also housed Picasso's *Guernica*. In 1938 he was sufficiently involved with the concerns of the time to express discontent with easel painting as too limiting for the contemporary artist. Nevertheless, his output remained abundant.

In the first month of the war he began his series of *Constellations* – his work had become a refuge from external events:

I felt a deep need to escape. I deliberately retired into myself. Night, music and the stars now played a major role in suggesting my pictures.

With the rapid German advance in 1940 Miró, who was at Varengeville on the Normandy coast, had a difficult decision to make. At first he thought of taking his family to America, but the boats were all full, so instead they travelled by train across France and into Spain. As a declared opponent of the now triumphant Franco régime, Miró had no idea of what reception he would meet. But he was not molested. Prudently avoiding Barcelona, he took refuge with his wife's relations in Palma. At first, however, he found himself unable to paint:

At this time I was very depressed. I believed in an inevitable victory for Nazism, and that all that we love and that gives us our reason for living was sunk forever in the abyss. I believed that in this defeat there was no further hope for us, and had the idea of expressing this mood and this anguish by drawing the signs and forms of which I had to be delivered on the sand so that the waves could carry them away instantly, or by making shapes and arabesques projected into the air as cigarette smoke, which would go up and caress the stars, fleeing from the stench and decay of a world built by Hitler and his friends.

In 1941, when he was still living in semi-clandestine fashion on Majorca, he received an important sign of international recognition. The Museum of Modern Art in New York devoted a large retrospective exhibition to him, with a catalogue which was the first monograph on his work. The next year he moved to Barcelona, where he started to experiment with ceramics, collaborating with his old friend Artigas, whom he had first met when they were students.

In 1947 Miró left Europe for the first time. He moved to New York in order to paint a large mural commissioned for a hotel in Cincinnati, and in 1948 he returned to Paris, after an absence of eight years. But it was not a permanent move: he had discovered that, for an artist of his reclusive temperament, life in Franco's Spain had distinct advantages. Since he was out of favour with the régime, he was completely ignored by the Spanish press. Elsewhere his reputation was growing rapidly. In 1950 he was commissioned to do another large mural, this time for the Graduate School at Harvard; in 1954–55 he returned to ceramics and was asked to make two large walls in glazed tiles for the new UNESCO headquarters in Paris. In 1959 he was the subject of a second

retrospective at the Museum of Modern Art in New York, followed in 1962 by a similar show at the Musée National d'Art Moderne in Paris. In 1964 the Fondation Maeght was inaugurated in the South of France, with a whole room devoted to Miró and a garden filled with his sculptures and ceramics. Large sculptures were an increasing preoccupation from 1963 onwards, as an extension of Miró's distinctive fantasy into a completely new field.

In 1956 Miró had once again left Barcelona for Palma. Once settled there, he lived the kind of life that suited him, spending long hours alone in the studio, seeing very few outsiders and going to Paris only at long intervals. In one of his rare public statements made in old age, he criticized what seemed to him Picasso's mania for publicity and his habit of surrounding himself with mediocre people. Nevertheless, he was by this time, after Picasso's death, certainly one of the two or three most famous survivors of the first generation of Modernists, rivalled only by Dalí and Chagall. He died in 1983.

RENÉ MAGRITTE

The one major Surrealist painter who remained a little detached from the extraordinary milieu surrounding André Breton was the Belgian René Magritte.

Magritte was born in 1898 at Lessines, and spent part of his youth in Charleroi. He was the eldest of three brothers; their mother committed suicide in mysterious circumstances when Magritte was thirteen. From quite early in his childhood Magritte thought of painting as a magical activity; he attributed this to a chance encounter which he and a female playmate had with an unknown painter in the romantic cemetery of the small country town where he spent part of his holidays.

In 1916 he persuaded his father to send him to the Académie des Beaux-Arts in Brussels, but attended only intermittently. He was convinced of his vocation as a painter when he encountered the work of Giorgio de Chirico in 1919, and in particular his painting *The Song of Love*. In this year he also showed his own work for the first time – a single painting influenced not by Italian Pittura Metafisica but by early Cubist Picasso. Some paintings shown the next year were also quasi-Cubist and reflected many influences, among them that of Matisse.

In 1920 Magritte re-encountered Georgette Berger, a childhood sweetheart. She became his wife in 1922, and an indispensable support thereafter. In his early adulthood Magritte had to make a living by painting cabbage roses in a wallpaper factory, and by designing posters and advertisements. Gradually, however, he was finding what he wanted to do, and in 1925 he produced his first fully realized work, *The Lost Jockey*, which shows a miniature horse and rider in a forest whose tree trunks resemble giant balusters. The bald, matter-of-fact style was to characterize the bulk of Magritte's production thereafter. He painted pictures rather as if they were inn-signs, with a deliberate disregard for nuance. The motifs in *The Lost Jockey* reappear, differently combined, in many other paintings – a feature typical of Magritte's art.

At this period he made some important friendships. In 1920, he met E. L. T. Mesens (1903–71), a Belgian poet, musician and collagist, who was to be an ally for many years. In 1927 Magritte went to Paris and joined the Surrealist milieu around Breton. His encounters with Breton, Max Ernst, Paul Eluard and others reinforced his enthusiasm for painting, but personal relationships were less easy. There was a clash of personalities with the

Top: RENÉ MAGRITTE with chessboard and body-bottle, 1960.
Photo Charles Leirens
Bottom: RENÉ MAGRITTE,
L'Esprit de géométrie
(The Mathematical Mind),
1936 or 1937

dictatorial Breton, precipitated by Breton's fanatical anti-Catholicism. At one Surrealist gathering Georgette Magritte was wearing a gold cross inherited from her family; without naming her, Breton remarked that it was in bad taste to wear religious emblems. Magritte lost his temper and escorted his wife from the room. The breach was never healed; shortly afterwards the Magrittes left for Brussels. He later burned all the relics of his Paris period – letters, pamphlets, even an overcoat, in the gas heater of his house, nearly setting the house on fire as a result.

After his return to Brussels Magritte deliberately identified himself with the ordinary Belgian bourgeois. He refused to travel; his life was a matter of habits fanatically adhered to: a morning walk with his dog to buy groceries, an afternoon visit to the Greenwich Café to play chess. His house, furnished with banal department-store objects, was as conventional as he could make it. A bowler-hatted figure who sometimes takes on the aspect of a self-portrait now appeared frequently in his work.

At the same time, Magritte was at the centre of a flourishing group of Belgian Surrealists, and regular Saturday meetings were held at his house. The paintings he produced in Paris, and in the first years after his return to Belgium, show troubled thoughts beneath his placid exterior: they are a mixture of melodrama and sardonic black humour, many inspired by the popular films and detective novels of the day. Like the poet Guillaume Apollinaire, Magritte had a particular interests in Fantomâs, the master criminal who invariably outwits the forces of the law, hero of a series of books and silent films which appeared just before the First World War.

The mid-1930s witnessed a significant change in Magritte's attitude towards imagery. He attributed this change to a single incident:

One night in 1936, I awoke in a room in which a cage and the bird sleeping in it had been placed. A magnificent error caused me to see an egg in the cage instead of the bird. I then grasped a new and astonishing poetic secret, because the shock I experienced had been provoked precisely by the affinity between two objects, the cage and the egg, *whereas formerly I used to provoke this shock by the encounter of unrelated objects.* Ever since that revelation I have sought to discover if objects other than the cage could not likewise manifest – by bringing to light some element peculiar to them and rigorously

predetermined – the same poetry the egg and the cage were able to produce by their first meeting.

Instead of seeking out incongruities, he now looked for hidden affinities. It was because he wished to point to these links, without fully disclosing them, that he spent so much time finding the right titles for his pictures, often debating the matter with his friends.

During the Second World War Magritte suddenly abandoned his now typical technique, with its deliberately cultivated flatness and blandness, and embarked on a kind of parody of Impressionism – of Renoir in particular – which disconcerted long-standing admirers. His defence for undertaking this shift is interesting:

The German occupation marked the turning point in my art. Before the war my painting expressed anxiety, but the experiences of the war have taught me that what matters most is to express charm. I live in a very disagreeable world, and my work is meant as a counter-offensive.

Another disconcerting stylistic episode followed. In 1947 there came the brief 'Epoque Vache' (so named by the artist: *vache* in French is slang for 'stupid'; it also serves as a kind of opposite to the word 'Fauve', used for Matisse and his followers). Magritte hoped that the deliberate crudity and clumsiness of this group of drawings and paintings would upset the complacency of the French post-war audience, which it did. When they were exhibited in Paris in 1948 the works caused a considerable scandal. Magritte bowed ironically to the verdict, returning to his former manner:

I should like to persist even more strongly with the 'approach' of my experiment in Paris – it's my tendency anyway: slow suicide. But there's Georgette to consider and the disgust I feel at being 'sincere'. Georgette prefers the well made pictures of 'yore'; alas, *especially* to please Georgette I shall exhibit only the painting of yore from now on. And I'll certainly find some way to slip in a big fat incongruity from time to time ...

True to his word, Magritte continued to paint in his old style, with little loss of quality, until his death in 1967.

SALVADOR DALÍ

Thanks to his genius for self-advertisement, Salvador Dalí was the most celebrated of all the Surrealist painters. His reputation, even after his death, remains controversial. Even more so is that of his wife and muse, Gala, inspiration for so many of his works.

Dalí was born at Figueras in Catalonia in May 1904. His father was a well known local notary, a Republican and an atheist; his mother was a devout Catholic. Despite these differences within the family his childhood was outwardly harmonious and well protected, though from the beginning Dalí showed himself to be both self-assertive and attention-seeking: these characteristics seem to have sprung from a morbid self-identification with a dead brother who had had the same Christian name. According to his father's principles, he was sent to the state school in Figueras, where he learned nothing, and then, when the experiment failed, to a local middle-class school run by the Christian Brothers. His early enthusiasm for drawing and painting was encouraged by a local Impressionist painter, Ramón Pichot, who had known Picasso. By 1918 Dalí had become sufficiently accomplished to show his work in an exhibition by local artists held at the municipal theatre in Figueras.

In 1921 Dalí entered the Academy of Fine Arts in Madrid. He learned little from his teachers, as his skills were already well developed, but he became a friend of the poet Federico García Lorca and the future film director Luis Buñuel. In 1923 he was suspended from the Academy for a year for insubordination, and on returning home was imprisoned for a month for taking part in an Anarchist demonstration against the then new dictatorship of Primo de Rivera. In 1924, after his return to his studies in Madrid, he began experimenting with a wide variety of Modernist styles, while at the same time building a reputation as an eccentric dandy. In 1925, at the Dalmau Gallery, then considered the most progressive in Barcelona, he held his first one-man exhibition which attracted very favourable critical attention.

The following year Dalí was expelled from the Academy of Fine Arts in Madrid for a second and final time for telling the three professors at his final viva voce examination that he was much more intelligent than they. He paid his first visit to Paris, where he saw Picasso, and went to Holland where he made a special study of the work of Vermeer (an enduring enthusiasm). He returned

Salvador Dalí with fly on his moustache, 1954. Photo Philippe Halsmann

home to take up an extremely active role in the Catalan avant-garde – in April 1928 he was one of the three signatories of a Catalan Anti-Artistic Manifesto which borrowed many of its ideas from Futurism. In his own work the influence of the Surrealists was beginning to show, particularly that of Tanguy.

Dalí was also affected by Buñuel's enthusiasm for the cinema, and it was a summons from Buñuel which brought him to Paris for a second time. The two men joined forces to make the astonishing and savage film *Un Chien Andalou*, an explicit rejection of the avant-garde cinema of the epoch, which was concerned with purely aesthetic effects. The film's most famous and horrifying image was early in its seventeen minutes – it showed a razor blade slicing an eye. *Un Chien Andalou* had its first showing in the early months of 1929, and provoked a riot.

Dalí inevitably attracted the attention of the Surrealists and in the summer of 1929, when he had returned to his home territory of Cadaqués, he was visited by a party of new friends from Paris – among them René Magritte and his wife Georgette and Paul Eluard and his wife Gala.

Double portrait of SALVADOR DALÍ and Gala, 1937. Photo Cecil Beaton

Gala began by finding Dalí strange and obnoxious, but was soon attracted to him. Dalí, who had never had a close relationship with a woman, was fascinated and terrified. Towards the end of the visit a decisive confrontation took place between them. Dalí's biographer, Fleur Cowles, describes the moment thus:

> His passion nearly reached the limit of dementia; one day was tempted to push Gala off the cliff on which they stood. Aware there was something she wanted him to do, he threw back her head, pulling her by the hair. Trembling in abject hysteria, he commanded her to tell him what she wanted him to do to her. 'But tell me slowly, looking me in the eyes, with the crudest, most ferociously erotic words that can make us both feel the greatest shame!'
>
> 'I want you to kill me,' she calmly replied.

Though Gala returned to Paris with Eluard at the beginning of September, her alliance with Dalí was firmly cemented from then on. She was to be both muse and manager to him for the rest of her life.

In November Dalí had his first one-man exhibition in Paris. The catalogue preface was written by Breton and he and a number of other leading Surrealists bought paintings. The most significant purchase was made by the great patron the Vicomte de Noailles, who acquired the most important picture in the show, *Dismal Sport*, despite scatalogical details which had disturbed even Breton, and hung it in his dining-room between a Watteau and a Cranach. It was Noailles who provided Dalí with the means to buy a fisherman's hut at Port Lligat, where he and Gala went to live after a bitter quarrel with his father. Gradually Dalí's genius for publicity and Gala's financial shrewdness made them very rich, and the house at Port Lligat was expanded in stages into a fantastic dream-castle.

Dalí's gift for publicizing himself soon began to irritate the other Surrealists, especially Breton who resented Dalí's indifference to the political debates which preoccupied the rest of the group during the 1930s, and what he saw as Dalí's attempt to seize control of the movement. Matters first came to a head in February 1934 when Dalí was summoned before a Surrealist tribunal held at Breton's flat, and accused of 'counter-revolutionary actions'. One cause of offence was the painting *The Enigma of William Tell*, which depicted Lenin half-naked, with one immensely elongated and flaccid bare buttock supported by a crutch; another was Dalí's apparent obsession with Hitler. Dalí sabotaged the meeting by claiming to have a bad cold – he appeared bundled up in sweaters and, sweating profusely, with a thermometer in his mouth which muffled his replies. He insolently played on Breton's well-known horror of homosexuality by half-threatening to paint a picture showing his accuser and himself engaged in anal intercourse – all in the name of Surrealist liberty. But eventually he knelt and swore that he was not an enemy of the proletariat. His final expulsion from the group was not until 1939.

During the late 1930s Dalí was extremely *à la mode*. He influenced women's fashions, especially those of his friend Elsa Schiaparelli, for whom he designed buttons and other trifles, and he had considerable impact on advertising and window-display. From 1935 onwards his chief patron was the eccentric English millionaire Edward James, who bought all his most important paintings and commissioned him to design Surrealist interiors for his country house in Sussex. Dalí continued to be as flamboyant as ever. One famous incident occurred at the International Exhibition of Surrealist Art in London in 1936 when Dalí gave a lecture while encased in a diving suit; the helmet stuck and nearly suffocated him.

He was also busy establishing a bridgehead in America. In 1936 he was accorded an honour given to few artists: his portrait appeared on the cover of *Time* magazine. His disputes with those who sought to profit from his promotional value made him legendary with the American public. He designed a special pavilion for the Amusement Area of the New York World's Fair of 1939 and had a noisy argument with the backers; and he designed a window for Bonwit Teller which was altered without his consent. In the ensuing fracas Dalí and a bathtub which was one of the props went crashing through the glass. Dalí was charged with criminal damage, but the charges were soon dropped and he gathered a magnificent harvest of publicity.

Somewhere at the back of his mind he remained very much aware of political events, particularly in Spain. In 1935 he made the first studies for one of his most striking paintings, *Soft Construction with Boiled Beans: Premonition of Civil War*, which shows the influence of Goya. This was followed by another Civil War picture, *Autumn Cannibalism*, the message of which is 'a plague on both your houses'. But Dalí, despite early Anarchist sympathics, never became involved on the Republican side like his compatriots Picasso and Miró. When the Germans invaded France he slipped across the frontier into Spain (where he was reconciled with his father), then went to America. His breach with the Surrealists remained open, and his passion for the rich (whose portraits he painted for high fees) was unabated. In 1941 his exhibition at the Julian Levy Gallery in New York was bitterly attacked by Breton, now living in America. The wound, if there was one, was quickly healed by the fact that the Museum of Modern Art in New York gave Dalí his first major retrospective exhibition the same year. During the war years Dalí collaborated with Walt Disney, and published his autobiography, *The Secret Life of Salvador Dalí* (1942), with great success.

Dalí returned to settle in Europe in 1948. His main base was now Port Lligat; the rest of his time he divided between Paris and New York. In both cities he was a familiar figure in café society, and an excellent source of material for gossip columnists. He became conservative in his politics – an enthusiast for the Franco regime – and a Roman Catholic. Long before this Dalí had begun painting ambitious religious works, some of which, like the *Christ of St John of the Cross*, now in Glasgow, convey genuine mystical fervour, undercut only by his reputation for charlatanry.

The last years of Dalí's career were marked by tragedies and scandals. Gala, who was ten years older than her husband, died in 1982 amid rumours that her legendary devotion to her husband had always been something of a sham. Dalí moved into the castle he had built for her at Figueras, which, during her lifetime, he was allowed to visit by invitation only (so great was his masochism, where she was concerned, that he made this stipulation himself). His residence there did not last for long. In August 1984 he was badly burned by a fire in his bedroom, and, when rescued and removed to hospital, was discovered to be suffering from extreme malnutrition. He lingered on amid rumours that he had become the centrepiece of a vast industry for the manufacture of faked prints, to die at last in 1989. Despite his miserable end, the importance of his Surrealist paintings of the early 1930s is acknowledged by most historians of Modernism. Their power to astonish is as strong as ever.

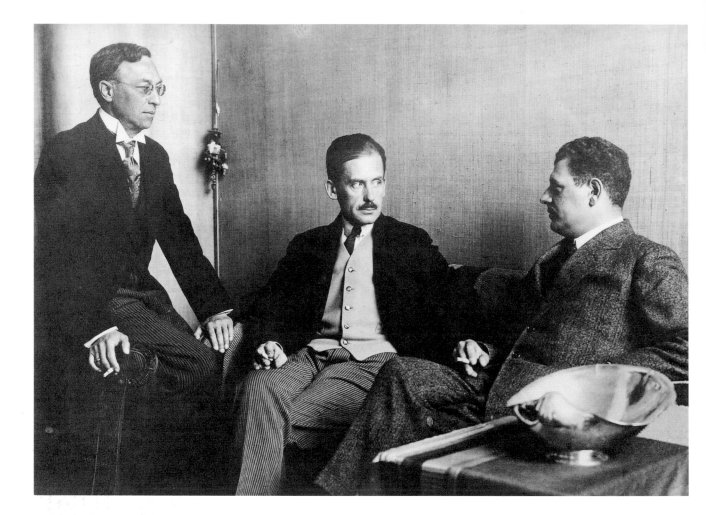

The Bauhaus was a school of architecture, design and craftsmanship founded in 1919 by the architect Walter Gropius (1883–1969) at Weimar, which moved successively to Dessau and to Berlin before being closed in 1933 by the Nazis. It stood for the application in the applied arts of the Constructivist principles which had evolved in Russia, and also of the parallel ideas of the Dutch avant-garde group De Stijl, of which Piet Mondrian had been a founder member. Its attitudes towards the fine arts cannot, however, be classified as neatly as these origins suggest; under Gropius's direction, the Bauhaus was never doctrinaire.

He succeeded in gathering about himself a remarkable band of artist teachers including Vasily Kandinsky, one of the founders of Der Blaue Reiter and the father of pure abstraction in painting; Paul Klee, who had frequented the same artistic circles as Kandinsky in Munich before the First World War; the German-American Lyonel Feininger; and the Hungarian Constructivist László Moholy-Nagy. Moholy-Nagy, who between 1923 and 1928 directed the all-important Preliminary Course taken by every Bauhaus student, was perhaps the teacher who in his own work came closest to projecting what we now think of as the Bauhaus style.

Above: (left to right) VASILY KANDINSKY, Walter Gropius and the Dutch architect J. J. P. Oud at the opening of the Bauhaus exhibition, 1923. Photographer unknown
Right: VASILY KANDINSKY with Gabriele Münter, March 1916. Photographer unknown

VASILY KANDINSKY

Vasily Kandinsky is one of the most important figures in the Modern movement in art, not merely because it was he who first arrived at the idea of total abstraction, but because he was at the centre of two major groups: the Blaue Reiter (the Blue Rider), and the artists who worked at the Bauhaus. Nevertheless, his personality remains mysterious: as he himself admitted, secretiveness was one of his outstanding characteristics.

He was born in Moscow in 1866, the son of a Siberian tea-merchant. As a small child he travelled with his parents to Italy and in 1871 they settled in Odessa. Soon after this his parents divorced. Kandinsky was educated largely by his mother's sister, and it was to her that he attributed his love of music, a source of emotional and spiritual refreshment throughout his life, and his interest in fairy-tales. From 1876 onwards he attended high school in Odessa, but once a year until 1885 he journeyed to Moscow to see his father.

In 1886 he went to Moscow University to study Economics and Law. His interests broadened to include Anthropology, and in 1889 he published his first essay, on some pagan relics of the East Finnish tribe of the Syrjaenen which he studied during an expedition to the remote Vologoda region. He was later to say that his art had been influenced by the bright colours and patterns he observed in the peasant houses there. For the moment, however, he returned to the law; he seemed set for an academic or bureaucratic career. In 1892 he married his cousin, Anja Chimiakin; in 1893 he became an attaché at the Faculty of Law, Moscow University, and published another legal dissertation; and in 1895 he became Artistic Director of a printing plant in Moscow. Behind the conventional façade, however, other ideas and feelings were at work. The Russian intellectuals of the time were in an apocalyptic mood, and like a number of them, Kandinsky was interested in the theosophy of Madame Blavatsky and in anthroposophical ideas which he united with the Orthodox faith which remained with him all his life.

In 1896 Kandinsky visited an exhibition of French painting in which he saw one of Monet's *Haystack* series; this made such an impression on him that he declined the offer of a professorship at the University of Dorpat, and moved to Munich to study painting. He settled in the artistic suburb of Schwabing, which he afterwards described as 'a spiritual state':

> Everyone painted ... or made poetry, or music, or began to dance. In every house one found at least two ateliers under the roof, where sometimes not much was painted, but where always much was discussed, disputed, philosophized and diligently drunk (which was more dependent on the state of the pocketbook than the state of mind).

At first Kandinsky studied at the private art school of Anton Ažbè, where he met his compatriots Marianne von Werefkin and Alexei Jawlensky, who were to become close associates. In 1900 he moved to the Munich Academy, to study under the celebrated Franz von Stück, and met Paul Klee, a fellow student in the same class. Perhaps because he was older than most of the students, with a better education and more experience of the world, and perhaps, too, because of his slightly grand ducal air (he never wanted to look bohemian), Kandinsky rose to a position of leadership amongst his contemporaries. In 1901 he was one of the founders of an artists' exhibiting association, Phalanx, of which he became President in the following year. He taught at the Phalanx Art School, and was responsible for no less than eleven exhibitions for the association. Through Phalanx he met Gabriele Münter, one of the students at the School, who became his mistress and a close collaborator for some years. In 1902 Kandinsky exhibited his work at the Berlin Sezession and

he continued to be represented there almost annually until 1911. He travelled extensively in Europe, and spent over a year in and near Paris in 1906–7. He had already shown his work at the Salon d'Automne in 1904, and exhibited there annually until 1910.

The Phalanx did not prosper: the school was closed in 1903, and the association itself was dissolved in 1904, the year in which Kandinsky obtained a legal separation from his wife Anja. Through Phalanx, he had been brought into close contact with the Arts and Crafts designers of the Jugendstil, who were already making boldly experimental use of abstract pattern.

In Munich around 1909 he experienced another revelation of the kind which had made him become a painter in the first place:

Once while in Munich I underwent an unexpectedly bewitching experience in my studio. Twilight was falling; I had just come home with my box of paints under my arm after painting a study from nature.

I was still dreamily absorbed in the work I had been doing when, suddenly, my eyes fell upon an indescribably beautiful picture that was saturated with an inner glow. I was startled momentarily and quickly went up to this enigmatic painting in which I could see nothing but shapes and colours and the content of which was incomprehensible to me. The answer to the riddle came immediately: it was one of my own paintings leaning on its side against a wall. The next day, by daylight, I tried to recapture the impression the picture had given me the evening before. I succeeded only half-way. Even when looking at them sideways I could still make out the objects and that fine coat of transparent colour, created by last night's twilight, was missing. Now I knew for certain that the subject-matter was detrimental for my paintings.

As he embarked on the adventure of creating a wholly abstract art which was to last from 1910 to 1914, Kandinsky was accorded an increasingly prominent place by his fellow artists in Munich. In 1909 the Neue Künstlervereinigung (New Artists' Association) was founded, and Kandinsky was elected President. Gabriele Münter bought a house at the summer resort of Murnau, which quickly became a meeting-place for radical artists. In 1910 Kandinsky met Franz Marc and August Macke, and the following year the three of them formed yet another group, Der Blaue Reiter (The Blue Rider). At this time Kandinsky renewed his acquaintance with Klee. The first Blaue Reiter exhibition was in December 1911, and was followed by more ambitious exhibitions in 1912 in Munich and Berlin. In March 1912 Kandinsky published what is perhaps his most significant text, *On the Spiritual in Art*; it ran to a third edition by the autumn.

The outbreak of the First World War put a stop to all this activity. Though Kandinsky was identified with the Munich art world, he had remained a Russian citizen and was forced to leave Germany immediately. He went to Switzerland, then crossed the Balkans to Odessa and Moscow. He left Gabriele Münter behind him – he had obtained a divorce from his wife in 1911, but his union with his mistress had never been legalized. They were to meet only once more, in Stockholm, which Kandinsky visited from December 1916 to March 1917. Later in 1917 he married a fellow Russian, Nina Andreevskaya.

Like most of the avant-garde artists in Russia, Kandinsky sympathized with the Revolution. In 1919 he

VASILY KANDINSKY's Paris studio as he left it at his death in 1944. Photo Alexander Liberman, 1954 helped to create the Institute of Artistic Culture (INKHUK) and the Museum of Pictorial Culture in Moscow; and in the following year he was given a one-man exhibition organized by the State. In the summer of 1921 he set up the Russian Academy of Artistic Sciences in Moscow, of which he became Vice-President. But in spite of these and other honours now showered upon him and the opportunities he was given to put his ideas into effect, Kandinsky soon became disillusioned with revolutionary Russia. In December 1921 he returned to Germany, arriving in Berlin on Christmas Eve, and in 1922 he moved to Weimar, where he had accepted a professorship at the newly created Bauhaus.

During the years that the Weimar Republic survived, Kandinsky was one of the most loyal and effective servants of the Bauhaus ideal. The courses for which he was responsible were of fundamental importance to the philosophy of the school – within the framework of the Preliminary Course, the foundation stone of all Bauhaus teaching, he taught analytical drawing, beginning with a still life which the students were asked to arrange for themselves, and also conducted a colour seminar.

During his Bauhaus period Kandinsky enjoyed increasing fame both in Germany and abroad. In 1923 he had his first one-man show in New York, with the Société Anonyme, the precursor of the Museum of Modern Art. In 1924 the dealer Galka Scheyer formed the Blaue Vier (Blue Four) group, which consisted of Kandinsky, Paul Klee, Lyonel Feininger and Alexei Jawlensky, and she succeeded in getting considerable exposure for their work. In 1926 Kandinsky published *Point and Line to Plane*, a summary of his Bauhaus teaching.

The Bauhaus closed in March 1933, and Kandinsky, who had striven to the last to save it, decided it was time to make a change in his own life. He had taken German citizenship in 1928 but felt no particular loyalty to a Germany dominated by Hitler. In December 1933 Kandinsky settled in the Parisian suburb of Neuilly-sur-Seine. He was already well known in the Parisian art world and soon became an influential and respected figure within it. He was largely responsible for inspiring the International Exhibition of Abstract Art which was put on at the Musée du Jeu de Paume in Paris in connection with the Exposition Universelle held in Paris in 1937. He remained at Neuilly for the brief remainder of his life, becoming a French citizen in 1939 and working almost to the end. He died on 13 December 1944.

LYONEL FEININGER

Lyonel Feininger was the link between American art and the Bauhaus. After spending the greater part of his career as an artist in Germany, he was finally driven out by the Nazis, and ended his days in the America he had left half a century previously.

He was born in 1871 in New York, of German stock. Both his parents were musicians – his father a well known violinist, his mother a singer and pianist. Feininger too showed signs of musical talent: at the age of twelve he was giving public performances as a musical prodigy. In 1887, at the age of sixteen, he was sent to Germany to continue his musical studies, and it was here that he decided to change to art. But music continued to mean much to him: he said that it was 'as much my life as air and creating in paint'. As an adult he continued to play and to compose, and in the 1920s he wrote a number of fugues which were performed in public in Germany.

His studies as an artist were undertaken with his father's approval, but in 1890 there was a disagreement between the two men (its immediate cause was that Feininger had pawned his father's watch) and the breach was never healed. The young man was briefly banished from Germany to Belgium, and from there made his first visit to Paris. In 1901, after his return to Germany, he married Clara Furst, by whom he had two daughters, although their marriage was short-lived. He now began to earn his living as a professional caricaturist, and had to struggle hard to make ends meet until 1906, when the *Chicago Sunday Tribune* gave him a contract to draw two weekly comic strips. This was also the year of his second marriage, to Julia Berg. Feininger seized the chance to return to Paris, where he lived for two years. 'For the first time,' he said later, 'I was able to think, feel and work for myself.' In 1911 he returned yet again to Paris, for a briefer visit; he showed six paintings at the Salon des Indépendants that year, and had a decisive encounter with Cubism. Despite this, he continued to think of himself as being basically an Expressionist, and his Expressionist colleagues in Germany always treated him as one of their own. In 1913 he was invited by Franz Marc to exhibit with the Blaue Reiter group (Marc, Kandinsky and Klee) at the First German Autumn salon in Berlin.

Feininger's own attitudes towards painting can be judged from a number of statements made at this period and later – for example, his remark in an open letter to

LYONEL FEININGER, self portrait cartoon in the *Chicago Sunday Tribune*, 1906

Paul Westheim, editor and publisher of *Das Kunstblatt*: 'We live in a state of perpetual longing and no release; only the stimulus to begin the work can come from outside ourselves.' The mood was accentuated by the black depression generated by the war: he was technically an enemy alien in Germany once America had joined the conflict.

In 1918 Feininger met Walter Gropius, the architect and founder of the Bauhaus. Feininger's symbolic woodcut, *The Cathedral*, adorned the cover of the Bauhaus manifesto published in 1919, and Feininger was Gropius's first appointment to the staff of the new school – he became master in charge of the Graphic Workshop. Despite the fact that Feininger remained associated with the Bauhaus until the very end, he was often out of sympathy with the directions it seemed to be taking. As early as 1922, when the Bauhaus was still at its first home in Weimar, he wrote in a letter to his wife:

It is a question of do or die ... we have to steer towards profitable tasks and mass production. That goes clearly against our grain, and we are aware of forestalling the process of evolution.

Later, when László Moholy-Nagy rose to power within the institution, Feininger criticized his attitudes:

What has been 'art' for ages is to be discarded – to be replaced by new ideals. There is talk only about optics, mechanics and moving pictures.

In fact, compared with Moholy-Nagy, Feininger was now part of a distinctly conservative faction – not least because he clung to figuration. His faceted, light-filled landscapes and seascapes applied the lessons learned from Cubism in a very personal way, giving his subject-matter mystical overtones which were traditionally Nordic. There is a kinship with the work of the great German Romantic artist, Caspar David Friedrich, in the paintings Feininger produced every year at West-Deep in Pomerania on the shores of the Baltic. The German Expressionists, notably Marc, also shared this affinity.

After the Bauhaus moved to Dessau in 1925 Feininger preferred to be artist-in-residence without remuneration, so as to have more time to pursue his own work. Alfred H. Barr, later to be Director of the Museum of Modern Art in New York, visited him as part of a pilgrimage to the Bauhaus:

There in the doorway of his severe, Gropius-designed house was one of the most American figures I had ever seen – tall and spare – though with nothing of the tight-lipped, rock-bound yankee about him. He seemed shy, but his smile melted my own shyness. And when he spoke, his American speech fascinated me with its strange purity of accent and antiquated slang – I was puzzled, too, until I realized that he had left America forty years before and was still speaking the American language of the 1880s, the language my father's generation had used in college.

By this time Feininger was reasonably successful. Between 1924 and 1934 he exhibited widely as one of the Blaue Vier (Blue Four) group. Its other members were Klee, Kandinsky and Alexei Jawlensky, and their work was seen not only in Germany itself, but in New York, California and Mexico. In 1929 Feininger was

LYONEL FEININGER, 1936. Photo Imogen Cunningham

shown at the new Museum of Modern Art in New York in an exhibition entitled 'Paintings by Nineteen Living Americans'. In 1931 he was given a large retrospective at the National Gallery in Berlin, in honour of his sixtieth birthday, followed by one-man shows in Hanover, Leipzig and Hamburg the following year.

The rise of the Nazis put a stop to his progress. He was asked to provide 'proof of Aryan descent' by the Nazi-organized Reichs Kulturkammer in 1935; his work was removed from museums, and in 1937 it was included in the notorious Degenerate Art Exhibition staged in Munich. Feininger decided to return to the United States. The process of readjustment was at first painful: it was not merely that he was comparatively little known in his native country, certainly compared to the considerable reputation he had built over many years in Germany, but he found it hard to adjust his sensibilities to a new range of subject-matter. Eventually New York's skyscrapers replaced the Gothic churches of Germany and the shifting lights of West-Deep. Exhibitions were organized for Feininger by friendly dealers, and in 1939 he was commissioned to paint two sets of murals for the New York World's Fair, one for the Marine Transportation Building and the other for the Masterpieces of Modern Art Building. The Metropolitan Museum bought his prize-winning painting *Church at Gelmerode XII* in 1942, and he was given a large retrospective at the Museum of Modern Art in 1944 which he shared with Marsden Hartley (1877–1943). Feininger died in New York on 13 January 1956.

Top: LYONEL FEININGER,
Lady in Mauve, 1922
Bottom: LYONEL FEININGER,
Church at Gelmerode XII, 1929

PAUL KLEE

The tiny scale of most of Paul Klee's paintings, drawings and watercolours is not in proportion to the vast influence they have exercized. In a sense, it was he who worked out the principles of Surrealist automatism before Surrealism itself was born. He was also a potent force within the Bauhaus, where he taught for a decade.

Klee was born in December 1879 at Münchenbuchsee close to Bern in Switzerland. His father, a German immigrant, was employed at the Cantonal School for Teachers at nearby Hofwyl. A bitter man with a sarcastic tongue, his personality contrasted with his wife's gentle and sensitive nature. As a child Klee shared her sensitivity and used to rush to her for comfort when the 'evil spirits' he was drawing became too real. Around 1906 she became partially paralysed, which intensified the bond of sympathy with her son.

Klee did well at school, but the only subject he was taught there which made any real impression on him was Ancient Greek. As an adult he continued to study Greek poetry in the original, reading Aeschylus and other texts in his spare time. From a very early age he showed a gift for music – he started to learn the violin at the age of

seven, and when barely ten was already playing with the Bern Municipal Orchestra. Nevertheless, he soon showed a determination to become an artist rather than a professional musician. In October 1898 he went to a private art school in Munich and then to the Munich Academy, joining the class of Franz von Stück in 1900. Those who taught him were enthusiastic about his abilities, but at this stage his work showed little individuality.

In the winter of 1899–1900 Klee met Lily Stumpf, the daughter of a Munich doctor. Their engagement was officially announced in 1902, but they did not marry until September 1906. At the conclusion of his studies Klee returned to Bern and earned money by playing as a regular member of the Bern Orchestra. His diaries at this time give many details of their performances, and record, for example, the impression made on him by the great cellist Pablo Casals, but they have surprisingly little to say about art. Klee made frequent trips to Munich to see his fiancée Lily and also paid brief visit to Paris and to Berlin. His first real, though minor, artistic success came when some of his etchings were shown in the Munich Sezession exhibition of 1906.

After their marriage the Klees settled in Munich. Their only child, a son, was born in November 1907. Lily, a talented pianist, supported the family by giving music lessons while Paul cooked and looked after the child. In 1910 he had his first one-man show, at the Bern Museum, where it was well received, then touring to Zurich, Basel and finally Winterthur. At Winterthur the public protested, and the museum authorities hastened to return his work. The whole exhibition was shown again in the following year at the Thannhauser Gallery in Munich.

By 1911 Klee came into contact with the avant-garde: in January he met Alfred Kubin, who praised him extravagantly, and in the autumn Kandinsky, by whom he was at first rather intimidated. Kandinsky and Franz Marc (who became a close friend) invited him to participate in the second Blaue Reiter exhibition, held in 1912, but Klee never played a leading role in the group. In 1912 Klee paid a brief visit to Paris and had a crucial three-hour meeting with Robert Delaunay in the latter's studio, which revealed the colouristic freedom modern art could now achieve.

The turning point in Klee's development came, however, as late as 1914, when he and August Macke paid a fortnight's visit to Tunis. The light and colour

PAUL KLEE,
Wiesbaden, 1924.
Photo Elain

of North Africa had an overwhelming effect. Klee wrote in his journal:

> Colour has taken hold of me; no longer do I have to chase after it. I know that it has hold of me forever. That is the significance of this blessed moment. Colour and I are one. I am a painter.

When war broke out Klee was already in his thirties and was not called up for some time. Despite the grief he felt at the death of close friends – Macke was killed almost at once, and Marc died at Verdun – he greeted the conflict itself with a certain detachment. 'I have carried this war within me for some time,' he wrote, 'and that is why it no longer concerns me internally.' He was conscripted in March 1915, into an escort unit which took convoys to the front. He then became a clerk at a Bavarian flying school, which enabled him to continue to work intermittently. His drawings were now beginning to sell through the *Der Sturm* Gallery in Berlin: in 1918 *Der Sturm* published a volume of Klee reproductions. When Klee was at last demobilized, in December 1918, he found himself with a certain amount of money in his pocket, and now felt sufficiently confident to start painting in oils.

Despite the chaotic conditions prevailing in post-war Germany, his reputation grew rapidly. In 1920 the dealer Walter Goltz, with whom he had signed a contract, organized a retrospective show in Munich, which caused something of a sensation, and in the same year three small monographs were published about his work. In November Walter Gropius asked him to join the staff of the Bauhaus and in January 1921 Klee left Munich for Weimar, where the new school was situated. Since the Bauhaus professors were supposed to be omnicompetent, he found himself taking charge first of glass-painting and then of weaving. The Bauhaus had a radical effect on him, as it forced him to analyse his own method of work to communicate it to others. He became a superb but undogmatic pedagogue. The Bauhaus was always a kind of pressure-cooker, full of powerful personalities, and Klee was from the beginning careful to keep himself aloof from internal disputes. His air of detachment earned him the nickname 'the heavenly father'. Klee himself had a keen sense of humour – Weimar was famous as the city of Goethe, with whom the painter ironically identified himself: he would pause in the street and strike poses

PAUL KLEE (right) and Vasily Kandinsky posing as Goethe and Schiller on the beach at Hendaye, France 1929. Photo Lily Klee

modelled on the most famous representations of the great poet. He formed a particularly close alliance with Kandinsky, and when the school moved to Dessau the two men had their homes and studios in the two halves of the same building.

From 1924 onwards, when the runaway rate of inflation had stabilized and Germans were able to travel freely again, Klee travelled abroad every year – to Italy, Corsica, and Brittany, and in the winter of 1928–29 to Egypt. The mosques and bazaars made little impression, but he was greatly struck by the desert landscape and by the ancient ruins.

The internal disputes within the Bauhaus came to a climax with the resignation first of Moholy-Nagy, who had been in charge of the Preliminary Course, and then, later in 1928, of Gropius himself. Klee was unsympathetic to the regime led by Hannes Meyer and increasingly fed up with the disputes which were tearing the institution apart. In April 1931 he resigned and accepted a part-time post at the Academy of Fine Arts in

PAUL KLEE, *The Tightrope Walker/Equilibrist*, 1923

PAUL KLEE, *Fire Source*, 1938

Düsseldorf, saying to friends that he preferred the more modest professors there to Bauhaus 'geniuses'. Because he was unable to find suitable accommodation for his family he retained his house in Dessau, and had not yet moved out of it when the Nazis came to power and dismissed him from his Düsseldorf post.

Klee had always resisted his wife Lily's view that one could not entertain any illusions about the Nazis. He stayed in Dessau for some months more, then suddenly abandoned everything and returned to Switzerland just before Christmas 1933. His house and studio were later packed up for him by friends. He settled into a small apartment in Bern with his wife and began to try to remake his career, but the process was a difficult one. He had never possessed Swiss citizenship, and now, when he applied for it, there were difficulties and delays. Worse still, in 1935 his health began to fail. He had an attack of measles which left behind it a rare disability, the gradual drying up of the mucous membranes. His friends did their best to help him, but like other refugee artists he was now cut off from the German public which had admired and understood his work. In January 1934 he was given his first show in London, by the pioneering Mayor Gallery, and in February 1935 a large exhibition at the Kunsthalle in Bern.

As his physical condition worsened, the technique and atmosphere of his work changed: the line grew rougher and took on a deliberate crudity, and a tragic Expressionism replaced the fantasy for which he had become famous. His imagery was full of premonitions of approaching death. Old friends and admirers whom he scarcely knew continued to visit him – in November 1937 he received a call from Picasso, who was then in Bern. But the milieu he inhabited was often unsympathetic. In February 1940 he was given another exhibition, this time at the Kunsthaus in Zurich. The Swiss press received it with jibes which distressed Klee because he thought they would affect the still pending matter of his application for Swiss citizenship. This was in fact granted the day after he died, on 29 June 1940.

On Klee's gravestone is inscribed the following extract from his diaries:

> I cannot be grasped in this world, for I am as much at home with the dead as with those yet unborn – a little nearer to the heart of creation than is normal, but still too far away.

LÁSZLÓ MOHOLY-NAGY,
early 1920s.
Photo H. Künstler

LÁSZLÓ MOHOLY-NAGY

One of the most important figures in the Bauhaus, and
the type of the modern technologically oriented artist,
László Moholy-Nagy was born on a wheat farm in
southern Hungary in 1895. Just before the First World
War he enrolled as a law student at Budapest University,
but then enlisted as an artillery officer in the Austro-
Hungarian army. At this stage he wanted to become a
writer – preferably a poet – a desire he never completely
lost. In 1929 he answered a questionnaire in the avant-
garde *Little Review*. Asked 'What has been the happiest
moment in your life?' he answered: 'I was still a small
boy when a friend pressed into my hand a paper in which
my first printed poem appeared.' He was wounded on
the Italian Front in 1916, and spent some time in various
field hospitals. After receiving little encouragement
from his friends for his poetry, he began to make
drawings of war scenes on military postcards. When
he was discharged from the army in 1918 he abandoned
his law studies and began to study art, working on his
own by day and attending life classes in the evening.

A political revolution in Hungary in 1919 brought to
power an extreme left-wing regime. Moholy-Nagy was
sympathetic to its aims but avoided becoming too deeply
involved, and at the end of the year, when a violent
counter-revolution had begun, he left Hungary for
Vienna. Sometime after the demise of the Hungarian
Soviet he allowed himself cautiously to lament its betrayal
of 'the spiritual and material needs of the wanting
masses'. The attractions of Vienna could not compete
with those of post-war Berlin, despite the disturbed situation there, and early in 1920 Moholy-Nagy moved again.
Once in Berlin he became associated with the Dadaists
(Berlin Dada had a distinctly left-wing flavour), and was
also appointed Berlin representative of the Hungarian
arts magazine in exile, *MA*, edited by his friend Lajos
Kassak. In 1921 he married a German, Lucia Schulz.

In October 1921 Moholy-Nagy was one of the
signatories of a 'Manifesto of Elemental Art' published
in the Dutch magazine *De Stijl*. The other signatories
included both Dadaists and Constructivists. By winter he
had become closely associated with the leading Russian
Constructivist El Lissitzky, newly arrived from Russia and
bringing with him news of recent artistic activities there.
Under Lissitzky's influence he began to work on abstract
constructions in various materials, which were shown at

his first one-man exhibition held at Der Sturm Gallery in the spring of 1922. The exhibition was seen by Walter Gropius, founder of the Bauhaus, who promptly offered him the headship of the Preliminary Course (the core of Bauhaus instruction), and also of the metal workshops. Moholy-Nagy accepted, but did not take up his appointment until the following year.

In the interim period he continued his association with Lissitzky, and the two artists showed their work jointly at the Kestner Gesellschaft in Hanover; Moholy-Nagy also shared a studio with the Dadaist Kurt Schwitters in the winter of 1922–23. This was the period of runaway inflation in Germany, and he followed Schwitters's example in making collages from devalued banknotes, which combined an aesthetic and a political point.

Once established at the Bauhaus, which was then still in Weimar. Moholy-Nagy set about putting his ideas into effect. He extended the Preliminary Course by one term and changed the policy of the metal workshop, which had until then concentrated on producing one-off arts-and-crafts items, to the production of prototypes for industry. Some designs for lamps and lighting fixtures which were the result of this policy are still available today. When the Bauhaus moved from Weimar to Dessau in 1925 Moholy-Nagy accompanied it, now established as Gropius's right-hand man. He was effective, but not altogether popular: his more conservative colleagues tended to resent his assertiveness, and in particular his advocacy of photography as the destined successor of easel painting. For the moment, however, his influence seemed unassailable. He and Gropius were now co-editing a series of Bauhaus Books which played an important part in spreading the School's reputation and influence. In a private capacity, Moholy-Nagy and his wife continued a series of photographic experiments which they had begun before coming to the Bauhaus. As early as 1921 Moholy-Nagy had begun making what he called 'photograms', abstract photographs made without the help of the camera. In 1926 he moved into film, producing his first documentary, *Berliner Stilleben* (Berlin Still-Lifes).

His eventual parting from the Bauhaus was due to political disagreements. Like Gropius, to whom he owed his position, Moholy-Nagy had become a political pragmatist: he was to state, towards the end of his life, that 'as an artist I never had any political affiliations' – a claim somewhat belied by his early history. But the

Bauhaus, like Germany itself, was becoming politically polarized in the late 1920s; in particular, there was a strong Communist faction among both students and staff which wished to see much greater emphasis placed on vocational training as opposed to general education. Moholy-Nagy had a violent quarrel with Hannes Meyer, the leader of this group, and resigned in January 1928; he was followed by Gropius and others in February, and Meyer was left temporarily in command.

Moholy-Nagy founded his own independent design office in Berlin a few months later, working in association with Gyorgy Kepes. From 1929–31 he also made stage designs for the new Kroll Opera, an experimental independent branch of the Berlin State Opera which had been placed under the direction of the conductor Otto Klemperer, and further designs for the left-wing theatre run by Erwin Piscator. His activities as a film-maker continued, and in 1930 he made his best-known film, the abstract *Light play, black and white and grey*, based on his own machine-powered mobile, the *Light Prop*.

In the same year he met Sybille Pietsch, a scenario-writer for a film company and former actress, who was to become his second wife (he separated from his first wife in 1929). In 1932 he joined the Abstraction-Création group in Paris, which brought him into contact with the English artist Ben Nicholson and, through Nicholson, with a new circle of English admirers. He made his first

LÁSZLÓ MOHOLY-NAGY,
Light Play: Black/White/Grey,
c. 1922–30

visit to London in November 1933, but did not at first respond to overtures to settle there. Nevertheless, from December of the same year, because of the deteriorating situation in Germany following the Nazi takeover, he worked chiefly in Holland, though he also made a further visit to London to study the Kodak colour-copy process. In November and December 1934 he was given a major retrospective at the Stedelijk Museum in Amsterdam, organized by the Dutch Society for Arts and Crafts.

In May 1935 he closed his design firm in Berlin and moved to London, following Gropius's example. After his arrival there were discussions about the feasibility of founding a new Bauhaus in England, but nothing came of them, and Moholy-Nagy found employment as an advertising, exhibition and film designer. He was appointed Design Consultant to Simpson's, the new department store in Piccadilly, and was employed by his Hungarian compatriot, Alexander Korda, to create special effects for the film *The Shape of Things to Come* based on a novel by H. G. Wells, but these were dropped from the final print. He was given a one-man exhibition at the Royal Photographic Society in 1936, and in the same year returned unmolested to Germany for the Olympic Games, to fulfil photographic and film commitments.

The project which remained dearest to his heart was that of a new Bauhaus, and in the spring of 1937 he received an offer from Chicago, where a group of backers were prepared to set up just such an institution. He crossed the Atlantic in July, and the new school was opened in October. By this time his work was being removed from public galleries in Germany as part of the Nazi campaign against 'degenerate art'. The New Bauhaus did not last long: it collapsed in the summer of 1938 because its backers were bankrupt. By supporting it with his own earnings as a commercial designer Moholy-Nagy was able to open a similar but more modest facility, the School of Design, in the spring of the following year. From 1940 onwards, thanks to the backing of Walter Paepcke, President of the Container Corporation of America, he was also able to run a summer school on a farm at Simonauk, Illinois. The School of Design ran into hard times because of the war, and nearly had to close its doors in 1942, but Moholy-Nagy was able to ensure its survival by having it designated as a certified school for camouflage personnel, and by providing occupational therapy for wounded servicemen. He also used the school as a research facility which looked for substitutes for materials which were in short supply because of the war. Gradually it became more prosperous and in the spring of 1944 it changed its name to the Institute of Design, to stress its connection with the Illinois Institute of Technology. Moholy-Nagy was now no longer forced to support it from his own resources, as he had found backing from a group of Chicago businessmen.

In November 1945 he fell ill with leukemia. Until his death a year later he continued to work on his book, *Vision in Motion*, which he regarded as his testament. It was published in 1947, and forms a permanent memorial to his ideas.

Group of students and teachers at the Bauhaus in Weimar. JOSEF ALBERS is seated on the floor on the right (with pipe), *c.* 1921–23. Photographer unknown

JOSEF ALBERS

Josef Albers was an inspired pedagogue and one of the principal channels through which Bauhaus influence and Bauhaus ideas reached the American art world. Like the very different Hans Hofmann, he achieved a considerable reputation as a creative artist in America towards the end of his life.

He was born at Bottrop in the Ruhr in 1888; his family had been craftsmen for generations, working as carpenters, blacksmiths or housepainters. From the beginning his decision was to be a teacher: in 1902–5 he attended Preparatory Teachers' Training School, then from 1905 to 1908 he studied at a Teachers' Training College in his native Westphalia. He then became an elementary school teacher. In 1908 he paid his first visit to Munich and to the Folkwang Museum in Hagen; these were his first encounters with modern art. In 1912–13 he took a two-year absence from his teaching job to attend the Royal Art School in Berlin. At this time he also made the rounds of the Berlin galleries, then in a particularly exciting phase. In 1915 he qualified as an art teacher, and from 1916 to 1919 he continued to teach at an elementary school in Bottrop while attending the Arts and Crafts School in Essen. It was during this period that he made his first prints, which were Expressionist in style. In 1919–20 he studied in Franz von Stück's class in the Munich Academy, at which point he heard about a newly founded school directed by Walter Gropius:

> All I knew of the Bauhaus was derived from a single sheet, the first manifesto, with one side giving Gropius's programme for reuniting arts and the crafts and the other showing Feininger's woodcut *The Cathedral*. This programme gave me the impulse to try out the new idea.

Albers destroyed most of the academic work he had done up to that point and joined the new school in Weimar where, at the age of thirty-two, he was the oldest student. Like all Bauhaus students he attended the Vorkurs (Preliminary Course), which was the heart of Bauhaus teaching, and at the same time he worked independently on 'glass paintings'. The first of these were made from bottle shards found on the town dump, and, by the very nature of the material, the forms used were irregular. Albers became obsessed with making them

Top: Josef Albers,
Factory, 1925
Bottom: Josef Albers,
study for *Homage to the Square Departing in Yellow*, 1964

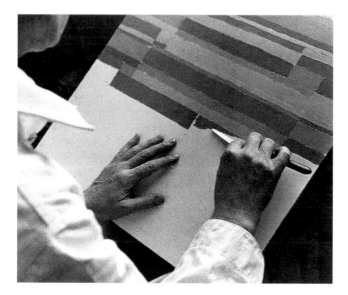

Top: JOSEF ALBERS in his studio,
North Forest Circle, New Haven, 1960s.
Photographer unknown
Bottom: JOSEF ALBERS
at Black Mountain College, North Carolina.
Photographer unknown

and did not want to join the mural painting class recommended for him by his instructors. He expected to be expelled from the school for his intransigeance, but instead, after his work had been shown in an exhibition of student work, he was invited to organize a glass workshop and was appointed a 'Bauhaus journeyman'. This slightly medieval title indicated a position intermediary between that of the student and that of the fully fledged teacher. In 1923, when Moholy-Nagy was appointed to run the Preliminary Course, Albers became his assistant; he was to feel afterwards that Moholy-Nagy had not been scrupulous enough about claiming credit for some of his assistant's ideas. There must have been a degree of influence one way or the other between the two since in 1923 Albers's glass paintings became quite different, and much more industrial in feeling – they were now panels of commercially produced flashed glass upon which geometric designs were sand-blasted. This quasi-industrial approach and use of an industrial material came close to Moholy-Nagy's own declared philosophy.

Albers moved to Dessau with the Bauhaus in 1925 and was appointed a full professor. In the same year he married the weaver Annie Fleischmann, who was to become a valued collaborator. In 1926 the glass workshop was closed, but he nevertheless continued to work on his own glass paintings. In line with the new industrial orientation of the Bauhaus, Albers designed typography, utilitarian glass and metal containers, and also furniture. In 1928 Moholy-Nagy left the Bauhaus, after a quarrel with the Communist faction led by Hannes Meyer, and was soon followed by Gropius; but Albers remained on the staff and took over the running of the Preliminary Course, and in the following year, exhibited his glass paintings as part of a joint exhibition in Zurich with Kandinsky, Klee and Feininger, who had also decided to remain at their posts. In 1930 Meyer was ousted and replaced by Mies van der Rohe, and when in 1931 the Bauhaus was forced to leave Dessau and move to Berlin, Albers continued to link his personal fortunes with that of the institution. He was extremely lucky that, when the new Nazi government suppressed the Bauhaus in 1933, he was almost immediately offered a post at the experimental Black Mountain College in North Carolina, on the recommendation of the Museum of Modern Art in New York. He launched himself into his new job with the declaration: 'I want to open eyes.' At this moment he spoke almost no English, and his command of the language remained shaky all his life – his idiosyncratic use of his adopted tongue may even have increased the effectiveness of his ideas.

Black Mountain College was never very large, nor particularly stable financially. From the moment they arrived Albers and his wife represented continuity, and Albers eventually became its Rector. His teaching was inspired and inspiring, but his manner could also be severe – Robert Rauschenberg was one student who felt his irritation and disapproval. The basic principle of all the teaching Albers offered was that art is 'the visual formulation of our reactions to life'.

His work was not confined to North Carolina: in 1934 he lectured in Havana, and in 1935 in Mexico – these were both the first of many visits and his links with Mexico became particularly close. From 1936 to 1940 he conducted regular seminars and lectures at the Graduate School of Design at Harvard University. After he left Black Mountain College in 1949 he lectured at the Cincinnati Art Academy, taught at the Pratt Institute, then became Chairman of the Yale Art School, a post from which he retired in 1958. Ouside America he taught in Chile and Peru and, in 1953, at the Hochschule für Gestaltung at Ulm.

Throughout these years Albers continued his career as a creative artist. Between 1936 and 1941 there were more than twenty one-man exhibitions of his glass paintings, oil paintings and prints in American galleries and museums. In 1946 he had a one-man exhibition at the Egan Gallery in New York, then closely associated with the beginnings of Abstract Expressionism. He carried out a number of decorative commissions, including a brick mural for Harvard Graduate School in 1950. In 1961 there was a retrospective of his work at the Stedelijk Museum in Amsterdam.

Albers's major international reputation was, however, made very late, by the 'Homage to the Square' touring exhibition, which was organized by the International Council of the Museum of Modern Art, and seen in ten South American museums and two museums in Mexico City during 1963–64. A second version of 'Homage to the Square' was seen in eight museums in the United States in 1966 and 1967. The pictures included in these exhibitions all belonged to one continuing open-ended series which examined the relationship of various hues to one another, and the way in which colours are affected by juxtaposition, using a square format canvas containing other squares, one within the other. These paintings have been categorized as examples of the Optical Art which was briefly fashionable in the 1960s, but this was a term Albers himself detested. 'To call any sort of pictorial art "optical art" ', he said, 'makes just as little sense as to speak of acoustic music or tactile sculpture.' Albers died in 1976.

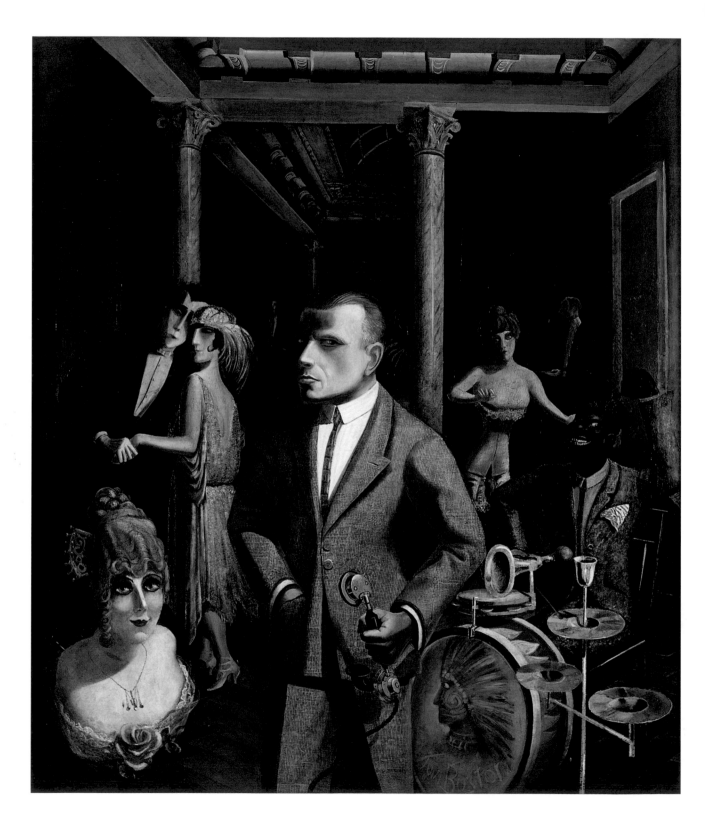

The New Objectivity (*Neue Sachlichkeit*) was the name coined in 1923 by G. F. Hartlaub, director of the Kunsthalle in Mannheim, for the 'realistic' tendency which was then beginning to show itself in German painting. The artists involved in it – chief among them George Grosz and Otto Dix – rejected what seemed to them the excesses of German pre-war Expressionism in favour of social criticism embodied in cutting satire. Nevertheless, for these artists realism was only relative. They continued to owe something to Expressionism in their use of distortion; and something, too, to the highly political Berlin Dada movement, which at one time numbered Grosz among its members.

Left: OTTO DIX,
To Beauty, 1922
Above: Otto and Martha Dix,
1927–28.
Photo August Sander

OTTO DIX

Otto Dix, perhaps the most representative artist of the New Objectivity, which challenged Expressionism in the 1920s, was notably taciturn. His utterances on art are few but pithy.

He was born in 1891 at Untermhaus near Gera in Thuringia, and from 1905 until 1909 was apprenticed to a local painter-decorator, which gave him a deep-rooted respect for the craft of painting. From 1910 until 1914 he was at the School of Arts and Crafts in Dresden. This was a period of artistic ferment in the city, and Dix was influenced by the Van Gogh exhibition held in Dresden in 1913, by the artists of Die Brücke – only a little older than himself – who lived there, and also by the Futurists, whose renown spread very rapidly throughout Europe.

Dix was mobilized in 1914 and joined an artillery regiment, being transferred in 1915 to Bautzen, where he painted portraits of a number of fellow soldiers in barracks. He then volunteered for a machine-gun unit which was due to be sent to the Front, for fear of missing the war. In old age he said: 'I needed to live all that intensely. I wanted to do it. I was far from being a pacifist.' He survived to create war paintings which shocked his contemporaries, though Dix himself claimed they were in no way expressions of emotion: 'I was painting still lifes. One has to paint things as they are ... one cannot paint indignation.' Yet it has also been said very justly that these works show that 'Dix believed in the war as a Catholic believes in the devil.'

He emerged from the conflict with a declared ambition to create what he described as 'anti-painting', something which would be 'objective, neutral, impassive'. His models were the artists of the German Renaissance – he had a particular admiration for Hans Baldung Grien. In 1922 he went back to school, this time to the Academy of Fine Arts in Düsseldorf, until 1925. During this period, as indeed later, he was very reluctant to become involved in the heated politics of the time: for example, he refused to take part in protests against the continued occupation of the Ruhr by the victorious allies. Yet he was, nevertheless, busy preparing a work which was to

become a *cause célèbre* – his lost masterpiece, *The Trench*.
In typically laconic fashion he once described how he
started work on this in 1922:

> One day I went to the dissection room and said
> 'I want to paint corpses!' I was taken to two female
> cadavers which had just been dissected and sewn
> up again in a hurry. I sat down and started to paint …
> I came back again and asked for some entrails and
> a brain. I was given a brain sitting on a dish and made
> a watercolour of it.

When the painting was finished the following year, it was
purchased by the Wallraf-Richartz Museum in Cologne
for the then considerable sum of 10,000 marks. Shown
in Berlin in 1925 it created a tremendous scandal because
of its apparent attack on German militarism. The Wallraf-
Richartz Museum lost courage and sold it, even though
the German Impressionist Max Liebermann, then
probably the most respected artist in Germany, defended
it warmly as 'worthy of the National Gallery'. *The Trench*
re-entered museum possession in 1930, when it was
bought by the Dresden Museums. The Nazis, who
detested Dix's horrific vision of war, confiscated it
when they came to power and it was one of the principal
items in the Degenerate Art Exhibition held in Munich
in 1937. The picture then disappeared.

The Trench, and the controversies surrounding it,
made Dix a celebrated artist, and in 1925 he was offered
a contract by the Galerie Nierendorf in Berlin. From
1927 until the Nazi takeover he was also a professor at the
Dresden Academy. But his enemies were unforgiving.
In April 1933 he was dismissed while absent on holiday,
without pension rights and with all access to the
Academy's premises specifically forbidden.

The new regime hated Dix not for his technique,
which was painstakingly traditional, nor for his political
convictions, which were almost non-existent, but simply
for his subject-matter. During the middle and late 1920s
the war paintings were succeeded by masterly depictions
of the German society of the time, in all its decadence.
Dix was fascinated by Berlin's feverish night-life: he
cherished the sight of the extraordinary figures he saw,
and particularly the swarming prostitutes.

After his expulsion from the Dresden Academy Dix
was forbidden to exhibit his work in Germany, though it
continued to be seen abroad – in 1935 he was shown at

the Museum of Modern Art in New York and at the
Carnegie Institute, Pittsburgh; and in 1938, the year
in which 260 of his works were removed from national
museums in Germany, there was a large one-man
show in Zurich. Under the Nazis, Dix lived quietly in
the country in the region near Lake Constance, first at
Randegg, and later at Hemmenhofen. He was now
painting traditional landscapes, as if to demonstrate
how mistaken the official view of his work was. Yet the
Gestapo continued to be suspicious, and in 1939 he
was briefly arrested. At the very end of the war, in 1945,
when the German army was desperate for men, he was
conscripted into the Volkssturm, though already over
fifty, and finished in a prisoner-of-war camp at Colmar
in Alsace, from which he was released in 1946. While
he was a prisoner he changed the laborious style with
multiple glazes which he had practised for so long,
and started to paint in a much more direct and
simple fashion, *alla prima*. The result was a kind
of belated Expressionism.

After the war he continued to live at Hemmenhofen,
but from 1949 onwards made annual visits to Dresden,
then in East Germany. In 1967 he went to Greece,
and while he was there suffered a paralytic attack which
affected his left hand. His last lithograph was produced
in 1968 and he died in hospital in July 1969.

Dix's attitudes towards art are summed up by a
paragraph from the only formal statement he ever
made about painting. It dates from 1927:

> At any rate what is new in painting for me is the
> widening of the area from which subject-matter is
> chosen, and also the intensified form of expression
> which essentially is already present in the Old
> Masters. For me, anyway, the object remains of first
> importance, and the form is created only through
> the object. That is why the question which has always
> been of paramount importance to me is whether I
> have come as close as possible to the object I see;
> for to me more important than the How is the What.
> It is only from the What that the How will develop.

GEORGE GROSZ

In many respects the artist most typical of the Weimar years, George Grosz professed a cult of America and things American which he shared with more than one of his contemporaries, among them the writer Bertolt Brecht. The irony of their situation was that neither of them, once in America, succeeded in acclimatizing a peculiarly German talent.

Grosz was born George Ehrenfried Gross in Berlin in 1893. His family background was comparatively humble; in 1898 the family moved to the provincial town of Stolp in Pomerania, where his father was caretaker at a free-masons' lodge. Gross senior died young, in 1900, and his widow and her three children moved back to Berlin where for two years she struggled to make a living as a seamstress. It was with profound relief that she returned to Stolp to take up a position as manageress of the Officers' Club of the Prince Blücher Hussars. The pictures in the Club, of battles and men in uniform, were Grosz's first exposure to art. His interest was supplemented by an enthusiasm for contemporary comic draughtsmen, such as Wilhelm Busch, creator of *Max und Moritz*, and for the illustrations in penny dreadfuls: he began by painstakingly copying these and drawing caricatures. In 1908 he was expelled from the local school for retaliating when a master boxed his ear, and in 1909 he entered the Dresden Academy of Art. His first professional success took place while he was a student there – he sold one of his caricatures to *Ulk*, the supplement to the Berlin *Tageblatt*. He completed the course and received his diploma, but his reaction to the experience was negative:

> In reviewing my two years at the Academy I can definitely say without reservation or hesitation that I did not learn very much. What I did learn or experience during that period came from my friends for the most part and from the books and pictures I hunted up myself.

In 1912 Grosz arrived in Berlin where he enrolled at the School of Arts and Crafts under Emil Orlik. He was now earning a living from his caricatures, which gave him a certain sense of superiority over his fellow students, and he started making sketches from life under the influence of Menzel. His subjects were the shabbier quarters of the city, the workers and the unemployed. In 1913 he went to Paris, where he enrolled at the Atelier Colarossi and met Jules Pascin, whose drawings he greatly admired. Perhaps due to Pascin's influence a strong erotic element now emerged in his work.

On the outbreak of war Grosz volunteered, but fell ill with what he afterwards described as 'a combination of brain fever and dysentery' and was discharged as unfit in May 1915, though with the threat that he would be recalled. His drawing style now began to change rapidly:

> In order to attain a style which would render the blunt and unvarnished harshness of my objects, I studied the crudest manifestations of the artistic urge. In public urinals I copied the folkloristic drawings; they seemed to me to be the most immediate expression and the most succinct translation of strong feelings. Children's drawings, too, stimulated me because of their lack of ambiguity. Thus it was that gradually I came to use the hard-as-nails drawing-style which I needed to transfer on to paper my observations which, at that time, were dictated by absolute misanthropy.

In January 1917 his worst fears were realized, and he was called up again. He lasted precisely one day; by his own account he was found 'semi-conscious, partially buried in a dung-pit'. He was threatened with court martial as a deserter, but through the intervention of his patron, Count Kessel, was placed instead in a mental hospital. In May 1917 he was discharged as permanently unfit.

He was still extremely active as a draughtsman, and during 1917 two portfolios of his prints were published in Berlin. The second of these, the *Small Grosz Portfolio*, had a prospectus designed in collaboration with John Heartfield and signalled the arrival of Dada in Berlin. By 1918 Grosz was a fully committed Dadaist. He took part in the first Dada 'recital' at the Berlin Sezession and was a co-signatory of the Dada Manifesto. In 1920, together with Raoul Haussman and John Heartfield, he was one of the organizers of the First International Dada Exhibition.

In Berlin, Dada took on a political implication – something which it had not possessed at its beginnings in Zurich. Grosz rapidly came to consider himself a socially committed artist:

> The sweep and surge of the movement influenced me so strongly that I considered art was useless unless it could be employed as a political instrument in the battle for freedom.

Above: GEORGE GROSZ,
Explosion, 1917
Right: GEORGE GROSZ,
*Daum marries her pedantic automaton
George in May 1920, John Heartfield
is very glad of it*, 1920

Yet he was also bitterly aware that in post-war Germany the artist was regarded as a kind of mountebank:

> I was neither a talented street singer, circus clown nor quick-change artist but I was included in this group. We were all highly paid and I almost became rich – just because we were permitted to make faces and show our behinds to the rich and mighty.

On a more superficial level Grosz relished his role as 'Propagandada', distributing stickers with slogans such as 'Come to Dada if you like to be embraced and embarrassed'; 'Dada kicks you in the behind and you like it'. He was soon to discover, however, that the tolerance of post-war German society had its limits. In 1920 he had his first brush with the law: he was tried for his anti-militarist print portfolio *Gott mit uns*, and fined 600 marks. The trial did nothing to diminish his popularity – rather the contrary – and by 1921 his portfolios were being published in large editions. He was now at the height of his brief involvement with the Communist Party: in

1922 he made a six-month visit to Russia and had a short meeting with Lenin. He is assumed to have left the party in the following year, but in 1924 he was still prepared to become chairman of the Rote Gruppe (Red Group), an association of German Communist artists.

In the mid-1920s Grosz achieved his greatest success. He was now represented by the important dealer Alfred Flechtheim, and in 1923 he had exhibitions in Berlin and Vienna; in 1924 in Paris; and in 1926 in Berlin, Cologne and Munich. He was included in the important Neue Sachlichkeit exhibition held at the Kunsthalle in Mannheim in 1925. This introduced the new post-Expressionist generation to the German public and gave it an identity. Around 1924 his style shifted towards a softened, more realistic manner, a signal that he was transforming himself from a figure in the class struggle into a more conventional kind of bourgeois moralist. By 1926 he had virtually severed his connection with the Communist periodicals and publishing houses which had helped to create his reputation and was working regularly for the solidly middle-class journal *Simplicissimus*.

There was to be one more major scandal during the Weimar years. From 1919 onwards Grosz had worked for the theatre, in association with the best experimental directors of the time. In 1928 he received a particularly imaginative commission – he was asked by Erwin Piscator to provide drawings to be made into a cartoon film, which would then be projected onto the backcloth for Piscator's production of *The Good Soldier Schwejk*. Grosz afterwards selected some of the most striking of these images and issued them as a portfolio which he called *Hintergrund* (Background). One drawing showed Christ on the cross, wearing a gas-mask. This and two other prints which were considered equally offensive led to a trial for blasphemy which was prolonged by various appeals until 1931.

In 1932 Grosz received an invitation to visit America to lecture at the Art Students' League in New York. He returned home to Germany, but soon decided to emigrate permanently. He was encouraged to take this step by the rapidly deteriorating political situation in Germany itself, and he afterwards claimed to have received at least two occult warnings that it would be wise to depart. One was a premonitory dream, the other came from his poet friend Theodor Däubler, then confined to a sanatorium.

'George,' said he, 'It's strange. When you walked in I saw something above your head. It was rather faint but you must believe me, there is no doubt about it being a rope and an axe. Please give me your word that you will leave Germany at once and take everything with you.'

Grosz emigrated in January 1933, and as soon as the Nazis took power they searched his house and his studio. Grosz afterwards believed that they would have killed him had they been able to lay hands on him.

Once settled in America he had to rebuild his career. In this he was never entirely successful, though he kept his head above water by making drawings for *Esquire* magazine, teaching, and giving private drawing lessons. His American patrons often hoped that he would depict the United States with the savagery he had shown in Berlin. But, Grosz reported, 'My eye could no longer see the grotesque; people did not readily lend themselves to distortion and caricature.' During his Berlin years, Grosz was one of the most urban of all artists; now he moved out of New York to live on Long Island, and even began drawing landscapes on Cape Cod.

In 1946 he published an amusing autobiography, *A Little Yes and a Big No*. The following year he was offered a professorship at the School of Fine Art in Berlin; he refused, saying that he would rather be poor and a failure in America than poor and a failure in Germany. He returned to Europe for the first time in 1951, but continued to avoid Germany. His prejudice against returning to his native country was only overcome in 1954, more than twenty years after his departure, when he visited Hamburg, Berlin and southern Germany. One of the old friends whom he saw was Otto Dix. In 1958 he paid a two-month visit to Berlin, where he was elected Extraordinary Member of the Academy of Art. He had now begun to make a series of collages which are an astonishing anticipation of the Pop Art of the 1960s, and close to the work of Richard Hamilton of the same period: their main subject was American consumerism. But he did not have much time left to explore this new source of satirical inspiration. He returned to Berlin in the middle of June 1959, and died there a few weeks later, on 6 July.

GEORGE GROSZ, 1928.
Photographer unknown

M exican Muralism was the first major movement in modern art to originate outside Europe. It owed its existence to the long drawn-out Mexican Revolution which began in 1910. This led to a great upsurge in national consciousness which in turn found expression in public art. The artists who participated evolved a style which combined European elements, chiefly borrowed from Cubism and Expressionism, with others from Mexico's Indian past and from the popular Mexican imagery of the late nineteenth and early twentieth centuries – in this case chiefly the prints of José Guadalupe Posada (1852–1913). The three leading muralists, Diego Rivera, José Clemente Orozco and David Alfaro Siqueiros exercized considerable influence outside Mexico, particularly in the United States. In recent years, their reputations have been challenged by that of Rivera's wife, Frida Kahlo. Her paintings, never on a large scale and many of which are self-portraits, are almost all autobiographical, in a style which owes much to that of Mexican *retablos*, the small votive paintings found in churches. Since the 1960s and 1970s, Kahlo has become a major feminist role model.

Above: José Clemente Orozco, New York 1933.
Photo Ansel Adams
Right: José Clemente Orozco, *La Evangelización*, 1938–39, detail of mural at the chapel of the Hospicio Cabañas, Guadalajara, Mexico

JOSÉ CLEMENTE OROZCO

The reputation of José Clemente Orozco has always been overshadowed by that of his prolific Mexican contemporary, Diego Rivera, a fact of which Orozco himself was always aware. Yet in some respects Orozco was the more original: his best murals fit their architectural settings less comfortably than Rivera's, but they have unique force. Ironically, it was his great rival who wrote what is perhaps the best description of him:

> Excessively conscious of his genius, his character is bitter because he never feels that he is sufficiently recognized and has been too long unappreciated. Profoundly sensual, cruel, moralistic and rancorous as a good, semi-blond descendant of Spaniards, he has the face and mentality of a servant of the Holy Office.

Orozco was born in 1883 into a middle-class family in Zapotlán il Grande (now Ciudad Guzman), in the province of Jalisco. In 1885 the family moved to Guadalajara, the capital of Jalisco, and in 1890 to Mexico City. Orozco's primary school was near a printing press whose publications were illustrated by popular artists such as José Guadalupe Posada, and it was from these that he received his first artistic stimulus. In 1897 he went to the School of Agriculture at San Jacinto, and then

continued his education at the Preparatoria, hoping to become an architect. But during this time he lost his left hand and part of his wrist in an accident with gunpowder, which made the profession of architect seem unattainable. In 1906 he decided that his vocation was to be a painter, and began full-time studies at the San Carlos Academy of Art. At first he was delighted by the situation he found there:

> There was no charge for the model. There were materials, a superb collection of Old Masters, a great library of books on art. The teachers were good. Above all there was unrivalled enthusiasm. What more could one want?

But eventually he was indeed to want more, and so were his fellow students. In 1910 he joined a historic strike at the Academy which lasted for nine months and resulted in the dismissal of the director. At about this time his father died, and the young artist was forced to fend for himself. He began work as a cartoonist for two radical newspapers, *El Imparcial* and *El Hijo del Ahuizote*; he was afterwards to say that their political position was a matter of indifference to him:

> I might equally well have gone to work for a government paper instead of the opposition, and in that case the scapegoats would have been the other side. No artist has, or ever has had, political convictions of any sort. Those who profess to have them are not artists.

In the same detached spirit Orozco witnessed the first stirrings of the Mexican Revolution which was to convulse the country for the next decade. 'To me,' he said, 'the revolution was the gayest and most diverting of carnivals, that is, of what I take carnivals to be, for I have never seen one.'

In 1912 Orozco was able to set up his own independent studio where he worked on a series of drawings called *The House of Tears* – scenes from the brothels which surrounded him – in a style influenced by the Jugendstil illustrations he had found in European magazines. The political situation grew much worse in 1913: there were ten days of heavy fighting in Mexico City, followed by the defeat and murder of President Madero, a tepid liberal. Orozco moved to the city of Veracruz and then in 1915 to Orizaba, capital of the State of Veracruz,

which was under the control of General Carranza, Madero's political heir. Here he provided cartoons and illustrations for the Carranzist newspaper *La Vanguardia*, whose editor was Dr Atl (Gerardo Murillo), a progressive painter whom he had met at the Academy in 1907. Siqueiros worked for a while as military correspondent for the same publication, before going off to take a more active part in the campaign.

In 1916, though the civil war was far from over, Orozco was back in Mexico City. But it was difficult for a young painter to make a living in the chaotic political and social conditions of the time, and he decided to try his luck in the United States. His first misfortune came at the border, where American customs officials confiscated a number of his low-life studies as indecent. He was unable to make any progress as an artist, and worked as a sign-painter in San Francisco and as a painter of dolls' faces in New York. In 1920 he returned to Mexico.

Immediately after his return he produced little but caricatures, and it was not until the American critic Walter Pach wrote appreciatively of him in 1922 that he was able to make some headway with his compatriots. In 1923 the Minister of Education, José Vasconcelos, engaged him to paint murals at the Preparatoria, where Rivera was already at work. At the same time he joined the Artists' Union founded by Siqueiros, who had also been asked to provide paintings for the same building. Orozco's work was immediately a focus of controversy; he had a foretaste of trouble when a conservative Catholic women's group took over the courtyard where he was working for a charity bazaar (he repaid them for their snubs by caricaturing them savagely), and in June 1924 the progress of his murals was halted when a group of conservative students staged a riot in protest against them.

In 1925 Orozco was commissioned to paint a mural in the historic and beautiful Casa de los Azuelos in Mexico City, and in the same year he was given an exhibition at the Bernheim-Jeune Gallery in Paris – his first taste of recognition abroad. He returned to the Preparatoria in 1926, and completed his commission there, repainting most of his previous work because he was now thoroughly dissatisfied with it. He was disappointed by the negative public reaction the completed paintings aroused, and decided to try his luck in the United States for a second time.

He arrived in New York in 1927, and by 1928 had achieved some minor successes. He was included in a group show of Mexican painters at the Art Center (he nevertheless described this in a letter to a friend as 'a total, absolute and definite failure'), and he also had a one-man show of drawings at a commercial gallery. He appreciated the opportunities to see art in New York, but chafed at the recognition which was already being accorded to Rivera: 'The idea that we are all his disciples is very well entrenched here,' he complained.

In 1930 Orozco received his first mural commission in the United States, when he was asked to paint a *Prometheus* at Pomona College, Claremont, California. Much of his not very generous fee came from a subscription raised by the student body. This was followed by a set of murals at the New School for Social Research in New York, painted more or less for the cost of the materials. Despite the effects of the Depression, Orozco's luck at last changed in 1932 when he was asked to create a major mural cycle for Dartmouth College, New Hampshire. The theme was entirely to his taste: his own personal interpretation of the evolution of civilization in America. With a little money now in hand he broke off in the middle of the task in order to make a three-month trip to Europe – his first and last – and he visited a number of major museums and galleries. The Dartmouth College murals were eventually completed in 1934, and Orozco returned to Mexico where he was promptly offered a wall at the Palacio de Bellas Artes in Mexico City – a sign of how far his reputation had risen in his own country.

In 1936 he moved to Guadalajara at the invitation of the governor of his native state of Jalisco. He spent the rest of the decade painting the magnificent series of murals which are his chief legacy to Mexican art. They include paintings for the Assembly Hall of the University of Guadalajara (1936), for the Government Palace there (1937), and for the deconsecrated chapel of the Hospicio Cabañas (1938–39). This large, severe space forms part of a complex designed by Mexico's greatest Neo-Classical architect, Manuel Tolsa, for use as an orphanage. Orozco's stormy expressionist images clash with the architecture, yet look magnificent within it. Orozco followed the Hospicio Cabañas paintings with a less ambitious cycle for the Gabino Ortiz library at Jiquilpan in the state of Michoacán, and then went back to Mexico City to work in the Supreme Court of Justice and to begin a cycle in the Church of the Hospital of Jesus, where the Conquistador Hernando Cortez is supposedly buried. Work on the latter cycle dragged on from 1942 to 1944, but funds for its completion were somehow never forthcoming. It is ironic that when Orozco was given the National Prize by President Camacho in 1946, it was these unfinished paintings which were especially mentioned in connection with the award.

During the 1940s Orozco was producing easel paintings, drawings and engravings, very often on anti-clerical and anti-military themes, as well as the murals which remained his principal interest. He was given a major retrospective at the Palacio de Bellas Artes in 1947, and had just begun an open-air mural in the Miguel Aleman housing complex in Mexico City when he died suddenly of heart failure on 7 September 1949. His best epitaph is something he wrote himself in 1946:

> Those who say I am an anarchist do not know me. I am a partisan of absolute freedom of thought, a real free thinker; neither a dogmatist nor an anarchist; neither an enemy of hierarchy nor a partisan of unyielding affirmations.

DIEGO RIVERA

If any man can be said to have changed the course of a nation's art single-handed, it is Diego Rivera. He was born in 1886 in the Mexican silver-mining town of Guanajuato. His father, a freemason with a 'liberal' background, was a teacher at the time of Diego's birth and later became a school inspector. Rivera was the elder of twin boys, but his brother died at the age of two. His family left his birthplace when he was six, driven out partly by the failure of certain mining speculations and partly by the unpopularity generated by his father's liberalism.

Rivera soon showed himself to be a precociously gifted artist and began to study in the evenings at the Academy of San Carlos at the age of ten. At sixteen Rivera joined a student strike at the Academy and was expelled. In due course he was officially reinstated, but never returned, instead working independently for the next five years.

Realizing that his son was getting nowhere in his chosen profession, Rivera senior helped Diego win a scholarship, awarded by the Governor of the Province of Veracruz, to study abroad. The young artist arrived in Spain in January 1907. Rivera made Spain his base for an extended tour which took in France, Belgium, Holland and England. He was in France in 1909, where he encountered the work of the Fauves and Cézanne, but he was later to claim that the artist who impressed him most was Henri Rousseau, 'Le Douanier' – 'the only one of the moderns whose works stirred each and every fibre of my being.'

In 1910 he made a trip home, and held a successful exhibition in Mexico City. The wife of the powerful President of Mexico, Porfirio Díaz, bought six of the forty paintings shown, and a number more were purchased by the Academy of Fine Arts. But Díaz, who had been in power for thirty years, was about to fall. Rivera watched the revolution which displaced him and put the liberal

Madero in power, but did not wait for subsequent events; he returned to Paris in 1911.

Rivera now made many friends in the cosmopolitan Parisian avant-garde, and at one time even shared a studio with Modigliani, who painted some striking portraits of him. But his chief contacts were with the Russians, largely because he had two Russian mistresses – this was the beginning of his career as a great womanizer. He was also becoming a legend in his own right, less for his talent than for his gargantuan stature and appetites. The Spanish modernist writer Ramon Gómez de la Serna wrote thus of Rivera:

They told fantastic tales about him; that he had the ability to suckle young at his Buddhic breasts ... that he was all covered with hair, which must have been true because on the wall of his study, by a Russian

DIEGO RIVERA,
Crossing the Barranca, 1930–31,
mural, Palacio de Cortés,
Cuernavaca, Mexico,

woman artist, Marionne [Marievna Vorobiev-Stebelska, one of Rivera's mistresses], who painted in his studio, in a man's suit, with the boots of a tiger-tamer and a lion's skin, was his portrait, nude, with legs crossed and covered in kinky hair.

From 1913 onwards Rivera was working within the orbit of Cubism. There was a particularly clear kinship between the work he was producing – still mostly landscapes – and the work of Robert Delaunay. The winter of 1917 was a time of emotional upheaval. The woman with whom he lived, Angelina Beloff, had a child. The baby was sickly (it died early in 1918), and Rivera, who resented the amount of attention Angelina gave to it, took himself off to her rival, Marievna, for five months. Marievna also became pregnant. Rivera was working like a demon, in isolation from his former friends and full of real or imaginary ills. It was soon after this that he decided to break with Cubism.

In 1919 he set off for Italy with David Alfaro Siqueiros, who had just arrived from Mexico, using money provided by Alberto Pani, the Mexican Ambassador to France. Together they studied the frescoes of the great Italian masters, and discussed the future of Mexican art. The decision to go back to Mexico was made in 1921. The homecoming was an emotional moment. 'On my arrival in Mexico,' Rivera said, 'I was struck by the inexpressible beauty of that rich and severe, wretched and exuberant land.' In November 1921 he accompanied the Minister of Education, José Vasconcelos, on a visit to Yucatán, an area where pre-Columbian influence was very strong. The two men got on well together, and Rivera was the first artist to be appointed when it was decided to experiment with murals at the Preparatoria (National Preparatory School). Rivera's first attempt was painted in encaustic, but he soon mastered traditional fresco technique, and shed stiff European allegories in favour of a new and popular style, where the influence of the Aztecs mingled with that of Cubism and Rousseau. At the same period Rivera joined the Communist Party, with which he was to have a long, complicated and stormy relationship.

Right-wing students rioted against the Preparatoria murals before they were completed, and Rivera was the only artist who stubbornly continued to work there, a pistol stuck in his belt. It was at this time that he attracted the attention of a ring-leader amongst the younger girls, Frida Kahlo. She was later to become his second wife.

Rivera soon proved that he was hugely prolific as well as energetic and determined. In 1923 he began a second series of murals at the Ministry of Education – this enormous cycle was to consist of 124 frescoes. He also embarked on a smaller cycle for the Agricultural School at Chapingo. His work was much criticized at home, but attracted increasing attention abroad. In 1927, when the murals at the Ministry of Education had at last been finished, Rivera was invited to go to Russia, for the tenth anniversary celebrations of the Revolution. He was flatteringly received – in November he signed a contract with the Minister for Culture, Lunacharsky, to paint a mural for the Red Army Club in Moscow. But every now and then Rivera had a moment of discomfort, of which the most acute occurred when he met Stalin:

I will always remember the day I met the undertaker [of the Revolution]. At eight we entered the offices of

DIEGO RIVERA, 1923.
Photo Edward Weston

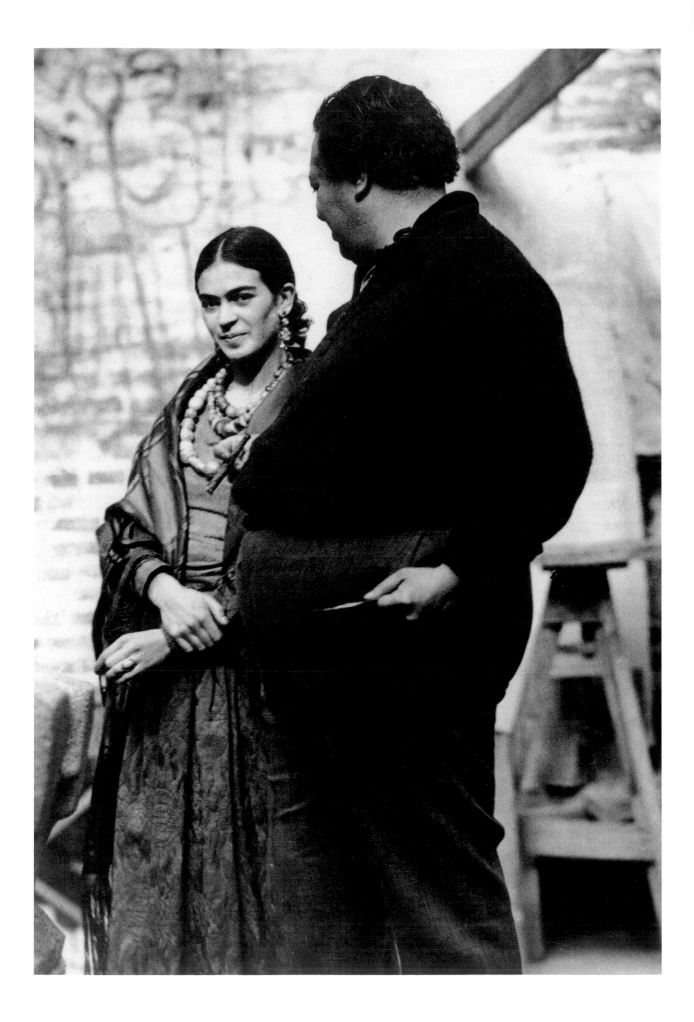

the Central Committee ... my fellow guests smirking with satisfaction, drooling with superiority ... they might have been entering paradise. ... Suddenly a peanut-shaped head, surmounted by a military haircut, decked out with a magnificent pair of long moustaches, rose above them ... one hand slipped into his overcoat and the other folded behind him *à la* Napoleon. ... Comrade Stalin posed before the saints and worshippers.

Rivera's Russian hosts found him rather more of a handful than they had bargained for. He got on badly with the assistants assigned to him, and the much heralded mural project was soon at a standstill. In May 1928 a solution was found to what had become a dilemma: Rivera was ordered home by the Latin American Secretariat of the Comintern as a prelude to his expulsion from the Party in 1929.

The year 1929 witnessed other momentous changes in his life. One reason for his eagerness to go to Russia was that he was tired of the tantrums of his first wife, the beautiful but termagant Guadalupe (Lupe) Marín. On his return home he decided to replace Lupe with his young admirer Frida Kahlo who was to become an important painter in her own right. Since he had gone through a church ceremony with Lupe, but never a civil one, the marriage was fairly easily dissolved, and he and Frida were married that August. In December he accepted a commission from the American Ambassador to Mexico to paint a series of frescoes in the loggia of the sixteenth-century Palace of Cortez in Cuernavaca. The building, splendidly proportioned, set in a superb landscape and full of historic overtones, inspired Rivera to produce some of his most memorable – and now best-loved – images.

In 1930 Rivera was invited to go to the United States, and decided to exploit his new-found fame north of the border, despite a deep-rooted suspicion of *gringos*. In November 1930 he arrived in San Francisco to paint a mural for the Stock Exchange. This was followed by a witty fresco for the California School of Fine Art showing the painter and his team at work: right at the centre of the composition is Rivera's enormous backside. He returned briefly to Mexico, then went to New York in November 1931 for a retrospective exhibition at the Museum of Modern Art. This was the Museum's fourteenth exhibition and only its second one-man show – the first had

been devoted to Matisse. It broke all previous attendance records and made Rivera and his wife into major American celebrities. His next stop was Detroit, where he had been invited to provide murals for the inner courtyard of the Detroit Museum. The reception given to them when they were officially unveiled in March 1933 was stormy, but Rivera and his partisans prevailed. The painter then moved back to New York to carry out a yet more prestigious commission – a mural for the RCA Building, part of the new Rockefeller Center. Rivera, more than ever filled with the spirit of provocation, and euphoric after his recent successes, tried the patience of his patrons too far by featuring a portrait of Lenin in his composition, which was supposed to depict 'Man at the Crossroads Looking with Hope and High Vision to the Choosing of a New and Better Future'. Work was abruptly halted and Rivera was paid in full according to his contract – which prevented him from having any further control over the fate of his work. It was first hidden from public view behind a curtain and then, despite assurances to the contrary, destroyed. The episode provided the biggest scandal of Rivera's career. He lingered for a while in New York, determined not to acknowledge defeat, filling his time painting a set of murals for the New Workers School and two small panels for the headquarters of the New York Trotskyites. Eventually he was forced to creep away with his tail between his legs.

After the New York fiasco Rivera found it difficult to secure commissions for murals, even at home. Between 1935 and 1943 he received no government commissions of any kind. The best he could get – in 1936 – was a mural commission for the new Hotel Reforma in Mexico City, from his old patron, Alberto Pani. But here, too, there was a disagreement, and as a result the murals were altered without the artist's consent. Mexican laws on this subject being different, and stricter, than those which prevailed in the United States, Rivera was able to bring a suit for damages and win it.

Since his expulsion from the official Communist Party Rivera had sided with the Trotskyites, and when Trotsky and his wife arrived in Mexico in January 1937 the Riveras were amongst the first to welcome them. Frida Kahlo, who had already put up with many infidelities on her husband's part, became Trotsky's lover, though the affair was soon over. Another admirer, to whom she did not respond so positively, was the 'pope' of Surrealism, André Breton, who arrived in Mexico in 1938.

Diego Rivera and Frida Kahlo
in San Francisco, *c.* 1930.
Photo Edward Weston

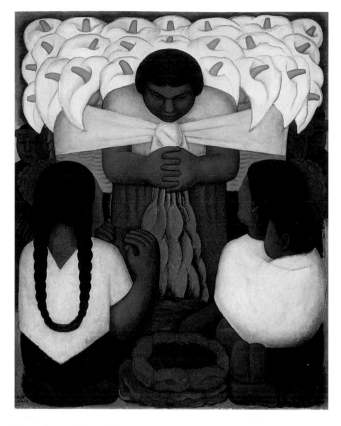

DIEGO RIVERA, *Flower Day*, 1925

The exact cause of Kahlo and Rivera's divorce in 1940 remains mysterious; but their lives were too much intertwined for them to remain apart, and they were soon remarried.

The late 1940s were marked by a series of humiliating attempts on Rivera's part to get back into the Communist party. He had quarrelled with Trotsky before the latter was assassinated, and the Mexican police even at one time suspected him of complicity in the crime. In 1946 Rivera made a major attempt to win the party's forgiveness, denouncing himself as a bad Communist, even saying that the quality of his work had suffered throughout the period of his separation from the Party. He was roundly rejected, and the same thing happened when he tried again a few years later. What counted against him was less his association with Trotsky than the fact that he had once painted an unflattering portrait of Stalin. He eventually grasped this, and when he was asked to provide a major work for the Mexican Exhibition in Paris in 1952 he produced a coarse piece of pro-Stalinist and anti-Western propaganda which contained a suitably

heroic likeness of the Soviet leader. The Mexican government refused to exhibit it, since by implication it insulted the French government, and Rivera was rewarded with a satisfactory uproar in the French press.

In September 1954 he was finally re-accepted by the Communists. But this dubious success came a little late since earlier in the year he had lost Frida. Due to an appalling accident suffered when she was still an adolescent she had been in poor health for many years, and in the last period of her life was in constant pain and often bedridden. Her husband was shattered by the loss. He was not in good health himself, and in 1953 he used his re-acceptance by the Party to go to Russia for medical treatment. On his return he had yet another surprise in store for the Mexican public which avidly continued to follow his activities. Some years previously he had painted a mural for the Del Prado Hotel in Mexico City, one of his most delightful compositions. (This was seriously damaged in the earthquake of 1985.) Called *Dream of a Sunday Afternoon on the Central Alameda*, it is an autobiographical work which shows the artist as a boy, hand in hand with a female skeleton in grand Edwardian costume – a typically gruesome piece of Mexican folklore. They are surrounded by characters from a fantastic *paseo*. The mural was kept covered after its completion because Rivera had included the slogan 'God Does Not Exist'. Now he ceremoniously painted out the offending words, thus announcing his reconciliation with the Church – though the reconciliation somehow did not involve another breach with the Communist Party. With the opposing forces in his life, and in Mexican culture, now neatly in balance, Rivera died in November 1957.

DAVID ALFARO SIQUEIROS,
Portrait of the Bourgeoisie, 1939,
detail of mural at the headquarters
of the Union of Electricians,
Mexico City

DAVID ALFARO SIQUEIROS

Of the great triumvirate of Mexican mural painters, David Alfaro Siqueiros was the youngest. Although he was the least talented, and the least admirable man, in some ways, however, he had the most significant impact on artists outside Mexico.

He was born into a middle-class family in Chihuahua in December 1896. His father was a lawyer and his mother the daughter of a politician and poet. After attending the Preparatoria (National Preparatory School) in Mexico City he entered the Academy of San Carlos, but his studies there were interrupted first by the strike of students in 1910–11 which resulted in the replacement of the Director, and secondly by General Victoriano Huerta's *coup d'état* in 1913 against the liberal regime of President Francisco Madero. This provoked a civil war which lasted for ten years. Like his older contemporary Orozco, Siqueiros moved to Orizaba, capital of the State of Veracruz under the control of the revolutionary forces of General Carranza. Here he was invited by the painter Dr Atl (Gerardo Murillo) to contribute to the paper *La Vanguardia*, the organ of the Carranzist forces. Soon he joined the revolutionary army and in 1914 became a member of the staff of General Manuel D. Dieguez and took part in numerous engagements.

In 1918 Siqueiros was in Guadalajara, where he engaged in passionate discussions with painter friends who had also been members of the Carranzist army. It was at this time that many of the ideas of Mexican muralism were formulated.

Carranza took control of Mexico City in 1917 and was subsequently elected President, but the war did not reach even a temporary halt until 1919, when his one-time ally, Zapata, was lured into an ambush and murdered. In this year Siqueiros was sent to Europe, with the salary of an army captain, to continue his studies as a painter. He visited Spain, France, Belgium and Italy, forming a friendship with Diego Rivera, who had already been resident in Europe for some time, and absorbing ideas from the Italian Futurists. In 1921 he published a single number of the review *Vida Americana* in Barcelona; this contained his 'Manifesto for the Artists of America', which set out his ideas on mural painting.

In 1922 Siqueiros returned to Mexico, where President Obregón was now in power after the flight and assassination of Carranza, the last episode in a revolution which is estimated to have cost over one and a half million lives. Obregón's Minister for Education was José Vasconcelos, and it was he who commissioned the first major Mexican murals, assigning jobs first to Rivera and then to Orozco and Siqueiros. The symbolic site for these was the Preparatoria. For all his theorizing, Siqueiros was

DAVID ALFARO Siqueiros in front of the *Polyforum Siqueiros, c.* 1970. Photo Daniel Frasnay not yet technically well equipped for the task and his mural made slow progress, which aroused Vasconcelos's impatience. Meanwhile, the painter was busy organizing an Artists' Union, the Syndicate of Technical Workers, Painters and Sculptors of Mexico. They issued a resounding manifesto, and Siqueiros and three assistants confronted Vasconcelos with a series of demands. But the Minister brutally refused to have any dealings with the delegation, threatening to spend the money set aside for murals on hiring more primary school teachers.

Siqueiros's mural at the Preparatoria was never finished, as the work was interrupted by student demonstrations and he and Orozco were expelled from the building, leaving only Rivera to continue, a pistol ostentatiously stuck in his belt. Siqueiros went to Guadalajara, to become assistant to another muralist, Amado de la Cueva, who was killed soon afterwards in a motorcycle accident. Siqueiros then abandoned art and devoted himself full-time to trade union organization amongst mineworkers. Eventually he became the Secretary General of the Mexican Federation of Trade Unions. He only returned to painting when he was imprisoned in 1930 for his political activities. His term of imprisonment lasted from May to December, and for a year after this he had to live under police supervision in Taxco. During this period he had long conversations with the Russian film director Sergei Eisenstein, then in the country to make *Que Viva Mexico!* From these exchanges grew his idea that mural painting should have the sweep, movement and multiple perspectives of the cinema.

Siqueiros left for the United States in 1932. He was engaged to give a course in mural painting at the Chouinard School of Art in Los Angeles, and established a group called the Mural Block of Painters. Local building techniques affected his approach: because he found himself painting on a white cement base which dried extremely quickly, he had recourse to the spray gun, a method he had envisaged more than ten years previously. He also began to use projectors as a means of getting the image he wanted on to a wall. After completing two murals in Los Angeles, one at Chouinard and the other at the Plaza Art Center, he left for South America, going first to Uruguay, where he made his first experiments with pyroxylin paints ('Duco') of the kind used in the automobile industry, and then to Argentina. He returned to Mexico in 1934, where he became President of the Militant League Against Fascism and War. Though he

had not as yet completed any major mural project in Mexico, this did not prevent him from engaging in controversy on the subject with Rivera, whose pre-eminence he resented. To the criticisms levelled at him by his rival, Rivera understandably retorted, 'Siqueiros talks; Rivera paints!'

Ever restless, Siqueiros left Mexico again in 1936. He went first to New York, where for a brief period he organized an Experimental Workshop for painters; one of the young artists who worked with him was Jackson Pollock. Siqueiros stressed not only the possibilities offered by industrial paints, but those offered by the 'pictorial accident', and it seems certain that the roots of Pollock's version of Abstract Expressionism were in ideas from the Mexican artist. The Spanish Civil War was now raging, and inevitably it attracted Siqueiros. Late in the year he abandoned the United States in order to join the Republican armies. According to his own account, his military experience during the revolutionary wars in Mexico soon earned him promotion: he rose to the rank of Lieutenant-Colonel and became a Brigade Commander. But this version of his service in Spain has recently been challenged. When the war reached its miserable conclusion, he returned to Mexico. In 1939 he as last completed a mural in his own country, although the site was not a government building: *Portrait of the Bourgeoisie* was created for the headquarters of the Union of Electricians in Mexico City.

In 1940 the most dubious incident of Siqueiros's career took place. Since the 1920s he had been a faithful follower of the political line laid down by Moscow, though his career had also been marked by two official expulsions from the Communist Party – one for indiscipline, and one for failing to carry out his mission as delegate to a conference. The presence of the exiled Trotsky in Mexico was a perpetual offence to Stalin, and now Siqueiros, at the instigation of Soviet secret agents, led a band of twenty armed men disguised in police uniform in an attack on the house where Trotsky lived. The would-be assassins machine-gunned the bedroom where their target and his wife were sleeping but succeeded only in wounding Trotsky's grandson, Seva, in the foot. Retreating, they carried off one of Trotsky's guards, who was later murdered in a mountain cabin and buried in quicklime under a floor. The scandal was considerable and Siqueiros had to flee the country. He did so by obtaining a visa from the Chilean Communist poet Pablo

Neruda, who was then his country's consul in Mexico City. Once Siqueiros was safely in Chile the Mexican attitude towards him became ambiguous; the Mexican Diplomatic Mission actually commissioned a mural from him for the Mexican School in the city of Chillán.

Siqueiros lived in Chile for a while, then resumed his restless travels and returned to Mexico in 1944. The following year he received a sign of official forgiveness: he was invited to paint a mural in the Palace of Fine Arts in Mexico City, which was already adorned with paintings by Rivera and Orozco. In 1950 he was allotted another wall in the same building, and was also chosen as the Mexican representative at the Venice Biennale. He won second prize for non-Italian artists – the first prize went to Matisse. In 1952 he undertook another major mural project, at the Hospital de la Raza in the northern area of Mexico City. The mural, *The Victory of Science Over Cancer*, is painted on an immense curved wall, and shows Siqueiros's characteristically sweeping treatment of space. Further travels followed in 1955 and 1956. In 1959–60 he was in Cuba for the celebrations marking the first anniversary of Castro's revolution and then went to Venezuela, where he made a speech bitterly attacking the Government of Mexico a few days before the Mexican President was due to make an official visit. This was less easily forgiven than his involvement in the Trotsky affair twenty years previously. He was arrested on his return home and, after a hunger strike in gaol in 1961 in which he was joined by other political prisoners, he was finally brought to trial in 1962 and condemned to eight years' imprisonment. The sentence was commuted in 1964 and he was released to resume work on a set of murals in the Natural History Museum in Mexico City. Despite a spinal injury he suffered in a fall from scaffolding shortly after his release he continued to paint with undiminished vigour for the rest of the decade. His most ambitious work is the immense and vulgar *March of Humanity in Latin America*, begun in 1963 and completed in 1969.

In his final years Siqueiros was showered with honours of all kinds. He was awarded the Lenin Peace Prize in 1967, and on the creation of the Mexican Academy of Arts in 1968 was named its first President. He died at Cuernavaca in 1974.

FRIDA KAHLO,
Las dos Fridas
(The Two Fridas), 1939

FRIDA KAHLO

In 1953, when Frida Kahlo had her first solo exhibition in Mexico (the only one held in her native country during her lifetime), a local critic wrote: 'It is impossible to separate the life and work of this extraordinary person. Her paintings are her biography.' This observation serves to explain both why her work is so different from that of her contemporaries, the Mexican Muralists, and why she has since become a feminist icon.

Kahlo was born in Mexico City in 1910, the third daughter of Guillermo and Matilda Kahlo. Her father was a photographer of Hungarian Jewish descent, who had been born in Germany; her mother was Spanish and Native American. Her life was to be a long series of physical traumas, and the first of these came early. At the age of six she was stricken with polio, which left her with a limp. In childhood, she was nevertheless a fearless tomboy, and this made Frida her father's favourite. He had advanced ideas about her education, and in 1922 she entered the Preparatoria (National Preparatory School), the most prestigious educational institution in Mexico, which had only just begun to admit girls. She was one of only thirty-five girls out of two thousand students.

It was there that she met her husband-to-be, Diego Rivera, who had recently returned home from France,

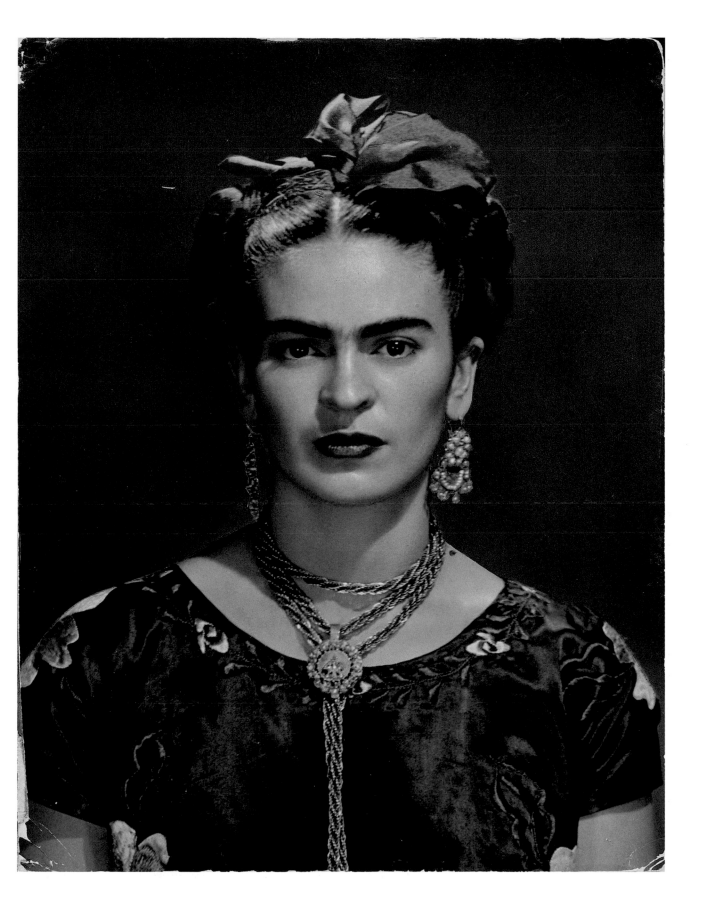

Frida Kahlo, *c.* 1939. Photo Nickolas Muray

and who had been commissioned to paint a mural there. Kahlo was attracted to him, and not knowing quite how to deal with the emotions she felt, expressed them by teasing him, playing practical jokes, and by trying to excite the jealousy of the painter's wife, Lupe Marín.

In 1925, Kahlo suffered the serious accident which was to set the pattern for much of the rest of her life. She was travelling in a bus which collided with a tramcar, and suffered serious injuries to her right leg and pelvis. The accident made it impossible for her to have children, though it was to be many years before she accepted this. It also meant that she faced a life-long battle against pain. In 1926, during her convalescence, she painted her first self-portrait, the beginning of a long series in which she charted the events of her life and her emotional reactions to them.

She met Rivera again in 1928, through her friendship with the photographer and revolutionary Tina Modotti. Rivera's marriage had just disintegrated, and the two found that they had much in common, not least from a political point of view, since both were now communist militants. They married in August 1929. Kahlo was later to say: 'I suffered two grave accidents in my life. One in which a streetcar knocked me down... The other accident is Diego.'

The political climate in Mexico was deteriorating for those with left-wing sympathies, thanks to the reactionary Calles government, and the mural-painting programme initiated by the great Minister of Education José Vasconcelos had ground to a halt. But Rivera's artistic reputation was expanding rapidly in the United States. In 1930, the couple left for San Francisco; then, after a brief return to Mexico, they went to New York in 1931 for the Rivera retrospective organized by the Museum of Modern Art. Kahlo, at this stage, was regarded chiefly as a charming appendage to a famous husband, but the situation was soon to change. In 1932 Rivera was commissioned to paint a major series of murals for the Detroit Museum, and here Kahlo suffered a miscarriage. While recovering, she painted *Miscarriage in Detroit*, the first of her truly penetrating self-portraits. The style she evolved was entirely unlike that of her husband, being based on Mexican folk art and in particular on the small votive pictures known as *retablos*, which the pious dedicated in Mexican churches. Rivera's reaction to his wife's work was, however, both perceptive and generous:

Frida began work on a series of masterpieces which had no precedent in the history of art – paintings which exalted the feminine quality of truth, reality, cruelty and suffering. Never before had a woman put such agonized poetry on canvas as Frida did at this time in Detroit.

Kahlo, however, pretended not to consider her work important. As her biographer Hayden Herrera notes, 'she preferred to be seen as a beguiling personality rather than as a painter.'

From Detroit they went once again to New York, where Rivera had been commissioned to paint a mural in the Rockefeller Center. The commission erupted into an enormous scandal, when the patron ordered the half-completed work destroyed because of the political imagery Rivera insisted on including. But Rivera lingered in the United States, which he loved and Kahlo now loathed.

When they finally returned to Mexico in 1935, Rivera embarked on an affair with Kahlo's younger sister Cristina. Though they finally made up their quarrel, this incident marked a turning point in their relationship. Rivera had never been faithful to any woman; Kahlo now embarked on a series of affairs with both men and women which were to continue for the rest of her life. Rivera tolerated her lesbian relationships better than he did the heterosexual ones, which made him violently jealous. One of Kahlo's more serious early love affairs was with the Russian revolutionary leader Leon Trotsky, now being hounded by his triumphant rival Stalin, and who had been offered refuge in Mexico in 1937 on Rivera's initiative.

Another visitor to Mexico at this time, one who would gladly have had a love affair with Kahlo but for the fact that she was not attracted to him, was the leading figure of the Surrealist Group, André Breton. Breton arrived in 1938 and was enchanted with Mexico, which he found to be a 'naturally surrealist' country, and with Kahlo's painting. Partly through his initiative, she was offered a show at the fashionable Julian Levy Gallery in New York later in 1938, and Breton himself wrote a rhetorical catalogue preface. The show was a triumph, and about half the paintings were sold. In 1939, Breton suggested a show in Paris, and offered to arrange it. Kahlo, who spoke no French, arrived in France to find that Breton had not even bothered to get her work out of customs.

The enterprise was finally rescued by Marcel Duchamp, and the show opened about six weeks late. It was not a financial success, but the reviews were good, and the Louvre bought a picture for the Jeu de Paume. Kahlo also won praise from Kandinsky and Picasso. She had, however, conceived a violent dislike for what she called 'this bunch of coocoo lunatic sons of bitches of surrealists.'

She did not renounce Surrealism immediately. In January 1940, for example, she was a participant (with Rivera) in the International Exhibition of Surrealism held in Mexico City. Later, she was to be vehement in her denials that she had ever been a true Surrealist. 'They thought I was a Surrealist,' she said, 'but I wasn't. I never painted dreams. I painted my own reality.'

Early in 1940, for motives which are still somewhat mysterious, Kahlo and Rivera divorced, though they continued to make public appearances together. In May, after the first attempt on Trotsky's life, led by the painter Siqueiros, Rivera thought it prudent to leave for San Francisco. After the second, and successful attempt, Kahlo, who had been a friend of Trotsky's assassin, was questioned by the police. She decided to leave Mexico for a while, and in September she joined her ex-husband. Less than two months later, while they were still in the United States, they remarried. One reason seems to have been Rivera's recognition that Kahlo's health would inexorably deteriorate, and that she needed someone to look after her.

Her health, never at any time robust, grew visibly worse from about 1944 onwards, and Kahlo underwent the first many operations on her spine and her crippled foot. Authorities on her life and work have questioned whether all these operations were really necessary, or whether they were in fact a way of holding Rivera's attention in the face of his numerous affairs with other women. In Kahlo's case, her physical and psychological sufferings were always linked. In early 1950, her physical state reached a crisis, and she had to go into hospital in Mexico City, where she remained for a year.

During the period after her remarriage, her artistic reputation continued to grow, though at first more rapidly in the United States than in Mexico itself: she was included in prestigious group shows in the Museum of Modern Art, the Boston Institute of Contemporary Arts and the Philadelphia Museum of Art. In 1946, however, she received a Mexican government fellowship, and in the same year an official prize on the occasion of the Annual National Exhibition. She also took up teaching at the new experimental art school 'La Esmeralda', and, despite her unconventional methods, proved an inspiration to her students.

After her return home from hospital, Kahlo became an increasingly fervent and impassioned Communist. Rivera had been expelled from the Party, which was reluctant to receive him back, both because of his links with the Mexican government of the day, and because of his association with Trotsky. Kahlo boasted: 'I was a member of the Party before I met Diego and I think I am a better Communist than he is or ever will be.'

While the 1940s had seen her produce some of her finest work, her paintings now became more clumsy and chaotic, thanks to the joint effects of pain, drugs and drink. Despite this, in 1953 she was offered her first solo show in Mexico itself – which was to be the only such show held in her own lifetime. It took place at the fashionable Galería de Arte Contemporaneo in the Zona Rosa of Mexico City. At first it seemed that Kahlo would be too ill to attend, but she sent her richly decorated four-poster bed ahead of her, arrived by ambulance, and was carried into the gallery on a stretcher. The private view was a triumphal occasion.

In the same year, Kahlo, threatened by gangrene, had her right leg amputated below the knee. It was a tremendous blow to someone who had invested so much in the elaboration of her own self image. She learned to walk again with an artificial limb, and even (briefly and with the help of pain-killing drugs) danced at celebrations with friends. But the end was close. In July 1954, she made her last public appearance, when she participated in a Communist demonstration against the overthrow of the left-wing Guatemalan president Jacobo Arbenz. Soon afterwards, she died in her sleep, apparently as the result of an embolism, though there was a suspicion among those close to her that she had found a way to commit suicide. Her last diary entry read: 'I hope the end is joyful – and I hope never to come back – Frida.'

Between the two World Wars America was the scene of a lively conflict of styles. Artistic attitudes covered a wide spectrum: there was the American Nationalism of Thomas Hart Benton and other Regionalists, who wanted to express what they felt to be the true nature of their country; though politically conservative, Benton has a good deal in common with the Mexican muralists, especially Diego Rivera. There was the sober Realism of Edward Hopper; and the Precisionism, influenced by photography and often veering towards abstraction, of Georgia O'Keeffe. There was also a great deal of abstract and semi-abstract painting which depended on established European styles. The most distinguished exponent of this tendency was the American Cubist Stuart Davis, who on some occasions seems to anticipate Pop Art.

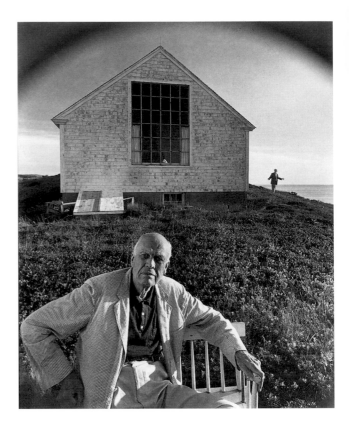

Above: Edward and Jo Hopper in South Truro, Massachusetts, 1960. Photo © Arnold Newman
Opposite top: EDWARD HOPPER, *House by the Railroad*, 1925
Opposite bottom: EDWARD HOPPER, *Nighthawks*, 1942

EDWARD HOPPER

Edward Hopper, the best-known American realist of the inter-war period, once said: 'The man's the work. Something doesn't come out of nothing.' This offers a clue to interpreting the work of an artist who was not only intensely private, but who made solitude and introspection important themes in his painting.

He was born in the small Hudson River town of Nyack, New York State, on 22 July 1882. His family were solidly middle-class: his father owned a dry goods store where the young Hopper sometimes worked after school. By 1899 he had already decided to become an artist, but his parents persuaded him to begin by studying commercial illustration because this seemed to offer a more secure future. He first attended the New York School of Illustrating (more obscure than its title suggests), then in 1900 transferred to the New York School of Art. Here the leading figure and chief instructor was William Merritt Chase (1849–1916), an

elegant imitator of Sargent. He also worked under Robert Henri (1869–1929), one of the fathers of American Realism – a man whom he later described as 'the most influential teacher I had', adding 'men didn't get much from Chase; there were mostly women in the class.'

Hopper was a slow developer – he remained at the School of Art for seven years, latterly undertaking some teaching work himself. However, like the majority of the young American artists of the time, he longed to study in France. With his parents' help he finally left for Paris in October 1906. This was an exciting moment in the history of the Modern movement, but Hopper was to claim that its effect on him was minimal:

Whom did I meet? Nobody. I'd heard of Gertrude Stein, but I don't remember having heard of Picasso at all. I used to go to the cafés at night and sit and watch. I went to the theatre a little. Paris had no great or immediate impact on me.

In addition to spending some months in Paris, he visited London, Amsterdam, Berlin and Brussels. The picture that seems to have impressed him most was Rembrandt's *The Night Watch* (in the Rijksmuseum, Amsterdam).

Hopper was able to repeat his trip to Europe in 1909 and 1910. On the second occasion he visited Spain as well as France. After this, though he was to remain a restless traveller, he never set foot in Europe again. Yet its influence was to remain with him for a long time: he was well read in French literature, and could quote Verlaine in the original, as his future wife discovered (he was surprised when she finished the quotation for him). He said later: '[America] seemed awfully crude and raw when I got back. It took me ten years to get over Europe.' For some time his painting was full of reminiscences of what he had seen abroad. This tendency culminates in *Soir Bleu* of 1914, a recollection of the Mi-Carême carnival in Paris, and one of the largest pictures Hopper ever painted. It failed to attract any attention when he showed it in a mixed exhibition in the following year, and it was this failure which threw him back to working on the American subjects with which his reputation is now associated.

In 1913 Hopper made his first sale – a picture exhibited at the Armory Show in New York which brought together American artists and all the leading European modernists. In 1920 he had his first solo exhibition, at the Whitney Studio Club, but on this occasion none of the paintings sold. He was already thirty-seven and beginning to doubt if he would achieve any success as an artist – he was still forced to earn a living as a commercial illustrator. One way round this dilemma was to make prints, for which at that time there was a rising new market. These sold more readily than his paintings, and Hopper then moved to making watercolours, which sold more readily still.

Hopper had settled in Greenwich Village, which was to be his base for the rest of his life, and in 1923 he renewed his friendship with a neighbour, Jo Nivison, whom he had known when they were fellow students under Chase and Henri. She was now forty; Hopper was forty-two. In the following year they married. Their long and complex relationship was to be the most important of the artist's life. Fiercely loyal to her husband, Jo felt in many respects oppressed by him. In particular, she felt that he did nothing to encourage her own development as a painter, but on the contrary did everything to frustrate it. 'Ed,' she confided to her diary, 'is the very centre of my universe… If I'm on the point of being very happy, he sees to it that I'm not.' The couple often quarrelled fiercely (an early subject of contention was Jo's devotion to her cat Arthur, whom Hopper regarded as a rival for her attention). Sometimes their rows exploded into physical violence, and on one occasion, just before a trip to Mexico, Jo bit Hopper's hand to the bone. On the other hand, her presence was essential to his work, sometimes literally so, since she now modelled for all the female figures in his paintings, and was adept at enacting the various roles he required.

From the time of his marriage, Hopper's professional fortunes changed. His second solo show, at the Rehn Gallery in New York in 1924, was a sell-out. The following year, he painted what is now generally acknowledged to be his first fully mature picture, *The House by the Railroad*. With its deliberate, disciplined spareness, this is typical of what he was to create thereafter. His paintings combine apparently incompatible qualities. Modern in their bleakness and simplicity, they are also full of nostalgia for the puritan virtues of the American past – the kind of quirky nineteenth-century architecture Hopper liked to paint, for instance, could not have been more out of fashion than it was in the mid-1920s, when he first began to look at it seriously. Though his compositions are supposedly realist they also make frequent use of covert symbolism. Hopper's paintings have, in this respect, been rather aptly compared to the realist plays of Ibsen, a writer whom he admired.

One of the themes of *The House by the Railroad* is the loneliness of travel, and the Hoppers now began to travel widely within the United States, as well as going on trips to Mexico. Their mobility was made possible by the fact that they were now sufficiently prosperous to buy a car. This became another subject of contention between the artist and his wife, since Hopper, not a good driver himself, resisted Jo's wish to learn to drive too. She did not acquire a driving licence until 1936, and even then her husband was extremely reluctant to allow her control of their automobile.

By this time Hopper, whose career, once it took off, was surprisingly little affected by the Depression, had become extremely well known. In 1929, he was included in the Museum of Modern Art's second exhibition, *Paintings by Nineteen Living Americans*, and in 1930 *The House by the Railroad* entered the museum's permanent collection, as a gift from the millionaire collector Stephen Clark. In the same year, the Whitney Museum bought Hopper's *Early Sunday Morning*, its most expensive purchase up to that time. In 1933 Hopper was given a retrospective exhibition at the Museum of Modern Art. This was followed, in 1950, by a fuller retrospective show at the Whitney.

Hopper became a pictorial poet who recorded the starkness and vastness of America. Sometimes he expressed aspects of this in traditional guise, as, for example, in his pictures of lighthouses and harsh New England landscapes; sometimes New York was his context, with eloquent cityscapes, often showing deserted streets at night. Some paintings, such as his celebrated image of a gas-station, *Gas* (1940), even have elements which anticipate Pop Art. Hopper once said: 'To me the most important thing is the sense of going on. You know how beautiful things are when you're travelling.'

He painted hotels, motels, trains and highways, and also liked to paint the public and semi-public places where people gathered: restaurants, theatres, cinemas and offices. But even in these paintings he stressed the theme of loneliness – his theatres are often semi-deserted, with a few patrons waiting for the curtain to go up or the performers isolated in the fierce light of the stage. Hopper was a frequent movie-goer, and there is often a cinematic quality in his work. As the years went on, however, he found suitable subjects increasingly difficult to discover, and often felt blocked and unable to paint. His contemporary the painter Charles Burchfield wrote: 'With Hopper the whole fabric of his art seems to be interwoven with his personal character and manner of living.' When the link between the outer world he observed and the inner world of feeling and fantasy broke, Hopper found he was unable to create.

In particular, the rise of Abstract Expressionism left him marooned artistically, for he disapproved of many aspects of the new art. He died in 1967, isolated if not forgotten, and Jo Hopper died ten months later. His true importance has only been fully realized in the years since his death.

GEORGIA O'KEEFFE

Georgia O'Keeffe was the most distinguished American female artist of the twentieth century. She was born in November 1887 near Sun Prairie, Wisconsin, the second of seven children. Her father was a farmer. According to

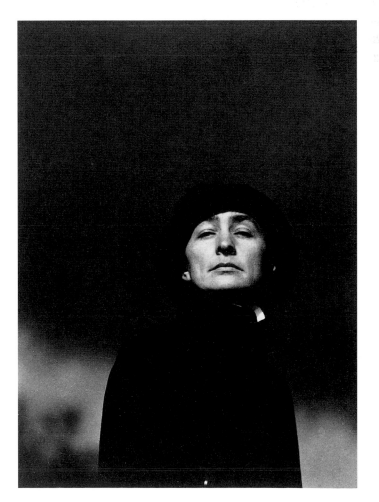

GEORGIA O'KEEFFE, 1927.
Photo Alfred Stieglitz

GEORGIA O'KEEFFE with *Pelvis, Red and Yellow, c.* 1960. Photo Michael Vaccaro

her own account, she decided to become an artist at the age of ten. For the next two years she had weekly drawing lessons, and these continued when she was sent to a convent boarding school run by Dominican nuns. In 1902 her family moved to Virginia, but at first she continued to look to the Middle West for her artistic education. She attended the Art Institute of Chicago in 1905–6, but her training was interrupted when she contracted typhoid fever. In 1907–8 she attended the Art Students' League in New York, where one of her tutors was William Merritt Chase. She saw Rodin's first US exhibition and an Henri Matisse exhibition at 291, Alfred Stieglitz's gallery in New York in 1908. She won the Chase Still Life Prize which enabled her to spend part of the summer of 1908 at the League Outdoor School at Lake George

in New York State, a place with which she was later to have a long association.

In 1908 she decided to abandon her ambitions to be a painter, and returned to Chicago where she worked as a commercial artist, drawing lace and embroidery for advertisements; she was forced to give up this work when her eyesight was affected by an attack of measles. Meanwhile the illness of her mother had led the family to move to Charlottesville, Virginia. In the summer of 1912 O'Keeffe visited an art class at the University of Virginia, which led to a renewal of her interest in art. In the autumn she took a job as Supervisor of Art in Public Schools at Amarillo, Texas – she had always felt a romantic attraction to the American West, and later declared: 'there was no place I would rather go'. She kept this job for two years, also teaching during the summers

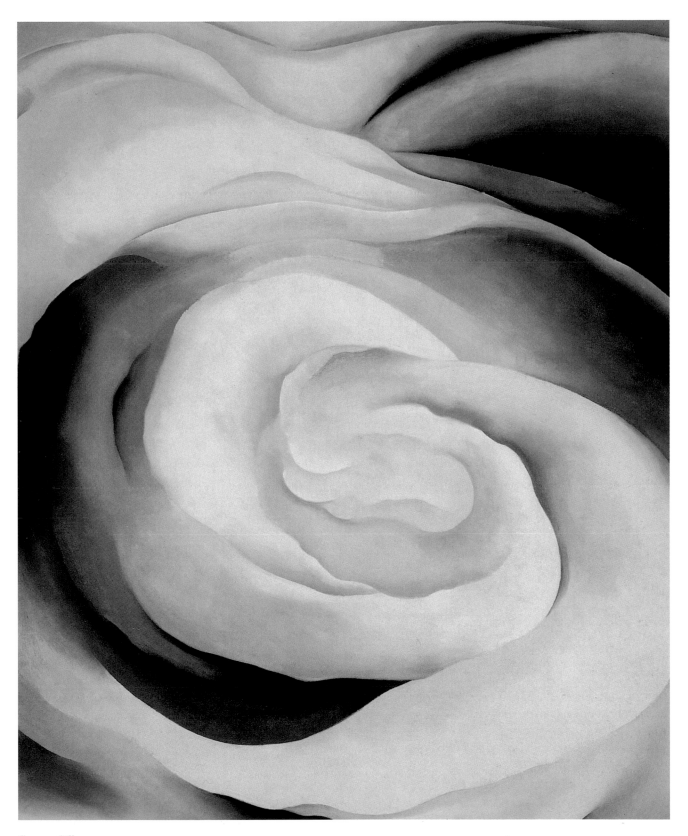

GEORGIA O'KEEFFE,
Abstraction, White Rose II,
1927

at the University of Virginia Art Department. In 1914 she went to New York to study at Teachers' College, Columbia University.

In the autumn of 1915 she accepted another teaching job, this time at Columbia College, South Carolina. It was at this moment that she reached a turning point: 'It was in the fall of 1915 that I first had the idea that what I had been taught was of little value to me except for the use of my materials as a language.'

She reviewed her existing work and decided to begin again, using only the simplest means. At first, in this period of exploration, she made only black and white drawings in charcoal:

This was one of the best times of my life. There was no one around to look at what I was doing – no one interested – no one to say anything about it one way or another. I was alone and singularly free, working into my own unknown – no one to satisfy except myself.

Eventually she bundled the drawings up and sent them to a girlfriend in New York, with strict instructions that they were not to be shown to anyone else. The friend disobeyed her, and took the sheets to the photographer-dealer Alfred Stieglitz at 291. Stieglitz was impressed, and kept them. In April 1916, still without O'Keeffe's knowledge, he hung them as part of a three-person show. As it happened, O'Keeffe was back in New York, and hearing of the matter, went to the gallery to make Stieglitz take them down. She failed; the result was the tentative beginning of a long relationship. In the autumn of 1916 she took another teaching post in Texas, this time as Head of the Art Department at West Texas State Normal School at Canyon. In May 1917 Stieglitz mounted a solo show for her, his last at 291, and O'Keeffe went to New York to see it. It had already been taken down, but Stieglitz rehung it so that she could judge the effect. At the same time he took the first of a long series of photographs of her. She returned to Texas for the rest of the summer, and visited New Mexico, with which she was later to become closely associated, on her way to Colorado.

In 1918 illness forced her to take leave of absence from teaching. Stieglitz then offered her a subsidy to enable her to take a whole year and do nothing but paint. She accepted, and resigned her post. For the next decade she was to divide her time between New York and Lake George, with occasional visits to Maine, and Stieglitz was to be her mentor, as well as her dealer. In 1919 she made what she considered to be her first fully mature oils – they were mostly abstracts, though she was never to abandon figurative painting altogether. 'Objective painting,' she once said, 'is not good painting unless it is good in the abstract sense.' In 1923 Stieglitz mounted a major show of one hundred of her paintings at the Anderson Galleries, and in the same year they married. It is clear that he was now having an aesthetic as well as a purely practical influence on what she did: in 1924 she made her first paintings of greatly enlarged flowers, and in 1926 her first of soaring skyscrapers, both of which series owe more than a little to the way the camera sees.

O'Keeffe was fortunate in never having to struggle once Stieglitz took charge of her affairs – unlike most Modernist painters she was favourably reviewed from the very first. The annual commercial exhibitions he arranged for her spanned a long period – from 1926 to 1946 – so her work was constantly in the consciousness of the gallery-going public. In 1927 her first retrospective was held, at the Brooklyn Museum. In 1929 she paid a planned visit to New Mexico, staying at Taos with Mabel Dodge Luhan, and living in a house recently vacated by D. H. Lawrence. She fell in love with the landscape, and from now on she summered in New Mexico and divided the rest of the year between New York and Lake George. In 1934 she spent her first summer at the remote Ghost Ranch, north of Abiquiu. She returned in 1935 and eventually bought the property in 1940. At the same time she began to venture rather tentatively abroad – in 1932 she went to the Gaspé country in Canada to paint the landscape and the stark farm buildings; in 1934 she went to Bermuda and in 1939 to Hawaii. Stieglitz's death in 1946 brought with it other major changes in the pattern of her life. In 1945 she had bought a house in Abiquiu itself, so that she could spend winters as well as summers in New Mexico – the ranch was too remote for severe winter weather. She now devoted three years' work to settling her husband's estate and setting up memorials to him, and then retired permanently to New Mexico.

In the 1950s O'Keeffe's output of paintings was relatively small, as she began to travel abroad for the first time. Her first visit to Europe was not until 1953, but during the 1950s and early 1960s she became a tireless traveller, visiting most parts of the world, and making a complete round-the-world trip in 1959. O'Keeffe received all the usual honours given to an American artist of her eminence, among them election to the American Academy of Arts and Letters in 1963, and to the American Academy of Arts and Sciences in 1966. In 1973, O'Keeffe was befriended by a talented potter, Juan Hamilton. Despite the difference in their ages (when they met, he was twenty-eight and she was eighty-six), he became her confidant and constant companion, to the point where he was accused of keeping old friends at arms' length and exerting undue influence over her. Hamilton managed her affairs and, as her eyesight deteriorated, attempted to teach her pottery skills. In 1984 O'Keeffe went to live with Hamilton and his family in Santa Fe, where she died in 1986.

THOMAS HART BENTON

Thomas Hart Benton was the leader of the so-called 'American Scene' painters, and represents the reaction against Modernism and the emphasis on national values which were conspicuous in American art during the 1930s.

He was born in Neosho, Missouri, in 1889, into a prominent political family. His great-uncle, after whom he was named, had been a United States senator; his father, who fought in the Confederate army during the American Civil War, was a member of the House of Representatives from 1897 to 1905. Benton spent much of his childhood in the lively atmosphere of camp meetings, rallies and barbecues, and heard many tales of the Confederacy and the old frontier from relatives and family friends.

His training as an artist began at the Corcoran School of Art when his father was in Washington, D.C., and continued at the Art Institute of Chicago. In 1908 he left for Paris, where he enrolled at the Académie Julian. In Paris he became at least partly aware of the immense changes which were taking place in French art, but was attracted chiefly to Neo-Impressionism, then slightly out of date.

When Benton returned to America he worked as a commercial artist and then, in 1914, as a set designer for the new motion-picture industry, which had not yet moved to Hollywood. At the same time he became involved with the Synchronist Movement, the earliest group of purely American Abstractionists. One of the founders of the group was Stanton Macdonald-Wright (1890–1973), a close friend of Benton's in Paris. But Benton never made a very convincing abstract painter.

Around this time he became involved with left-wing politics and at one point, in the 1920s, by his own account conspired 'to provide secret meeting-places for the Communist Party, one of which was my own apartment in New York.'

Benton's break with Modernism was first precipitated by his enlistment into the American navy at the end of the First World War. He worked as an architectural draughtsman at the Norfolk Navy Base:

My interests became, in a flash, of an objective nature. The mechanical contrivances of building, the new

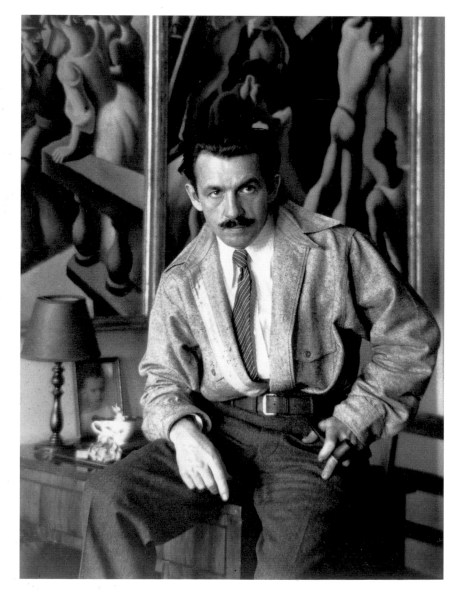

Left: THOMAS HART BENTON,
late 1920s. Photographer unknown
Above and right (detail):
THOMAS HART BENTON,
Independence and the Opening of the West,
1959–62, mural at Harry S. Truman
Library, Independence, Missouri

airplanes, the blimps, the dredges, the ships of the base, because they were so interesting in themselves, tore me away from all my grooved habits, from my play with colored cubes and classic attenuations, from my aesthetic drivelings and morbid self-concerns. I left for good the art-for-art's-sake world in which I had hitherto lived.

The break in fact took place more gradually than this reminiscence from the 1930s suggests, though Benton did indeed begin to concentrate on specifically American subject-matter. He conceived the idea of depicting the whole history of America in a series of murals. Despite the fact that *The American Historical Epic*, as he called it, was never completed, the project paved the way for his subsequent activity as a muralist. His desire to give expression in painting to his feelings about America was reinforced by his father's last illness and death in 1924:

I cannot honestly say what happened to me while I watched my father die and listened to the voices of his friends, but I know that when, after his death, I went back East I was moved by a great desire to know more of the America which I had glimpsed in the suggestive words of his old cronies ... I was moved by a desire to pick up again the threads of my childhood.

At about this time he began to loosen his connections with left-wing politics, though he did not finally break from the Left until about 1930. This was when he achieved sudden prominence as a painter, through a series of controversial mural commissions. The first two were for buildings in New York, the New School for Social Research and the Whitney Museum of American Art. In both cases the theme was contemporary – the mural at the New School was entitled *Contemporary American Life*, that at the Whitney *The Arts of Life in America* – and both enabled Benton to make vigorous, confident statements about the nature of his country. The New School murals have an especially immediate effect: they are designed like the pictorial section of a newspaper of the time, with the figures bursting out of interlocking compartments.

In 1932 Benton was offered an opportunity in the Middle West: he was asked to paint *The Social History of the State of Indiana* for the approaching Chicago Exposition. He toured the state, researched its history,

undertook many interviews and completed twenty-two panels measuring a total of 45,000 square feet – all within six months.

Benton's mural commissions, and the strong opinions which he did not hesitate to express in public, embroiled him with two powerful factions in the New York art world. One consisted of the urban Social Realists, with whom he had broken politically, the other of the followers of the School of Paris, with whom he had broken aesthetically. In spite of the fact that he had once been on friendly terms with him he described Alfred Stieglitz and the artists associated with him as 'an intellectually diseased lot, victims of sickly rationalizations, psychic inversions and godawful self cultivations'.

His pugnacious statements now caused Benton to be baited and heckled at public meetings, rejected by students and ostracized by many of his old friends. He was therefore ready for a change, and when, in 1934, he was invited to paint a series of murals for the Missouri State Capitol in Jefferson City and at the same time to become the Director of the Kansas City Art Institute, he accepted gratefully. He shook the dust of New York from his feet and departed to live permanently in the Middle West. From this new base he continued his outspoken attacks on all the things he disliked – among them museums and their curatorial staff. His American patriotism became even more extreme. His reaction to Pearl Harbor was to return home immediately from a speaking tour in order to create ten large paintings designed to rouse Middle Westerners to the perils now facing them. He said that he wanted to awaken 'the kind of hard ferocity that man must have to beat down the evil that is now upon us.' Nevertheless, with the coming of the war the world was changing rapidly, and Benton found that he had lost his confident grip on American reality. Critical taste increasingly rejected him and after the war he became a symbol of provincialism and jingoism. Jackson Pollock, who had been his pupil, said: 'My work with Benton was important as something against which to react very strongly, later on.'

Benton retreated. Instead of depicting the present, he became a historical painter, in a style which lacked his old turbulent energy. He nevertheless continued to receive important commissions, including one for a mural entitled *Independence and the Opening of the West* for the Harry S. Truman Memorial Library, in Neosho, where he had been born. Thomas Hart Benton died in 1975.

STUART DAVIS

Stuart Davis is the link between the American art world of the 1930s, in many respects still isolated and provincial, and the triumphant internationalism of the post-war epoch. He is also the most distinguished American Cubist, who gives the style a peculiarly personal twist.

Davis was born in Philadelphia in 1894. His mother was a sculptor and his father, the art director of the *Philadelphia Press*, was friendly with the artist Robert Henri and his circle who worked for the paper as illustrators. In 1901 Davis moved with his family to East Orange, New Jersey: his father was now both editor and cartoonist of the *Newark Evening News*. His family expressed no opposition to Davis's wish to become an artist, and in 1909 he went to New York to study with Henri at the Henri School. The curriculum was unusually progressive, and the young man wrote enthusiastically to a cousin:

> Henri's is different than any other school in the world, and if he should stop I would never go to any other

teacher because the rest of them don't know what *real* drawing is, an' that's straight.

Henri had recently become the leader of 'The Eight', a group of Popular Realists in revolt against the academicism of the National Academy of Design. The precociously talented Davis soon mastered their manner, and in 1910 showed an astonishingly mature painting in one of their exhibitions.

In 1912 Davis left the Henri School, and with a friend set up his own studio in the Terminal Building in Hudson Street, Hoboken, just across the river from New York. He had five watercolours chosen for the Armory Show in 1913. For Davis, as for many other Americans, this provided the first opportunity to see the full panorama of avant-garde art. He reported later:

> I was enormously excited by the show and responded particularly to Gauguin, Van Gogh and Matisse because broad stylization of form and the non-imitative use of colour were already practices within my experience. I also sensed an objective order in these works that I felt was lacking in my own ... I resolved that I would quite definitely have to become a 'modern' artist.

In 1913 he joined the staff of the radical periodical *The Masses*, working under John Sloan, one of Henri's associates and followers, and formerly one of his father's employees on the *Philadelphia Press*. He also began to work for *Harper's Weekly*. At this stage he was still using the style he had acquired from The Eight, who had now broadened their base to become the Ash-Can School. His style only started to change radically in 1915–16, and the change coincided with his discovery of the port of Gloucester, Massachusetts, where he was to spend the summer almost every year until the mid-1930s. Among the attractions of the place were the brilliant light and 'the important additions of topographical severity and the architectural beauties of the Gloucester schooner'.

When he first arrived in Gloucester Davis used to carry around a mass of equipment on his back, but at length he learned to restrict himself to a sketchbook and a fountain pen.

> It seems that in all this tramping round with full equipment I had actually learned something. All that

STUART DAVIS in front of
Summer Landscape, 1930.
Photographer unknown

was required to cash in on some of this information was to stop lifting things up and putting them down ... I have scrupulously followed this discipline ever since.

He was beginning to develop away from the circle which had originally nurtured him. In 1916 he resigned from *The Masses* because an editorial group headed by Max Eastman, Art Young and John Reed tried to insist that his work, and that of the other artists connected with the magazine, should correspond more closely with its ideals, as narrowly defined by themselves. He was also showing steady professional progress. In 1917 he held his first one-man exhibition of watercolours and drawings, at the Sheridan Square Gallery in New York.

The war only briefly interrupted his career. In 1918 he spent a period making maps for U.S. Army Intelligence. He was working steadily towards a new and different style; by 1921 his painting showed a sophisticated understanding of Synthetic Cubism, the more impressive because he had not yet visited Paris. In 1925 he had another one-man exhibition, this time including paintings, at the Newark Museum, and in 1926

he was included in the International Exhibition of Modern Art arranged by the Société Anonyme at the Brooklyn Museum, and in addition was given a retrospective at the Whitney Studio Club, the predecessor of the Whitney Museum.

Despite these external signs of success, Davis was not satisfied. He decided to subject himself to drastic discipline:

One day I set up an eggbeater in my studio and got so interested in it that I nailed it on the table and kept it there to paint. I called the pictures *Eggbeater*, number such and such, because it was from the eggbeater that the pictures took their impulse ... Their subject is an invented series of planes which was of interest to the artist.

Davis worked at the *Eggbeater* series in 1927–28. Because of the deliberate banality of their subject-matter the pictures have sometimes been described as the precursors of Pop Art. In May 1928 he had the good luck to sell two paintings to the Whitney Studio Club 'for an

STUART DAVIS, *Eggbeater No. 1*, 1927

unheard of price; nine hundred dollars.' He promptly used the money to go to Paris, where he remained for just over a year. During this period he married his first wife, Bessie Chosak, and after his return to New York they settled in Greenwich Village. The marriage itself did not last long: Bessie died around 1932, the year in which Davis's work was included in the First Biennial of American Painting at the Whitney Museum.

Since he had a background in radical politics through his early connection with *The Masses*, it was logical that Davis should become increasingly involved in the political controversies of the 1930s. In 1935 he enrolled in the Public Works of Art Project, and in 1939 in its successor, the Federal Art Project of the Works Project Administration. He joined the Artists' Union when it was founded in 1934 and was elected its President. From January 1935 to January 1936 he was Editor of the periodical *Art Front*. He was then at the height of his radical phase – he declared that the single acceptable political theory was Marxism 'because it was the only scientific social viewpoint', and bitterly attacked the American Scene artists, particularly Thomas Hart Benton and his propagandist the critic Thomas Craven, condemning their right-wing political tendencies as well as stylistic conservatism. In 1936 he was a charter member of the American Artists' Congress, and was elected National Secretary; he became National Chairman in 1938. Davis stuck closely to the orthodox Communist line: he actually signed a letter to *The Masses* in 1938, condemning victims of the Moscow show-trials as 'Trotskyite-Bukharinite

traitors'. He had already quarrelled with a number of artist friends, among them Arshile Gorky, for being less committed to political causes than himself, and also for preferring their own studios to the numerous committee rooms and public meetings he would have liked them to frequent. It is not surprising that Davis's own output dwindled both in quality and in quantity during the late 1930s. It was perhaps a sign of malaise when he severed his long-time relationship with the Downtown Gallery in 1936: Edith Halpert, who owned it, had represented him for nine years. The relationship was resumed in 1941.

Davis's change of direction may perhaps be dated from his second marriage in 1938, to Roselle Springer. In 1939 he left the Federal Art Project, and in 1940 he resigned, disillusioned, from the American Artists' Congress. One of the primary purposes of the Congress had always been to oppose both war and Fascism. Now a Communist faction succeeded in defeating a statement of support of Finnish War Relief, because the Finns were at war with Russian invaders.

During the 1940s Davis returned to the somewhat elitist Modernist attitudes which he had professed before the Depression, but always with an American twist. One of his enthusiasms was jazz, in succession to his early interest in ragtime. He and Mondrian, now exiled in New York, used to attend jazz concerts together. Late in life Davis said:

> For a number of years jazz had a tremendous influence on my thoughts about art and life. For me at that time jazz was the only thing that corresponded to an authentic art in America ... I think all my paintings, at least in part, come from this influence, though of course I never tried to paint a jazz scene.

In 1945 a major retrospective of Davis's work was put on by the Museum of Modern Art in New York, and his characteristically combative autobiography was published the same year. In 1952 he was included in the 26th Venice Biennale, and his son (and only child), George Earl Davis, was born. In 1956 he was elected to the National Institute of Arts and Letters, one of the pillars of the American cultural establishment. There was a touring retrospective in 1957, which was seen at the Walker Art Center, Minneapolis, in Des Moines, San Francisco, and finally at the Whitney. Davis died in June 1964, a few months before his seventieth birthday.

Left: STUART DAVIS,
Pad No. 4, 1947

The English art of the inter-war period gives the impression of being unpolarized, partly because English painters and sculptors had great difficulty in securing patronage. This was due to innate cultural conservatism, but also to the fact that leading critics were obsessed with the achievements of the Ecole de Paris (see pp. 88–105), and reluctant to recognize native talent.

In the 1920s the most distinguished artists tended to be individualists who fell into no particular category – chief among them were Jacob Epstein and Stanley Spencer. In the 1930s, a more coherent English avant-garde began to emerge. Though the artists were united in their effort to obtain recognition, and were on very friendly terms from a purely personal point of view, the leading painters and sculptors of the period can be placed in two broad categories. There were those, such as Henry Moore, who inclined towards Surrealism without fully committing themselves to it, and those – chiefly Ben Nicholson, but also to some extent Barbara Hepworth – who were more attracted by Constructivism.

JACOB EPSTEIN in his Chelsea studio in front of his Oscar Wilde Memorial, 1912. Photo E. O. Hoppé

JACOB EPSTEIN

Between the two World Wars the most notorious and controversial artist in Britain was undoubtedly the sculptor Jacob Epstein. Even now his stature is not fully established and he remains a contentious figure.

He was born in 1880, in the Jewish ghetto on the Lower East Side of New York, the third son of Russian immigrants. His father at least was unsympathetic to his desire to become an artist, because of the sanctions imposed by their Orthodox faith and observances. When his family moved to a more respectable part of the city Epstein remained behind, though he ventured out of the ghetto to study at the Art Students' League. At this time his ambition was to become a painter; he went to see Thomas Eakins (1844–1916) in Philadelphia, and Eakins was sufficiently impressed to offer to take him into his own home and teach him. The young Epstein, however, decided that the atmosphere in the Eakins household was too fusty for his taste, and declined.

It was at about this date that Epstein decided that his vocation was to be a sculptor, not a painter. He found enough money for a steamship ticket to France (opportunities for sculptors to study or to work were limited in America at that time). His mother came to see him off, and had to be torn from him by force when the ship sailed. Her premonition proved right: she never saw her son again. Epstein arrived in Paris just in time to attend Zola's funeral the day after his arrival, and was accepted at the Ecole des Beaux-Arts. Very soon, however, he fell out with his fellow students, and transferred himself to the Académie Julian. His fees were covered by a small allowance from his mother, sent in all probability without his father's knowledge. Of this period Epstein wrote afterwards:

The whole student period in Paris I passed in a rage of work. I was aflame with ardour and worked in a frenzied, almost mad manner, achieving study after study, week after week, always destroying it at the end of the week to start a new one the following Monday.

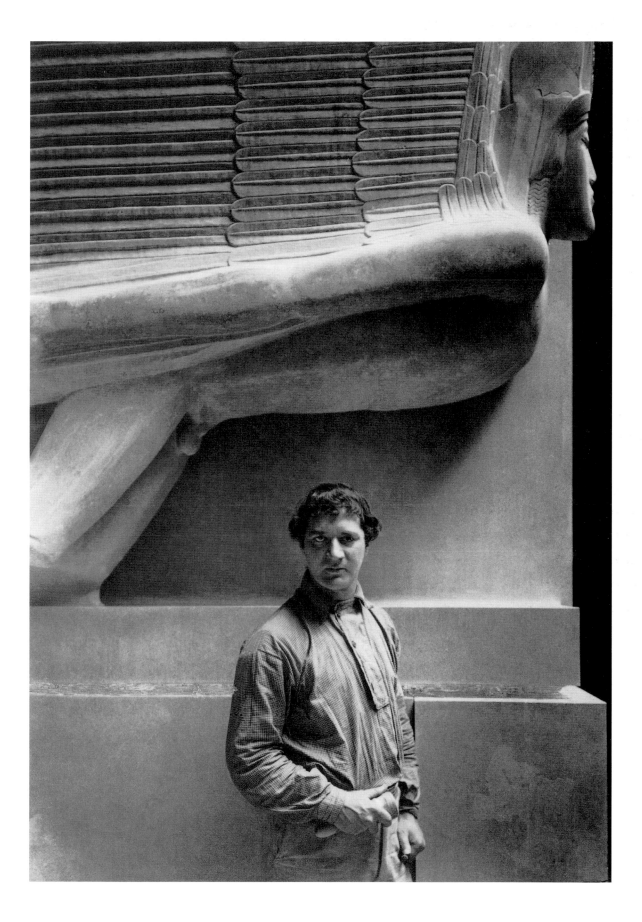

He paid a brief visit to Florence, and another to London, where he fell in love with the British Museum. In 1905 he decided to move to London permanently – he had now married a Scottish girl named Margaret Dunlop whom he first encountered at the house of a Belgian anarchist.

Once in London, Epstein experienced feelings of inadequacy. He travelled steerage to New York and spent a fortnight there, but returned to England again and in 1907 became a British citizen. This was also the year in which he received his first major commission, for eighteen figures, one-and-a-half times life-size, for the new British Medical Association building in the Strand. The first Epstein scandal broke when the scaffolding was removed from the first four sculptures. The *Evening Standard* wrote: 'They are a form of statuary which no careful father would wish his daughter or no discriminating young man his fiancée, to see.' They brought the young artist enough notoriety for him to be offered another commission – to create a tomb for Oscar Wilde in the Père Lachaise cemetery, paid for by a subscription raised among Wilde's friends, who belonged to the progressive party in art. He also began to receive commissions for portrait busts. An early sitter was the Irish writer Lady Gregory, whose portrait was paid for by her nephew, the celebrated collector Sir Hugh Lane. Epstein had a disagreement with his sitter about her hairstyle, and Lane, when he saw the bust, remarked: 'Poor Aunt Augusta. She looks as if she could eat her own children.'

The Wilde tomb was finished and installed in 1912, and caused another rumpus. Epstein took it to Paris and arrived at Père Lachaise to add the finishing touches, to find the sculpture covered by a tarpaulin and guarded by a gendarme because of its alleged indecency. It represents a rather Asiatic-looking angel who is undoubtedly masculine in gender. The French put a bronze plaque over the figure's sexual organs, and this was promptly removed by a night raid of poets and artists. The tarpaulin went on again and stayed until the First World War gave the authorities other things to think about.

During the summer and autumn of 1912 Epstein met many of the leading avant-garde artists in Paris, among them Picasso, Modigliani and Brancusi. He also re-encountered Gertrude Stein, who found he had changed for the worse since they had last met: he was no longer 'a thin rather beautiful rather melancholy ghost who used to slip in and out among the statues in the Luxembourg Museum'. In 1913, on his return to London, he was undoubtedly an important member of the new avant-garde which was rooting itself in England. He was one of the founders of the London Group, and became involved with the Vorticists, led by Wyndham Lewis. He contributed two drawings to the first number of the Vorticist magazine, *Blast!* One of these was for the sculpture *Rock Drill* which many critics consider his most important work. 'Here was the armed sinister figure of today and tomorrow,' Epstein wrote; 'No humanity, only the terrible Frankenstein's monster we have made ourselves into.'

During the first years of the war Epstein lived quietly in the country. He received some prestigious portrait commissions, but he found it difficult to keep in touch with what was going on, and his neighbours were suspicious of his foreign name. He resettled in London and then was called up in 1917. He joined the Artists' Rifles and was posted to Plymouth. He fell ill and spent some time in hospital before being demobilized in 1918.

His reputation as a troublemaker revived almost immediately the war was over. In 1920 he exhibited a figure of the *Risen Christ* at the Leicester Galleries and was denounced by a fashionable Jesuit, Father Vaughan:

> I felt ready to cry out with indignation that in this Christian England there should be exhibited the figure of a Christ which suggested to me some degraded Chaldean or African, which wore the appearance of an Asiatic-American or Hun-Jew, which reminded me of some emaciated Hindu, or a badly grown Egyptian smothered in the garments of the grave.

This racialist outburst fed Epstein's already well developed persecution-mania. Yet, if he was abused, he was also celebrated. To pose for Epstein was the summit of many a young woman's ambition. Epstein had an eye for female beauty, the more exotic the better. In 1921 he met Kathleen German, who became his mistress as well as his model and eventually his second wife. Other favourite models included the beautiful Indian Sunita, who lived in his household for a while, and the fiery Dolores. Epstein remembered ruefully that the latter

even gave as an excuse to a magistrate, before whom she appeared for some indiscreet conduct in Piccadilly, that my being in America had disoriented her, and this was taken as sufficient excuse, together

JACOB EPSTEIN in his studio, September 1947. Towering on the right is his study of Christ exhibited in 1935, *Behold the Man*. Epstein is standing by his new bust of the film producer Gabriel Pascal. Photographer unknown with a small fine, by a magistrate indulgent to a Phryne of modern times.

Those of his sitters who were not beautiful were usually famous. Among them were George Bernard Shaw, Paul Robeson, Haile Selassie, Chaim Weizmann and Albert Einstein.

It was not his portraits which caused Epstein trouble, but his other work, especially his stone carvings, with their sometimes brutal primitivism. *Rima*, commissioned by the Royal Society for the Protection of Birds in 1924 as a memorial to W. H. Hudson, the writer and naturalist, and set up in Hyde Park, was tarred and feathered and threatened with removal. *Genesis*, shown in 1931, was denounced as a 'Mongolian moron that is obscene' by the *Daily Express*, and described as 'unfit to show' by the *Daily Telegraph*. It was still considered shocking nearly thirty years later. With three other major Epstein carvings it was bought by a wax museum in Blackpool and made part of a peepshow for holidaymakers. Epstein rather naïvely tempted the fates with this kind of work. *Genesis*, which for him represented 'the profoundly elemental in motherhood, the deep down instinctive female', is hugely pregnant. *Adam*, which also finished up in the Blackpool waxworks, after being toured for years round fairgrounds, is, as the father of all mankind, gigantically endowed.

Epstein ceased to be controversial only in the last decade of his life, and even then he was occasionally subjected to the old anti-semitism. As late as 1956, when he was proposed as the sculptor for *St Michael and the Devil* for the rebuilt Coventry Cathedral, a member of the Reconstruction Committee objected: 'But he is a Jew'. His first public work to be almost universally admired was the 1953 *Madonna and Child* for Cavendish Square in London. By this time Epstein's health was already failing, and his work was no longer as forceful as it had once been. The large-scale commissions now being offered to him came too late. He died of heart disease in 1959.

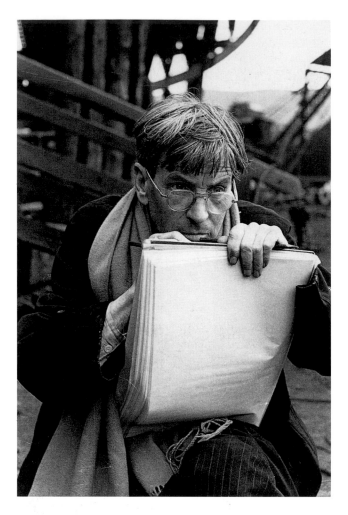

STANLEY SPENCER

Spencer fits uncomfortably into the structure created by art historians to explain the Modern movement, but his eccentric vision undoubtedly makes him one of the most important British artists of the first half of the twentieth century. He was born in 1891, in Cookham-on-Thames, the eighth child of an organist and piano teacher. He was brought up in a sheltered environment with a strong emphasis on music and the Bible. The stories from the Old and New Testaments fused in his mind with the familiar Cookham environment which surrounded him during his childhood and adolescence to create a personal mythology which would serve him for the rest of his life.

After a year spent at Maidenhead Technical Institute drawing from casts, Spencer went to the Slade School, University College, London, where he studied under the formidable Henry Tonks, then generally considered the best teacher of drawing in England. He travelled up from Cookham every morning, and back again at night. He was physically small, and seemed childish in comparison to his fellow students, some of whom were inclined to tease and bully him. In 1912, Spencer left the Slade, and worked at home. He was always to believe that he produced his best work in the few years after his graduation:

> I entered a kind of earthly paradise. Everything seemed fresh and to belong to the morning. My ideas were beginning to unfold in fine order when along comes the war and smashes everything.

The war took Spencer far from home for the first time. He served as a medical orderly first at Beaufort War Hospital in Bristol and then in Macedonia, and later as a private soldier on the Macedonian front. His war service added to his stock of personal imagery; suffering became connected in his mind with eroticism:

> During the war, when I contemplated the horror of my life and the lives of those with me, I felt the only way to end the ghastly experience would be if everyone suddenly decided to indulge in every degree and form of sexual love, carnal love, bestiality, anything you like to call it. These are the joyful inheritances of mankind.

After the war he returned to Cookham, but its spell was temporarily broken: 'My life was in a sort of abeyance. I was tired of not being me, of being a corpse watching other people be alive.' Some uncertain years followed, until in 1925 he married Hilda Carline, who had also been a student at the Slade and who had originally been courted by his brother Gilbert. After their marriage the Spencers lived in Hampstead, where they formed the focal point of a large circle of artists.

In 1927 Spencer began work on what was to be his most important commission, the Sandham Memorial Chapel at Burghclere in Hampshire. The imagery which covers the walls of the chapel is based on what he had experienced during the war, and culminates on the east wall in a huge *Resurrection of the Soldiers* which took nearly a year to complete. In this visionary composition – the artist's first attempt at what was to become a favourite theme – the resurrected soldiers bear a multitude of white crosses towards Christ, who stands awaiting them.

Spencer returned to live permanently in Cookham in 1932. He was now a successful artist – he was elected an

STANLEY SPENCER on a working visit to the Clydeside shipyards at Port Glasgow, October 1943. Photographer unknown

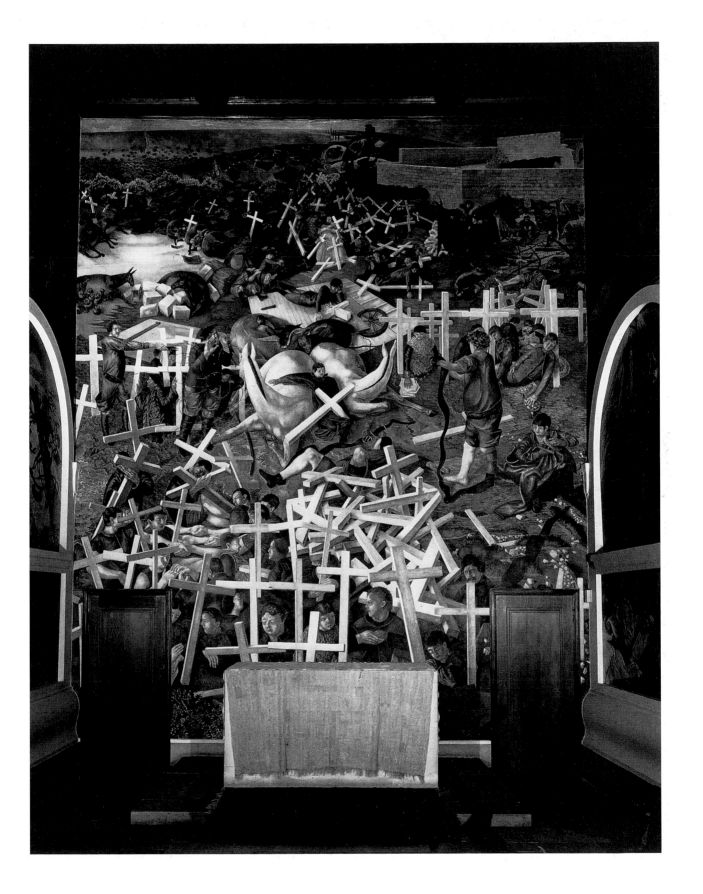

STANLEY SPENCER,
Resurrection of the Soldiers (detail)
at the Oratory of All Souls at
Burghclere, Berkshire, 1928

Associate of the Royal Academy that year, and showed five paintings and five drawings at the Venice Biennale. The 1930s, however, brought a series of personal crises. In 1929 he had met Patricia Preece in a Cookham tea-shop. She lived in the village and after his return he felt a growing infatuation for her. In 1933 he announced to his wife that he intended to become Preece's lover. Though his finances were insecure, he showered Preece with gifts of clothes and jewellery. His real hope was to possess both women, but even Hilda's essential passivity rebelled at this. In 1937 they divorced, and Spencer and Preece were married. Preece had demanded a high price for the marriage: the freehold of Spencer's house in Cookham. The honeymoon was a disaster. The new Mrs Spencer went to a rented cottage in Cornwall accompanied by the female friend with whom she had shared her life for many years while Spencer remained in Cookham for the weekend and was joined by Hilda at Patricia's suggestion. When he arrived in Cornwall to meet his new bride, she reproached him for his inconstancy and said that, in the circumstances, she could not possibly live with him. Spencer now found himself without either woman, when he had hoped to have both. Patricia was in full command of his financial affairs, and forced him to leave the house he had given to her.

Disconsolately, Spencer migrated to lodgings in Hampstead to be near Hilda, who was now living with her family. He visited her often and repeatedly begged her to remarry him; she always refused, though she continued to see him. Spencer also wrote her numerous letters which he would read to her at their meetings. This continued when Hilda had a mental breakdown in the 1940s, and Spencer visited her regularly in hospital. Even after she died in 1950 Spencer continued to write the letters, up to one hundred pages long, as he obsessively reviewed the course and nature of their relationship.

Some of Spencer's most powerfully idiosyncratic paintings belong to the period of the collapse of his first marriage and include a number of erotic nudes of Patricia Preece. In the two most striking of these (*Self-Portrait with Patricia Preece* and *The Leg-of-Mutton Nude*) Spencer includes his own naked likeness. Slightly earlier than the nudes is a painting entitled *The Dustman* or *The Lovers*. Spencer describes this enigmatic composition as showing 'the glorifying and magnifying of a dustman. The joy of his bliss is spiritual in his union with his wife who carries him in her arms and experiences the bliss of

union with his corduroy trousers.' When this and another painting were rejected by the Royal Academy Hanging Committee in 1935, Spencer resigned his membership.

This public rejection of, and by, the artistic establishment did not prevent Spencer from being given an important commission during the Second World War. He was asked by the War Artists Advisory Committee to paint a series of scenes showing shipbuilding on the Clyde at Port Glasgow. This project broadened into a series of *Port Glasgow Resurrections*, painted between 1945 and 1950, when Spencer was re-elected to the Royal Academy. Despite this gesture of reconciliation he was now in some ways much more isolated than he had been in the 1920s. He did not lack patrons, but artistic fashion had passed him by. He had moved back to the outskirts of Cookham in 1943, and now lived at Cookham Rise in conditions of considerable squalor. Some years previously he had written in a notebook (it is now his most often quoted remark): 'I am on the side of the angels and dirt.' In his later years his appearance confirmed at least the last part of this, as he trundled his painting materials through Cookham in a dilapidated pram.

For some years before his death he was in poor health: he suffered from intestinal cancer and eventually had to have a colostomy. Despite the pain, he struggled to complete one final ambitious project, a large painting of *Christ Preaching at Cookham Regatta*. This combined his love of the Edwardian Cookham of his childhood with his deep identification with the Gospel story – the first studies for the composition had been made nearly thirty years previously, in the late 1920s. In the end the vast canvas was left less than half-completed, but enough had been done to show the unique force of his imagination. Spencer was knighted in 1959, just before he died.

BEN NICHOLSON

Ben Nicholson was a private person, and reticent in his painting and sculpture. He was born in April 1894, in Denham, Buckinghamshire, the son of the painter William Nicholson by his first wife, Mabel Pryde, an artist and sister of James Pryde. William Nicholson and James Pryde worked together as the Beggarstaff Brothers.

Nicholson was sent to the Slade School of Art in 1911, at the height of its reputation for producing talented and

BEN NICHOLSON, St Ives 1956. Photo Bill Brandt

skilful artists, but he did not get on with its presiding genius, Henry Tonks. Throughout his life Nicholson resisted the idea of a slickly professional finish, though his art was always essentially stringent. At the Slade he spent much of his time playing billiards rather than studying (he always had an English passion for games of all kinds, and later invented his own variety of ping-pong). He claimed, tongue-in-cheek, that the rectangle of the billiard table, and the precise angles which had to be chosen for a successful shot, taught him more about composition than the teaching given at the Slade.

Later in 1911 he went to Tours to learn French, then in 1912 to Milan to learn Italian. When he was young his health was poor, which meant that he did not fight in the First World War; he spent the winter of 1913–14 in Madeira and that of 1917–18 in Pasadena, California. He returned to England when his mother died.

In 1920 he married Winifred Dacre, also a painter, the first of his three wives. Until 1931 the couple divided their time between Cumberland, where they spent their summers, and Castagnola in Switzerland, where they spent the winters, varying this with occasional visits to London and Paris.

Nicholson saw his first Cubist Picasso in Paris in 1921. It was the handling of colour rather than the design which impressed him. In the middle of the composition was 'an absolutely miraculous *green* – very deep, very potent and absolutely real. In fact, none of the actual events of one's life have been more potent than that.' He was still uncertain of his own direction as an artist, and during the 1920s he made and destroyed hundreds of experimental paintings – his output at this time consisted of modest landscapes and still lifes. He had his first one-man show in London at the Adelphi Gallery in 1922, followed later in the decade by shows shared with Winifred Nicholson (1923), Christopher Wood and the potter William Staite Murray (1926). In 1924 he joined the '7 and 5 Society', a rather timid and unfocused group of would-be avant-gardists whose lack of direction was typical of the English art scene at that time.

Christopher Wood was an attractive young man, a homosexual who was pushing his slender but charming talent as a painter as far as it would go in Paris at the time. He varied bouts of self-promotion with restless travelling, and in August 1928 it was he who introduced Nicholson to the Cornish fishing village of St Ives:

This was an exciting day, for not only was it the first time I saw St Ives, but on the way back from Porthmeor Beach we passed an open door in Back Road West and through it saw some paintings of ships and houses on old pieces of paper and cardboard nailed up all over the wall, with particularly large nails through the smallest ones.

For Nicholson the author of these works, retired fisherman Alfred Wallis, was the personification of the creative impulse, as opposed to the production by rote of the sophisticated art of his father's generation. Wallis had much the effect on him that 'Le Douanier' Rousseau had on the original Cubists.

In the 1930s Nicholson's orientation changed, and he became a much more considerable and original artist. The beginning of the change was a period of some weeks spent on the Norfolk coast in 1931, in the company of Barbara Hepworth, Henry Moore and Ivon Hitchens. Hepworth became his second wife. They were anxious to discover more about what was going on in Paris, which at that period seemed the fountainhead of artistic originality, and in 1932 they paid the city a visit and met Picasso, Braque, Brancusi and Arp. Later they went to Dieppe, where they stayed with the American sculptor Alexander Calder, and to Varengeville where they again saw Braque. In the autumn of the same year he and Hepworth had a joint exhibition at the Tooth Gallery in London. In the summer of 1933 they were in Paris again, and now met Mondrian for the first time. His work made a slightly confusing impact on Nicholson: the Dutchman's severe abstracts were, he recalled, 'entirely new' to him. 'I did not understand them on this first visit (and indeed only partly understood them on my second trip a year later).' But he saw at once that they were important.

Nicholson and Hepworth were now sufficiently well known in Paris to be asked to join Abstraction-Création, an international alliance of abstract artists. At home, Nicholson, thanks to the forcefulness of his personality, was becoming one of the accepted leaders of the English avant-garde. He was a founder member of Unit One, a far more stringent group than the 7 and 5, set up in 1933, and in 1937 he joined with the architect J. L. Martin (later Sir Leslie Martin) and the sculptor Naum Gabo, to edit an international survey of constructive art, entitled *Circle*. From 1934 to 1939 he produced some of his most distinguished work, a series of completely non-figurative carved low reliefs, which brought him growing recognition. He was invited to show at the Stedelijk Museum, Amsterdam, in 1938, in its large survey exhibition, Abstract Art, and in the British Section of the New York World's Fair in 1939.

During the latter part of the decade he formed part of a tight-knit group of artists, some British and some foreign and most of them living in Hampstead. With Hepworth, Henry Moore and Paul Nash, the group included Gabo, Mondrian, Moholy-Nagy and the Bauhaus architects Walter Gropius and Marcel Breuer. They were dispersed by the threat of war: Nicholson, Hepworth and their young family took refuge in St Ives in 1940. Nicholson was to remain there until 1958, and Hepworth for the rest of her life. St Ives inspired a partial return to figuration, which made work more accessible, and after the war was over his international reputation grew rapidly. Important landmarks were a one-man exhibition at the Phillips Memorial Gallery in Washington, D.C. in 1951, and the first prize at the Carnegie International of 1952. In 1954 he had retrospectives in Amsterdam, Brussels and Zurich, and at the Tate Gallery in London.

Nicholson's marriage to Hepworth broke up, and in 1957 he married the Swiss photographer Felicitas Vogler. In the same year he was awarded the Order of Merit. A few months later he moved to Switzerland – to his beloved Ticino – and based himself there for a number of years until this third alliance collapsed in turn. He then came back to end his days in England. He died in 1982 at the age of eighty-eight.

BEN NICHOLSON, *White Relief*, 1935

Henry Moore, Much Hadham 1954. Photo Ida Kar

HENRY MOORE

Henry Moore was the most celebrated sculptor of his time, and the second part of his career, in particular, demonstrated that Modernist sculpture was, after all, surprisingly adaptable to official needs. In this sense, Moore was the contemporary equivalent of the great Neo-Classical sculptors such as Canova and Thorwaldsen.

Moore was born in July 1898 in Castleford, Yorkshire, the seventh child of a mine manager who had worked at the pit face. Both parents were strong and supportive personalities, and Moore's childhood was a happy one. He became a student teacher in 1915, and by 1916 was teaching in the local elementary school which he had attended in his boyhood. At seventeen he joined the army, as the youngest member of his regiment, the Civil Service Rifles. For him the First World War was not the traumatic experience it was for so many others: he remembers the army as being 'just like a bigger family' and says that 'for me the war passed in a romantic haze of trying to be a hero.' He was gassed at Cambrai but made a swift recovery, and finished the war as a physical training instructor.

In September 1919, after a brief return to elementary-school teaching, he went to Leeds School of Art on an ex-serviceman's grant. He was soon recognized as a star pupil, and in 1921 won a scholarship to the Royal College of Art in London:

I was in a dream of excitement. When I rode on the open top of a bus I felt that I was travelling in Heaven almost. And that the bus was floating on the air.

Moore made the most of the opportunities London offered, regularly visiting the museums, where he acquired a great interest in primitive art: he was particularly struck by pre-Columbian sculpture. In his first year at the Royal College of Art he went to Paris with his fellow student Raymond Coxon, who had been with him at Leeds; these visits were to be many times repeated. In 1925 he visited Italy on a travelling scholarship – something which caused a certain creative blockage as he tried to work his way through what he had seen and experienced.

Even before he went to Italy Moore had been fortunate enough to be offered a part-time post as Assistant in the Sculpture Department at the Royal College of Art. In 1926 he held his first one-man show, which attracted some distinguished purchasers including Augustus John, Henry Lamb and Jacob Epstein. He was also commissioned to provide a sculpture for the new London headquarters of the London Underground – the job came to Moore on the recommendation of Epstein, who was also employed there.

Moore married a beautiful Russian, Irina Radetzsky, in 1929, and in 1931 they bought a small cottage in Kent where he could work during the Royal College holidays. He was still obsessed, as he had been from the beginning, with the idea of direct carving, and at this time everything was laboriously hewn by hand. His second one-man exhibition also took place that year, and it was Epstein who wrote the catalogue introduction, saying: 'For the future of sculpture in England Henry Moore is vitally important.' By this time he was sufficiently well known to have become a controversial figure. His show was savagely attacked in the *Morning Post* and a number of other newspapers and periodicals. The *Morning Post* review was brought to the attention of the Royal College of Art and played a role in the non-renewal of his teaching appointment in 1932, after seven years. Fortunately Moore was able to move to the Chelsea School of Art, which had already approached him.

In 1934 he sold his cottage in Kent and bought another, equally small, but with five acres of ground attached to it which enabled him to see his work in the open air. In London the Moores lived in Hampstead, where they came together with the group which included Ben Nicholson and Barbara Hepworth, and the critic Herbert Read. Nicholson inclined to Constructivism, but Moore, though reluctant to join any stylistic grouping, was more interested in Surrealism, and showed at the International Exhibition of Surrealist Art held in London in 1936. This was also the year in which his work was first seen in the USA: he was included in an exhibition entitled *Cubism and Abstract Art*, at the Museum of Modern Art in New York.

After the outbreak of the Second World War in 1939 Moore commuted from his cottage in Kent to London in order to teach. When the Chelsea School of Art was evacuated he resigned and applied to Chelsea Polytechnic for training as a munitions toolmaker. Before the application could have any effect (the course was oversubscribed) he began making the first drawings of people sheltering in the London Underground during the Blitz.

These came to the attention of the War Artists Advisory Committee, and Moore was commissioned to make larger and more finished versions. When the drawings were shown in 1940 and 1941 Moore began to attract a wide public, who recognized their own feelings in what he had to show them.

Moore's studio in Hampstead was damaged by bombing during the Blitz. As a result he moved to Much Hadham in Hertfordshire, where friends had told him there was a house available. In 1942 he continued his work for the War Artists Advisory Committee, drawing miners in his native Yorkshire. It was only in 1943 that he was able to return to sculpture, with a commission for a figure of a Virgin and Child for the church of St Matthew's, Northampton. This was his first draped figure and a more traditional and accessible image than anything he had made so far. The theme of mothers and children continued in his post-war sculpture, inspired now by something personal – the birth of a daughter in 1946.

The year 1946 also marked an important stage in the growth of Moore's public reputation – a retrospective exhibition of his work at the Museum of Modern Art in New York was a triumphant success. The show later travelled to Chicago and San Francisco, and then on to Australia. In 1948 Moore was asked to take part in the first post-war Biennale in Venice, and carried off the main prize for sculpture. His stature as an artist of international reputation was thus confirmed.

Moore now began to shift from direct carving to the modelling he had once despised. He began in 1952 by building an experimental foundry at the bottom of his garden, in order to learn the fundaments of the process; the shift from one method to another was accelerated after 1954 when he had a brief illness which seems to have given him a sense of his own mortality. Later, in 1960, he said: 'The difference between modelling and carving is that modelling is a quicker thing, and so it becomes a chance to get rid of one's ideas.'

There was another reason for reverting to techniques he had once scorned – the fact that he was now being offered commissions for works on a massive scale. Some of these, like the screen for the Time-Life building in London executed in 1952, could be carved, but others, like the massive *Reclining Figure* for the Lincoln Center in New York (1961–65), had to be cast. Others again, like another *Reclining Figure* made for the Unesco

Headquarters in Paris (1957–58), though still made of stone, were largely shaped by assistants. Moore's ever expanding studios and gardens came to resemble a factory as the work came to be organized along quasi-industrial lines, with maquettes and models of gradually increasing size being made until the final full-scale result was achieved. Maquettes for rejected ideas would also be cast, so that there was a steady flow of small bronzes from Moore's studio, as well as drawings and prints.

All this was a reversion to a pattern widespread in the sculptors' studios of the nineteenth century but rejected by the early Modernists. In his final years, Moore was increasingly criticized for the amount of work he was prepared to leave to his assistants, and for the resulting insensitivity of surface in many of his larger works. The best of his late work is to be found in his drawings. While those of his active maturity nearly always seem to have been made with sculpture in mind (almost the sole exception to this being the celebrated series of *Shelter Drawings* made during the Second World War), the very late drawings are often pictorial rather than sculptural. Moore's studies of trees, made in old age, can be compared to similar sheets by Rubens and Van Dyck.

In the post-war years Moore was loaded with official honours – it is difficult to think of any which he might have coveted which were not offered to him. He was made a Companion of Honour in 1955, and a member of the Order of Merit in 1963. These marks of distinction showed the extent to which Modernist art had now been absorbed and accepted by the traditionally conservative British cultural establishment. They also demonstrated the extent to which Moore himself now identified with this establishment. Though his work remained in demand to the end of his life, and continues to fetch high prices at auction, it now seems very far from the mainstream of sculptural development. Moore died on 31 August 1986 at the age of eighty-eight.

Opposite above: BARBARA HEPWORTH with her husband John Skeaping, Hampstead, 21 March 1933. Photographer unknown
Opposite below: BARBARA HEPWORTH, *Pelagos*, 1946

BARBARA HEPWORTH

Of the three major sculptors of the first half of the twentieth-century who lived and worked in England Hepworth was the most limited, but her achievement was still remarkable, and in many ways complementary to that of Ben Nicholson to whom she was married for twenty years.

She was born in 1903, the eldest of four children and the daughter of a civil engineer who lived and worked in the West Riding of Yorkshire. Unlike many artists, she had a gift for mathematics, and her closeness to her father and his work familiarized her with technical drawings. At the age of sixteen she won a scholarship to the Leeds School of Art, where Henry Moore was studying. Instead of doing the compulsory two years at the School she fitted the course into a single year, and went to the Royal College of Art in 1921 on a senior scholarship. She spent three years there, and in 1924 was a finalist for the Prix de Rome and runner up to John Skeaping, her future husband. Despite her failure to win the prize, a grant from the West Riding enabled her to

live and travel in Italy for a year. She and Skeaping travelled to Florence together, and married in the Palazzo Vecchio. Later they went to Siena and then to Rome. In Rome she received a thorough training in carving, which was not then taught at the Royal College since sculpture was considered to be mainly a matter of modelling.

Hepworth reported that Italy brought her two crucial insights. The first was 'the experience of *light*' (her italics) missing from her youth in the north; the second was brought into focus by a chance remark made by the Italian master-carver Ardini, that marble changed colour under different people's hands. This, she said, made her 'decide immediately that it was not dominance which one had to obtain over material, but an understanding, almost a kind of persuasion, and above all a kind of co-ordination between head and hand.'

She returned to London in November 1926, and in December of the following year she and Skeaping held a joint exhibition in their own studio in St John's Wood – their first major patron was George Eumorfopoulos, owner of a great collection of Chinese art. The studio show was followed by a second, held at the Beaux-Arts Gallery in London in June 1928. In 1929 her son Paul was born. During this early period in London Hepworth was in frequent contact with Henry Moore, with whom she had been a student, both at Leeds and at the Royal College, and in 1930 and 1931 the two sculptors formed part of a group holidaying on the Norfolk coast. The second of these vacations brought Hepworth close to Ben Nicholson, who was also a member of the party, and in that year she went to live with him. They later married.

During the 1930s Hepworth and Nicholson lived in Hampstead and were at the centre of the small group of

BARBARA HEPWORTH, *Assembly of Sea Forms*, 1972

avant-garde artists living and working in London. They travelled on the Continent, and made the acquaintance of leading artists in France, most notably Picasso, Brancusi, Braque and Mondrian. Hepworth's personal life was greatly changed by the birth of triplets – two daughters and a son – in November 1934. Her work, partly under Nicholson's influence, was shifting in the direction of greater formality and abstraction, but there were strong overtones of neolithic art, as the physicist J. D. Bernal noted in an introduction for a show of her sculpture held at the Reid & Lefevre Gallery in London in 1937.

The Nicholsons' financial position remained precarious throughout the 1930s, partly due to the heavy burdens imposed by a large family of young children. After 1938 in particular it was difficult for avant-garde artists to make any kind of living in England. They decided to leave London, and five days before the declaration of war in 1939, set out for the Cornish fishing village of St Ives, where they had been lent a house by their friend, the critic Adrian Stokes. They were to remain in the area for more than a decade, and Hepworth was to settle there permanently.

For the first three years of the war she ran a nursery school and was not able to carve at all, though she drew at night, after the day's duties were over. This was a period of intense discussion with the Constructivist sculptor Naum Gabo and other artists and writers who had settled in the same area. In 1942 the Nicholsons moved into a roomy house with its own garden, and conditions became a little easier. In 1949 Hepworth acquired a new studio in a sheltered position where she was able to carve out of doors nearly all the year round.

Like many of the 'advanced' artists of the 1930s Hepworth won increasing recognition in the decade that followed the Second World War – her work was shown in the Venice Biennale of 1950, though its impact was somewhat muffled after Henry Moore's triumph there in 1948. But the early 1950s were also years of personal crisis. Hepworth's marriage to Ben Nicholson was dissolved in 1951, and in 1953 her first child, Paul Skeaping, who had become an aircraft designer and professional pilot, was killed in an air-crash over Siam. In 1954 she made a journey to Greece in an attempt to reconcile herself to her son's death and, in her own opinion, succeeded. She wrote at this period: 'Sculpture to me is primitive, religious, passionate and magical – always affirmative.'

As was the case with Henry Moore, her sculpture increased in scale as greater and greater opportunities were offered to her. She began to turn away from carving and to make some works, especially the larger ones, in bronze. Gradually she was able to buy many of the properties surrounding the studio she had acquired in 1959, and create an environment where her output could be properly displayed. In the 1960s Hepworth's repertory of forms extended, from the strict geometry of her earlier work to the more composite structure and monumental scale of her later work. In 1962–63, a large bronze was commissioned to stand next to the United Nations Building in New York, in memory of Secretary General Dag Hammarskjöld. Other monumental works in bronze were commissioned in the 1960s, a period which some consider to have yielded examples of her best work. However, cancer was diagnosed in 1964, and ill health increasingly limited her imaginative scope and energy.

Hepworth was made Commander of the British Empire in 1958. In 1965 she was appointed a Trustee of the Tate Gallery in London, and was created Dame Commander of the British Empire, which marked her acceptance by the British artistic establishment.

Hepworth's final years were beset by increasing ill health – eventually she had to take to a wheelchair. Her living conditions continued, despite her success, to be very simple, even primitive. In 1975 she died as the result of a fire in her studio, perhaps caused by a cigarette setting light to the bedclothes. The studio itself was opened as a museum in 1976.

Barbara Hepworth, 1963. Photo Cornel Lucas

The birth of Abstract Expressionism was perhaps the most significant event in the history of modern art since the birth of Cubism, and it marked a decisive shift in influence, from Paris to New York. Abstract Expressionism, despite its name, owed less to European Expressionism than it did to Surrealism. Its main source was the Calligraphic Surrealism associated with Miró; Arshile Gorky, recognizably Surrealist yet equally recognizable as an American artist, marks the point of transition.

The Abstract Expressionists can be divided into several groups. Within New York itself there were the 'wild men from downtown' – Pollock, De Kooning and Kline – and the more bourgeois uptown artists, such as Rothko. He, in turn, was closely allied to Clyfford Still, who spent little of his career in New York. The personalities of Rothko and Still were very similar: both made vaunting claims for their art; both were self-centred, ambitious and temperamental. Newman and Reinhardt were the intellectuals of the movement, and their work is markedly less thickly painted, and less dependent on physical gesture than that of their peers: Newman, in particular, anticipates some of the characteristics of Post-Painterly Abstraction.

Above: MARK ROTHKO, New York City 1964. Photo Hans Namuth
Right: Opening of Franz Kline's exhibition at Sidney Janis Gallery, New York, March 1960. Visible are Harriet Janis (left), Franz Kline, William Baziotes (eyes only), Robert Goldwater, Louise Bourgeois (with hat), Ethel Baziotes (right), Mark Rothko (with hat), David Sylvester (rear centre), Willem de Kooning (rear right). Photo Fred W. McDarrah

MARK ROTHKO

Mark Rothko was born Marcus Rothkovich in Dvinsk, the largest city of the province of Vitebsk in Russia, in 1903, the youngest of four children. His father, Jakob, was a Jewish pharmacist, and the children were brought up in a traditional way – Rothko afterwards claimed that he remembered his resentment at being kept in swaddling bands – and received a strictly religious upbringing. In 1910 Jakob Rothkovich emigrated to America, and the following year his two elder sons, who were threatened with conscription, fled from Russia to join him. The rest of the family followed in 1913, and settled in Portland, Oregon: seven months after their arrival Jakob Rothkovich died unexpectedly. Young Marcus had to deliver newspapers to help pay for his education, and he said later that he recalled being perpetually hungry throughout his adolescence. Despite these disadvantages, he did well at school and graduated at the age of only seventeen.

In 1921 he and two classmates went to complete their education at Yale, where they had all been promised scholarships. After six months, however, these were withdrawn, perhaps because of the concealed anti-semitism prevalent in Ivy League colleges at that time, and Rothko was told that the authorities would, instead, give him a loan to complete his education. During his college years he worked as a waiter and then as a delivery boy for an establishment run by his cousins. At this stage he intended to be an engineer, and was interested in politics rather than in art. In 1923 he dropped out of college 'to wander around, bum around, starve a bit'. He went to

MARK ROTHKO, *Orange, Yellow, Orange*, 1969

New York and lived in various tenements, working in the garment district, where he cut patterns for clothes. In 1924 he enrolled at the Art Students' League, where he attended classes for the next two years – despite this, he always regarded himself as being essentially self-taught as a painter. At this time he also seems to have had some experience as an actor, scene-painter and illustrator.

He became a part-time teacher of art in 1929, at Central Academy in Brooklyn, a parochial school attached to a synagogue. This was the start of a teaching career which lasted for thirty years. In 1929 he first exhibited his own work, at the aptly named Opportunity Gallery. At the beginning of the 1930s he married a Brooklyn Jewish girl, Edith Sacher, who designed jewellery and made a modest commercial success of it. The marriage was not happy – Rothko disliked the small menial tasks his wife made him do in connection with her business: she, in turn, despised his artist friends and brutally criticized their work.

However, his career as an artist was making some progress. In 1933 he had two solo exhibitions – one at the Contemporary Arts Gallery in New York, and another in Portland. These helped to qualify him for the Federal Art Project: he was hired by the easel-painting division and

paid just over $23.50 a week. He was also beginning to make contact with other 'dissident' artists. He already knew Milton Avery, and in the early 1930s he met Jackson Pollock, Willem de Kooning and Arshile Gorky. He formed a close friendship with Adolph Gottlieb, and in 1935 Rothko and Gottlieb were two of the founder-members of 'The Ten', a group of Expressionists who exhibited together regularly during the next decade and even managed to hold an exhibition in Paris. In 1938 Rothko received his US citizenship papers, and it was at this point that he officially altered his surname. About now, too, he abandoned the dream-like urban landscapes he had been producing hitherto, and began to use ideal-ized Greek gods and goddesses and archaic symbols as themes for calligraphic abstractions.

Rothko's first marriage came to an end during the war, and in late 1944 he met Mary Alice (Mell) Beistle, a twenty-three-year-old illustrator of children's books. Despite their differences in background (she was not Jewish) and in age, they were married within six months. In 1945 Rothko also had his first important one-man exhibition at Peggy Guggenheim's Art of This Century Gallery, and won critical praise. In the same year his work was included in the Whitney Annual, but his relationship with this institution was to be stormy: they were early buyers of his work, but by 1947 he was already refusing to be included in one of their Annuals on the grounds that he did not wish to be shown next to 'mediocrity'.

When Peggy Guggenheim closed her gallery in 1946, the only dealer with the courage to take on her more difficult artists was Betty Parsons. She signed up three painters who had already shown at Art of This Century: Rothko, who was now painting Surrealistic seascapes, Pollock and Clyfford Still. In the summer of 1946 Rothko had shows at the San Francisco Museum of Art and the Santa Barbara Museum. He taught in California that summer, and was fascinated by Still's work. His own painting was still evolving, and 1947 witnessed the emergence of his mature style – abstractions with floating blocks of colour.

Despite his growing fame, he was still very poor. His comments at this time show a mixture of bitterness and resignation:

> The unfriendliness of society to his activity is difficult for the artist to accept. Yet this very hostility can act as a lever for true liberation. Freed from a false sense of security and community, the artist can abandon

his plastic bank book, just as he had abandoned other forms of security ... free of them, transcendental experiences become possible.

Yet Rothko was ambitious and was mocked by the bohemian painters who worked in lofts in Greenwich Village for his insistence on living as near to the Museum of Modern Art as he could (in a tiny apartment) and his determination to cultivate the friendship of its formidable Director, Alfred H. Barr. When Rothko had a successful show at the Betty Parsons Gallery in 1950 Barr wanted a picture for his Museum; knowing he had no chance of forcing a purchase through his acquisitions committee, he persuaded the Modernist architect Philip Johnson to donate the canvas he wanted, feeling that his trustees would be reluctant to reject a gift from this source. They did indeed agree to accept it, but the process took two years, and one of the Museum's founders, A. Conger Goodyear, resigned in consequence.

In 1950 Rothko encountered another controversy. His daughter Kate had just been born, so he resigned his part-time job at Central Academy in order to take a higher-salaried full-time post at Brooklyn College. He was opposed to the Bauhaus philosophy espoused by the rest of the staff and his relationship with them deteriorated to the point where, in 1954, he was denied tenure, because he was considered 'too inflexible'.

Meanwhile, the inflexibility of his character was being demonstrated elsewhere. In 1952 he refused to sell two paintings to the Whitney, which he now referred to privately as a 'junk-shop'. In the same year he was included in the prestigious *Fifteen Americans* show at the Museum of Modern Art. The curator, Dorothy Miller, had expected trouble with some of the other artists, but it was Rothko who caused her most problems by sending more and different pictures from those agreed upon, and by interfering with the hang. Old friends began to notice his competitiveness: he destroyed his friendship with Barnett Newman by boasting that he had 'taught Barney how to paint'; and he offended Pollock when he invited Rothko to his studio to see the incomplete *Blue Poles*. 'Isn't it the greatest?' Pollock exclaimed exuberantly. 'Don't forget we are all painters,' Rothko retorted sourly.

Rothko's reputation grew steadily throughout the 1950s, and his financial position improved accordingly. In 1954 he had important exhibitions at the Rhode Island School of Design and at the Chicago Art Institute – the latter bought a painting for $4,000. In 1958 he was chosen, together with Mark Tobey, as American representative at the Venice Biennale. He could now afford a studio for the summer months in the artists' colony at Provincetown, Massachusetts. Yet he was growing increasingly neurotic and depressive, and was drinking heavily. For him, the making of his apparently tranquil canvases involved enormous emotional effort:

> You might as well get one thing straight. I'm not an abstract artist ... I'm not interested in the relationship of colour or form or anything else. I'm interested only in expressing basic human emotions – tragedy, ecstasy, doom and so on. And the fact that a lot of people break down and cry when confronted with my pictures shows that I can communicate these basic human emotions ... The people who weep before my pictures are having the same religious experience as I had when I painted them.

Because the creation of the work was a kind of rite Rothko was extremely secretive about how it was done and insistent about controlling the way the finished canvases were shown. He did not sleep well, and tended to work between the hours of five and ten o'clock in the morning. He once admitted to fellow artist Robert Motherwell that he worked under high-intensity lights arranged like stage lights, but when his work was shown he liked the light to be extremely low, so muted that the colour blocks would seem to float in indefinite space.

In 1961 Rothko was offered a kind of apotheosis – a full-scale retrospective at the Museum of Modern Art, New York. Peter Selz, the exhibition's curator, wrote a catalogue preface so fulsome that it immediately attracted parodies. Despite this – or even because of it – the painter's reputation continued to soar. His prices were high and his position apparently unassailable – he even found himself courted by the Kennedys at the White House. But inwardly Rothko felt ever more threatened: the beginnings of Pop Art both frightened and enraged him. He denounced its practitioners as 'charlatans and opportunists', and declared that 'the young artists are out to murder us ...' In the spring of 1968 he suffered an aneurysm, and his bouts of depression, which had become increasingly frequent, now gave way to an all-pervasive melancholia.

Rothko's second marriage, once successful and supportive, had been deteriorating for some time; most of the couple's friends were aware of their drunken brawling. Mell Rothko had little physical tolerance for alcohol, but she had begun to drink as a defence against her situation and was well on the way to becoming an alcoholic. On New Year's Day 1969, Rothko walked out. He retired to his studio where, during the last year of his life, he produced a stark series of black on grey paintings which are a painful evocation of his state of mind. His own drinking was out of control, and he was taking heavy dosages of barbiturates and anti-depressants. Early in 1970 he committed suicide, slashing the veins inside the crooks of his arms and bleeding to death. It was a messy end to what had become an intolerably miserable existence.

CLYFFORD STILL

Of all the Abstract Expressionists of the first generation, Clyfford Still's connection with the New York art scene was most peripheral; and of all the major figures in the movement, his reputation seems the least secure.

Still was born in 1904 in Grandin, North Dakota, the son of an accountant. In 1905 his family moved to Spokane, Washington, and after 1910 began to spend much of their time in southern Alberta, when the area was opened to homesteaders by the Canadian Government. They did, however, keep their home in Spokane, and Still attended Edison Grammar School there. He early developed an interest in art and music, and in 1925 went to New York to 'visit the Metropolitan Museum and see at first hand the paintings I had learned to love through study of their reproductions.' Characteristically, he found them disappointing. In November that year he enrolled at the Art Students' League in New York but left after forty-five minutes: 'The exercizes and results I observed I had already explored for myself some years before, and had rejected most of them as a waste of time.'

During 1926 he attended Spokane University, but dropped out after the spring session of 1927 and returned to his family in Canada. In 1931 he was awarded a teaching fellowship in art at Spokane – this was the beginning of a long career as a teacher, during which Still usually seems to have had easier relations with his students than with his colleagues. From 1933 until 1941 he taught at Washington State College, Pullman, Washington (now Washington State University), where he was successively Teaching Fellow, Instructor and Assistant Professor of Fine Arts.

Crucial at this stage in his development were two summers spent on a fellowship at Yaddo – he described this as the first absolutely free time of his life:

> From [a] momentarily emancipated position I was able to collect my resources and begin an intense probing of the instrument I had intuitively chosen as an open means in a field of closed alternatives.

At Yaddo he painted a number of Expressionist figure studies on old green window shades, since at that stage in his career he could not afford proper canvases.

In 1935 Still exhibited professionally for the first time. He was persuaded by the academic portrait painter Sidney E. Dickinson, who had recommended him to Yaddo, to submit a painting to the annual exhibition of the National Academy of Design in New York. It was one of sixty-eight paintings accepted out of fifteen hundred entries; this was almost the last occasion on which Still submitted his work to a juried exhibition.

In 1941 he resigned his teaching post and moved to California, where for two and a half years he worked in the war industries, first for a shipbuilding firm in Oakland, then as a materials release engineer for the Hammon Aircraft Company in San Francisco. He continued to paint in his limited spare time:

> By 1941, space and figure in my canvases had been resolved into a total psychic entity, freeing me from the limitations of each, yet fusing into an instrument bounded only by the limits of my energy and intuition. My feeling of freedom was now absolute and infinitely exhilarating.

The new style which Still had forged for himself was related to the Abstract Expressionism emerging in New York, though he was probably at first unaware of the similarities. His paintings were now large, thickly impastoed, virtually monochromatic abstracts – a version of the manner he was to practise for the rest of his career. The San Francisco Museum was sufficiently impressed to give him a retrospective in March 1943, and later the same year he met Rothko, who had come out to Berkeley to teach at the summer school. The two men immediately recognized a kinship of aim and temperament.

In 1943 Still moved to Richmond, Virginia, where for two years he was Professor at the Richmond Professional Institute. At the conclusion of the spring term in 1945 he went to New York and found himself a studio. Rothko introduced him to Peggy Guggenheim, who promptly invited him to take part in the Autumn Salon at her Art of This Century Gallery which opened in October. Still accepted – he had not yet fully formulated his objections to mixed exhibitions. In the same year Guggenheim brought the Surrealist 'pope', André Breton, with her to Still's studio. The occasion was marked by mutual incomprehension – a gap which she vainly attempted to bridge in translating Still's comments for Breton's benefit:

> Without a dialectic and a set of verbs, Breton was lost. Guggenheim had no doubts, seemed eminently confident. Breton expressed interest but seemed at a loss when he discovered I had no titles to my pictures to give him a key to their meaning. He only recognized I was not a part of his Surrealist theology.

In February 1946 Still had a one-man show at Art of This Century – an event which caused him some trepidation. He noted in his diary: 'I await the opening of the show with a strange mixture of anticipation and cynicism. I have taken the precaution to prepare myself for flight back to Western Canada.' In the event, he did in fact take to his heels. He left New York for Alberta in the spring of 1946, spent the summer building a small house there single-handed, and in the autumn went to San Francisco to take up a teaching position at the California School of Fine Arts, where he remained until 1948. He nevertheless maintained close contact with the New York art world he had briefly inhabited, chiefly through Rothko, with whom he had left a number of paintings in store. In 1946 Rothko sent one of these, without asking Still's permission, to a group show at the Betty Parsons Gallery and was sharply rebuked by Still for doing so. Usually quick to take offence, Rothko seems always to have been slightly in awe of Still. During the late 1940s a mutual friend would make periodic trips to New York to visit Rothko, and then report to Still in California. Rothko invariably asked how big Still's latest painting was, then attempted to make a larger one. Still noted this pattern and then said: 'Tell him I'm now doing paintings the size of postage stamps.' It is one of the few jokes attributed to him. In general he was inclined to hint, and to encourage others

Top: CLYFFORD STILL in his studio, 1953.
Photo Hans Namuth
Bottom: CLYFFORD STILL,
1957-D no. 1, 1957

to believe, that Rothko owed the final style which made him famous to his example.

Still's opinion of his own work was never modest. At about this period he said:

> I had made it clear that a single stroke of paint, backed by work and a mind that understood its potency and limitations, could restore to man the freedom lost in twenty centuries of apology and devices for subjugation.

In California, by the late 1940s, his reputation stood extremely high. But he still hankered after New York, and in 1948 he resigned his teaching position and went East with the intention of establishing an artist-directed school, as he had often discussed with Rothko. He soon discovered that his intended colleagues were unable to make up their minds about the project and returned to San Francisco, where the California School of Fine Arts allowed him to establish a graduate school which was immediately over-subscribed. The school he had planned for New York did eventually open its doors after he had lost patience with the project and returned to the West Coast; it was an immediate failure.

In the autumn of 1950 Still resumed his assault on the recalcitrant New York art world. He moved back to the city and the following year had a one-man show with Betty Parsons, now the chief impresario of Abstract Expressionism. In 1952 seven of his paintings were shown in the influential *Fifteen Americans* show at the Museum of Modern Art; Rothko was another exhibitor. Still justified his appearance in a mixed exhibition by stressing the fact that each exhibitor was allowed a separate compartment. His reputation was at last rising rapidly in the East, but he remained impatient with the New York critical establishment; his view of his own painting was also becoming more and more Hemingwayesque. In 1956 he noted in his diary:

> Like Belmonte weaving the pattern of his being by twisting the powerful bulls around him, I seem to achieve a comparable ecstasy in bringing forth the flaming life through these large responsive areas of canvas.

Meanwhile, he became increasingly reluctant to exhibit. In 1957 he refused to show at the Kunsthalle in

Zurich, in an exhibition he would have shared with Rothko, Kline, De Kooning and Sam Francis. He was, he noted later, 'the only artist in this country who would have refused an exhibition in Europe at this time'. In December of the same year he made the first of numerous refusals to appear at the Venice Biennale.

He did find the kind of conditions he was looking for in 1959, when he had a major one-man show at the Albright-Knox Art Gallery in Buffalo. The catalogue contains what is perhaps his most extravagant statement about his own art:

> It was a journey that one must make, walking straight and alone. No respite or shortcuts were permitted. And one's will had to uphold against every challenge of triumph, or failure, or the praise of Vanity Fair. Until one had crossed the darkened and wasted valleys and come at last into clear air and could stand on a high and limitless plain. Imagination, no longer fettered by the laws of fear, became as one with Vision. And the Act, intrinsic and absolute, was its meaning, and the bearer of its passion.
>
> Therefore let no man undervalue the implications of the work or its power for life; – or for death if it is misused.

This provoked a brutal riposte from painter and critic Ad Reinhardt, who found in it everything he disliked about Abstract Expressionism.

After his triumph at the Albright-Knox, Still was finally ready to abandon New York and moved to Maryland in July 1961. In 1964 he marked his gratitude to Buffalo, at the same time creating a shrine to himself, by presenting the museum with thirty-one major paintings, with the stipulation that the majority were to be kept permanently on view. In 1965 he betrayed his own declared principles by agreeing to appear in a major survey exhibition of Abstract Expressionism at the Los Angeles County Museum. He wrote to his daughter, after her visit to the show, that this was

> a negative matter, since I felt I should not be in it, yet had no alternative, since I had such an important role in forming many of the ideas and paintings that you saw. Thus to be seen explicitly, rather than in incompetent parody, became the pressure point which induced me to show the eight works.

Like other leading Abstract Expressionists, he signed up with the Marlborough-Gerson Gallery in the 1960s, and in 1969 they exhibited the paintings they had purchased from him. In 1975 he gave twenty-eight paintings to the San Francisco Museum of Art, again with the condition that some should be permanently on view. In his final years he received most of the standard honours given to eminent American artists, which culminated in his election to the American Academy of Arts and Letters in 1978. He died in 1980.

WILLEM DE KOONING

Among the giants of Abstract Expressionism Willem de Kooning had the most varied artistic personality. He once said to the critic Harold Rosenberg, 'I am an eclectic painter by choice; I can open almost any book of reproductions and find a painting I could be influenced by.'

He was born in Rotterdam in 1904 to Cornelia Nobel and Leandert de Kooning. His parents divorced when he was about three years old, and he confessed to having missed his absent father, for whom he had a warm affection. His mother, on the other hand, behaved abusively towards him, and he had little love for her. In 1916 he was apprenticed to a local firm of commercial artists and decorators, attending night-classes at the Rotterdam Academy of Fine Arts and Techniques, where he continued to study until 1924. At this stage he encountered the art and thought of the Dutch artists grouped around the central figure of Mondrian:

> When we went to the Academy – doing painting, decorating, making a living – young artists were not interested in the painting per se. We used to call that 'good for men with beards'. And the idea of a palette, with colours on it, was rather silly. At that time we were influenced by the De Stijl group. The idea of being a modern person wasn't really being an artist in the sense of being a painter.

As he grew up De Kooning became restless and impatient with his limiting Dutch environment. In 1924 he travelled through Holland and Belgium, and in 1926 he took a far more decisive step and found his way to the United States as a stowaway:

WILLEM DE KOONING, 1950. Photo Rudolf Burckhardt

I didn't expect there were any artists here. We never heard in Holland that there were artists in America. There was still the feeling that this was where an individual could get places and become well off, if he worked hard; while art, naturally, was in Europe ... When you're about nineteen and twenty, you really want to go up in the world, and you don't mind giving up art.

I was here only about three days when I got a job in Hoboken as a house-painter. I made nine dollars a day, which was quite a large salary, and after being around for four or five months doing that, I started looking for a job doing applied art-work. I made some samples and I was hired immediately. I didn't even ask the salary because I thought that if I made twelve dollars a day as a house-painter, I would make at least twenty dollars a day being an artist. Then at the end of two weeks, the man gave me twenty-five dollars, and I was so astonished that I asked him if that was a day's pay, he said 'No, that's for the whole week.' And I immediately quit and went back to house-painting.

Nevertheless, in 1927 he suffered another change of heart, moved to New York from New Jersey, and worked at various commercial art jobs, among them making signs and displays for a group of shoe-shops. In 1929 De Kooning met Arshile Gorky, to whom he was introduced by fellow painter, Mischa Reznikoff. De Kooning said: 'I was lucky when I came to this country to meet the three smartest guys on the scene: Gorky, Stuart Davis and John Graham'. Gorky and De Kooning developed an almost brotherly relationship, and for a period they shared a studio.

I met a lot of artists – but then I met Gorky. I had had some training in Holland, quite a training, the Academy. Gorky didn't have that at all. He came from no place; he came here when he was sixteen, from Tiflis in Georgia, with an Armenian upbringing. And for some mysterious reason he knew more about painting and art – he just knew it by nature – though I was supposed to know and feel and understand, he really did it better.

De Kooning was able to teach Gorky new techniques. His work as a house-painter and sign-painter had made him a virtuoso in handling the painter's materials.

In the 1930s and 1940s De Kooning had a widespread reputation among his fellow New York artists for never finishing a picture, though a fairly large body of work still survives to prove them wrong. He also had to get to grips with the heritage he brought with him from Europe. In one later interview, commenting on this, he remarked: 'Style is a fraud. It was a horrible idea of Van Doesburg and Mondrian to try to force a style. The reactionary strength of power is that it keeps style and things going.' But in another context he added: 'I'm crazy about Mondrian. I'm always spellbound by him.'

There was another, more immediate problem, too, in the 1930s, and that was keeping alive. De Kooning took a sanguine view of this struggle:

When the Depression came, I got on the WPA ... I was on the Project about a year and a half, and that really made it stick, this attitude [of wanting to be a serious artist], because the amount of money we made on the project was rather fair; in the Depression days one could live modestly and nicely.

Above: WILLEM DE KOONING, 1950. Photo Rudolf Burckhardt.   Right: Willem and Elaine de Kooning, 1950. Photo Rudolf Burckhardt

De Kooning's period on the Federal Art Project, set up to help artists survive the Depression by giving them a small stipend to work for the government, began in 1935 – he worked on both murals and easel painting – but he was eventually removed as an illegal immigrant, and the struggle to make a living began all over again. Gradually, however, he was becoming better known. In 1937 he was commissioned to design one section of a mural for the Hall of Pharmacy at the New York World's Fair, and in 1940 he designed the sets and costumes for *Les Nuages* for the Ballets Russes de Monte Carlo. In 1936 De Kooning met the intelligent and dynamic Elaine Fried (1918–89). Of Irish and German stock, Elaine was also a painter. She was, however, both very good-looking and a gifted promoter of her husband's work. Sometimes, it is alleged, she extracted good reviews from critics in return for sexual favours. In due course, she became an influential critic herself, writing chiefly for *Art News*, and, though she never reviewed her husband's work, she helped to create a favourable context for it through what she wrote about other artists. From the first Willem and Elaine seem to have enjoyed an open relationship, each taking other partners when it pleased them. Having married in 1943, they separated in 1954, both because of the tensions created by other relationships (at this time De Kooning

had a daughter, Lisa, by another woman) and because of their descent into alcoholism.

In the 1940s De Kooning was still forced to undertake some commercial work, and he also experimented with portrait painting which, as he said, provided a free model, but the sitters were rarely satisfied with the results. His work was occasionally seen in public – in 1942 he shared a show at the McMillen Gallery, New York, with John Graham, Stuart Davis, Jackson Pollock and Lee Krasner. This was followed in 1946 by a group show at the Charles Egan Gallery, generally considered the headquarters of the downtown bohemian set, and in 1948 by his first one-man show, again at the Egan Gallery. The powerful black-and-white paintings which he showed created a considerable stir amongst the New York avant-garde, and success was at last almost within reach, though it was to be some years yet before prosperity accompanied it. Characteristically, De Kooning took the opportunity to reflect on his art and where it was taking him. In 1949 he wrote: 'The only certainty today is that one must be self-conscious. The idea of order can only come from above. Order, to me, is to be ordered about, and that is a limitation.' Just when his career seemed to be set on the right course, he decided on a drastic change of direction. In 1950, the year in which his work was shown at the 25th Venice Biennale, he began work on *Woman 1*, the first in

WILLEM DE KOONING, *Excavation*, 1950

a series of Expressionist figurative paintings of women, and a direct rejection of Abstraction. The picture was to cost him much effort and he almost despaired of finishing it.

In 1951 De Kooning's painting *Excavation*, generally considered one of the key works in the evolution of Abstract Expressionism, won the Logan Medal and Purchase Prize at the Sixtieth Annual of American Painting and Sculpture in Chicago, and in 1953 six of the paintings of women were shown at the Sidney Janis Gallery in New York and caused a sensation. In the same year he was given his first small retrospective exhibition, at the Boston Museum School. These events seemed to put him on the same footing as Pollock, with whom he

had long had a rancorous rivalry, fomented on either side by their wives. In the late 1950s, following Pollock's death, De Kooning had a very public affair with Ruth Kligman, once Pollock's mistress, and a survivor of the car crash in which Pollock killed himself. The circle of artists and critics who had created the Abstract Expressionist movement understood the symbolic force of this alliance.

Even this and his increasingly wild drinking were no impediment to De Kooning's now-inevitable acceptance first by the American cultural establishment, and then in Europe. In 1960 he was elected a member of the National Institute of Arts and Letters (ironically, this event took place before he had regularized his status as an illegal immigrant – he did not become an American citizen until 1962), and in 1964 he received the Freedom Award Medal from President Lyndon Johnson. In 1968 he returned triumphantly to the Netherlands, for the first time since he had left as a stowaway in 1926, for a large retrospective exhibition at the Stedelijk Museum in Amsterdam. While he was in Amsterdam he was presented with the first Talens Prize International 'in recognition of the quality of his entire work'. The retrospective show was seen subsequently at the Tate Gallery in London and the Museum of Modern Art in New York.

Five years before this in 1963, De Kooning had made a symbolic gesture, moving from New York, where he had long been considered the quintessential artist-bohemian, to a vast new purpose-built studio at The Springs, Long Island. This could not, however, halt the steady deterioration of his physical and mental condition, which (especially the artist's lapses of memory) had become painfully obvious to many of his old friends by the mid-1970s. In 1976, Elaine de Kooning, who had been scraping a living on her own as a visiting professor at various American universities, returned to take charge of the situation. She herself had given up alcohol, and she now did her best to curb her husband's drinking. She got rid of studio assistants and others who encouraged it for their own purposes, and succeeded in putting some order into his working conditions. De Kooning's career took on a new impetus under her guidance, and she successfully concealed his increasing mental incapacity from most people – it has since been attributed by journalists not merely to sustained alcohol abuse, but to the onset of Alzheimer's Disease. This regime lasted until her own death, from lung cancer caused by heavy smoking, in 1989. De Kooning's guardianship then passed into the hands of his lawyer and into those of his daughter.

From the mid-1980s onwards there was controversy about the paintings which belong to De Kooning's late phase. Claims were made that these are not the artist's own unaided work but are instead composite efforts in which others played a part – either Elaine de Kooning herself, or studio assistants working either under her direction or that of his dealer in the 1980s, Xavier Fourcade. Willem de Kooning died in March 1997.

ARSHILE GORKY

Arshile Gorky's work marks the transition not only from Surrealism to Abstract Expressionism, but from American dependence on imported styles to proud originality.

He was born Vosdanig Adoian in 1905, in a village near Lake Van in Turkish Armenia, the third of four children. His father was a trader and carpenter, who deserted the family for America in 1908 in order to avoid conscription into the Turkish army. Gorky's mother and the two younger children fled from Turkey during the First World War, driven out by the Armenian massacres, and settled temporarily at Erevan in Russian Armenia. His mother died in Russia, and Gorky and his sister were attached to a party of refugees and shipped to the United States to join their estranged father, who was living in Providence, Rhode Island. In later years, somewhat to the disapproval of his more sophisticated artist friends, Gorky liked to parade the Armenian peasant he might have been: he performed folk-songs and peasant dances at parties.

During his first five years in the United States he did a variety of jobs, working at a rubber factory in Watertown, Massachusetts, and as a sketch artist in a Boston theatre. He also managed to build up an education as an artist, studying at the Rhode Island School of Design, at Providence Technical High School, and at the New School of Design in Boston. At the age of twenty-one he went to New York, and was first a student and later an instructor at the Grant Central Art School – it was when he began to make headway as an instructor that he seems to have decided to change his name: he passed himself off in a newspaper interview as a cousin of the Russian writer Maxim Gorky, apparently unaware of the fact that the writer's surname was a pseudonym. Rechristened, the young painter took a romantic view of his vocation. He is

ARSHILE GORKY,
The Liver is the Cock's Comb, 1944

reported to have imported a Hungarian violinist to play for his class, and he himself experimented with a variety of roles: sometimes he wore a coat with a fur collar, and pretended to be a successful European portrait painter; sometimes he grew an impressive beard. The critic Harold Rosenberg, who knew him, wrote:

> When, on arriving in America, Gorky decided to become an artist, he decided at the same time to *look* like an artist. I place great importance on this comic-opera side of Gorky, sustained by his taste for an elegance tuned to the red-plush era and by his DuMaurieresque appearance, tall, dark and handsome, with pleading war-orphan eyes.

Role-playing extended from Gorky's appearance to his art. At first he was a Cézanne follower; then in 1927 he took the step from Cézanne to Cubism. Later still, he was specifically an imitator of Picasso. His dependency on this exemplar became something of a joke in the New York art world, and was the subject of many anecdotes. For instance, when it was maliciously pointed out that

Picasso had abandoned the clean-cut edge Gorky had been at such pains to cultivate, the latter retorted unabashed: 'If Picasso drips – I drip!'

The Depression hit Gorky hard, as it did so many American artists, and there was a period when he was too poor even to buy paint and canvas. This left a permanent mark: later he was famous as a hoarder of artist's materials. His first wife, Marny George, whom he married in 1935 but lived with only briefly, remembered that in spite of usually having to scrape for food (which Arshile often cooked in or over a wood stove) he could never pass by an art supply store without coming home with new tubes and paints and brushes.

Gorky made slow progress in the 1930s. In 1930 he was included in a show at the Museum of Modern Art, *Forty-Six Painters and Sculptors Under Thirty-Five*; in 1932 he became a member of the Abstraction-Création Group in Paris; in 1934 he had his first one-man show, at the Mellon Gallery in Philadelphia. This year also saw the end of his friendship with the veteran American Cubist Stuart Davis and the beginning of a long, quasi-brotherly relationship with Willem de Kooning. It was a great epoch for artists' organizations, and Davis later wrote in a brief memoir of their broken friendship:

> I was in these things from the very beginning and so was Gorky. I took the business as seriously as the serious situation demanded and devoted much time to the organizational work. Gorky was less intense about it and still wanted to play. In the nature of the situation our interests began to diverge and finally ceased to coincide altogether. Our friendship terminated and was never resumed.

Gorky wanted above all else to paint, and the help offered to artists by the Roosevelt administration enabled him to do this. He was in the first group of New York artists hired by the Civil Works Administration (later the Works Project Administration), and in 1935, despite doubts about the 'abstract' nature of his style, he was commissioned to paint an important set of murals on the theme of aviation for Newark airport. These paintings, now lost, marked the end of one stylistic phase and the start of another: in 1936 Gorky moved from a purely Cubist Constructivism to an idiom marked by the use of sweeping organic shapes which prepared the way for the emergence of his mature manner. People who had

Arshile Gorky, 1946.
Photo Gjon Mili

formerly laughed at him, or who had dismissed him as a mere pasticheur, now began to take him more seriously. In 1937 the Whitney Museum bought a painting – his first museum purchase – and in 1938 he had his first one-man exhibition in New York.

The 1940s brought triumph and tragedy. In 1941 Gorky married for a second time. His new wife was Agnes Magruder, the daughter of an American admiral. Gorky nicknamed her 'Mougouch', an Armenian term of endearment, and at first they were very happy, though Gorky's volcanic temperament meant that their alliance was always full of high drama. In 1946 Agnes wrote:

> It is like riding a roller coaster, a huge dipping one to be sure with dizzy heights of elation that I can't describe for my heart is in my mouth.

In 1944 he met the exiled Surrealist group in New York. He formed a particularly close bond with their formidable leader, André Breton, who (and this was a signal honour) wrote the catalogue preface for Gorky's 1945 show at the Julian Levy Gallery in New York. Gorky also formed a friendship with a leading Surrealist younger than himself, the Chilean painter, Matta (Roberto Sebastián Matta Echaurren, born 1911). Contact with Matta's art finally liberated Gorky from the tyranny of imitation.

In 1946 Gorky suffered the first two of a series of ultimately crushing misfortunes. In January a fire at his studio in Sherman, Connecticut, destroyed about twenty-seven paintings and many notebooks and drawings. In February he underwent a serious operation for cancer, and around this time he began to form jealous suspicions about the relationship between his friend Matta and his wife. Worse was to follow. In 1947 the Gorkys moved permanently to Sherman, and on 26 June 1948 he was involved in a serious automobile accident in which his neck was broken and his painting arm temporarily paralysed. The weather was hot and his convalescence was extremely uncomfortable because of the assortment of apparatus he was forced to wear. After he was released from hospital the situation between him and his wife became so tense that she decided that the only possible solution was to separate. On 21 July Gorky committed suicide. His friend and dealer Julian Levy describes this final act in a preface to the retrospective exhibition of

Gorky's work held at the Museum of Modern Art, New York, in 1962:

> After carefully and curiously trying half a dozen favoured spots in which to die (several nooses were found) on hilltops with a view or in intimate valleys with the trees and hilltops pressed close-up to his face, Gorky finally chose the rafters of a little woodshed in Connecticut where he was found swinging nearby a wall-board on which he had chalked: 'Goodbye My Loveds'.

ARSHILE GORKY,
The Artist and His Mother,
1929–42

BARNETT NEWMAN

Barnett Newman's work marks the point of transition
between Abstract Expressionism and the 'colour field'
painting which succeeded it. Newman himself had to
wait considerably longer than most of his contemporaries
for recognition of his true status.

He was born in Manhattan in 1905 of Polish Jewish
stock: his father Abraham had built up a successful
clothing manufacturing company after arriving in
America as a penniless immigrant. Barnett was the
eldest surviving child – after him came a brother and two
sisters. Thanks to his father's success in business he was
brought up in comfortable circumstances and in 1911 the
family moved to a semi-rural part of the Bronx. Newman
remembered his childhood and adolescence as exceptionally happy. His father, with whom he got on well, had
been an expert Talmudic scholar while still in Russia,
but was now easy-going and not particularly orthodox:
his loyalty to Judaism expressed itself not in rigorous

adherence to religious law, but in enthusiastic Zionism.

Newman soon developed an obsessive interest in art –
he played truant from high school to spend whole days in
the Metropolitan Museum of Art. In 1922, when he was
about to graduate, he obtained his mother's permission
to enrol at the Art Students League. In the beginners'
class he attended, many students seemed to have more
flair than he did, and he was delighted when a careful
drawing he had made of a cast of the Belvedere Torso
was picked for the annual students' exhibition. He
continued to attend the Art Students League (and made
an important friend of the painter Adolph Gottlieb) while
he studied at the City College of New York from 1923 to
1927. The years here made little impression on him –
he afterwards claimed that he had gained from only
one class.

When Newman graduated his father asked him to
come into the family clothing business, promising that if

Barnett Newman and his wife Annalee
at the Guggenheim Museum, 1966.
Photo Bernard Gotfryd

Barnett Newman, *Onement I*, 1948

he worked for two years in the business as a full partner he could retire with about $100,000 in capital and lead his life as he wished. But the crash of 1929 changed Newman's future completely: the family business was almost wiped out, but Abraham Newman stubbornly refused to go into bankruptcy. Nearly ten years of struggle and bad luck followed, during which Newman worked part-time with his father and part-time as a substitute art teacher. He also went back to the Art Students League. It was a period of great strain and frustration, but Newman refused to be embittered. He said later:

> They weren't wasted, the years I spent with my father, in the business. I learned about the nature of plasticity in the cutting room, the meaning of form, the visual and tactile nature of things: how to take a rag and make it come to life. I learned the difference between a form and a shape, for instance, I learned that women's clothes are painting and that men's clothes are sculpture ... Soft sculpture ... And I got to know my father as a man ...

In 1937 he was at last released from this family obligation, when his father had a heart attack and retired from the company, which Newman was then able to liquidate.

During these difficult years he was nevertheless able to find time for other activities. He was busy building the reputation as a controversialist in which he was to revel all his life. In 1933 he stood as an independent candidate for Mayor of New York, against Fiorello LaGuardia. His manifesto, which mingled the serious and the comic in typical fashion, had four planks: a municipal art gallery; pavement cafés; a city opera; and playgrounds for adults.

He also found time to marry. The courtship began in characteristic fashion: he was upholding the glory of Mozart at a teachers' meeting, and a young woman defended Wagner. The discussion grew so heated that she finally stormed out of the room. This unpromising encounter was the beginning of a successful relationship – Newman and his opponent, Annalee Greenhouse, were married in 1936.

In the 1930s, his career as an artist was virtually at a standstill. He did not join the various government-sponsored art projects, for two reasons: first, low as the wages were, he could make slightly more money as a teacher; and secondly, he was reluctant to accept what he viewed as a handout from the artist's traditional enemy,

the State. He was later to say rather ruefully: 'I paid a severe price for not being on the project with the other guys; in their eyes I wasn't a painter; I didn't have the label.' At the end of the 1930s he passed through what he described as a 'limbo' period. On one occasion he said despairingly to Gottlieb: 'Painting is finished; we should all give it up.'

It was no doubt Newman's disillusionment with art which diverted him into a serious study of botany, geology and (especially) ornithology in the early 1940s, and in 1941 he took a summer course in ornithology at Cornell University. He was particularly fascinated by the 'wildness – the idea of freedom' which he found in birds, and clashed with his tutors over what they described as his animistic attitude towards them. His studies supply the background to his famous demolition of the philosopher Suzanne Langer when they appeared on a panel together in 1952: 'Esthetics is for artists as ornithology is for the birds.' It is his best-remembered remark.

In 1944 he began a series of drawings of seed and growth motifs – his first continuous work as an artist for nearly a decade. At the same time he destroyed nearly all his previous work. In the winter of 1945–46 he rented a small cold-water flat on the top floor of a building on Lower Fourth Avenue in New York, across the road from Willem de Kooning's studio, and settled down to discover what he could now accomplish as a painter. He did not achieve a real breakthrough until he painted a small picture called *Onement I*, in January 1948. This was a small monochromatic canvas of dark red with a single stripe of light orange running down the middle, and it was the herald of his mature style.

He had by now already established a reputation as a champion of the new American art. When Adolph Gottlieb had his first show with Betty Parsons's Gallery at the Wakefield Bookshop in 1944, Newman wrote the catalogue foreword. Impressed by the intelligence of his text, Betty Parsons asked him to organize two exhibitions of primitive art for her. In 1947, when she moved to the Mortimer Brandt Gallery, Newman organized a show of contemporary American painting, *The Ideographic Picture*, which did much to establish the boundaries of the new art.

Newman's own first one-man show did not take place until January 1950, again with Betty Parsons. Since Newman was, within the confines of the New York avant-garde, an extremely well known figure thanks to his activities as a controversialist and propagandist, his colleagues attended *en bloc*. They reacted violently against his large, smoothly painted, apparently empty canvases – the paintings which had evolved from *Onement I*. Newman received only one good review, from Aline Saarinen of the *New York Times*, who printed a shortened version of Newman's own explanations to her. A second one-man show followed in April 1951, and was an even worse disaster than the first. Very few people, and certainly very few of those whom Newman regarded as his peers, bothered to visit it. He felt the lack of support keenly, especially in view of all he had done for those who now spurned him, and 1951 marked the cooling of old friendships with Mark Rothko, Adolph Gottlieb and Clyfford Still. The one important figure who began to show a slight attraction to Newman's work was the critic Clement Greenberg, who felt that any exhibition which excited so much controversy amongst fellow artists was likely to have something to offer, if only he could find it.

Meanwhile, Newman continued to be in very low water financially. He described 1955–56 as the blackest years of his whole career. Some of his remedies were bizarre: at one time he resolved to give up painting altogether and work as a fitter with a tailor; he entertained a fantasy about 'chalking up' the suit of the President of the Museum of Modern Art, getting him a good fit and then brusquely showing him the door.

In the late 1950s the tide began to turn. In 1958 four of his paintings were included in the Museum of Modern Art's show *The New American Painting*, which toured Europe for two years and introduced post-war American art to an astonished European audience. In the same year he had a retrospective exhibition at Bennington College for which Greenberg wrote the catalogue introduction, and in the autumn of 1959 Greenberg again provided a preface when French & Company opened their prestigious new exhibition space on Madison Avenue with a Barnett Newman exhibition. From this point onwards Newman's reputation was solidly established, and it reached a peak with the exhibition of his *Stations of the Cross* at the Solomon R. Guggenheim Museum in 1966. Newman was then seen as being simultaneously the defender of the idea of the Sublime against the cynicism of Pop Art, and as the forerunner of what was soon to be identified as Minimalism.

In his final years – he died in 1970 – Newman was loved, respected, and occasionally laughed at, chiefly for his irrepressible flow of words. A colleague described him as 'an artist of the 1940s – perhaps the only one left; you meet him on the street and stop for a six-hour conversation.'

LEE KRASNER

Lee Krasner occupies an ambiguous position in the history of Abstract Expressionism. On the one hand she is seen as someone who subsumed her artistic identity in that of her husband, Jackson Pollock, and who later became the ferocious guardian of his work and reputation. On the other she has become a feminist icon, and an emblem of the neglect which is often the lot of gifted women artists.

She was born Lena Krassner in Brooklyn in 1908, the sixth child of Russian Jewish immigrant parents, and the first member of her family to be born in the United States. Her father was a market trader, selling fruit, vegetables and fish. After schooling in Brooklyn, she transferred to Washington Irving High School in Manhattan, which was the only public high school in the city where a girl could study art. Later, from the spring of 1926 to the spring of 1928, she studied at the Women's Art School of the Cooper Union. In 1928 she transferred to the Arts Students' League, where the teaching was less structured and more imaginative; then, finding the instruction did not suit her, to the National Academy of Design. Here she linked up with a fellow student, a young man of White Russian descent named Igor Pantuhoff, who was later to make a career as a society portraitist. They lived together for some years.

In the 1930s, having changed her name to Lenore Krasner, she enrolled in the Public Works of Art Project, like the majority of artists in New York. Since she had no seniority, the tasks she was assigned were not very interesting. In 1936, according to some accounts, she met Jackson Pollock, four years younger than herself, at an Artists Union party. In 1937 she began to study again, this time with Hans Hofmann.

During this period her work, like that of many New York artists of her generation, was extremely eclectic. She was a strong draughtsman of the figure – stronger than

Pollock was ever to become. Her paintings showed the influence of Cézanne, Matisse and the then fashionable Surrealists. There were even a few in a Social Realist vein. Krasner was almost as interested in politics as she was in art, taking part in numerous demonstrations on behalf of the Artists Union, and sometimes being jailed. Her relationship with Pantuhoff degenerated as she came to realize the limitations of his talent, and in 1939 they separated, by most accounts amicably.

In 1941 she was introduced to another Russian, the painter John Graham (Ivan Dabrowski), who claimed to have fought in the Russian civil war in the early 1920s, as a cavalry officer for the Whites. Graham was regarded by many younger New York artists as a kind of prophet, and he had widespread influence. He liked Krasner, and in December 1941 he invited her to participate in a prestigious show he was organizing for the design firm of McMillen Inc. Among the participants were some of the great names of European Modernism – Picasso, Braque and Matisse. Among the Americans was Jackson Pollock. Learning that Pollock lived only a block from her own apartment, she decided to go over and introduce herself.

By the autumn of 1942 they were living together. Lenore, now 'Lee', decided to devote most of her immense energy to promoting her new partner, whose outstanding gifts she had immediately recognized. She played a major role in manoeuvring Pollock into Peggy Guggenheim's fashionable Art of the Century Gallery, where he had his first one-man show in November 1943, and in obtaining a contract for him.

In 1945, largely because of Pollock's alcoholism, the couple decided to move out of New York and live in Long Island, which seemed to offer a much less stressful environment. They married. Lee adjusted very well to country life, and Pollock, at least for a two-year period from 1948, stopped drinking. Both were painting prolifically – this was the period at which Lee produced her *Little Image* series. These are some of her most characteristic works, their small scale dictated by the fact that she used their small living room as her studio, while Pollock used the barn.

By 1951 Pollock was drinking again, and Lee had her first solo show with Betty Parsons, now her husband's dealer. It was a mild critical success but a commercial

LEE KRASNER and JACKSON POLLOCK, *c.* 1950. Photo Wilfred Zogbaum

failure, and when Pollock left the Parsons stable in the same year, his wife was told to go with him. She used the unsold canvases as backgrounds for the collages which she made for her next show, held at the Stable Gallery in 1955. In destroying paintings which had been rejected, she expressed her rage not only at the New York art world's attitude to her work, but also her feelings about her own personal dilemma. Her marriage was now under severe strain. Pollock was drinking more heavily than ever, and seemed unable to paint. In 1956, he began an affair with a young model named Ruth Kligman and Lee started to contemplate divorce.

Friends persuaded her to take a European vacation to think matters over, and during her absence Pollock was killed in a drunken car crash. Krasner returned to organize his funeral and look after his estate, now suddenly very valuable. In the years that followed she earned herself a reputation as the quintessential 'art widow' – the term first coined to describe her in a 1965 article written for *Esquire* by the critic Harold Rosenberg. She knew this, and was unrepentant. In her view she simply did what had to be done to secure her husband's legacy, artistic as well as financial. Meanwhile, she took

over Pollock's studio and began to paint on a very much larger scale than previously. One work from this period, *The Seasons* (Whitney Museum), is seventeen feet long.

Her third solo show, held at the Martha Jackson Gallery eighteen months after Pollock's death, attracted much more attention than the two previous ones, but both Krasner and others found it hard to decide if this was due to her own merits or her newly acquired status as an important 'player' in the game of art.

At Christmas 1962, perhaps as a result of the cumulative stresses of the past seven or eight years, Krasner was struck down by a cerebral aneurysm – the first in a succession of accidents and illnesses. Her luck did not turn again until 1965, when she was offered a show by the Whitechapel Art Gallery in London, the launch pad for many American reputations in Europe. The exhibition was a substantial success.

The tide, however, did not really begin to turn for her in the United States until the early 1970s. Two events coincided: she gave up the administration of her husband's estate to concentrate on her own work, and she was discovered by the emergent feminist movement in the arts. The interest was reciprocated – in 1972, after an absence from political activism of more than thirty years, she returned to the picket lines to protest about the Museum of Modern Art's neglect of female artists.

Her leading role in the emergence of the Abstract Expressionist movement had first been recognized in 1969, when she was the only female artist included in the survey show *The New American Painting and Sculpture: The First Generation*, staged at the Museum of Modern Art. Less than ten years later, she was prominently included in another major survey, *Abstract Expressionism: The Formative Years*, organized by the Herbert F. Johnson Museum, Cornell University, in conjunction with the Whitney. From this time onwards she was the recipient of numerous honours. In 1983 the Houston Museum of Fine Arts opened a full retrospective of her work. After showings in San Francisco, in Norfolk, Virginia and in Phoenix, this reached New York in the autumn of 1984. Krasner had been able to attend the Houston opening, but she died before the show reached New York. Thanks to Pollock, and to her own care for his legacy, she died an extremely wealthy woman. Her estate funded the Pollock-Krasner Foundation, set up under the terms of her will, which provides funds for struggling artists.

LEE KRASNER,
Noon, 1947

FRANZ KLINE

Franz Kline was a member of the second Abstract Expressionist generation. His warm and likeable personality made him popular, though memoirs of the time recall him as a hard drinker, he was not an 'ugly' drunk like Jackson Pollock and (on some occasions) Willem de Kooning. A leading figure at the Cedar Bar, the Abstract Expressionists' downtown hangout in New York, he was also a companion of the literary beats, especially of Jack Kerouac.

Kline was born in Wilkes-Barre, Pennsylvania in 1910, the second of four children. His parents were both immigrants – his father, a saloon-keeper, came from Hamburg and his mother from Cornwall. In 1917 his father committed suicide, and his mother remarried three years later. From 1919 to 1925 Kline attended

Girard College, Philadelphia, an institution for fatherless boys which he afterwards referred to as 'an orphanage'. In retrospect, he also lengthened his stay there to 'eleven years', which hints that it may have been a traumatic experience. After his mother withdrew him from Girard, Kline attended Lehighton High School. Though not a big man, he was athletic and was Captain of Varsity Football in 1929. While at high school, he had an accident in football practice which immobilized him for a while, and this was when he developed an interest in drawing and decided to become a cartoonist and illustrator.

In 1931 he left home and went to Boston to begin his training. He studied first at the Boston University School of Education and later at the Boston Art Students' League. At this time Kline, a handsome and vain young man, was attracted by everything which seemed upper-class and English, so it was natural than in 1935 he should decide to go to England to study art. He crossed the Atlantic in 1935, and in 1936 enrolled at Heatherley's School of Fine Art in London. This was a thoroughly conservative, old-fashioned institution, and it suited Kline perfectly as he was not at that time interested in anything avant-garde but was, on the contrary, fascinated by the work of the great Victorian illustrators, such as Phil May.

He did a great deal of life-drawing in London, and it was at Heatherley's that he met his future wife, Elizabeth Vincent Parsons, a dancer who had worked with the Sadlers' Wells Ballet Company (later the Royal Ballet) and with the Ballet Rambert, and who modelled for classes at the school. Her family was upper middle-class, and Kline's identification with all things English reached the point where he wanted to adopt British citizenship. However, to achieve this he would have had to remain in Britain for eight years without permission to work. This was impossible, so he returned to America in 1938. Elizabeth followed him, and they were married shortly after her arrival. Kline then spent a brief period in Buffalo as a display designer for a women's clothing store before settling in New York, where he was to live for the rest of his life.

He began his career in the New York art world at the bottom of the ladder, showing his work at the Washington Square Outdoor Show in 1939. During this period he was producing competent urban views, usually of New York, with an Expressionist tinge. He painted murals in bars, and also worked briefly with the well known set designer Cleon Throckmorton, who employed

FRANZ KLINE,
New York, N.Y.,
1953

a large number of assistants and often provided useful contacts for them. In 1943 and 1944 he showed successfully at the annual exhibitions put on by the conservative National Academy of Design, winning one of the major prizes in 1943.

This was also the year in which he met Willem de Kooning, who was to exercize a great influence over his art. It was De Kooning who in 1949 borrowed a Bell-Opticon projector to enlarge some of his own drawings. Offered the use of it, Kline took a small drawing of a favourite chair and projected this on to canvas on such a large scale that it completely overlapped the edges. He was fascinated to note that the design, in these circumstances, became completely abstract.

Its effect on him was the more powerful because he had already begun to experiment with abstraction some three years earlier. The transition from figuration to abstraction was a curious one, demonstrated through a series of heads based on a photograph of the dancer Nijinsky in the role of Petroushka. Kline identified with clowns. In 1938 he wrote to his wife: 'I have always felt that I am like a clown, and thinking that life might work out as a tragedy, a clown's tragedy.' The Nijinsky paintings also have strong elements of self-portraiture.

There may also have been another, very personal factor connected with Kline's move into abstraction, and this was the illness of his wife. She suffered repeated attacks of depression and schizophrenia, perhaps exacerbated by their lack of money and nomadic, unstable life. Between his arrival in New York in 1938 and 1957 Kline moved house no less than fourteen times, including at least three evictions because he was unable to pay the rent. In 1946, Elizabeth Kline entered Central Islip State Hospital for six months, and in 1948 she returned to hospital and remained there for twelve years, being finally discharged in 1960. Her husband visited her, often at long intervals, but from the time of her second hospitalization the marriage was effectively over. Kline, handsome, outgoing and charming, was not slow to find consolation elsewhere, and became especially attractive to women when he started at long last to enjoy success.

Kline's experiments with the Bell-Opticon projector had finally convinced him that he ought to abandon representation altogether. In 1950 he had his first one-man exhibition, made up entirely of paintings in his new manner. It took place at the Egan Gallery, then the

FRANZ KLINE, c. 1960. Photo Walter Auerbach

usual showcase of the 'downtown' group of Abstract Expressionists. His calligraphic images in black-and-white were well received, and after a second show in the same space in 1951, Kline's reputation grew very rapidly.

He was included in a number of key exhibitions in the 1950s: various Whitney Annuals, starting in 1952; *Twelve American Painters and Sculptors* at the Museum of Modern Art in 1955; the São Paulo Biennial in 1957, and the key anthology show *New American Painting*, which toured Europe in 1958–59. The Museum of Modern Art acquired *Chief*, one of his most impressive paintings, in 1952 – the underlying image is a streamlined locomotive (Kline's stepfather was a railway employee). The Whitney Museum bought *Mahoning* in 1955. Prices for Kline's work escalated rapidly, especially after he moved to the Sidney Janis Gallery in 1956. For the first time, he had plenty of money.

He was not to enjoy this prosperity for very long. In 1961 Kline fell ill and entered Johns Hopkins Hospital for tests which revealed long-standing rheumatic heart-trouble, with more recent and dangerous deterioration of the heart-muscle. He was put on a strict diet and told to curb his lifestyle, but his illness was incurable. He died in hospital in New York in May 1962.

Kline's talk ranged over many subjects – his favourite English illustrators, the lives of Baron Gros and Sir Joshua Reynolds, Géricault's way of depicting horses, old silver and pewter, the finer points of vintage cars. Many people remembered being amused by his accurate imitations of the actor Wallace Beery. However, the core personality remained difficult to identify. His attitudes towards art were basically those of the Abstract Expressionists, mingled with some loosely existentialist ideas. Kline frequently spoke of a painting as a 'situation', and of the first strokes of paint on canvas as 'the beginning of the situation'. When painting, he said, he tried to rid his mind of everything else and 'attack it completely from that situation'. The real criterion was the feeling a given work conveyed: 'The final test of a painting, theirs [that of artists he admired, such as Daumier], mine, or any other, is: does the painter's emotion come across?'

JACKSON POLLOCK

Jackson Pollock represents an extreme point in the development of the artist's attitude towards his own vocation. He once said in a radio interview given in 1951:

> The thing that interests me is that today painters do not have to go to a subject-matter outside themselves. Modern painters work in a different way. They work from within.

He was not merely a modern artist who summed up in his own career many of the developments which had taken place since Fauvism, but a specifically American one, functioning just at the moment when America came of age as a world power. In Pollock's career American and Modernist elements were symbolically intertwined.

He was born on 28 January 1912, on a sheep ranch in Cody, Wyoming, the youngest of five brothers. Before he was a year old the family moved to California, then to Arizona, and they continued to divide their time between California and Arizona throughout Pollock's childhood. Their frequent moves were dictated by his father's lack of success in business.

One of the things which Pollock gained from life in the West was at least superficial contact with American Indian culture. In particular, he may have been attracted by the Indian custom of making sand-paintings on the floor as part of religious ritual. He also came into contact

Above: JACKSON POLLOCK, *Portrait and a Dream*, 1953
Right: Pollock at work, seen from above, 1950.
Photo Rudolf Burckhardt

with a more modern kind of mystical thought, that of the Hindu prophet and poet Krishnamurti, then in fashion with the volatile Californian public, and was taken to several of Krishnamurti's camp-meetings at Ojai, north of Los Angeles. One of the teacher's sayings must certainly have struck him: 'Fall in love with yourself and you fall in love with the truth.'

Pollock was already studying at the Manual Arts High School in California when he had this early brush with Eastern thought. In 1930 he abandoned California, going to New York to continue his studies. He was, however, for some years to make periodic forays across America, savouring its vastness, and the fluidity of the passing landscape as seen from a speeding automobile – a sensation which had not been available to the painters who first tried to pin down some kind of American identity.

In New York, he enrolled at the Art Students' League under Thomas Hart Benton, the leader of the American Regionalists. To begin with the young Pollock fell completely under Benton's influence and strove to

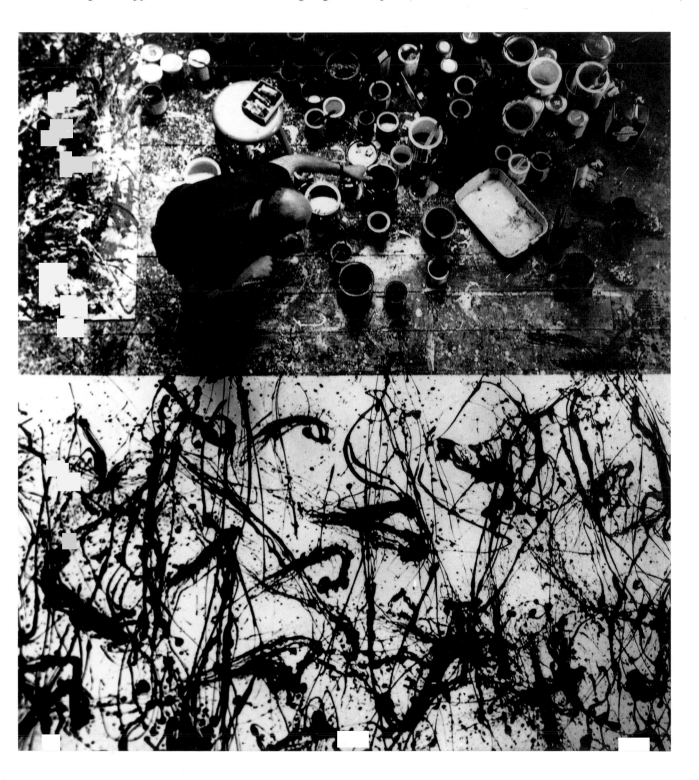

imitate his work. He was also attracted, at a more personal level, by Benton's cult of hard-drinking masculinity; alcoholism was to dog Pollock throughout his life. He tried many forms of treatment, including Jungian psychotherapy – indeed, Jung's idea of archetypal images rising from the deepest subconscious was to exercize considerable influence over his work. Such images made their appearance in a transitional phase in his painting before it became for a while entirely abstract, and they also reappeared sporadically towards the end of his career.

Many people came to identify Pollock's alcoholism with his creative capacities, and perhaps he did so himself, thinking that drink released something in him which nothing else could. Drink became part of his legend, that of the artist as roaring-boy, rebel and outcast, doomed even when apparently successful.

Success in any guise was a long time in coming. During the early 1930s Pollock remained totally unknown, and, like other American avant-garde artists, had a harsh struggle to survive through the years of the Depression. He did find a place on the Federal Art Project, and a small wage from this source enabled him to continue painting. An important influence during this period was that of the Mexican muralists. It was not the political content of their work which interested Pollock, but their emotionalism and their bold disregard for accepted formats and techniques. Pollock had personal contact with David Alfaro Siqueiros, who briefly ran an experimental workshop in New York. Siqueiros advocated both unconventional methods, such as stencilling, spattering and spraying, and also the use of new materials such as Duco (pyroxylin paint of the kind used in the automobile industry) and other industrial lacquers and enamels. He introduced Pollock to the idea of the 'controlled accident', and at the same time convinced him that a wholly personal art could ally itself to the industrial world. But the strain remained great. In June 1938 Pollock had a nervous breakdown which lasted for six months. Nevertheless, he had begun to convince one or two people that he had enormous talent.

In 1942 Pollock achieved his first real breakthrough. A painting of his was included in a show at the McMillen Gallery in New York, which was part of a firm of interior decorators. The exhibition included a distinguished French contingent, among them Picasso, Bonnard and Braque. Another American painter shown was Lee Krasner, a brilliant young woman who began introducing Pollock to a broader art world. A year later, after doing a variety of menial odd jobs (one of them was hand-painting neckties), Pollock met the patron Peggy Guggenheim. Guggenheim had recently returned to New York because of the war and had opened the Art of This Century Gallery, providing a link between a large contingent of European Surrealists in exile and the younger generation of American artists. She was impressed by Pollock, apparently as much by his machismo as by his talent, and offered him a contract.

It was at this point that the scribbled, calligraphic style soon to be associated with the artist began to emerge. His new manner was noted by one very important expert. In a review of Pollock's first one-man show, printed in the intellectual weekly *The Nation* in November 1944, the young critic Clement Greenberg hailed Pollock as the author of 'some of the strongest paintings I have yet seen by an American'. From this point onwards Pollock's reputation grew steadily, though his art still brought him little money and much of the attention he received was uncomprehending or malicious. He married Lee Krasner in 1945 (Peggy Guggenheim was invited to be a witness but did not attend), and together they moved to a farmhouse on Long Island, just outside East Hampton – a town which was later to become an artist's colony consisting largely of the Pollocks' friends.

Pollock's work became increasingly radical. By 1947 he was working with the canvas laid on the floor, using paint poured directly from a tin. Painting had now become for him a purely subjective act, the direct and instinctive expression of the artist's psyche. A series of photographs taken in 1950, and two films made in the following year, show that making a picture had been transformed into a kind of complex, improvised ritual dance, the equivalent of the Indian ceremonies Pollock might have witnessed in Arizona when he was a boy.

Pollock's main problem now was that the undisturbed conditions he needed in order to enact the ritual properly (he painted at most for a few hours, sometimes only minutes a day) were increasingly hard to obtain. He had begun to attract the attention of the mass media. In 1947 *Time* magazine devoted a column to him, and in 1949 *Life* made him the subject of a major article. For a wide public, Pollock became one of the symbols of modern art – incomprehensible, perhaps fatuous, but undoubtedly exciting. His painter contemporaries, on the other hand, began to see him as someone who had 'made it'; they envied him, yet regarded him as a talisman, and his known moodiness became a challenge. When Pollock visited New York in his later years, the habitués of the Cedar Bar, then the chief artists' haunt in the city, made it almost a point of honour to get him drunk. 'For them,' one eye-witness wrote, 'Jackson was a freak, part of the entertainment, a notorious figure in the art world who had somehow succeeded in spite of himself.'

Pollock held his last one-man show in 1954. His rate of production slowed to a trickle; then he stopped painting altogether. In February 1956 he began an affair which led to a separation from his wife. On the night of 10 August Pollock, driving with his young mistress and another passenger, crashed his car on a road near his home in East Hampton. He was flung out of the vehicle and killed instantly. To many of his friends his end seemed curiously inevitable. For them Pollock was an artistic frontiersman, a being who combined the myth of Modernism with an even more potent American myth: that of the solitary individual who tames a dangerous wilderness and who makes it possible for others to colonize it at the sacrifice of his own life.

AD REINHARDT

Ad Reinhardt played two rather different roles in the New York art world of the post-war epoch. First, he was the self-appointed conscience of his fellow artists, and second, he provided the point of transition between Abstract Expressionism and Minimal Art.

He was born in New York on 24 December 1913. His father was an immigrant from Russia; his mother came from Germany. He showed some talent for art early on – he reported in a autobiographical sketch that he won a flower-painting contest in 1920, and that in 1927 he won a prize for his pencil portraits, which included one of the boxer Jack Dempsey. In 1931 he went to Columbia University, where one of his instructors was the distinguished art-historian Meyer Schapiro, who guided him to the various radical groups which then existed on campus. In 1935 he was elected to the Columbia Student Board on a promise to abolish fraternities, and the same year he became editor of the campus magazine *Jester*, in succession to the novelist Herman Wouk.

Reinhardt only began to study painting seriously in 1936, but soon found his way into the very centre of the New York avant-garde:

I got out of Columbia and I got on to the WPA project and then into the American Abstract Artists group, which had almost all the abstract artists in the country in it, about forty or fifty. There weren't many abstract artists not in it. I think Stuart Davis didn't belong, because he still liked belonging to social protest groups.

Reinhardt never seems to have had any doubt that Abstraction was what he should be producing. He once declared, when speaking of abstract art: 'I was born for it, and it was born for me.' The man who hired him for the Federal Art Project was Burgoyne Diller, one of the most distinguished American abstract painters of the inter-war period.

The Federal Projects Administration (FPA) supported Reinhardt comparatively handsomely until 1941, when he was forced to leave it and turn his hand to whatever work was available:

In the early forties I ran the gamut of commercial and industrial jobs around the New York World's Fair ... I guess I could do any commercial or industrial job and then I got on *PM* in forty-four.

PM was a newspaper, and Reinhardt's experience of this kind of work was to stand him in good stead later. First, however, there was the interruption of the war:

I was drafted and I was a sailor for a year. They didn't know what to do with me, so they made a sort of photographer out of me. I was in Pensacola and San Diego. I was always thrown in with a bunch of kids. I was 29 then. I was called Pop. I was the old man of every outfit. ... The dropping of the bomb prevented me from getting anywhere near anyone shooting at me.

Reinhardt was discharged from the US Navy in 1945, and returned to *PM*, which fired him the following year. But, thanks to his experience in journalism, he was then offered a job at Brooklyn College, where he taught for most of the rest of his career. His view of this occupation

Top: AD REINHARDT in his Broadway studio,
New York, 1961.
Photo Fred W. McDarrah
Bottom: AD REINHARDT,
Red Painting, 1952

was sardonic. In 1966 he declared: 'I've been teaching for almost twenty years. I've never been called a good teacher, incidentally. I'm proud of that.' Nevertheless, he took a keen interest in the foibles of American art education and art educators, just as he did in those of the art world in general. 'Brooklyn', he noted, 'was the first to be struck by the Bauhaus thing, and it swept the country.'

In the post-war epoch Reinhardt's reputation made steady but not spectacular progress. In 1946 he had a show with Betty Parsons, and by 1955, to his incredulous amusement, the business magazine *Fortune* listed him as one of the twelve best investments in the art market. Reinhardt himself never longed for commercial success, and he despised the increasing number of artists who made concessions in order to achieve it in the 1950s and 1960s. In 1966 he said:

I haven't done any cartoons or satires for a long time because it doesn't seem possible, the art world is no longer satirizable. I suppose there isn't much going on except business, and that's not funny. Ten years or fifteen years ago (perhaps it was longer), it was possible for one artist to call another artist an old whore. It's not possible any more. The whole art world is whorish and one artist couldn't possibly call another an old or a young whore.

His own progression was towards increasingly difficult, introspective work. In a note on his own art he analysed his progress from 'late-classical mannerist post-cubist geometric abstractions of the late thirties', to 'rococo semi-surrealist fragmentation', and then to 'archaic colour brick-brushwork impressionism and black and white constructivist-calligraphy of the late forties.' In 1953, just as Abstract Expressionism was beginning to achieve real success, he gave up all traces of asymmetry and irregularity and began to produce monochrome canvases in red, blue and black, patterned by barely visible squares in different tones of the same colour. Finally, in the 1960s, all his canvases became what he described as 'classical black-square uniform five-foot timeless trisected evanescences'. He described the black paintings as 'the first paintings that cannot be misunderstood', to make the point clear he added: 'Art is art. Everything else is everything else.'

Reinhardt's quarrel with the Abstract Expressionists was prolonged and intimate. Artists like Clyfford Still,

Mark Rothko and Robert Motherwell were very much part of his social circle. His attitude towards their work, however, was essentially that of an uncompromising moralist, and this was why he remained, until the end, an outsider, a man who gloried in making those who surrounded him feel uncomfortable: referring to Clyfford Still's 1959 show at the Albright-Knox Gallery, Buffalo, he said:

> It is not right for an artist to make his bag of tricks a matter of life and death. Artists who send chills, however delicious, up curators' spines with warnings like 'Let no man undervalue the implications of this work, or its powers for life, or for death, if it is misused,' should be charged with arson and false alarm.

In the last decade of his life Reinhardt, though far from being one of the most successful artists in New York, was making enough money to be able to travel extensively in the Near and Far East. In 1958 he visited Japan, India, Persia and Egypt; in 1961 he went to Turkey, Syria and Jordan. In these places he found things which seemed to confirm his own attitudes towards art, though he was also quite sure of his own status as a member of the Modern movement. He even claimed, only half in jest, to be 'the only painter who's been a member of every avant-garde movement in art of the last thirty years'. He had a triumphant retrospective exhibition at the Jewish Museum, New York, in 1966, and died in 1967.

AD REINHARDT,
Abstract Expressionism: No. 15,
1952

Whereas American art in the immediately post-war epoch was relatively unified, this was far from being the case in Europe. Giacometti, Bacon, Balthus and Dubuffet – the four most important artists of the period – were all figurative (the European effort to rival American abstraction was never successful). Each evinced a very different attitude towards the problem of depicting reality. Giacometti and Bacon have both been described as 'existentialist' and have been aligned by critics with the philosophy elaborated by Jean-Paul Sartre. In each case the connection is doubtful, though Giacometti belonged to the social circle that surrounded Sartre in the years immediately after the war. Dubuffet was fascinated with *art brut* (raw art) – the images produced by children, by the mad and by furtive urban graffitists. These had previously interested the Surrealists, and Parisian graffiti had already been extensively recorded by the photographer Brassaï, who had links with the Surrealist Group. Balthus deliberately distanced himself from Surrealism before the war, and his figures are much closer to the developed tradition of European figurative painting, as typified by artists such as the nineteenth-century realist Gustave Courbet, though Balthus did also borrow ideas from 'popular' art of the nineteenth century – from provincial Swiss painters of regional costumes, from the creators of signs for inns and shops, and from crude prints known as *images d'Epinal*, after the town in which they were manufactured.

Left: ALBERTO GIACOMETTI installing his sculpture at the Galerie Maeght, Paris 1961.
Photo Henri Cartier-Bresson
Above: ALBERTO GIACOMETTI's eye, 1963.
Photo Bill Brandt

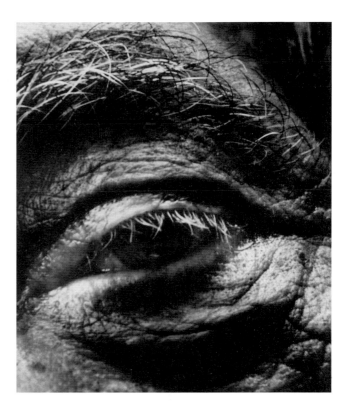

ALBERTO GIACOMETTI

Alberto Giacometti is, both because of the nature of his work and because of his close friendship with the philosopher Jean-Paul Sartre, the artist most closely identified with the Existentialist movement. Part of his art-historical importance springs from his defence of figuration at a time when the advantage was with abstract art.

He was born in October 1901 in Italian-speaking Switzerland and came from an artistic background – his father, Giovanni, was a well known Post-Impressionist painter. Alberto was the eldest of four children and was always especially close to the brother nearest to him in age, Diego. From the beginning, he was interested in art:

As a child, what I most wanted to do was illustrate stories. The first drawing I remember was an illustration to a fairy-tale: Snow White in a tiny coffin, and the dwarfs.

He remembered his youth as being very happy; he also recalled his own arrogant self-confidence: 'I thought I could copy absolutely anything, and that I understood it better than anybody else.' This self-confidence began to waver in 1919:

Once in my father's studio, when I was eighteen or nineteen, I was drawing some pears which were on a table – at the usual still-life distance. But they kept getting smaller and smaller. I'd begin again, and they'd always go back to exactly the same size. My father got irritated and said: 'Now start doing them as they are, as you see them.' And he corrected them to life-size. I tried to do them like that, but I couldn't help rubbing out; so I rubbed them out, and half an hour later my pears were exactly as small to the millimetre as the first ones.

His father allowed him a break from school in order to find himself, but instead of returning to school afterwards, Giacometti went to the School of Arts and Crafts in Geneva, where he studied with a member of Archipenko's circle. In May 1920 he went to Venice for the Biennale, where his father was an exhibitor, and discovered Tintoretto, who inspired him with a kind of euphoria. But on the way back he visited Padua, where he discovered Giotto in the Arena Chapel: 'The frescoes of Giotto gave me a crushing blow in the chest. I was suddenly aimless and lost, I felt deep pain and great sorrow.' He made two more visits to Italy in quick succession. During the second one, an old Dutchman whom he had agreed to accompany, and whom he in fact scarcely knew, was suddenly taken ill and died. His death made a great impression on the young Giacometti – he later said it was the reason why he had always lived provisionally, with as few possessions as possible:

Establishing yourself, furnishing a house, building up a comfortable existence, and having that menace hanging over your head all the time – no, I prefer to live in hotels, cafés, just passing through.

In 1922 Giacometti went to Paris, to study under the sculptor Bourdelle at the Ecole de la Grande Chaumière, and in 1925 he and his brother Diego set up an atelier together. In 1927 he had his first one-man exhibition, at a gallery in Zurich, and in the same year the brothers moved to the cramped studios in the rue Hippolyte-Maindron which they were to use for the rest of Alberto's life. In 1928 he exhibited two sculptures at the Galerie Jeanne Bucher. These not only sold immediately, but brought Giacometti into contact with the Paris avant-garde: in particular, he met Masson and the circle surrounding him. In 1929 he signed a contract with Pierre Loeb, then the Surrealists' preferred dealer, and this was followed by an invitation to join the Surrealist Group. His first one man show took place in 1932, and set a fashion for Surrealist objects with symbolic or erotic overtones. Much of Giacometti's art at this time was influenced by primitive sculpture seen at the Musée de l'Homme – an influence which was to persist even after he changed direction as an artist.

Like many avant-garde artists of the time, Giacometti found himself in a dilemma. His clientele was a fashionable one, and in addition he supplemented his income by making decorative objects, in collaboration with his brother Diego, for the leading decorator Jean-Michel Frank; but he was keenly aware of the class struggle in France and sympathized with the underdogs. Louis Aragon, the member of the Surrealist Group with whom he felt the closest bond of sympathy, reacted to the same tensions by becoming a committed Communist. Giacometti moved in a different direction: he gradually separated himself from the Surrealists and returned (a great heresy) to working from the model – he began with a series of portrait busts of Diego. Breton did not like this development and Giacometti was tricked into attending what turned out to be a Surrealist tribunal. Before the proceedings could be fully started, he said, 'Don't bother. I'm going,' and turned his back and walked out. There was no public excommunication, but his friends in the movement deserted him.

In the late 1930s his career was repeatedly interrupted – first by an accident when a car ran over his foot, then by the outbreak of war. In 1941, in wartime Paris, he made very important new friendships, with the philosopher Jean-Paul Sartre and Simone de Beauvoir. But as the Occupation tightened its grip, he moved to Switzerland, arriving in Geneva on the last day of 1941. He lived and worked in a small hotel room and supported himself by making furniture and doing interior decoration work passed on to him by his brother Bruno, who was an architect. While living in Geneva, he met Annette Arm, whom he later married.

ALBERTO GIACOMETTI,
*Annette in the Atelier with 'Chariot'
and 'Four Figures on a Pedestal'*, 1950

Alberto Giacometti 271

An important development in Giacometti's work took place during the war years. In the period 1935–40 he had worked from the model, and had also made some paintings; he then began to make heads and standing figures from memory, but had an experience which paralleled his attempt in his late teens to draw the still life of pears in his father's studio:

To my terror the sculptures became smaller and smaller. Only when small were they like, and all the same these dimensions revolted me, and tirelessly I began again, only to end up, a few months later, at the same point.

When he packed up to leave Geneva, his total output while he was there fitted into half-a-dozen matchboxes. It was only when he returned to Paris after the war that he found himself able to make sculptures of more normal dimensions, but now they were tall and thin. He reoccupied his studio, which was still intact, and shortly afterwards he was rejoined by Annette.

In January 1948 Giacometti's new work was exhibited at the Pierre Matisse Gallery, New York. The catalogue preface, written by Sartre, did much to propagate the idea that Giacometti's art was now one 'of existential reality'. From this point his post-war reputation as a sculptor (the paintings were neglected until the late 1950s) grew rapidly. He held his first European one-man show of the new work at the Kunsthalle in Basle in 1950, and his first Paris exhibition since the war at the Galerie Maeght in 1951.

The year 1956 saw a further development in his work – he was now seized with a desire to produce paintings which were recognizable likenesses. Each portrait required many sittings – the business of sitting for Giacometti has been described in a lively book by James Lord, who stresses the artist's half-humorous despair at his continual inability to catch precisely what he wanted. Giacometti himself once said:

If I could make a sculpture or a painting (but I'm not sure I want to) in just the way I'd like to, they would have been made long since (but I am incapable of saying what I want). Oh, I see a marvellous and brilliant painting, but I didn't do it, nobody did it. I don't see my sculpture, I see blackness.

He was awarded the major prize for sculpture at the Venice Biennale of 1962, and the award brought with it worldwide celebrity. He was philosophical about the penalties of fame:

I refused the intrusion of success and recognition as long as I could. But maybe the best way to obtain success is to run away from it. Anyway, since the Biennale it's been much harder to resist. I've refused a lot of exhibitions, but one can't go on refusing forever. That wouldn't make any sense.

In the 1960s Giacometti's health began to fail. In 1963 he underwent an operation for cancer of the stomach (he made the curiously characteristic remark: 'The strange thing is – as a sickness I always wanted to have this one.'). The cancer did not recur, but in 1965 heart disease and chronic bronchitis were diagnosed. Giacometti died in June 1966 at the Kantonsspital in Chur, Switzerland.

JEAN DUBUFFET

The immensely prolific Jean Dubuffet probably exercized a greater influence over both his European and his American contemporaries than any other artist of the immediately post-war epoch. He did this not only through his own work but also through his exploration and documentation of the phenomenon he named 'Art Brut' – art produced by completely untrained artists, including children and psychotics, in which the artistic impulse seems to express itself in a completely 'raw' state.

Dubuffet was born in Le Havre in 1901, the son of a prosperous wine merchant. Among his contemporaries at the Lycée in Le Havre, which he entered in 1908, were Armand Salacrou, Georges Limbour and Raymond Queneau, all to become well known as writers, and all to have a connection with the Surrealist movement. Dubuffet's ambition was to be an artist, and in 1916 he began his studies at the Ecole des Beaux-Arts in Le Havre, transferring to Paris in 1918 to work at the Académie Julian. After six months, dissatisfied with the instruction he was receiving, he left the Académie and set up a studio

épreuve HC
III / VIII   Nez carotte   J.Dubuffet 62

JEAN DUBUFFET, *Nez carotte*, 1961

of his own in Paris, in a building which belonged to a subsidiary of the family firm. At this time he met the painter Suzanne Valadon and the poet Max Jacob, but he did not mingle further with the Parisian art world. The years 1920 to 1922 were a period of isolation, during which he studied literature, languages and music as well as art. In 1923 he made a trip to Italy, and this was followed by a period of military service during which he used his enforced leisure to learn Russian.

By 1924 he had begun to feel growing doubts about all cultural and artistic values and decided that, if these truly existed, they did so only among the common people. He gave up painting and went first to Switzerland, then to Buenos Aires, where he worked for a firm of central heating engineers. In 1925 he returned home and entered the family business in Le Havre. He married Paulette Bret in 1927, the year in which his father died, and in

1930 expanded his operations by founding a wholesale wine business which eventually became very prosperous. In 1933, after an interval of eight years, he began to paint again, and also to make marionettes. The following year he handed over his business to trustees in order to devote himself entirely to art. He divorced in 1936 and in the same year met Emilie Carlu, who became his mistress. They married in December 1937, by which time he had once again abandoned painting and returned to the wholesale wine trade.

When war broke out in 1939 Dubuffet was mobilized into the meteorological service and assigned to the Air Ministry in Paris. He was removed to Rochefort for indiscipline, and after the great exodus of 1940 found himself in Céret, where he was demobilized. He immediately returned to Paris and business. But the impulse to paint remained strong, and in 1942 he rented a studio and took up painting for a third time. The subject-matter of his earliest mature works, produced in 1943, was very simple and down to earth – he depicted, in a deliberately crude and childish style, people in the Metro and views of Paris in wartime. In 1944 the writer Jean Paulhan, editor of the prestigious clandestine review *Les Lettres Françaises* during the German Occupation and later editor of the *Nouvelle Revue Française*, introduced Dubuffet to the dealer René Drouin. Drouin gave him his first show in the heady atmosphere of newly liberated Paris. It was accompanied by a catalogue preface written by Paulhan, but despite this distinguished support, opinion was sharply divided because of the apparent brutality of handling in the paintings.

In 1946 Dubuffet published a collection of theoretical and critical texts entitled *Prospectus aux amateurs de tout genre*, in which he spelled out his future programme. He was now beginning to experiment with the so-called 'Hautes Pâtes', which made use of a surface built up of plaster, glue and putty, which was afterwards scribbled and scratched to give the appearance of graffiti on old walls. The portraits Dubuffet exhibited in the autumn of 1946 make use of this technique and are amongst his most striking works. Their subjects included some of the best-known writers in Paris: Ponge, Paulhan, Limbour, Léautaud, Michaux and Artaud – a roll-call of the French literary avant-garde of that period. Dubuffet described these portraits as being 'anti-psychological' and 'anti-individualist', and said of them:

Georges Limbour and JEAN DUBUFFET,
Farley Farm, 1959.
Photo Lee Miller

Jean Dubuffet in the *Jardin d'hiver*, 1970. Photographer unknown

JEAN DUBUFFET sculpting a piece of polystyrene, Paris, 1970.
Photo Kurt Wyss

It seemed to me that in *depersonalizing* my models, in generalizing their appearance and turning them into elementary human figures, I was able to set free, and put at the service of painting, certain mechanisms which stirred the imagination and greatly increased the power of the effigy.

By this time Dubuffet's reputation had already begun to spread to the United States, through exhibitions organized by the Pierre Matisse Gallery. He put together the first show of Art Brut in 1947, and followed this by creating a permanent organization, the Compagnie de l'Art Brut, to collect and study such material. He declared at this time:

There are (there are everywhere and always) two different orders of art. There is the art everyone is used to – polished or perfect art, baptised according to the fashion of the moment either classic art, or romantic art (or whatever else one likes – it always comes to the same thing). And there is also, untamed and furtive as some wild creature, Art Brut.

Having committed himself to an artistic career after so many hesitations, Dubuffet now entered a period of tireless creativity. His tendency was to work in series, and amongst the most notable groups of paintings produced at this epoch were the 'Texturologies', inspired by his visits to the Sahara, and the 'Corps de Dames'. These latter, which date from 1950, seem to have something in common with the paintings of women which Willem de Kooning was producing at the same time as celebrations of the wonder, horror and terror of female sexuality. In 1954 Dubuffet had his first retrospective exhibition, which took place at the Cercle Volnay in Paris. The following year, after the example of similarly successful artists of an earlier generation, he moved to the south of France and settled in Vence.

In 1961, ever restless, he began to research into experimental music, sometimes with the collaboration of the CoBrA Group painter Asger Jorn. In 1962 he built himself another house and studios at Le Touquet, a seaside resort in the north of France, but tended to stay there for brief periods only.

From about 1950 onwards the story of Dubuffet's life is one of almost uninterrupted success. In 1962 he was given a retrospective exhibition at the Museum of Modern Art in New York, which was also seen in Chicago and Los Angeles. In the same year the collection of Art Brut he had brought together was installed in the new premises of the Compagnie de l'Art Brut in Paris, at 137 rue de Sèvres. In 1965 he had a major show at the Palazzo Grassi in Venice, and in 1966 retrospectives were held at the Tate Gallery in London, the Guggenheim Museum in New York, and the Stedelijk Museum in Amsterdam. In 1967 an important group of Dubuffet's paintings and sculptures was given to the Musée des Arts Décoratifs in Paris. Throughout his period, and indeed later, he experimented restlessly with different materials: there were sculptures made from tree-roots and lumps of coal; collages made from butterfly wings; and three-dimensional works made from painted metal and carved polystyrene.

As his career progressed, it became possible to see certain limits to Dubuffet's talent. His tireless inventiveness could not quite conceal an element of the facetious and the frivolous; his use of intractable or apparently unsuitable materials seemed increasingly like the last refuge of a talent fleeing from its own refinement. The late works often lack the charm and inventiveness of the earlier ones – they are coarse in detail, unsympathetic in texture and garish in colour. But Dubuffet worked unflaggingly, and apparently with complete personal satisfaction, until his death in 1985. Nearly forty years previously he had said in a lecture: 'I draw and I paint for pleasure, out of mania, out of passion, for myself, in order to keep myself happy, and not in the least because I want to make fun of anybody.' He would probably have considered these words a good epitaph.

BALTHUS

The art of Balthus represents the survival of classical values within Modernism, though these are mingled with many strange and disturbing elements.

Balthus was born Balthazar Klossowski de Rola in Paris in 1908. His father Erich, of noble Polish origin, was a painter and art historian who became a successful stage designer. His mother Baladine, who was Jewish, and his elder brother, Pierre, were also painters. In 1914 the Klossowskis, who held German passports, were forced to leave France. In 1917 the parents separated. Baladine and her sons went to Switzerland, and in 1919 she began an intense relationship with the German poet Rainer Maria Rilke, which lasted until Rilke's death in 1926. Like all Rilke's relationships with women, this seems to have been conducted as much by correspondence as in person. But it was the poet who first encouraged Balthus's precocious talents as an artist: he admired a series of drawings made by the eleven-year-old boy illustrating his adventures with a stray cat, wrote a preface for them and arranged for them to be published.

Cats have been a passion for Balthus throughout his life. As a young man he painted a self-portrait of himself as *The King of the Cats*, and later a splendid signboard for a fish restaurant showing a happy cat seated at table, with a rainbow arc of fish landing on his plate.

In 1921 Baladine was forced back to Berlin by lack of money, and the family endured a difficult period in the near-anarchic post-war city. Because his mother could not afford to pay for private schooling, the young Balthus was left to his own devices. From 1918 onwards he spent his summers at Beatenberg in Switzerland, as pupil and assistant to a sculptor called Margrit Bay who belonged to a small arts-and-crafts group there. He was to paint some murals for the church in Beatenburg in 1927, but they were afterwards erased.

In 1923 Pierre Klossowski obtained a visa, after many difficulties, and went to study in Paris under the protection of André Gide. Balthus followed early in 1924; he earned a living building sets for *Les Soirées de Paris*, a series of avant-garde theatrical presentations financed by Court Etienne de Beaumont. This marked the beginning of his long association with the theatre. He also copied Old Masters in the Louvre and attended sketching classes at the Grande Chaumière, and he attracted the attention of senior artists – Pierre Bonnard, Maurice Denis and Albert Marquet visited his studio. This period of study was followed by another in Italy, where Balthus copied the frescoes in Arezzo of Piero della Francesca, a painter much admired by his father. These paintings had a profound influence on his art, where references to them are often evident.

Balthus did not become a mature artist until the early 1930s, after his military service in North Africa – an experience which seems to have had a minimal impact on him. His first major painting was *La Rue* (The Street) of 1933. This is a rigorously structured, wilfully archaic representation of ordinary life which owes something to Piero, something to nineteenth-century popular prints and illustrations to children's books, but most of all to a series of rather wooden late eighteenth-century paintings of Swiss costumes which he had studied in the Historisches Museum, Bern. *La Rue* contained an erotic detail, since altered: an adult male fondling a pubescent girl. This introduced one of Balthus's recurrent themes, the erotic attraction of girls on the eve of sexual awakening. His first important exhibition, held in 1934, contained only four major works. It caused a scandal, and established the artist's reputation. One painting, the notorious *Guitar Lesson*, was placed in a back room, accessible only to certain visitors. It seems to represent a sexual assault made by an older girl (the teacher) on a younger one; the abandoned pose of the latter blasphemously recalls that of Christ in the fifteenth-century *Pietá of Villeneuve-lès-Avignon*. Balthus, writing to his old teacher Margrit Bay, said he had wanted to disturb people's consciences.

Though none of the major pictures in his exhibition sold, Balthus was able to make a living painting portraits of fashionable sitters, among them the beautiful Lady Abdy and the Vicomtesse de Noailles, who kept one of the most influential salons in Paris. He also designed the sets and costumes for Antonin Artaud's production of Shelley's *The Cenci*. The production, which was a resounding flop, and ran for only fifteen performances, exemplified Artaud's theories about the 'Theatre of Cruelty' discussed in his book of the same title published in 1935, which advocated the use of gratuitous violence as a necessary theatrical ingredient. However, Balthus's contribution was much admired. At the same period he made a set of illustrations for *Wuthering Heights*, a novel which meant so much to him that he even made a painting in which he portrayed himself as Heathcliff.

When the Second World War broke out Balthus was mobilized. He fought briefly in the campaign of 1940 and then retired with his wife, the former Antoinette de Watteville (whom he had married in 1937), to the remote farmhouse at Champrovent in the French Savoy where they had spent holidays in the late 1930s. They lived there until 1941 when, perhaps threatened by the fact that Balthus was half-Jewish, they went to Switzerland, where they remained for the rest of the war. During this period they had two sons. Soon after the war Balthus separated from his family and went alone to Paris.

A busy interlude followed, mainly occupied by designing for the stage, but culminating in another Paris street scene, *Le Passage du Commerce-Saint-André*, which was even more classical than *La Rue*, but just as alien in its atmosphere. In 1953 Balthus left Paris as abruptly as he had arrived, and settled at the austere Château de Chassy in the Morvan in central France. There he remained until he was appointed Director of the French Academy in Rome in 1961 by his friend André Malraux, then General de Gaulle's Minister of Culture. Here Balthus, who had never been prolific, painted extremely slowly, hampered by his official duties, and by the need to

BALTHUS, *The Guitar Lesson* (detail), 1934

restore the Villa Medici which housed the French Academy. His technique involved the use of layer upon layer of casein tempera so thick that the images sometimes seem modelled or carved instead of painted. He produced only thirteen major pictures in seventeen years.

In 1963, on an official visit to Japan, Balthus's interpreter in Kyoto was a young woman called Setsuko Ideta. She followed him back to Rome later in the same year, modelled regularly for him thereafter, and in due course became his second wife. Some of the paintings she inspired are based on Japanese *shunga* – popular erotic images symbolizing the renewal brought by a new spring.

On his retirement in 1977, Balthus returned to live in Switzerland, sharing a tranquil existence with his Japanese wife and their daughter. Even into his nineties he was painting almost every day in his studio. His reputation remained high in his later years, with major retrospective exhibitions in New York (1984), Lausanne (1993) and Madrid (1996). A catalogue raisonné of his complete works was published in 1999. When he died at the age of ninety-two, in 2001, his funeral was attended by artists, politicians and celebrities, among them his friend the photographer Henri Cartier-Bresson, the Irish rock star Bono and the President of France.

FRANCIS BACON

Together with Giacometti, Francis Bacon has the chief claim to be described as an 'existentialist' artist. His work also has a relationship to Surrealism, though unlike Giacometti, Bacon was never formally a member of the Surrealist Movement.

He was born in Dublin in October 1909, a collateral descendant of the essayist Sir Francis Bacon. His father was a well known horse-trainer whom Bacon described as 'very narrow-minded. He was an intelligent man who never developed his intellect at all.' Bacon also said that he 'never got on with either my mother or my father. They didn't want me to be a painter, they thought I was just a drifter, especially my mother.' Bacon was asthmatic, and received very little conventional schooling. His childhood background was one of violence: his family lived in London during the First World War, when his father worked for the War Office, and returned to Ireland during the Civil War in the early 1920s. Bacon spent some time living with his grandmother 'who married the Commissioner of Police for Kildare amongst her numerous marriages – the house was therefore sandbagged to protect it against attack.' It was at this period that Bacon seems to have discovered his own homosexuality – he has since claimed that his father was the focus of his sexual attraction, though he did not know it at the time. His earliest sexual experiences were with his father's grooms, who also beat him at his father's behest. This seems to have set the pattern for his life as an adult. In sexual matters he was a masochist, and he was often attracted to burly working-class types. At the age of sixteen, he left home for good.

He went first to London, then in 1927–28 spent two months in Berlin, a wide-open city in every possible sense. It attracted him enormously with its air of risk and freedom. He later made his way to Paris, where he scraped a living by securing occasional commissions for interior decoration. At this time he saw a Picasso exhibition at the Galerie Paul Rosenberg, which inspired some drawings and watercolours of his own. Picasso was to be almost the only contemporary artist who retained Bacon's respect – in later years, he seldom had a good word to say about other contemporary painters.

By 1929 Bacon was back in London. He had a studio in Queensberry Mews, where he exhibited rugs and furniture made to his own designs. These were close to

BALTHUS with his wife Setsuko
and daughter Haruni, 1990.
Photo Henri Cartier-Bresson

Francis Bacon 279

the work of the Bauhaus designers of the period, and Bacon was later to dismiss them as completely derivative. In 1930 he held a joint studio exhibition with the painter Roy de Maistre, in which he showed gouaches and drawings as well as furniture. He now gradually began to abandon his decorative work in order to devote himself to painting. In 1933 he painted a *Crucifixion* which sufficiently impressed the leading critic Herbert Read for him to reproduce it in his book *Art Now*, and in 1934 he had his first one-man show, at the so-called 'Transition Gallery' – in fact, in the basement of a house belonging to a friend.

Though far from mature as a painter, Bacon had already started to collect his characteristic stock of images. In 1935, he saw Sergei Eisenstein's film *Battleship Potemkin* for the first time, and was enormously impressed by it, most of all by the celebrated Odessa Steps sequence. At about the same time, when on a visit to Paris, he bought a medical treatise on *The Diseases of the Mouth*, attracted by its hand-coloured plates.

Bacon submitted work to the International Surrealist Exhibition of 1936, only to have it rejected as 'insufficiently surreal'. In the following year he was included in an important show at Agnew's entitled 'Young British Painters'. Despite this and other early successes, he always dated his own emergence as a distinct personality to about 1939 or 1940:

> When I was very young, you see, I was incredibly shy, and later I thought it ridiculous to be shy, so I tried deliberately to get over this because I think old shy people are ridiculous. And when I was thirty or so I gradually began to be able to open myself out.

During the war Bacon destroyed almost all of his own earlier work. Because of his asthma, he was declared unfit for military service, and was assigned to civil defence duties in London. The atmosphere of wartime London suited him well, just as it suited other homosexuals, and he began to emerge as one of the leading figures in a bohemian society which frequented a series of pubs and out-of-hours drinking clubs in Soho. Heavy drinking did not get in the way of art, however. Towards the end of 1944 he painted *Three Studies for Figures at the Base of a Crucifixion*, the acknowledged start of his mature work:

Francis Bacon on the Underground, London. Photo Johnny Stiletto

FRANCIS BACON, *Three Studies for Figures at the Base of a Crucifixion, c.* 1944

It was a thing that I did in about a fortnight, when I was in a bad mood or drinking, and I did it under tremendous hangovers or drink; I sometimes hardly knew what I was doing. And it's one of the only pictures I've been able to do under drink. I think perhaps the drink helped me be a bit freer.

When the triptych was exhibited in April 1945, it caused a sensation – in its horror and its terror it seemed to reflect the mood of the time. Bacon's reputation was immediately established.

He had become a heavy gambler as well as a heavy drinker, and in the years immediately following the war he spent much of his time in Monte Carlo. He liked what he called the 'impersonality' of roulette, his preferred game of chance:

When I was never able to earn any money from my work, I was able sometimes in casinos to make money which altered my life for a time, and I was able to live on it and live in a way that I would never have been able to afford had I been earning it.

During this period his work began to achieve wider recognition. The Museum of Modern Art in New York purchased a painting as early as 1948, while the Tate Gallery in London bought *Three Studies for Figures at the Base of a Crucifixion* in 1953.

At the end of 1950 Bacon went to South Africa to see his mother, who had settled there. On the way, he spent some days in Cairo, where he became fascinated by Ancient Egyptian art; and in South Africa he visited Kruger National Park where he took numerous photographs of wild animals, some of which he was afterwards to use as the basis for paintings.

He then settled permanently in London, changing studios restlessly and also travelling occasionally, usually to Paris or Tangier, the North African 'free port' which was then a magnet for homosexuals from all over Europe. When in London, he was the unchallenged king of his own small bohemian group, whose social centre was the Colony Room in Soho, better known as Muriel's, after its formidable proprietress Muriel Belcher. Muriel had originally offered Bacon a commission if he brought drinkers to her establishment, and even in the days of increased prosperity he did not desert her.

Despite his homosexuality, he maintained close friendships with a number of women, among them Isabel Rawsthorne, married successively to two leading composers, Constant Lambert and Alan Rawsthorne, and Henrietta Moraes, wife of the poet Dom Moraes. Like Muriel Belcher, their likenesses appeared frequently in his paintings. Male lovers also appeared, but male friends more seldom. Bacon maintained a slightly rivalrous relationship with Lucian Freud, and made some likenesses of him. The friendship ended, after many years, in a major breach. Bacon also knew – but did not paint – the neo-romantic artist John Minton. There is a story about Bacon pouring a bottle of champagne over the unfortunate Minton's head, exclaiming as he did so:

'Champagne for my real friends; real pain for my sham friends.' Minton was left in no doubt as to the category in which he had been placed. This illustrates the way in which Bacon's innate masochism could often express itself as its opposite – sadism. Minton, who was a depressive, committed suicide not very long afterwards, and the incident may have been a contributory factor.

Likenesses of friends were incorporated into the small, extremely personal repertoire of images which Bacon continued to build up. Most of these were borrowed (indeed, even where friends were concerned, Bacon preferred to use photographs taken for him by the raffish Soho photographer John Deakin, rather than working from life). Prominent in this repertoire were the *Portrait of Pope Innocent X* by Velazquez (which he knew only from reproductions), the shot of a screaming nurse from the Odessa Steps sequence in *Battleship Potemkin*, and various photographs illustrating human and animal motion by the Victorian photographer Eadweard Muybridge. One of these, showing two nude men wrestling, Bacon transformed into the unmistakably erotic *Two Men on a Bed* of 1953. Granted the moral and legal climate which prevailed in England at that time, the image is astonishingly forthright, especially as the two figures are recognizably Bacon himself, and his then lover, Peter Lacy. A somewhat less bold homoerotic scene, *Two Figures in the Grass*, was shown in Bacon's first retrospective exhibition, held at the Institute of Contemporary Arts in London, but could not be illustrated in the catalogue.

Despite the boldness of some of his imagery, Bacon always remained somewhat evasive about acknowledging the actual content of some of his paintings. The following statement is characteristic:

I've used the figures lying on beds with a hypodermic syringe as a form of nailing the image more strongly into the reality of appearance. I don't put in the syringe because of the drug that's being injected but because it's less stupid than putting a nail through the arm, which would be even more melodramatic.

Bacon's second retrospective, and the first major showing of his work, took place at the Tate Gallery in 1962, and was later seen in Mannheim, Turin, Zurich and Amsterdam. It confirmed that Bacon was now a painter with a major international reputation. At about this time, Bacon's style began to change – his compositions grew larger, and the handling, except for that of the figures themselves, was now less painterly, with large expanses of plain, unworked colour. The triptych format, already seen on a smaller scale in *Three Studies*, now established itself as a major means of expression. Some of the most important of these triptychs are devoted to the death of another of Bacon's lovers, George Dyer, whom he met in 1963, and who committed suicide in Paris in 1971, on the eve of the opening of the artist's great retrospective at the Grand Palais.

Bacon's pattern of life, from this time until his death, was fairly fixed. He worked obsessively, always more or less dissatisfied with what he produced, spent time with old friends in Soho (always insisting on picking up the bill at the restaurants they frequented), and visited Paris often. He now had a pied-à-terre near the Place des Vosges, which also served as a studio. He was the subject of several major exhibitions all over the world, including a second comprehensive retrospective at the Tate Gallery in 1985. An exhibition at the House of Artists in Moscow in 1988 had a sensational impact on the Russian public, comparable to the sensation Bacon's work had caused in Latin America thirty years previously when his work was shown at the São Paulo Biennial of 1958. The artist died in 1992, while on a visit to Madrid. According to his wishes, his corpse was disposed of without ceremony – despite his preference for triptych formats, and his allusions to Christian imagery in his paintings, Bacon had been a militant atheist throughout his life.

None of the three artists included under this heading can plausibly be described as an Abstract Expressionist, but it also seems clear that none would have pursued the course they did without Abstract Expressionism to show the way. David Smith took ideas from the welded sculpture made by Picasso and Julio Gonzalez between the wars, and adapted them to the American industrial ethos. The work of Louise Nevelson may owe a debt to Kurt Schwitters, but a more direct inspiration was the way in which New York itself was being torn down and rebuilt all around her. Abstract Expressionism offered Smith and Nevelson the liberty to improvise with found elements just as Pollock did with paint.

Morris Louis was one of the leaders of Post-Painterly Abstraction, a movement promoted by the influential critic Clement Greenberg in opposition to Pop Art. The technique of Louis's painting, though different from that of the Abstract Expressionists, remained dependent on the idea of improvisation. Louis mixed his pigment with an extremely dilute acrylic medium which was allowed to soak into unprimed canvas, its flow regulated not by brushing and dripping, but by manipulating and folding the canvas itself.

LOUISE NEVELSON, 1978.
Photo Cecil Beaton

LOUISE NEVELSON

Born in Russia, of Russian Jewish stock, and brought to America as a child, Louise Nevelson's background was similar to that of a number of leading members of the Abstract Expressionist movement. She was slow to establish a major reputation, perhaps for two reasons – her gender, and the lack of a sculptural tradition in the United States. There is also the fact, however, that Nevelson was slow to mature as an artist.

She was born Leah Berliawsky, near Kiev, in 1899, and moved to the United States in 1906. Her family settled in the small town of Rockhampton, Maine, where her father was a pedlar and junk-dealer, and later a prosperous real-estate dealer and builder. Some of the scavenging instincts she displayed as an artist may have been inherited from him.

An attractive young woman, in 1920 she married Charles Nevelson, an apparently wealthy shipping-broker, and left Rockhampton for a conventional bourgeois life in New York. Her son Myron (Mike) was born in 1922 – their relationship, though often competitive and stormy, was to be perhaps the most stable of her long life. Her husband's business soon began to go downhill, and at the same time Louise, as she was now called, became increasingly restless. Like many fashionable women of the period she became interested in esoteric cults, particularly in theosophy. For some time she regarded herself as a disciple of Jiddu Krishnamurti, the theosophists' 'new Messiah', after attending one of his lectures in the spring of 1928.

In 1929 she began to study art full time at the Art Students' League in New York. This decision exasperated her husband and foreshadowed the break-up of their marriage. After two years at the League she decided to broaden her experience, and left for Munich in order to study with Hans Hofmann, already well known in America thanks to his summer school classes at the University of California at Berkeley. She arrived in Germany at an unpropitious moment – the Nazis were about to take power, and Hofmann was preoccupied with the idea of emigrating and was only interested (Nevelson

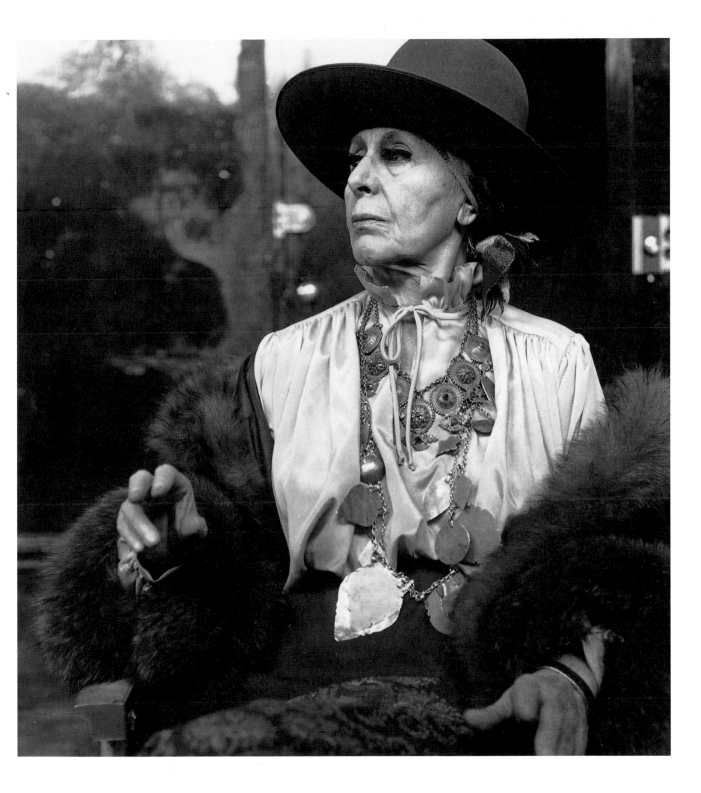

thought) in those of his students who might help him to do so. After three months she dropped out of his school and began to travel round Europe. During a visit to Paris she seems to have had a brief affair with the leading art dealer Georges Wildenstein. It was the first of a series of affairs with celebrated men. During the 1930s, her lovers ranged from the anti-semitic French writer Céline (Louis-Ferdinand Destouches), whom she met on an Atlantic liner, to the Mexican painter Diego Rivera. There were many other liaisons.

LOUISE NEVELSON, *Sky Cathedral*, 1958

Her marriage now effectively at an end (though she and Charles Nevelson did not divorce until 1941), Louise began to lead an independent bohemian existence in New York, frequently moving studios, and living from hand to mouth. Like most of the leading American artists of the period, she received some help from the Works Project Administration, but it was a measure of her lack of status that she was employed as an art teacher, rather than being part of the more prestigious fine arts section of the Art Project, where artists were paid to do their own work. During the 1930s she gradually made the transition from painter to sculptor. She struggled hard to establish herself as a professional artist, showing in the huge non-juried exhibitions popular at the period, and also in some of the small co-operative galleries which were springing up in Greenwich Village.

She did not, however, achieve her first major solo show until 1941, when she exhibited at the then very prestigious Nierendorf Gallery. The exhibition excited an unusual amount of comment, but nothing was sold. Nevelson enjoyed some other successes as well. In January 1943 she was included in a show of women artists at Peggy Guggenheim's new Art of This Century Gallery, the launch pad of the new Abstract Expressionist movement. In the same year she had a large solo exhibition at the Norlyst Gallery – a loft-space operated by Jimmy Ernst, the artist son of the surrealist painter Max Ernst. This show, on a circus theme, was her boldest to date. The totality of the experience counted for as much or more than the individual sculptures, and many of the items shown were made from pieces of wood and other materials salvaged from the streets, because during the war years they were both free and abundantly available. Once again, no works sold, and for lack of storage space nearly all the sculptures had to be destroyed after the closure of the show. In 1946 there was another tantalizing indication of possible success when Nevelson's work was included in the Whitney Annual for the first time.

Nierendorf continued to support and exhibit her work until his unexpected death from heart failure in 1947. His death was a heavy setback for Nevelson. She spent the 1950s struggling to re-establish herself, but now without the help of a powerful and sympathetic dealer. Because of her difficult situation, her sculpture was in many respects more conservative than it had been in the previous decade – she was now making a great deal of work not in wood but in terracotta. In this medium it was difficult to make sculptures on a really large scale. She exhibited wherever and whenever she could, without caring too much about the company she found herself in. It has been estimated that she appeared in at least sixty exhibitions in the course of the 1950s. Her persistence was rewarded by the fact that, by the middle of the decade, she was a regular prize-winner in juried shows.

In 1945 her family, worried about the instability of her life, had clubbed together to help her buy a run-down brownstone on East 30th Street. In 1954 this was compulsorily purchased as part of a slum clearance scheme. Nevelson remained in possession as a tenant. As the neighbourhood became more and more derelict, she continued to gather material from the demolition sites all around her, and started to work in wood again, making frequent forays with a wheelbarrow at three and four in the morning in order to beat the garbage trucks to her spoils.

At this crucial moment she found a new dealer, Colette Roberts, who ran a small non-profit gallery called Grand Central Moderns on East 56th Street. Her first exhibition there, in January 1955, foreshadowed the emergence of her fully mature style, and in particular her fascination with black, which for her had come to represent both the darkness of night and the mystery of the unconscious. Her first all-black show took place at Grand Central Moderns early in 1956.

Roberts, born Lévy-Rothschild, was French by birth, and she brought Nevelson's work to the attention of a circle of leading French intellectuals and artists, whose members included Marcel Duchamp, and the painters Pierre Soulages and Georges Mathieu. Their interest and support gave her work an intellectual respectability which it had not previously possessed in the eyes of American critics. In 1958 the first serious critical appraisal of Nevelson's work was written by Hilton Kramer, one of the leading pundits of the day, for *Arts* magazine. Kramer's article led to a feature about Nevelson and her sculpture in *Life*. Marcel Duchamp, meanwhile, persuaded Alfred Barr Jr., Director of the Museum of Modern Art, to accept Nevelson's assemblage of boxes, *Sky Cathedral*, as a gift from Nevelson's sister and brother-in-law, Lilian and Ben Mildwoff. Though Nevelson made no money from the transaction, the acquisition marked a crucial turning point: Nevelson was now, at long last, fully recognized as a leading figure in the American art community. She was almost sixty.

The years from 1958 to Nevelson's death thirty years later, in 1988, were a period of increasing wealth and fame, but her essential idiom did not change a great deal. She now experimented with colour, painting first in white, then gold, and also with materials, making sculptures in plexiglas and lucite in the mid-1960s. She exhibited with a series of prestigious commercial galleries, beginning with the Martha Jackson Gallery in 1958. It was Jackson who laid the foundations for her international reputation, taking her to Daniel Cordier in Paris, where she had her first show outside America in 1960, to the Staatliche Kunsthalle in Baden-Baden, the scene of her first European museum show in 1961, and to the Hanover Gallery in London. In 1962 Nevelson was one of four American exhibitors at the Venice Biennale. Hopeful friends expected her to win the prize for sculpture, but this went instead to Giacometti.

After a brief, unhappy association with Sidney Janis, she settled at the Pace Gallery in 1964. Arnold Glimcher, the owner-director, was the most successful of all her dealer-collaborators. During the 1970s, he made Nevelson into a prolific and sought-after public sculptor.

After initial resistance to the idea, she moved under his guidance into making works in metal, since this would endure stringent physical outdoor conditions. Working alongside the metalworkers, she adapted their techniques to her own spontaneous and instinctive way of creating sculpture, but the metal pieces were necessarily less varied and capricious in their forms than the wooden ones with which she had made her reputation.

Nevelson immensely enjoyed her role as a conspicuous 'sacred monster' on the New York art scene, sallying forth to openings and other gatherings from her new home in Spring Street in a variety of splendidly outlandish costumes. Success had come to her late, but she left no one in any doubt that she intended to enjoy every moment of it. Nevelson died in 1988.

DAVID SMITH

David Smith was the most important American sculptor of the twentieth century, a claim reinforced by his wide-spread influence over other artists, both in the United States and abroad.

He was born in 1906, at Decatur, Indiana. His father worked for the telephone company, and was an unsuccessful inventor in his spare time; his mother, the stronger personality of the two, was a teacher with a firm belief in the puritan virtues. As a child Smith was fiercely independent, and would often run away to his grandmother's house. On one occasion, aged three or four, he was tied to a tree in the yard to stop him wandering, and modelled a figure of a lion from the surrounding mud. This was later taken to be the first sign of his artistic vocation.

In 1921 the family moved to Paulding, Ohio, where Smith seems to have passed an ordinary American boyhood, playing pranks and working rather reluctantly at odd jobs to pay for his education. He studied mechanical drawing for two years at high school, and followed a correspondence course in art, making a local reputation as a cartoonist. In 1924 he spent an unhappy year at Ohio University, and passed the following summer working at the Studebaker car factory in South Bend. This gave him a feeling for industrial forms and a basic knowledge of factory tools and equipment; it also gave him an almost mystical sense of identification with working men.

'I know workmen, their vision,' he claimed later, 'because between college years I have worked on Studebaker's production line.'

A restless period followed, during which Smith worked at a variety of jobs interspersed with brief spells at two different colleges. In 1926 his employers, Acceptance Corporation (a branch of Morris Plan Bank), transferred him to New York where he met an art student from California who happened to be living in the same boarding house. Her name was Dorothy Dehner, and, on hearing of his ambition to be an artist, she recommended him to try the Art Students' League. Smith enrolled immediately, and studied there off and on for five years, while continuing to work at various jobs. In 1927 he and Dorothy Dehner were married. Through friends at the League they got to know the summer resort of Bolton Landing, on the western side of Lake George, and bought a property there in 1929. This was to be Smith's base for the rest of his life. Through the same friends they also met John Graham (1881–1961), a painter who claimed to have fought the Bolsheviks as a White Russian cavalry officer before coming to America, and who was now an important link between the European Modernists and the still struggling American avant-garde.

Graham introduced Smith to the work of Julio Gonzalez, and he now began to experiment with welded metal sculpture, which gradually displaced painting as his primary artistic interest. His first welded piece, a head, was made in 1932. The Brooklyn apartment the Smiths used in the winter was not suited to this sort of work, and their landlord began to object because of the fire risk. At his wife's suggestion Smith approached a neighbouring ironworks for working space. They agreed, and he immediately made friends, not only with the men in charge, but with all their cronies, who used to meet at a nearby 'men only' saloon: 'It was the social hall for blocks around. Any method of technique I needed, I could learn it from one of the habitués, and often get donated materials besides.' Smith's blue-collar identification was further reinforced by a growing interest in left-wing politics, encouraged by John Graham.

In 1935 the Smiths set off for an extended tour of Europe, partly under Graham's guidance. He met them in Paris, introduced them to artists, and opened the doors of several private collections for them – he himself was a well known dealer in ethnographical objects, in addition to being a painter. Later they went to Greece, and finally spent a month in the Soviet Union.

The general pattern of their lives was now fixed. They spent most of the summer and autumn at Bolton Landing and returned to New York for the winter, living in rented apartments in Brooklyn. Smith worked for various New Deal art programmes and became an active member of the Artists' Union. He rather uneasily defended Abstraction, to which he remained committed, as a vehicle for political and social meanings. 'The great majority of abstract artists,' he claimed around 1940, 'are anti-fascist and socially conscious.'

The year 1940 marked a major turning point in Smith's life. His connection with the Federal Art Project came to an end, and he moved away from New York. Though he had slowly begun to gain recognition, his chief need during the war years was for an income of any sort. He worked first as a machinist at Glen Falls, then as a welder in the American Locomotive Company Plant at Schenectady. After the war he returned permanently to Bolton Landing, where he and his wife rebuilt their house with very little outside help. From 1947–48 onwards he was able to make a living teaching and lecturing. The financial hazards they had been forced to undergo and their life of isolation took their toll. Dehner afterwards accused her husband of being a wife-beater – certainly he was subject to fits of temper when drunk. Smith separated from his wife in 1950 and they were divorced in 1952. Some notes he wrote at this period give a picture of his feelings:

> The heights come seldom – the steadiness is always chewing the gut – seldom without a raw spot – the times of true height are so rare, some seemingly high spots being suspected later as illusion ... the future – the factory or the classroom, but in twenty years neither will be open ... and nothing has been as great or wonderful as I envisioned.

At the same moment, however, he could write: 'I believe that my time is the most important in the world – that the art of my time is the most important art.'

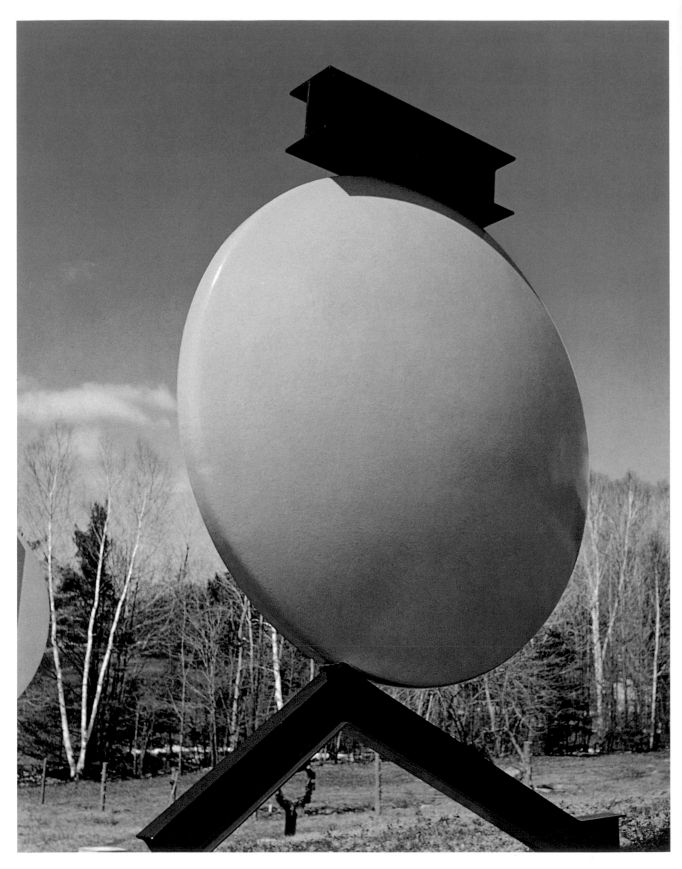

DAVID SMITH, *Bec-Dida Day, July 12, 1963*

A second marriage, in 1953, to Jean Freas, produced two much loved daughters, but ended in 1961. His artistic reputation gradually became widespread, reaching a peak when the Museum of Modern Art in New York held a major retrospective of his work in 1957. By this time he had shed many of his old friends, though he had also acquired new ones, among them Robert Motherwell and Helen Frankenthaler. His public pronouncements now often held a note of arrogance and harshness.

His creativity, if anything, increased to meet the opportunities he was offered: in 1962 the Italian government invited him to spend a month at Voltri, near Genoa. The authorities made available to him an abandoned factory and its contents, and provided several workmen as helpers. He made twenty-six huge sculptures in thirty days. By this time he was a major beneficiary of world-wide interest in the new American art: he was the subject of many articles and catalogue essays, sought after for interviews on television and radio. His work featured in numerous exhibitions in America and abroad. In February 1964 President Lyndon Johnson appointed him to the National Council for the Arts – convincing proof that he was now a member of the American establishment. In May 1965 Smith died as the result of an accident in his pick-up truck.

MORRIS LOUIS

Morris Louis, the standard-bearer of Post-Painterly Abstraction, is an outstanding example of the power of critics in moulding careers.

He was born Morris Bernstein in Baltimore, Maryland, in November 1912, the third of four sons of Russian Jewish immigrants. He attended schools in Baltimore, and just before graduation won a scholarship to the Maryland Institute of Fine Art. He studied here from 1929 until 1933, but left just before completing his course. He then signed on with the Works Projects Administration (WPA) and painted a mural for Baltimore High School. Like many aspiring artists, he was also forced to do odd jobs to support himself – they included working in a restaurant and in a laundry, and as an opinion gatherer for the Gallup Poll. His steadiest employment was with one of his brothers, who was

a pharmacist. He was sufficiently respected to be elected President of the Baltimore Artists Association in 1935, when he was still only twenty-two.

From 1936 until 1940 Louis lived in New York (it was at this time that he adopted his new surname), working with the Mexican artist David Alfaro Siqueiros at the latter's short-lived experimental workshop, and employed by the easel-painting division of the WPA. Among the artists he knew in New York was Arshile Gorky. In 1940 he went back to Baltimore, and for six years supported himself by private teaching.

Louis married Marcella Brenner in 1947, and moved to his wife's apartment in Silver Spring, Maryland, a commuter suburb of Washington, D.C. During the next three years he showed his work with some success in local exhibitions, and in 1950 he accepted a commission to design an exhibition on tuberculosis for the United States Public Health Service. In 1952 he moved to a house in Washington itself and became an instructor at the Washington Center, teaching adult groups two evenings a week. Through this job he met Kenneth Noland, an artist twelve years younger than himself, who was also teaching in the same institution. At this time Louis's work was heavily derivative from Jackson Pollock.

Top: MORRIS LOUIS,
Point of Tranquility, 1959–60
Bottom: MORRIS LOUIS,
Beta Kappa, 1961

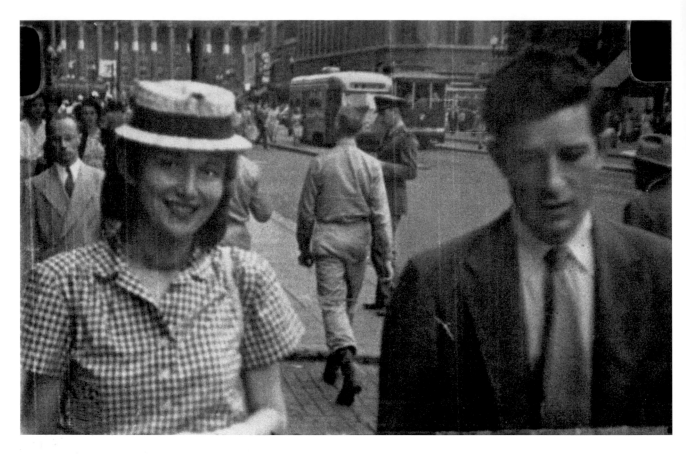

Morris and Marcella Louis on honeymoon in New York City, 1947. Photographer unknown

In 1953 he held his first one-man show at the Workshop Art Center Gallery and taught for one semester at Howard University.

Louis was always extremely reluctant to go to New York, but in early April 1953 he was persuaded to spend a weekend there with Noland. At the beginning of their visit Noland introduced him to the critic Clement Greenberg, perhaps the most eloquent and influential advocate of Abstract Expressionism – the two men had met at Black Mountain College some years earlier. Later Louis, Noland and Greenberg, in the company of the dealer Charles Egan, the painter Franz Kline and several others, went to visit Helen Frankenthaler's studio. Here they saw her painting *Mountains and Sea*, created by a new technique of pouring and staining. The two painters from Washington were extremely enthusiastic about this picture, and on their return they spent several weeks working together, sometimes on the same canvas, evaluating what Frankenthaler's methods might do for their own work, and at the same time attempting to break down their own

previous assumptions about painting. The following January Greenberg came to Washington and selected three of Louis's paintings for a show entitled *Emerging Talent* at the Sam Kootz Gallery.

The paintings Greenberg selected for this exhibition were tentative efforts, but in the winter of 1954 Louis, at the critic's request, sent a batch of paintings for submission to the dealer Pierre Matisse. In these his mature style – or at least a style Greenberg fully approved of – emerged for the first time. The canvases were covered with veils of colour, produced by an elaborate technique of soaking and staining using a very liquid medium. Little is known about Louis's technical methods, as he worked strictly in private and was secretive about how his effects were achieved; it is known that he later suffered from chronic back problems, caused by constant stooping and bending as he manipulated the unstretched canvas. Despite Greenberg's enthusiasm for the new work, Pierre Matisse decided not to give Louis a show. His next public exposure was a second one-man exhibition at the Workshop Art Center in Washington, attached to the school where he taught. Louis later destroyed most of his output for this year.

In 1957 he was included in a group show at the new Leo Castelli Gallery, and paintings were sold to the Baltimore Museum and to at least one major private collector. Later in the same year he had his first one-man show in New York, with Martha Jackson. Greenberg found the new work disappointingly conventional, and encouraged Louis to return to what he had been doing in 1954. Most of the paintings in the Martha Jackson show were later destroyed by the artist.

Greenberg became artistic adviser to a prestigious new gallery of contemporary art opened by French & Company at the end of 1958, and here he gave Louis two one-man exhibitions in quick succession – in April 1959 and in March and April 1960. Louis's reputation at long last began to take off. In the spring of 1960 he had his first foreign exhibition, with the Institute of Contemporary Arts in London. In September of that year he signed a contract with the influential dealer Lawrence

Rubin; in October he had a show at Bennington College in Vermont, and in November one in Milan. In 1961, when French & Company closed the doors of its contemporary gallery, Louis moved to André Emmerich, another prestigious dealer, who gave him a show in October 1961.

Louis had little time to enjoy his success. In July 1962 cancer of the lung was diagnosed and his left lung was removed. He was never well enough to paint again. He died in Washington in September 1962. He left little in the way of anecdote behind him, and seems to have been entirely obsessed by his work, both before and after his moment of breakthrough. Michael Fried, one of his champions, writes:

Louis seems to have had little taste for artistic gatherings of any kind. He never learned to tolerate light conversation about painting, nor to reconcile himself to the circumstance that his students were often less passionately devoted to painting than he.

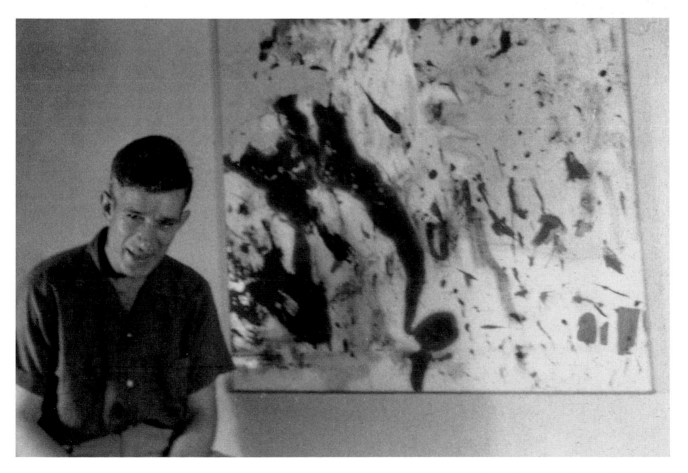

MORRIS LOUIS, 1957. Photographer unknown

During the second half of the 1950s Robert Rauschenberg and Jasper Johns engaged in a period of intense private experimentation. Many of the ideas they used were borrowed from the Dada movement, particularly from Duchamp, but they also made use of popular American imagery in a way that foreshadowed Pop Art. They took collage and assemblage, both Dada techniques, to new heights of elaboration. Characteristic of one aspect of the post-war American scene is the ambitious scale of much of their work.

Left: ROBERT RAUSCHENBERG,
Untitled (Red Painting), 1954
Above: ROBERT RAUSCHENBERG,
Front Street Studio, New York 1958.
Photographer unknown

ROBERT RAUSCHENBERG

Robert Rauschenberg pioneered the revival of the Dada spirit in American art. His early career also marked a decisive shift in the mores and manners of the New York art world. The blustering machismo of the Cedar Bar, the downtown haunt frequented by Jackson Pollock, Franz Kline and Willem de Kooning, was replaced by deliberate coolness and ambiguity.

Rauschenberg was born in the oil-refinery town of Port Arthur, Texas, in 1925. His given name was Milton, changed when he was an art student to Bob and finally to Robert. He was the older of two children, and his father was employed by Gulf States Utilities, a local light and power company. His family background was austere, as both parents were members of a fundamentalist sect called the Church of Christ. Rauschenberg had a difficult childhood and adolescence: he was a poor scholar and (to his father's disappointment) a poor sportsman. After

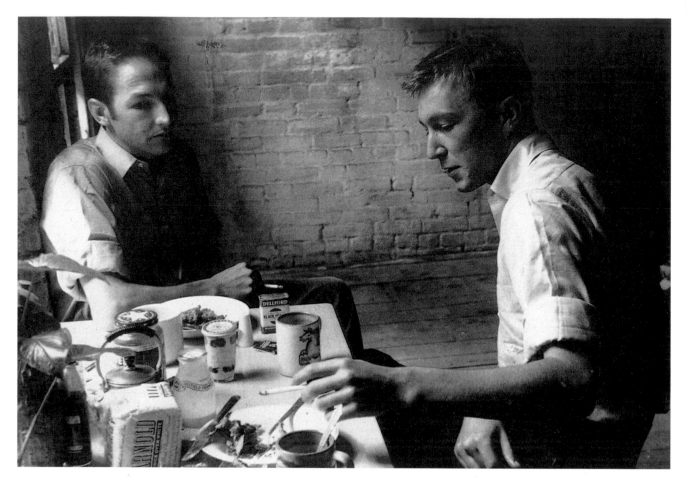

ROBERT RAUSCHENBERG and Jasper Johns, *c.* 1954. Photo Rachel Rosenthal

a brief spell in the School of Pharmacy at the University of Austin (from which he was expelled for refusing to dissect a live frog), he was drafted into the US Navy as a neuro-psychiatric technician. He commented later: 'This is where I learned how little difference there is between sanity and insanity and realized that a combination is essential.' While he was stationed in San Diego he had his first conscious encounter with art, stumbling on the collection of English eighteenth-century portraits in the Henry E. Huntington Library near Pasadena. He was discharged in 1945, and returned to Port Arthur to find that his family had moved without informing him, and that their house was occupied by strangers. He tracked them down to their new home in Lafayette, Louisiana, but, disillusioned by his lack of contact with them, soon returned to California where he did a series of menial jobs.

A friend suggested that he could study art by enrolling at the Kansas City Art Institute under the GI Bill of Rights, and he followed her suggestion. He remained

in Kansas City until February 1948, studying hard and earning money doing part-time jobs. He then used the money he had saved to go to Paris, where he enrolled at the Académie Julian. A fellow student there was Susan Weil, his future wife. They both found the atmosphere at the Académie disillusioning and spent most of their time in museums and galleries. Impressed by an article he had read in *Time* magazine about Black Mountain College and the teaching of Josef Albers, and influenced further by the fact that Susan Weil already planned to go, Rauschenberg decided to return to America to study there too. Once at the College, he soon discovered that he and Albers were temperamentally at odds – Albers detested what he thought of as Rauschenberg's 'frivolity'. Despite this conflict of temperaments, Rauschenberg still regards Albers as his most important teacher:

He was a beautiful teacher and an impossible person. He did not teach you how to 'do art'. The focus was on your own personal sense of looking. When he taught you watercolour, for example, it was about learning the specific properties of watercolour, not about making a good picture.

In the spring of 1949 Rauschenberg left Black Mountain College, though he maintained his connection with it for some years to come, and in the autumn he enrolled at the Art Students' League in New York. He and Weil were married in 1950 and were now experimenting jointly with large-scale photographic blueprints. Through these they got a commission to create a window display for the department store Bonwit Teller, and this was followed by an article in *Life*, which appeared in April 1951. One blueprint was also included in a photography exhibition at the Museum of Modern Art. In May 1951 Rauschenberg had his first one-man exhibition, at the Betty Parsons Gallery, which received rather condescending reviews. In July his son Christopher was born, but there was already a feeling that his marriage was under strain; at the end of the year he returned briefly and alone to Black Mountain College. He also spent the summer of the following year there, working with the avant-garde composer John Cage. Partly as a result of Cage's influence, Rauschenberg's work moved towards extreme minimality with all-white and all-black paintings. At Black Mountain College, that summer, Rauschenberg and Cage participated in *Theater Piece No. 1*, an improvised performance whose various elements had little apparent connection with one another, which has since been recognized as the precursor of the 'Happening'.

Rauschenberg's bisexuality was now becoming apparent, and he and his wife decided to divorce in the autumn of 1952. Soon afterwards he left for Europe, accompanying fellow artist Cy Twombly. After a period in Rome with Twombly, he continued alone to North Africa and returned to America in 1953, paying his way with an exhibition in Rome and one in Florence, of small fetish objects he had made during his travels. He settled in a loft on Fulton Street in downtown New York, and soon re-established his relationship with Cage. Through Cage he also made friends with the experimental choreographer Merce Cunningham, for whom he now began to design sets and costumes. Meanwhile, his own independent work was creating a reputation for him as an *enfant terrible*.

In 1954 he met Jasper Johns, then working quietly in a bookshop with scarcely any contacts with the New York art world. Johns and Rauschenberg formed a freelance window-display partnership and moved into different studios in the same building in Pearl Street. An intense interchange of aesthetic ideas developed between them which has reminded some of the interchange between Picasso and Braque during the early years of Cubism. Rauschenberg was later to say to his biographer Calvin Tomkins:

He and I were each other's first serious critics. Actually he was the first painter I ever shared ideas with, or had discussions with about painting. No, not the first. Cy Twombly was the first. But Cy and I were not critical. I did my work and he did his. Cy's direction was always so personal that you could only discuss it after the fact. But Jasper and I literally traded ideas. He would say, 'I've got a terrific idea for you,' and then I'd have to find one for him.

Absorbed in their own work, Johns and Rauschenberg remained isolated from the New York art world, then dominated by Abstract Expressionism. This changed when they attracted the attention of Leo Castelli, who started his own gallery in February 1957, having long nourished an interest in avant-garde art. The story of Castelli's initial visit to the Pearl Street studios is well known: invited there by Rauschenberg, he and his wife Ileana Sonnabend were immediately fascinated by the work of Johns. In the end, however, both artists were invited to join the new gallery. Rauschenberg's first show there, in March 1958, had less impact than the Johns show which preceded it in January, but his *Monogram*, a stuffed angora goat encircled by a car-tyre, had a memorable effect when it was first exhibited in a three artist group show in 1959.

In 1959 Rauschenberg decided to try to build a more serious reputation and produced a series of illustrations to Dante's *Inferno*, based on images borrowed from news-papers and magazines: the figure of Dante came from a *Sports Illustrated* advertisement for golf clubs. The project was completed in a deserted store-room at the end of a wharf, which belonged to a dilapidated motel in Florida. The six months Rauschenberg spent there in isolation seem to have marked the beginning of a deterioration in his relationship with Jasper Johns. In the summer of

1962 they went together to Connecticut College, in order to work with Cunningham, who was on a dance residency. During the residency their relationship finally foundered, amid considerable bitterness.

For Rauschenberg, the early 1960s were a period of technical experiment. He used large-scale silk-screen to produce images in his paintings and began making prints. In March 1963 he was given a retrospective at the newly refurbished Jewish Museum in New York, and this was followed, less than a year later, by another at the Whitechapel Art Gallery in London. In 1964, amidst violent controversy, he was awarded the major prize at the Venice Biennale. The Vatican newspaper *L'Osservatore Romano* went so far as to describe the award as 'the total and general defeat of culture'. At the time Rauschenberg was on a major foreign tour with the Merce Cunningham Dance Company, for which he had designed costumes and scenery, and which arrived for a series of performances at La Fenice in Venice two days before the Festival opened. Cage and Cunningham were not pleased with the amount of attention their collaborator attracted, and as the tour continued – to London, Stockholm, Helsinki, Prague, Warsaw, Antwerp and Toulon, and finally to India and Japan – his relationship with them disintegrated.

Rauschenberg had nevertheless acquired a taste for performance, and for a while after his return from the tour most of his creative energy went into this. In 1965 he bought an enormous new studio, financed by ever-rising earnings from his art. This became the rehearsal space for 'Nine Evenings: Theater and Engineering', an ambitious collaboration between artists and scientists put together by Rauschenberg and the research scientist Billy Klüver. The performances were not a success – they were spoilt by numerous technical failures – but they spawned a non-profit-making foundation called Experiments in Art and Technology which attempted to cement the link between art and science. In the late 1960s Rauschenberg showed a series of ambitious technologically inspired works: *Revolver* (1967), where revolving Plexiglas discs printed with silk-screen imagery turned at the touch of a switch, offering a multitude of random combinations; *Solstice* (1968), where the spectator passed through four rows of automatically opening Plexiglas doors; and *Soundings* (also 1968), where interior lighting was triggered by ambient sound.

Rauschenberg's personal life was not happy at this time. Calvin Tomkins quotes the abstract painter Brice Marden, who worked for Rauschenberg at this time:

Technically you're his assistant, but you're also being paid to sit around and drink with him. He was very lonely then, and sort of shaky in other ways, he couldn't really go out in bars because people would just hassle him. And then there was the question of whether he was ever going to be able to paint again.

In 1969 he was able to make a new start. At the invitation of NASA he went to the Kennedy Space Center to watch the launch of Apollo 11, which landed the first men on the Moon. This inspired a series of thirty-three lithographs entitled *Stoned Moon*, which Rauschenberg did with the print workshop Gemini GEL of Los Angeles. When the project was finished he remained in California because his studio in New York had been rendered uninhabitable by a fire. In 1971 he moved from California to the house on Captiva Island off the coast of Florida which he had bought as a retreat in 1962 but which he had up to that point used very little. Gradually he came to New York less and less and extended his operations on Captiva, establishing the Untitled Press there with Robert Petersen. Both his reputation and his prices rose throughout the 1970s, aided by a major retrospective at the National Gallery of Art in Washington, D.C., in 1976, the year of the United States bicentennial. The exhibition was seen later in New York (at the Museum of Modern Art), in San Francisco, Buffalo and Chicago.

Rauschenberg continued to travel widely and initiated a number of collaborations with artists abroad. These culminated in the Rauschenberg Overseas Culture Interchange project from 1985 to 1991, a testament to his belief in the power of creative collaboration to engender social change. In the 1990s he continued to produce his signature collage pieces, often working on a large scale, though these somewhat lacked the potency of his earlier 'Combines'. Despite this, his reputation as a key figure of postwar American art remained strong, and a major retrospective of his work was organized by the Guggenheim Museum in New York in 1997.

After a stroke in 2002 that left his right side paralysed, Rauschenberg learned to work more with his left hand, aided by a team of assistants. He died from heart failure on 12 May 2008.

JASPER JOHNS

Jasper Johns is one of the most elusive of contemporary artists, both personally and in terms of the interpretation of his work. The powerful legend that surrounds him often finds little in the way of facts to support it.

He was born in May 1930, in Augusta, Georgia. Shortly after he was born his parents separated, and he spent his childhood being passed back and forth between his grandparents and an uncle and aunt, all of whom lived in Allendale, South Carolina. The family were neither well off nor particularly cultivated, but Johns's grandmother painted, and he decided very early that he wanted to be an artist. He remarked later: 'People would say I was talented. I knew it was good to use one's talents, but I also knew I couldn't do that where I was – there weren't any artists there – so I guess it was also a form of escape.' He was eventually reunited with his mother, who had remarried, and who was now living in Columbia, South Carolina, but his period with her did not last long – he was sent to stay with another aunt who taught in a one-room school in a tiny community called The Corner where he remained for six years. He eventually finished high school in Sumter, South Carolina, living with his mother, stepfather and their new family of three children.

To please his parents, he enrolled in the University of South Carolina, but dropped out after a year and a half and went to New York in 1949, where he entered a commercial art college. After two terms he applied for a scholarship, and was told that he would be given one on the basis of need, since he did not deserve it on grounds of merit. He refused to accept these terms, and left to work as a messenger and shipping clerk before being drafted into the army. He spent part of his two year service back in South Carolina, and the final six months in Japan. After his release he returned to New York and entered City College on the GI Bill, but lasted there only one day. After dropping out, he got a job at the Marlboro bookshop and did figurative watercolours and drawings in his spare time.

In the winter of 1954 Johns was introduced to Robert Rauschenberg by a mutual friend. Gradually they became friends, then later lovers in a triangular relationship with a girl named Rachel Rosenthal. For a while Johns and Rosenthal occupied apartments one above the other in the same downtown loft building, until Rosenthal's space was taken over by Rauschenberg (already living nearby) in the summer of 1955; the emotional relationship between the two men was now in addition an intense professional one. Even before Rauschenberg moved into the same building, he and Johns had formed a partnership to design window displays for smart New York shops such as Bonwit Teller and Tiffany, earning money to support their artistic experiments.

In 1954 Johns decided to destroy all the work he had done up to that point:

Before, when anybody asked me what I did, I said I was going to become an artist. Finally I decided I could be going to become an artist all my life. I decided to stop *becoming* and *be* an artist.

The work which was the turning point in his development of a new and individual style came into being as the result of a dream that he was painting an American flag, and soon afterwards he did so, filling the whole field of the canvas. The technique he chose was encaustic, with the colour in a wax medium which gave a delicately sumptuous surface to contradict the flat literalism of the image. He also began to paint targets as well as flags, in the same literal way.

The first work by Johns to be seen in a museum was *Green Target*, included in an exhibition at the Jewish Museum in New York entitled *Artists of the New York School: Second Generation*, which had been selected by the eminent art historian Meyer Shapiro. The show opened in February 1957, and was seen by the dealer Leo Castelli, who had then just opened his gallery. Two days later Castelli and his wife Ileana Sonnabend came to visit Rauschenberg's loft because they were thinking of giving him a show. Johns's name was mentioned, and Castelli, recalling the impression *Green Target* had made on him, asked to see Johns's work as well, and was duly taken downstairs to the latter's studio. When the paintings were produced Castelli was thunderstruck: 'I saw evidence of the most incredible genius,' he declared later, 'entirely fresh and not related to anything else.' Ileana Sonnabend bought a painting at once, and her husband decided to give Johns a show.

The exhibition opened in January 1958 and was an instantaneous success. The Museum of Modern Art bought four works for its own collection, and several of its trustees made private purchases; only two works remained unsold. From this time onwards Johns was a major celebrity in the New York art world – a situation which he found difficult to deal with. His fame increased so rapidly that three of his paintings were shown at the Venice Biennale in October 1958, less than a year after his first show at Castelli. In December he was awarded the International Prize at the Pittsburgh Biennale at the Carnegie Institute.

Johns's work underwent a rapid evolution after his first show. He began making small sculptures, abandoned encaustic for oil paint, and became preoccupied with the work of Marcel Duchamp (whom he first heard of in 1958 and met personally the following year), and with the philosophy of Ludwig Wittgenstein. In 1960 he began printmaking, with the encouragement of the remarkable Tatyana Grossman, and after many experiments and reworkings his first lithographs were published in 1963. Printmaking was henceforward to be an important part of his artistic activity.

In 1961, in order to get away from some of the pressures of celebrity, Johns purchased a house on Edisto Island, off the coast of South Carolina. The time he spent there marked the beginning of a drift away from Rauschenberg, and the end of their intense artistic relationship. The personal relationship did not survive, and broke up amid some bitterness in the summer of 1962.

Johns's first major retrospective was held from February to April 1964 at the Jewish Museum in New York. He then visited Hawaii and Japan (for a second time) before going to London for another retrospective at the Whitechapel Art Gallery. By 1967 Johns was rich enough to buy a large building, a former bank, on the Lower East Side for use as a studio. In 1969, during his third visit to Japan, his house and studio on Edisto Island were destroyed by fire. This was a small setback in a career which continued to soar. In 1973, at an auction of works from the Robert C. Scull Collection, his painting *Double White Map* fetched $240,000 – then a record for a living American artist. In 1988, however, this record was to be far surpassed when another painting, *False Start*, was sold for $17 million to the publishing magnate S. I. Newhouse. In the midst of the major art boom of the early twenty-first century, that same painting was sold in 2006 to an American hedge-fund manager for a breathtaking $80 million.

Critics now divide Johns's career into three main periods. First come the literal representations of banal objects – the American flag, maps, targets, numbers – for which he became celebrated. These were followed, from 1972, by abstract works using cross-hatched patterns (derived from something seen on a moving car) and another pattern taken from painted flagstones (first seen on the side of a building in Harlem). In the third period, from about 1978, figurative imagery re-entered his work. Johns constantly claims not to be able to draw, but these later paintings show the influence of American turn-of-the-century *trompe l'œil* specialists such as William M. Harnett and John F. Peto, as well as more orthodox sources of inspiration, such as the work of Cézanne, Picasso and Matthias Grünewald.

Ever since he achieved fame, Johns has been famously reclusive. From 1970, he used a house at Stony Point, New York, as his main residence. He subsequently moved to a 100-acre estate in Connecticut, two hours north of New York City, and now spends the winter months in his house on the island of St Martin in the Caribbean, with his dogs Pepper and Pumpkin. His most recent retrospective was held at the Art Institute of Chicago in 2007, touring to New York's Metropolitan Museum of Art the following year.

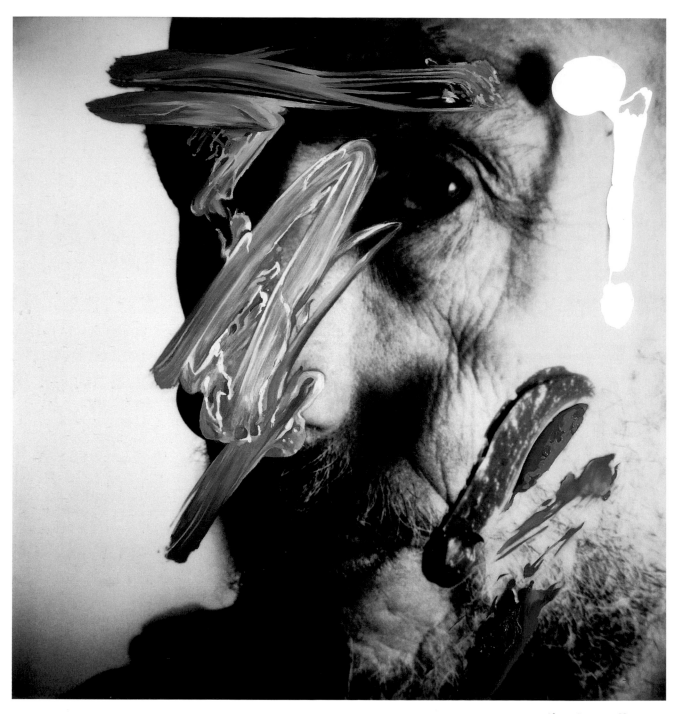

Above: Richard Hamilton,
O5.3.81.d, 1990
Right: Richard Hamilton,
*Just what is it that makes today's homes
so different, so appealing?*, 1956

There are two paradoxes connected to the British Pop Art movement. One is that it actually started somewhat earlier than its American counterpart; its basis was not an exploration of the familiar, but an excited appreciation of life which, viewed from the other side of the Atlantic, seemed full of romance and exoticism. The second is that many of the leading artists who have been given the Pop label feel that this is inappropriate to their work. Richard Hamilton is a Neo-Dadaist of a more didactic and academic sort than Johns and Rauschenberg; Hockney is an explorer who investigates many styles, inhabiting each in turn without inhibition.

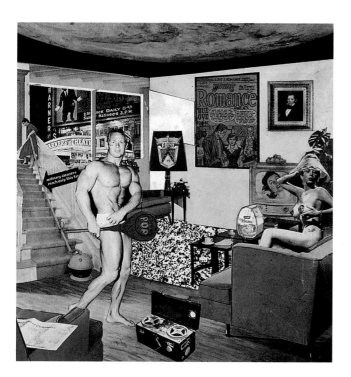

RICHARD HAMILTON

Richard Hamilton, though associated with the British Pop Art movement, is best thought of as the chief English disciple of Marcel Duchamp.

Born in London in 1922, he began an exceptionally long process of art education in 1934, when he started attending classes at his local adult education institute while still under age. After leaving elementary school in 1936 he attended evening classes at Westminster Technical College and St Martin's School of Art while working as an office boy, and as a display assistant at Reimann Studios. He then studied painting for two spells at the Royal Academy Schools, from which he was finally expelled in 1946 for 'not profiting by the instruction given in the Painting School'. He was married in 1947 to Terry O'Reilly, who was killed in a car accident in 1962. From 1948 to 1951 he studied at the Slade. These periods in education were interrupted during the war by some years as a jig and tool draughtsman, and immediately after it by an eighteen-month spell of military service.

When he graduated from the Slade, Hamilton entered the art teaching profession, but never as a teacher of painting. He first taught design at the Central School of Arts and Crafts in London. From 1953 he was a lecturer in the Fine Art Department at King's College, Durham University (later the University of Newcastle-upon-Tyne), where he devised and taught an influential Basic Design Course. From 1957 he taught interior design one day a week at the Royal College of Art.

In 1952 he was one of the founder-members of the Independent Group which met at the Institute of Contemporary Arts in London – one of its main objects was the study of popular imagery. Hamilton also helped to design a number of influential exhibitions inspired by the philosophy of the Group, the most famous being the *This is Tomorrow* exhibition at the Whitechapel Art Gallery, London, in 1956. This included Hamilton's small collage *Just what is it that makes today's homes so different, so appealing?* which draws on popular advertising imagery and is usually considered to be the first recognizably Pop Art work.

Hamilton showed a group of engravings at the Gimpel Fils Gallery in 1950, but his first major one-man show, a small retrospective of work executed since 1956, did not take place until 1964. After this show, at the Hanover Gallery, London, Hamilton met with rapid recognition and was widely exhibited, especially in the second half of the 1960s, when he had exhibitions in Kassel, New York, Milan, Hamburg and Berlin.

In 1960 he published his typographic version of Marcel Duchamp's *Green Box*, and in 1965 he began his reconstruction of the *Large Glass*. In 1966 he was responsible for organizing the Duchamp retrospective 'The Almost Complete Works of Marcel Duchamp', at the Tate Gallery, London.

Through his teaching at the Royal College of Art and the University of Newcastle-upon-Tyne, Hamilton influenced a generation of British artists, including Mark Lancaster, Stephen Buckley, Tim Head, Tony Carter and Rita Donagh, who became Hamilton's second wife.

Since he stopped teaching in 1966, Hamilton has explored a number of other techniques and media alongside painting. In the 1960s his interest in commercial advertising media led him to explore different reproduction techniques, such as photography and print. In 1968 he produced the pristine, white, blind-stamped and individually numbered sleeve for the Beatles' 'White Album', achieving the widest distribution of any of his work. During this preoccupation with mass production, Hamilton created an edition of 5000 of the print *Kent State* (1970), derived from a photograph taken from a television image. He has collaborated with many eminent printers in Europe and the United States to produce masterful screenprints and etchings. In the late 1980s Hamilton began exploring the techniques of digital manipulation of images using computers. A large printer and several computers now form part of his studio, a converted farm in the Oxfordshire countryside.

In 1992 the Tate Gallery in London organized a major retrospective of his career, and the following year Hamilton represented Great Britain at the Venice Biennale, winning the Golden Lion lifetime achievement award. His creativity has continued to flourish and in the late 1990s he completed his illustrations to James Joyce's novel *Ulysses*, a project he had begun more than fifty years earlier while studying at the Slade. In 2008 he won the prestigious Praemium Imperiale award, a sign of the high international esteem in which his work continues to be held.

RICHARD HAMILTON
reflected in *Interior 2*, 1966.

DAVID HOCKNEY

David Hockney has always denied being a Pop artist but is included under this heading because this is how the public perceives him. The most highly publicized British artist since the Second World War, he occupies a position analogous to that which was once accorded to Augustus John – one irony of this being that for John's exuberant heterosexuality Hockney substitutes a publicly acknowledged homosexuality.

He was born in Bradford in 1937, the fourth of five children. By the time he won a scholarship to Bradford Grammar School at the age of eleven he had already decided that he wanted to be an artist. He drew for the school magazine and produced posters for the school debating society as a substitute for homework. At sixteen he managed to persuade his parents to let him go to the local art school, and this was followed by two years of working in hospitals as an alternative to National Service, as he had registered as a conscientious objector. After this he went to the Royal College of Art in London to continue his studies, arriving there in 1959:

> Immediately after I started at the Royal College I realized that there were two groups of students there: a traditional group, who carried on as they had done in art school, doing still life, life painting and figure compositions; and then what I thought of as the more adventurous, lively students, the brightest ones, who were involved in the art of their time. They were doing big Abstract Expressionist paintings on hardboard.

Hockney duly tried his hand at abstraction, but found it too barren. He was at this moment in a phase of rapid self-discovery on both artistic and personal levels, coming to terms with his own sexuality, and at the same time searching for a style. His stylistic experimentation was fuelled by discussions with R.B. Kitaj, who was a student at the Royal College over the same period. Since figure-painting seemed 'anti-modern' Hockney began by including words in his paintings as a way of humanizing them, but these were soon joined by figures painted in a deliberately rough and rudimentary style which owed a great deal to Jean Dubuffet. Hockney's ebullient personality soon made him well known, even outside the Royal College, and he made his first major impact as a painter with the Young Contemporaries Exhibition of

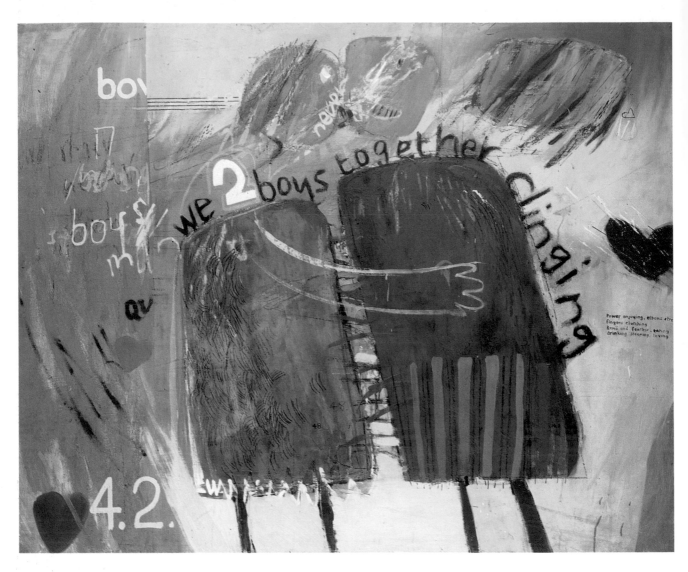

David Hockney, *We Two Boys Together Clinging*, 1961

January 1961. This show marked the public emergence of a new Pop movement in Britain, with Hockney (apparently) as one of its leaders.

In the same year Hockney made a series of discoveries. He visited New York, and was struck by the freedom of American society – it was at this stage that he bleached his hair and began to present a new image, fuelled not only by the United States but also by his discovery of the poetry of Whitman and Cavafy. He had begun to make etchings, and on his return to England set to work on a series of prints which were a modern version of Hogarth's *Rake's Progress*, and which reflected his American experiences. He also visited Italy for the first time in December 1961, and Berlin in 1962.

Hockney's success was so rapid that he became independent very soon after leaving the Royal College and did not, like the vast majority of his contemporaries, have to rely on teaching in order to make a living. In 1963 he travelled to Egypt at the invitation of the London *Sunday Times*, then at the end of the year went to Los Angeles, a city he had always fantasized about:

Within a week of arriving there in this strange big city, not knowing a soul, I'd passed the driving test, bought a car, driven to Las Vegas and won some money, got myself a studio, started painting, all within a week. And I thought, it's just how I imagined it would be.

David Hockney with *A Neat Lawn*, 1972. Photo Jorge Lewinski

The Los Angeles lifestyle and landscape became important features of Hockney's work. There were other important changes in his work as well: he started using acrylics rather than oil paint and he made increasing use of photography for purposes of documentation. His life was professionally successful – he had no fewer than five one-man exhibitions in Europe in 1966 – and personally happy. In 1966 he met Peter Schlesinger, a young Californian art student who became his lover and favourite model.

In 1968 Hockney returned to England with Peter, who enrolled at the Slade. But gradually the relationship came under increasing strain, and in 1970 it broke up. This break-up was recorded in Jack Hazan's film, *A Bigger Splash*, a candid documentary about Hockney's life and work, which was being made at this time. This was also the year in which Hockney had his first major retrospective exhibition, at the Whitechapel Art Gallery in London.

In 1973 Hockney went to live in Paris for a while. He took the opportunity while he was there to work with Aldo and Piero Crommelynck, who had been Picasso's master printers, and produced a series of etchings in memory of Picasso who had died earlier that year, and who had been one of Hockney's heroes since he saw the Picasso exhibition at the Tate Gallery in the summer of 1960. In 1974 there was a large exhibition of Hockney's work at the Musée des Arts Décoratifs in Paris.

Hockney is instinctively gregarious, and he has always been interested in the full spectrum of the arts, not merely in painting. It was therefore natural that he should be drawn into designing sets for the theatre. His first commission of this sort was for a production of Jarry's *Ubu Roi* at the Royal Court Theatre in London in 1966. In 1974 he returned to stage design when he was approached by the Glyndebourne Festival to design sets for Stravinsky's *Rake's Progress*. This was followed by a second collaboration with Glyndebourne, on Mozart's *Magic Flute* in 1978, and a commission from the Metropolitan Opera in New York to design sets and costumes for a triple bill of works by Satie, Poulenc and Ravel. In 1983, a large touring exhibition, *Hockney Paints the Stage*, showed a selection of his designs for opera and ballet. He later designed sets for a Stravinsky triple bill at the Metropolitan Opera, Wagner's *Tristan und Isolde* in Los Angeles, Puccini's *Turandot* in San Francisco and Strauss's *Die Frau ohne Schatten* at Covent Garden.

During this period Hockney was also experimenting both with large composite photographs and with works made of paper pulp impregnated with colour – the *Paper Pools*. From 1982 Hockney explored the use of the camera, making composite images of Polaroid photographs arranged in a rectangular grid. Later he used regular 35-millimetre prints to create photocollages, compiling a 'complete' picture from a series of individually photographed details.

After working with master printer Ken Tyler in the 1980s on making etchings and lithographs, in 1986 Hockney explored ways of creating work with colour photocopiers. 'The works I did with the copying machine ... were not reproductions,' he said later, 'they were very complex prints.' Subject to the same curiosity about new technical methods, he began to experiment with the fax machine, and in 1989 even sent work for the São Paulo Biennale to Brazil via the telephone line. Experiments using computers followed, composing images and colours on the screen and having them printed directly from the computer disk without preliminary proofing.

A major retrospective of Hockney's work opened in February 1988 in Los Angeles, and visited New York and London. Technical experimentation has continued to inform his work, without taking it over. His easel paintings made during the 1980s show the influence of Matisse and Picasso. He has designed for the stage in the 1990s, and in 1995–96 a retrospective exhibition of his drawings was mounted at the Royal Academy in London. Hockney works in his studio in the Hollywood Hills near Los Angeles in California, where he has lived permanently since 1978, and also, increasingly often, in a small house he has purchased in Malibu.

In recent years, however, he has shown a renewed interest in the landscape of his birthplace. From about 2004 he began to paint a series of elegiac views of the East Yorkshire countryside, working on the pictures in the open air before completing them in his studio. He has also started to produce paintings on an epic scale. In 2007 his largest ever work, *Bigger Trees Near Warter*, was hung majestically as the centrepiece of the Royal Academy's Summer Exhibition in London. Hockney later decided to donate the work, 5 × 12 metres (15 × 40 ft) long and made up of fifty individual canvases, to the British nation, generously giving it as a gift to the Tate.

DAVID HOCKNEY,
Artist and Model, 1974

Pop Art in America arose from a fascination with the new urban mass-culture, with its characteristic cults and artefacts: advertisements, pin-ups, comic-strips and badges. There was also a self-conscious interest in different conventions of representation – a theme which Roy Lichtenstein, for example, explored in some depth. But there was in addition a deliberate rejection of the claim made by many leading Abstract Expressionist artists that art conferred high moral status on those who committed themselves to it with sufficient energy and seriousness. These ideas, already rejected from within Abstract Expressionism by Ad Reinhardt, were deliberately flouted by artists such as Andy Warhol. Warhol, passive, frivolous, coolly uninterested in everything which artists like Rothko and Still believed to be important, rapidly emerged as one of the greatest showmen of his time. In contrast to the work of the rest of the group is that of Claes Oldenburg and Jim Dine, which is linked to both Dada and Surrealism, and much less impersonal in tone. Dine was one of the main progenitors of the 'Happening', a plotless theatrical event which used gestures, props, sounds and incidental effects of all kinds as ingredients in a kind of collage which dissolved as soon as it had been created.

Above: Roy Lichtenstein,
Yellow and Green Brushstrokes, 1961
Right: Roy Lichtenstein, 1985.
Photo Grace Sutton

Roy Lichtenstein with his wife
Dorothy in their kitchen
in Southampton, c. 1977.
Photographer unknown

ROY LICHTENSTEIN

Roy Lichtenstein was the master of the stereotype, and the most sophisticated of the major Pop artists in terms of his analysis of visual convention and his ironic exploitation of past styles. The work for which he is now known was the product of a long apprenticeship.

He was born in New York City in October 1923. His parents were middle-class and he described himself as having had a quiet and uneventful childhood. Though art was not taught as part of the curriculum at his high school, in his junior year he started to draw and paint as a hobby. His first subjects were jazz musicians (the product of a youthful enthusiasm for their music), and his work was affected by Picasso's Blue and Rose Period paintings, which he knew from reproductions.

In his last year of high school, 1939, he enrolled for summer art classes at the Art Students' League under Reginald Marsh. His subject-matter was then strongly influenced by Marsh's own work. On his graduation from high school, Lichtenstein decided to leave New York and study art. He went to the School of Fine Arts at Ohio State University, but his artistic education was interrupted by the war. He was drafted in 1943 and served in Britain and continental Europe. During his time in the services he was able to do some work as an artist, particularly drawing from nature. Demobilized in 1946, he returned immediately to Ohio State University and gained his Bachelor of Fine Art in June. He then joined the graduate programme, as an instructor. In 1949 he gained his Master of Fine Art and held his first one-man exhibition at the Ten Thirty Gallery in Cleveland. At this time he started to introduce broad references to Americana in his work: in 1951 he had a show in New York consisting largely of assemblages made of found objects. He moved to Cleveland and worked on and off as an engineering draughtsman for various companies while continuing to paint and intermittently show his work in New York. His earliest proto-Pop work was painted in 1956 – a picture of a dollar bill – but it had no immediate successor. From 1957 until 1960 his work could, broadly speaking, be classified as Abstract Expressionist; he had previously passed through Geometric Abstraction and a version of Cubism.

In 1960 Lichtenstein was appointed Assistant Professor at Douglas College at Rutgers University of New Jersey, which put him within striking distance of New York. He met and had long discussions with Allan Kaprow, and he also met Claes Oldenburg, Jim Dine, Lucas Samaras and George Segal. He attended a number of early 'Happenings', but did not participate in them actively. These contacts revived his interest in Pop imagery, and a more immediate stimulus was provided by a challenge from one of his sons, who pointed to a Mickey Mouse comic book and said; 'I bet you can't paint as good as that.' In 1961 Lichtenstein produced about six paintings showing characters from comic-strip frames, with only minor changes of colour and form from the original source material. It was at this time that he first made use of devices which were to become signatures in his work – Ben-Day dots, lettering and speech balloons.

Lichtenstein took in his comic-strip paintings unannounced to the new Leo Castelli Gallery, and was almost immediately accepted for exhibition there, in preference to Andy Warhol, who had started doing similar work. His first one-man show with Castelli in 1962 launched him on a career which was thereafter uniformly successful. In 1963 he moved from New Jersey to New York, having taken leave of absence from his job at Rutgers; in 1964 he resigned from teaching altogether. In 1966 he showed at the Venice Biennale, and in 1969 he was given a retrospective at the Guggenheim Museum, which later toured America. He was elected to the American Academy of Arts and Sciences in 1970, and then moved to Southampton, Long Island, thus following a pattern set by many successful American artists.

Lichtenstein's development as a mature painter was marked by his propensity for working in successive series or thematic groups. The later groups tended to be interpretations and to some extent parodies of earlier Modernist styles – Cubism, Futurism and Surrealism. In the early 1980s Lichtenstein created sculptural maquettes constructed from flat shapes as three-dimensional graphic imitations of German Expressionist woodcuts. These, like his series of painted or sculpted brushstrokes of the 1980s, painstakingly created an ironic suggestion of spontaneity. In the late 1980s and early 1990s he returned to the use of Ben-Day dots in a new and refined application of his earlier style. Roy Lichtenstein died in September 1997.

ANDY WARHOL

Andy Warhol was perhaps the most celebrated of all the American Pop artists – his celebrity, carefully cultivated by himself, came as much from his lifestyle as from the work. He was born Andrew Warhola, in Pittsburgh in 1928. His parents were Czech immigrants, and the family were working class; his father worked in the West Virginia coal mines, and died in 1942. Warhol studied painting and design at Carnegie Institute, and graduated with a BA in 1949. He left immediately for New York, living at first in a communal apartment, and surviving as an illustrator and commercial artist. A friend who remembers him from that time said later:

> Although he may ... have been nineteen at the time, he seemed even younger. And so shy – he rarely spoke at all. One of the girls in the apartment got so mad at Andy for not talking to her that she threw an egg at him and hit him on the head with it.

Despite his shyness, Warhol rapidly became success-ful – his speciality was drawing shoes, and he worked for the most prestigious glossy magazines and the more exclusive New York department stores. In 1957, he was sufficiently well known to be awarded the Art Directors' Club Medal for his work as a commercial illustrator. There were a number of reasons for Warhol's success, one of which was his skill at presenting himself:

> Andy never wore anything but old clothes. He would show up at *Vogue* or *Bazaar* looking like some street urchin in his torn chinos and dirty sneakers – Raggedy Andy – and the editors and art directors found him irresistible.

Even more important were his co-operativeness, prompt-ness and professionalism. In the course of his work he gained a thorough knowledge of processes of mechanical reproduction, and in addition invented some techniques, such as a personal use of monotype to create a blurred and softened line, which made his drawings distinctive – in fact, the work of this phase strives for exactly the per-sonal, 'hand-made' look which his most characteristic paintings avoid.

Warhol never gave up his early ambitions to be recognized as a fine artist rather than as a purely commercial one. He exhibited regularly in the late 1950s, mostly derivations from his bread-and-butter work, but his drawings aroused little interest from the critics. He also became involved with an avant-garde theatre group working on the Lower East Side for whom he designed

Left: ANDY WARHOL in front of a
self-portrait at an exhibition at the
Anthony d'Offay Gallery,
London 1986.
Photographer unknown
Above: ANDY WARHOL,
Marilyn, 1967

ANDY WARHOL with members of the Factory, 1968. Photo Philippe Halsman

sets. It was probably through this group that he became acquainted with Bertolt Brecht's theory of alienation – the idea that the work of art deliberately distances the spectator and invites judgment, rather than identification with what is shown.

In 1960 he made a series of paintings based on newspapers and fragments of comic strips – the images he selected were photographed, projected on to canvas and filled in by hand. These works were shown as window decorations at the Bonwit Teller store on Fifty-Seventh Street in April 1961, following a precedent set by Robert Rauschenberg and Jasper Johns. But no established gallery would accept them, despite the fact that Pop imagery was beginning to surface regularly in art. This was part of Warhol's problem: Roy Lichtenstein was doing work which looked superficially similar, and which was clearly more accomplished and better presented.

Warhol felt he had reached an impasse – until, at the joking suggestion of a friend, he made his first paintings of dollar bills and Campbell's soup cans, objects so familiar that people had ceased to notice what they looked like. At first he painted the images freehand, but soon, as literalism was the aim, it seemed logical to silk-screen them on to the canvas. The soup cans were quickly followed by portraits of Marilyn Monroe from photographic originals – these were ironic allusions to the cult of the 'star' which was an important part of the new Pop mythology. The Campbell's soup cans were exhibited in the summer of 1962 in Los Angeles, and in the autumn of the same year Warhol had a show at the Stable Gallery in New York. The timing was exactly right, and the exhibition caused a sensation.

He now took a studio on East Forty-Seventh Street, which he renamed 'The Factory', and began to mass-produce silk-screened paintings with the aid of friends. New subjects were found – Jackie Kennedy, Elvis Presley, a series of 'disasters', another one devoted to images of the electric chair. In 1963, he also started to make films.

ANDY WARHOL in front of his cow wallpaper at a press conference to open an exhibit at the Whitney Museum of American Art, 1971. Photographer unknown

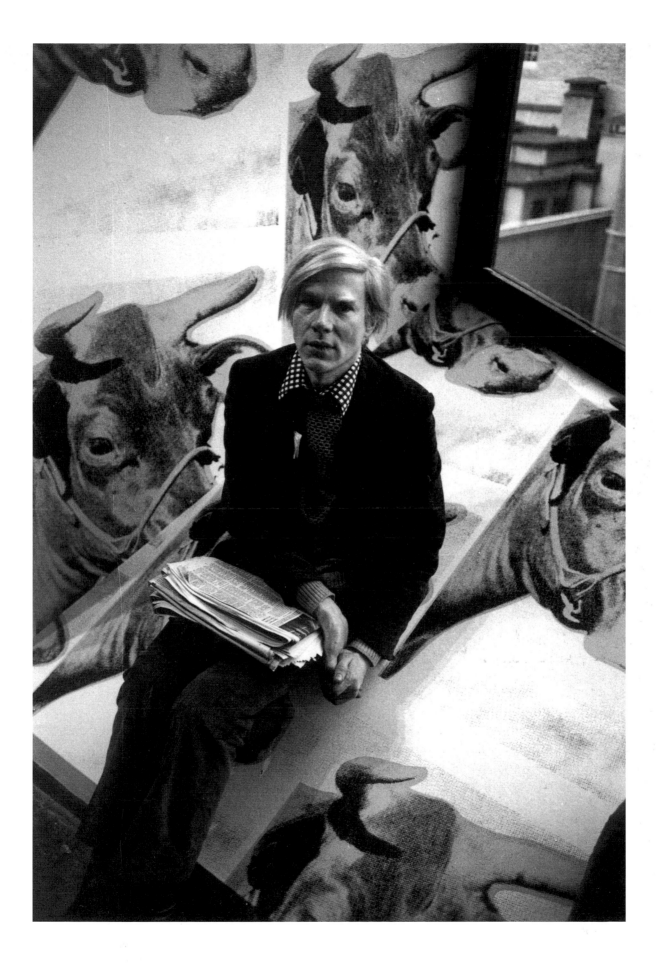

At first these were extremely primitive, and their main subject seemed to be boredom. The camera was simply left to stare at an object or person, sometimes for hours on end. As Warhol said:

I like boring things. When you just sit and look out of a window, that's enjoyable. It takes up time. Yeah. Really. You see people looking out of the window all the time, I do. If you're not looking out of a window, you're sitting in a shop looking at the street. My films are just a way of taking up time.

Soon, however, they became rather more than that – they developed into a voyeuristic examination of the 'superstars' with whom Warhol now surrounded himself. These were people of very different kinds – runaway girls from 'good' families, like the tragic Edie Sedgwick, who was to die of a drug overdose; aspiring New York socialites, like Baby Jane Holzer; transvestites, hustlers and addicts. They acted out their traumas and fantasies in the presence of their seemingly passive host. 'I don't know where the artificial stops and the real begins,' Warhol once declared. 'With film you just turn on the camera and photograph something. I leave the camera running until it runs out of film because that way I can catch somebody being themselves.'

By the mid-1960s, Warhol was surrounded by an extraordinary atmosphere of hysteria. His first retrospective exhibition, held in 1965 at the Institute of Contemporary Art, University of Pennsylvania, generated a near riot at its opening, as guests pressed close to the hero of the occasion. Warhol and Edie Sedgwick had to be smuggled out of a side-door, as did many of the exhibits, to save them from damage. By this time Warhol had already moved to the prestigious Leo Castelli Gallery where he exhibited two series of paintings. The first of these was of *Flowers*, based on a photograph he had discovered in a woman's magazine; it had won second prize in a contest for the best picture taken by a house-wife. The Factory produced over nine hundred *Flowers* in all sizes. In 1966 there was a further exhibition, of *Cow Wallpaper* and *Silver Clouds* – the latter were floating plastic pillows filled with helium. By the time the exhibition opened Warhol had announced his retirement from painting on the grounds that it was no longer interesting.

April 1996 also marked Warhol's début in the rock-music business – the Velvet Underground band, which was his creation, gave its first performance, in a setting provided by the mixed-media show Exploding Plastic Inevitable, which he directed.

In June 1968, he became the victim of his self-created legend. He was shot and critically injured by an unbalanced young woman called Valerie Solanas, who had appeared in his film *Bikeboy*. Six months previously she had founded an organization with the acronym SCUM – the Society for Cutting Up Men. Warhol was the particular male on whom she chose to vent her anger. Characteristically, he later displayed the scars left by his terrible injuries in his portrait painted by the veteran American Expressionist Alice Neel.

Though he announced early that he would retire from painting, Warhol never really did so. He continued, sometimes under protest, to produce vast quantities of work, in intervals snatched from other, more fascinating but less reliably lucrative activities, such as film-making and running the periodical *Interview*. He was also one of the most enthusiastic party-goers of his time, as is amply recorded in the *Andy Warhol Diaries* published after his death. One of his chief sources of income was a series of commissioned portraits of otherwise unremarkable German businessmen. When painting portraits, Warhol, a good businessman himself, invariably gave a discount for quantity. Despite the apparent cynicism of his attitudes, Warhol continued to be highly regarded by the international visual arts establishment. In 1981, for example, he was the only American Pop artist to be included in the exhibition *A New Spirit in Painting*, held at the Royal Academy, London – the show announced the triumph of the new German Expressionism, which one might have thought inimical to everything Warhol stood for. One of his ways of constantly repositioning himself was through shared exhibitions and collaborations. He shared a show with Le Roi Neiman, chiefly famous for work commissioned for *Playboy*, and collaborated with the young New York graffiti painter Jean-Michel Basquiat.

Warhol died as the result of a botched gall-bladder operation in 1987. The immensely successful sale at auction of his vast collections (everything from fine American Empire furniture to cookie-jars) proved how successfully he had established himself in the popular imagination.

CLAES OLDENBURG,
Lipsticks in Piccadilly Circus, 1966

Piccadilly Circus, London.   ET .2987R

CLAES OLDENBURG

Claes Oldenburg is an upholder of ideas originated by the Surrealists between the two World Wars. He was born in Stockholm in 1929, the elder son of a Swedish diplomat; his mother was a Christian Scientist with an interest in spiritualism. After three years in the United States, the family moved to Oslo in 1933. They finally settled in Chicago, where Oldenburg's father was appointed consul. When Oldenburg arrived in Chicago he spoke no English and compensated for the isolation this imposed by developing a rich fantasy life, centred round the imaginary country of 'Neubern', an island between Africa and South America whose language was half-Swedish and half-English. All aspects of this country were carefully documented in a series of scrapbooks which contain many images which were to recur later in Oldenburg's art – he himself said defiantly in 1966: 'Everything I do is completely original – I made it up when I was a little kid.'

He attended the Chicago Latin School for boys, and, in reaction to this traditional classical education, explored Chicago's raunchy burlesque houses in his teenage years, talking to the dancers and gathering a store of sexual images which were to influence his work. In 1946 he left Chicago for Yale University, where he was chosen to participate in the experimental Directed Studies Programme designed to combat specialization. He concentrated on literature and art (his formal art studies began in his last year at university), and also took a drama course. In 1950 he returned to Chicago to work as a novice reporter with the City News Bureau, covering the police beat. It was not until he was rejected by the Army in 1952 that he decided to concentrate on art. During this period he worked at a variety of jobs – he even sold sweets in Chicago's Dearborn Station. Meanwhile, he attended classes at the Art Institute of Chicago, and got to know

CLAES OLDENBURG, *The Store*, front window looking into The Store, 107 East Second Street, New York, December 1961. Photographer unknown

them Allan Kaprow and Red Grooms. Through them he was asked to co-found a gallery in the Judson Memorial Church, which was used for dance, theatrical and poetry events as well as for showing experimental work by new artists.

Oldenburg held his first public one-man show in this gallery in May and June 1959. What he showed were fragile sculptures made by dropping newspaper into wheat paste, then modelling this substance on to rough chickenwire armature. The exhibition started off a period of intense self-analysis: 'My procedure was simply to find everything that means something to me, but the logic of my self-development was gradually to find myself in my surroundings.' At this time he was determined to 'revel in contradiction, bringing out of myself numerous identities.' He invented an *alter ego*, Ray Gun, who saw himself as 'only alive when he [was] constantly arranging to upset his existence.' One of the associations this figure had for Oldenburg was with Hart Crane's 'religious gunman', identified by the poet with Christ. Ray Gun played a part in Oldenburg's next exhibition, *The Street*, which was influenced by Louis-Ferdinand Céline's magnificently pessimistic novel, *Mort à Crédit* (Death on the Instalment Plan), by the art of Jean Dubuffet, and most of all by what Oldenburg saw around him on the Lower East Side. A notebook entry for 1960 reads:

My position and that of others like me is one of the supersensitive and superintellectual in an insensitive and unintellectual society WHO DO NOT WISH TO ESCAPE or who realize that escape is impossible. We thus become clowns or wits or wise men. The danger is to forget art and merely construct parables, to become a wise man rather than an artist ...

The Street, with its frightening, sometimes scatological vision of city life, was shown in two versions, at the Judson Gallery, and then at the Reuben Gallery, also in New York. It was followed by a much more optimistic show, *The Store*, a celebration of mass-market consumerism which established Oldenburg's reputation with the New York avant-garde. Installed in an actual shop, this was planned to run for the month of December 1961, but was extended by popular demand until the end of January 1962.

The next step, which turned him into one of the high priests of the new cult of Pop Art, was his exhibition held

members of the budding Chicago School, among them Leon Golub and H. C. Westermann. Eventually he decided that Chicago was provincial from an artistic point of view, and that it was necessary for him to live and work in New York.

He arrived in New York in June 1956, just after the death of Jackson Pollock. Though Pollock had been his hero, Oldenburg found himself out of sympathy with the derivative second generation of the Abstract Expressionists who were then dominant in the New York art world. He took a part-time job, which he held until 1961, shelving books in the libraries of the Cooper Union Museum and Art School. This enabled him to embark on a process of self-education – in particular, he studied the drawings of Watteau and Tiepolo, an important stage in his development as a draughtsman. From 1958 onwards his continuing interest in the theatre brought him into contact with a group of environmental artists, among

CLAES OLDENBURG and Coosje van Bruggen, *Spoonbridge and Cherry*, 1988

<small>CLAES OLDENBURG with model. Photo Julian Nieman</small>

at the Green Gallery on Fifty-Seventh Street in 1962. This contained the first giant soft sculptures made of vinyl stitched together by his wife Pat, whom he had married in 1960. Many were enlargements of familiar domestic appliances, which in their new form took on a distinctly erotic air.

In March 1965 Oldenburg was able to move into a vast, block-long studio on New York's Fourteenth Street. The size of this space, plus the amount of air-travel he had been doing in previous months as a result of his new-found success, encouraged him to think in terms of even bigger objects than he had made hitherto. The first result was a series of 'monument' drawings, proposals for monumental sculptures which would be further enlargements of trivial domestic objects. Here the original intention was to satirize the banality of American

<small>CLAES OLDENBURG walking down the street with a monumental tube of toothpaste, London 1966. Photo Hans Hammarskiöld</small>

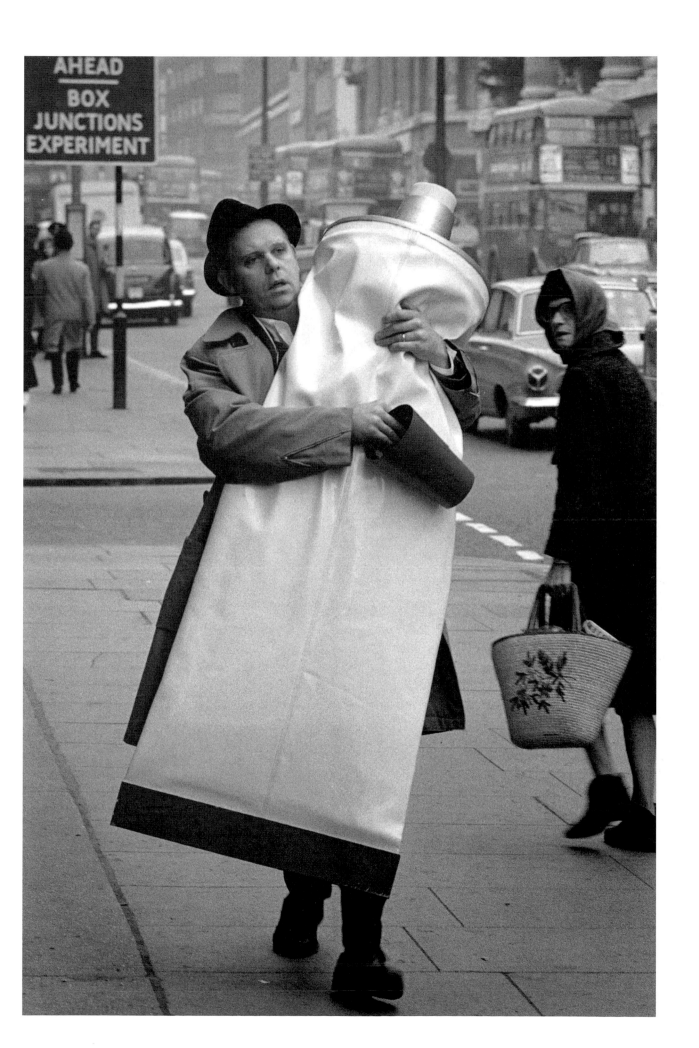

life, sometimes with an element of the erotic or scatological thrown in: for example, *Dam Fall*, a drawing now in the Sonnabend Collection, features a dam sluice transformed into gigantic male genitalia. Soon Oldenburg was given the opportunity to create some of these fantasies in real life, at which point the humour began to drain out of them. In the early 1980s he was still making them and was given an accolade which could only have come to a thoroughly established artist: he was asked to create a feature for the central atrium of the magnificent new Dallas Museum. He came up with an immense version of the *Stake Hitch* – the metal peg and rope used to tether cattle and horses – as a tribute to the local ethos. The sculpture itself, and even more so its presence in these surroundings, was an ironic echo of Oldenburg's best-known public statement, a manifesto issued in 1961, which read in part:

> I am for an art that is political-erotical-mystical, that does something other than sit on its ass in a museum.
> I am for an art that grows up not knowing it is art at all, an art given the chance of having the starting point of zero.
> I am for an art that embroils itself with the every-day crap and still comes out on top.
> I am for an art that imitates the human, that is comic if necessary, or violent, or whatever is necessary.
> ... I am for an artist who vanishes, turning up in a white cap, painting signs and hallways ... I am for an art that is smoked, like a cigarette, smells, like a pair of shoes. I am for an art that flaps like a flag, or helps blow noses, like a handkerchief. I am for an art that is put on and taken off, like pants, which develops holes, like socks, which is eaten, like a piece of pie.

In 1977 Oldenburg married Coosje van Bruggen, a former museum curator, and his collaborator on a series of large-scale projects and performances. Since the 1970s they have created oversized sculptures of objects such as pool balls, clothespins, trowels and shuttlecocks, which have been installed in cities and parks across the US, Europe and in Japan. Many of these projects have blurred the boundaries between sculpture and architecture, some in collaboration with architects, others in dialogue with iconic buildings, such as their 2006 dustpan-and-brush sculpture sited in front of Denver Art Museum, Colorado.

JIM DINE

Jim Dine is the youngest of the major American Pop artists of the first generation, the most closely linked to Neo-Dadaists such as Rauschenberg and Johns, and, paradoxically, the most Expressionist of the whole group in style.

He was born in June 1935 at Cincinnati, Ohio, and his first contact with art was children's classes at the Cincinnati Art Museum. His mother died in 1947 and he went to live with his maternal grandparents:

> My family were immigrants, hardware store owners on a very simple level. My grandpa, who raised me, thought he was a carpenter – he fixed things and made all kinds of things, but he wasn't a very good craftsman. He did it with such bravado, such self-confidence, that we believed him. He let me play with his tools, but I think I would have had the same obsession if no one in my family had had anything to do with these primary objects. They are the link with our past, the human past, the hand.

While at high school Dine attended adult evening classes at the Cincinnati Art Academy. He then went to Ohio University in Athens, where he took his Bachelor of Fine Art in June 1957, and worked for a year as a postgraduate before moving to New York in 1958. Here he taught at Rhodes School and soon became part of a

JIM DINE,
Large Boot Lying Down, 1985

Jim Dine, *Self-Portrait Next to a Coloured Window*, 1985

flourishing East Village scene of as yet unestablished artists. He was one of the founders of the Judson Gallery together with Claes Oldenburg.

Dine was the true father of the 'Happening', which combined both planned and improvised theatrical activity. In 1959 he gave the first performance of *The Smiling Workman*, which was an affirmation of optimism, of Dine's enjoyment of his 'job' as an artist. This was followed in 1960 by the more celebrated *Car Crash,* which was based on a real accident involving the artist and his wife. Nevertheless, Dine never really felt at ease in New York in spite of the fact that he had so rapidly achieved a central position in the Pop scene. In 1962, a year after he joined the Martha Jackson Gallery, with a subsidy which enabled him to paint full-time, he entered psychoanalysis. This had been preceded by a period of peculiarly intense work:

It was an unusual summer. I didn't leave the house apart from when I walked to my studio and back. I could do that, but otherwise ... I couldn't leave the house. That summer I really painted like crazy.

Dine was not interested in the impersonality which characterized the work of other Pop artists. In an interview given in 1963, he said:

I'm interested in personal messages, in making paintings about my studio ... I'm working on a series of palettes right now. I put down the palette first, then within that palette I can do anything – clouds can roll through it, people can walk over it, I can put a hammer in the middle of it. Every time I do something, the whole thing becomes richer; it is another thing added to the landscape.

His field of activity continued to broaden. In 1965 he made his first cast-aluminium sculptures and designed a theatre production – *A Midsummer Night's Dream* – for the Actors' Workshop in San Francisco. In 1966 he started to write poetry under the influence of members of the so-called New York school of poets, some of whom had become friends. He now calls this poetry 'not very good, but not without interest, because the poetry is painter's poetry.'

Dine's excursion into poetry coincided with his move to London in 1967 – he had visited England for the first time in 1966. He did not go to Paris until 1969. In 1970 he had a retrospective exhibition at the Whitney Museum in New York, and in 1971 he moved from London to spend part of the year at a farm he had bought in Vermont. In 1973 he started working in Paris with the master printers Aldo and Piero Crommelynck, who had been Picasso's collaborators in making the later part of his graphic output. It was perhaps etching, with its emphasis on line, which made Dine want to work in a more traditional fashion. In 1975 he began drawing from the figure every day, and continued to do this for the next six years.

From the beginning of his career Dine had always tended to work in series, the paintings in each series being devoted to one motif – ties, tools, bathrobes, hearts etc. In 1980 he began making paintings of single trees which revealed more clearly than any previous pictures his link with Expressionism: they can be compared, for example, with Mondrian's paintings of the same subject. In 1981 he found another motif – the wrought-iron gate outside the Crommelyncks' home and workshop in the rue de Grenelle – which he used the following year as the basis for a piece of sculpture. He has continued to make sculptures in very different styles – some, such as his versions of the Venus de Milo, are reminiscent of Magritte; others, like the large heads of his wife, Nancy, seem to show the influence of Giacometti.

In the mid-1990s Dine began to explore a new motif that originated in a childhood fascination with the nineteenth-century story of the wooden puppet Pinocchio. Since then he has made numerous paintings and sculptures of the boy, as well as creating a new version of the book, complete with his own lithographs and updated typography. 'This idea of a talking stick becoming a boy,' he has said, 'is like a metaphor for art; it's the ultimate alchemical transformation.'

Above and left: JIM DINE,
Car Crash, 1960.
Photos © Robert McElroy

The six artists in this section bring new approaches to the problems of making art. Their work often lies at extremes, challenging not only our assumptions about what art is but what it does. For Yves Klein, and perhaps even more so for Joseph Beuys, the physical objects produced by the artist assumed importance, not for their innate aesthetic value, but as relics, memories and reflections of a particular personality. Eva Hesse and Louise Bourgeois give the same attitudes a distinctively feminist twist. Their sculptures seem spun out of themselves, out of their very viscera, as the spider spins its web, and the personality and the artwork become part of a single continuum. The African-American painter Jean-Michel Basquiat and the Chinese artist Zhang Xiaogang form an interesting contrast. Part Haitian and part Puerto Rican, Basquiat grew up between New York and Puerto Rico, but always identified with the culture of the former. His art appropriates imagery from a number of cultures – European and African images are combined with the 'popular' urban culture of the moment. Zhang, a key figure in the sudden upsurge of Chinese contemporary art that began in the mid-1980s, focuses on a single episode in recent Chinese history – the Cultural Revolution. In both cases the artists seem to be trying to work out what kind of place can be found for art in the contemporary world. Beuys, generally regarded as introspective, often referred to his art as 'social sculpture'. Basquiat and Zhang are 'social' artists' but in a very different sense. What they share with Beuys is a keen sense of the impact made by historical events.

LOUISE BOURGEOIS,
Cell (Arch of Hysteria), 1992–93

LOUISE BOURGEOIS

The late flowering of Louise Bourgeois's reputation was one of the more remarkable by-products of the feminist movement. She was born in Paris in 1911, and spent much of her childhood at Aubusson, where her parents ran a workshop which renovated old tapestries. From the age of ten, Louise helped with the restoration. Her first assignment, she remembers, was to redraw a foot, since it was the lower borders of these tapestries which had often rotted away thanks to damp and age.

Bourgeois had a complex relationship with her parents, and particularly with her father – she often said in interviews that it was these traumas of childhood and adolescence which continued to provide the basic material for her art. Her parents had three children – Bourgeois had an older sister and a younger brother. Named after her father, Louise became his favourite, because she looked like him. On the other hand, he often subjected her to sadistic teasing. 'My father would often make me feel small,' she said. 'Teasing, you see, is a permissive form of cruelty.'

He was also a philanderer. Bourgeois's mother became ill with emphysema (the result of a severe attack of Spanish influenza immediately after the First World War), and from 1922 to 1932 the family spent the winters in the south of France for the sake of Madame Bourgeois's health. They were accompanied there by a young English governess called Sadie, who was also her father's mistress. 'My mind, as an artist,' Bourgeois said, 'was conditioned by that affair, by my jealousy of that dreadful intruder.' She added: 'I learned that the way to survive is to make yourself indispensable to someone else. My father needed me. I pleased him. I was never rejected. But it often made me sad.'

As Louise grew older, her father began to take her to the nightclubs of Pigalle and Montmartre, and this gave Bourgeois a taste for bohemianism which she never quite lost, even after she married and went to America. These experiences also inform the erotic content of some of her sculptures.

In 1932 Louise Bourgeois's mother died. Her father, sadistic in this as in everything else, teased her about her grief, and as a result she attempted suicide by throwing herself into a river. Her father had to leap in to rescue

LOUISE BOURGEOIS, 1982.
Photo Robert Mapplethorpe

her. Her mother's death marked the first major turning point in Bourgeois's life. 'When [she] died... this rage to understand took me over. If you fear abandonment, it keeps you in a state of dependency, which makes you feel unable to cope.' She decided to study mathematics at the Sorbonne, because 'you could trust the principles on which it is constructed. It is a reliable system. It will not betray you.' However, she gave up the subject, and began to study art at the Ecole des Beaux-Arts in Paris, then transferred to the free academies, working at the Ranson, Julian, Colarossi and Grande Chaumière. She also worked with a number of the leading artists of the time – Fernand Léger, Marcel Gromaire, Othon Friesz and André Lhote.

She was particularly influenced by Léger, who allowed her to study with him free because, with her excellent English (which she owed to the detested Sadie), she was able to serve as his translator with American students. It was in Léger's atelier that she realized that it was her destiny to be a sculptor. He told his students to draw a wood shaving, curled like a lock of hair, which he had pinned under a shelf so that it fell freely. Bourgeois found she was very interested in the form itself, 'and its trembling quality. I did not want to make a representation of it. I wanted to explore its three-dimensional quality.'

Bourgeois made two trips to Russia, in 1932 and 1934, as a member of one of the left-wing cultural delegations popular at the time. In 1937 she met the American art historian Robert Goldwater, and married him in the following year. 'He told me his father had never been unfaithful to his mother. I couldn't believe this was true, but it made me interested in him.' After adopting a son, Michel, the couple moved to New York. Bourgeois found she liked the puritan temperament of her new husband and new country, but nevertheless missed aspects of her old life. She turned to art to help her reconstruct what she had left behind: 'I ran away from people at home, in Paris, because I couldn't stand them, and as soon as I got away I started to rebuild them.'

Bourgeois had two sons in America, but also, slowly, began to build a career as an artist. She worked at the Art Students' League in New York during the war years, and, somewhat under protest, mingled with the Surrealist exiles who had now begun to arrive in New York: 'It was the Left Bank again, and though I was now close to them, I objected to them violently. They were so lordly and pontifical.' She had her first solo show in 1945, and

a second show in 1947, both as a painter. In 1949 she had her first exhibition of sculpture, at the Peridot Gallery. These contained a number of abstracted wooden figures or 'personages' based on people she knew and perhaps influenced by her husband's study of African art. From this point she showed her work regularly, but often at rather long intervals. She became an American citizen in the 1950s.

In 1960, Bourgeois also began teaching regularly, which brought her into closer contact with the rest of the New York art world. In 1966, she was included in the feminist critic Lucy Lippard's survey show *Eccentric Abstraction* at the Fischbach Gallery (which also featured Eva Hesse), and in the closing years of the decade she became more and more involved in the feminist movement, though she always said that she did not see herself as a true feminist but, rather, as a 'specialist in the feminine'.

She now began to experiment with an ever wider range of materials – plaster, latex, rubber, bronze and marble – and to make work which was more and more outspokenly erotic. Some of the most characteristic pieces of this time are intended to be shown not on pedestals, but suspended – they were inspired by memories of her father's collection of antique chairs, which were displayed suspended from the rafters in a vast attic.

In 1973 Robert Goldwater died, and Bourgeois had to re-orientate her life. She did so by committing herself more deeply to her art. In 1978, she achieved a major breakthrough with two much noticed exhibitions in New York, one at the Hamilton Gallery of Contemporary Art and the other at Xavier Fourcade. Her success had perhaps taken so long to arrive because of her own 'self-defeatism'. 'I'm more afraid of success,' she once said, 'than I am of failure.' But the moment was, in any case, ripe for recognition of an artist with few stylistic affiliations, but with strong autobiographical and feminist content.

In 1993 Bourgeois was the American representative at the 45th Venice Biennale – the first time this honour had been given to an artist over eighty years old. She is now recognized as one of the most significant sculptors of the twentieth century. In 2007 a major retrospective exhibition of her life's work, with more than 200 works spanning seven decades, began a tour at London's Tate Modern before travelling to Paris, New York, Los Angeles and Washington.

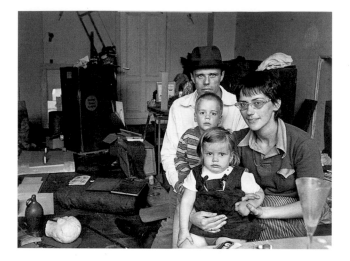

JOSEPH BEUYS

Joseph Beuys produced relatively little work which fits into conventional categories. He acted partly as a modern shaman, and partly as a catalyst for social change – he spoke of making 'social sculpture'. More decisively than any other artist he shifted the emphasis from what the artist makes – the creation of objects – to his actions, opinions and personality.

Beuys was born in Krefeld, Germany, in 1921, and spent his childhood and adolescence at Rindern, near Cleves, where his father had a flour and fodder business. His relationship with his parents was not close, and the local community was narrow and rigorously Catholic. Beuys was deeply interested in science, and built himself a laboratory in his parents' apartment, played the piano and the cello, and studied Nordic history and mythology. He was also interested in art, and regularly visited the studio of a local sculptor called Achilles Moortgat. He decided on leaving school to become a paediatrician, because of his scientific interests, but the war prevented him from training for this. Instead, he served in the German Air Force as a dive-bomber pilot, stationed in southern Russia, the Ukraine and the Crimea. In 1943 his aircraft was shot down and crashed in a desolate area of the Crimea. Though badly injured, Beuys survived, and was looked after by nomadic Crimean Tartars for eight days until he was found by a German search-party. Though he was unconscious for most of the time, he afterwards came to regard his brief period with these nomads as a seminal experience. Later in the war he served as a member of a scratch paratrooper unit.

He was wounded five times in all, and was finally taken prisoner at Cuxhaven after fighting in Holland and on the North Sea coast of Germany.

In 1946 Beuys returned to Cleves, and decided to become a sculptor. He studied privately with Walter Brüx, a local Cleves artist, and then enrolled at the Düsseldorf Academy of Art when he joined the studio of Ewald Mataré, who had been dismissed from his teaching post as a 'degenerate' in 1933, and reinstated in 1946. Mataré's ideas in some respects anticipated those of Beuys: 'Sculpture', he said, 'must be like a footprint in the sand. I do not want any more aesthetic art-work, I am making myself a fetish.' Beuys found him a difficult taskmaster – 'monomaniacal' was the adjective he afterwards used – and not prepared for discussion with students, but his emphasis on spontaneity appealed to Beuys. Later he was to become a strong opponent of his one-time pupil.

When Beuys graduated he was given a studio as a mature student at the Düsseldorf Academy, and began to participate in local exhibitions in a comparatively conventional way. He was concerned chiefly with the archetypal representation of animals, which for him were symbols of the primitive, untouched by civilization and technology. He had become interested in the anthroposophical ideas of Rudolph Steiner, and in particular he was influenced by Steiner's lectures 'About Bees' delivered in 1923, with their description of the way in which bees generate wax and create honeycombs. This led to the beginnings of a personal theory of sculpture:

> What had interested me about bees, or rather about their life system, is the total heat organization of such an organism and the sculpturally finished forms within this organization. On the one hand bees have this element of heat, which is a very strong fluid element; and on the other they produce crystalline sculptures; they make regular geometric forms.

Beuys was now gaining steadily in reputation – he was given a one-man show at the Von der Heydt museum in Wuppertal in 1953. Nevertheless, he became depressed and exhausted by his lack of progress and suffered a kind of nervous breakdown:

> Certainly incidents from the war produced an after-effect on me, but something also had to die. I believe that the phase was one of the most important for me

Above: JOSEPH BEUYS at home with his family in Oberkassel, 1965. Photo Leonard Freed in that I had to reorganize myself constitutionally. I had for too long dragged a body around with me. The initial phase was a totally exhausted state, which quickly turned into an orderly phase of renewal. The things inside me had to be totally transplanted, a physical change had to take place in me. Illnesses are almost always spiritual crises in life, in which old experiences and phases of thought are cut off in order to permit positive changes.

From April to August 1957 he worked in the fields, on the farm of the brothers Hans and Franz Joseph van der Grinten, who had been generous patrons since 1951. It was during this phase of breakdown and renewal that Beuys came to the conclusion that

the concepts of art and science in the development of thought in the western world are diametrically opposed, and that on the basis of these facts a solution to the polarizations of conceptions must be sought, and that expanded views must be found.

In 1961 Beuys was appointed to the professorial chair of monumental sculpture at the Düsseldorf Academy. This appointment not only demonstrated to him that teaching was as much part of his vocation as art itself, but provided a base for the launching of a new international art movement, Fluxus (the name means 'the flowing'), which was intended to combat traditional expectations about art and its place in society. In particular, the art object was dismissed as 'a useless piece of merchandise whose only purpose is to provide the artist with an income.' Beuys was not at first one of the central figures in Fluxus, but through his association with it he acquired the international reputation he had hitherto lacked, and in return he was able to offer the Academy as a base. In 1964 he was invited for the first time to participate in the Kassel *documenta*, the most important avant-garde showcase in Europe.

Beuys's work during this period was deeply mysterious and poetic. In 1965 he performed one of his most important 'actions', stringing together a series of memorable if ephemeral images. The piece was called *How to Explain Paintings to a Dead Hare*. Beuys, with his head covered in a mixture of honey and gold leaf, wearing an iron sole on his right foot and a felt sole on his left, held the dead hare in his arms and carried it from picture

JOSEPH BEUYS, *Chair with Fat*, 1963

to picture at an exhibition held at the Schmela Gallery in Düsseldorf. He talked to the hare as he carried it, and touched each item with its paw. Then he sat down on a chair, still holding the corpse, and began a more thorough explanation of the various works 'because I do not like to explain them to people'. During this 'action' the gallery was closed to the public, and what was going on was visible only from the doorway and the window opening to the street. The artist described his performance as:

A complex tableau about the problems of language, and about the problems of thought, of human consciousness and of the consciousness of animals, and of course the abilities of animals. This is placed in an extreme position because this is not just an animal but a dead animal. Even this dead animal has a special power to produce.

In 1967 Beuys's career again changed direction, in response to a changing political climate within Germany itself which led to increasing polarization, with the forces of conservatism and law on the one hand and those of rebellion and sometimes terrorism on the other. He founded the 'German Student Party as Metaparty' which immediately brought him into conflict with his colleagues in Düsseldorf. The inaugural meeting of the new party was to have been held on the Academy's premises, but this was forbidden by the administration. The following year nine members of the Academy staff signed a manifesto condemning the 'presumptuous political dilettantism' of their fellow professor. Six months later, the Academy was briefly closed by the police who had been called in by the Director. Matters reached a climax in October 1972, at a time when the Baader-Meinhof terrorist group was receiving maximum publicity in Germany. Beuys led an occupation of the Düsseldorf Academy's secretariat in protest against the refusal to admit all students who had applied (the second time he had done this) and was summarily dismissed from his teaching post for 'trespassing'. Asked to meet

him to resolve the conflict, Johannes Rau, then Minister of Education for the province of North Rhine-Westphalia, retorted: 'I cannot and will not let myself be made into a portable art object.' A series of legal actions followed, and these were not finally resolved until a settlement was reached in October 1978. This was precipitated not only by the fact that Beuys won a final appeal to the German Supreme Court, but by his threat to accept a newly established professorial chair at the University of Applied Arts in Vienna. Intimidated by the thought that it might be blamed for costing the country the man who was now Germany's most celebrated artist, the Ministry for Education of North Rhine-Westphalia, now under a new Minister, negotiated a settlement whereby Beuys was allowed continued use of his studio at the Academy, and was also permitted to hold the title of Professor there, though his actual teaching contract ceased to exist.

Throughout these troubles Beuys continued to perform and to teach, frequently giving instructions and criticism to students outside the main doors of the Academy itself. The German Student Party became the 'Organization for Direct Democracy through Referendum',

JOSEPH BEUYS, *How to Explain Paintings to a Dead Hare*, Galerie Schmela, Düsseldorf, 1965. Photo Ute Klophaus

which was given an 'information office' as part of the 1972 Kassel *documenta*. Here Beuys indefatigably debated his ideas with allcomers. Asked why it seemed appropriate to him to mix politics with art in this fashion, he replied: 'Because real future political intentions must be artistic. This means that they must originate from human creativity, from the individual freedom of man.'

In his final years Beuys became a peripatetic all-purpose sage, prophet and performer, exhibiting his work (and usually himself as well) in major museums and conferring with a wide range of personalities, from Andy Warhol (1979) to the Dalai Lama (1982). His political activity, though it remained maverick, was linked to that of the Greens (the West German Ecology Party) and he was responsible for planting thousands of trees. He seemed so self-contained and *sui generis* that it came as a surprise to most people, when he died of heart failure in January 1986, to learn that he left a wife, Eva, and two children.

YVES KLEIN

In his introductory essay to the Yves Klein retrospective held in Houston, Chicago, New York and Paris in 1982–83, twenty years after the artist's death, Thomas McEvilley wrote the following:

> Yves Klein was a myth-making artist. He declared that his *manner of existence* would be the foremost event of our time, and his strategy for achieving the goal involved the preparation of an explicit personal myth, left behind as the trace, or ashes of his life.

Klein was born in Nice in 1928. He spent a disturbed childhood being shuttled about between his parents, his grandparents, and a childless aunt who became a somewhat possessive surrogate mother. His parents represented bohemian carelessness, his aunt piety and respectability. The boy was not a good student and soon became a confirmed truant. His studies were further disrupted by the war, and in 1946 Klein failed his baccalaureate examination. This made it impossible to go on to the Merchant Marine Academy, as he had planned to do. For the rest of his life he was to be ashamed of his lack of formal education, and sometimes laid claim to credentials to which he had no right.

Yves Klein, *Leap into the Void*, Nice, 1962. Photo © Harry Shunk

After a brief visit to England with his parents Klein found himself back in Nice again, running a small bookshop in one room of his aunt's electrical appliance store. It was a dull existence for a lively young man. In 1947 he found an escape by enrolling in judo classes at the police school in Nice and thus found both new friends and a vocation. One of his friends was Armand Fernandez (later known as Arman), who was to become an artist like himself, and a comrade-in-arms in the French avant-garde. Shortly afterwards Klein discovered Rosicrucianism, which was to absorb him intellectually for the next decade, and which provided a mystical basis for many of his artistic experiments.

Klein did his military service in Germany, then returned to England for a longer stay in order to learn the language. It was here, in 1950, that he first began to feel a serious vocation as an artist – something he had always resisted because of a wish to be different and separate from the world of his parents. In 1951 he went to Spain to study Spanish, and for the first

YVES KLEIN, *Ant. 96. People Begin to Fly*, 1961

time began to teach judo; this was to be his source
of livelihood for much of the rest of his life. Finally,
in 1952, with the financial help of his aunt, he was
able to go to Japan and enter the Kodokan Judo
Institute in Tokyo – the most prestigious judo school
in the world.

It was in Japan that Klein began taking stimulants
to prepare himself for judo contests, including
amphetamines, which were legally obtainable. He
continued to use these thereafter, and they were perhaps
responsible for the intensity and grandiosity of his
character, and also for an inability to sleep which later
became well known; they probably also contributed to
his early death. Through intense work, Klein succeeded
in reaching the rank of black belt, fourth dan – a higher
grade than that held by any judo expert in Europe. Early
in 1954 he returned to Paris, determined to take over the
world of French judo. The French Judo Federation was
equally determined to reject him. It refused to recognize
his Japanese qualifications, stopped him from taking part
in the European championships, and even refused to let

him join the Federation itself. The publication of his book
Fundamentals of Judo in October made no difference.

Klein retired to Spain and began to think more
seriously about his vocation as an artist. His first step
was characteristic – he prepared a little book of reproductions of non-existent monochrome paintings, back-dated
in a carefully ambiguous way, to give himself something
of a track-record.

His first attempt to make a place for himself in
the French art world was a failure. He sent an orange
monochrome to the Salon des Réalités Nouvelles in 1955;
it was rejected. He then arranged a small one-man show
of monochromes. This was marginally more successful,
because it attracted the attention of an eloquent and
ambitious young critic, Pierre Restany, who wrote the
catalogue preface for his next show, held in 1956. It was
in 1956 that Klein launched his *Monochrome Propositions*
using a variety of colours, of which he chose blue as
the focus of his creative attention. He showed many
manifestations of the same shade of blue – canvases,
objects, sculptures, and casts of sculptures by others,

notably Michelangelo's *Dying Slave*, sprayed blue. He experimented with many canvases of pure saturated colour, altering and refining the shade endlessly. He is associated with a shade of blue named uniquely for him, International Klein Blue (IKB). Good fortune then led Klein to the lively dealer Iris Clert, at that very moment making a place for herself in the Parisian avant-garde. Clert became Klein's co-conspirator – her gallery provided a stage where he could act out an evolving personal myth. His second show with her in 1958 was a triumph of scandalous publicity. The exhibition was called *Le Vide* (The Void). The gallery entrance was draped with blue and was flanked by members of the Garde Républicaine in full uniform. Within, as the fashionable crowd at the vernissage discovered, there was precisely nothing – a pristine white space. The opening night ended in a near-riot, as dealer and artist had undoubtedly hoped.

Klein's star was now rising rapidly in Europe, and he enjoyed a series of successes. He won an important commission for the decoration of the new Gelsenkirchen Opera house, held a further show with Iris Clert, and found himself the centre of a group put together by Restany – the New Realists. A bombastic collection of Klein's writings was published in Belgium, full of prophecies of immediate evolution into an age of levitation, telepathy and immateriality.

During this period Klein had tremendous energy. According to an official catalogue raisonné, he produced no less than 1,077 artworks between 1956 and 1962. He was also increasingly difficult and unstable – many of his friends now saw him as the archetypal spoilt child. He also became increasingly celebrated. Early in 1961 he was given a major retrospective in Germany, at the Museum Haus Lange in Krefeld; he was also invited to show at the Leo Castelli Gallery in New York, which was already becoming an important space. He responded to the opportunities which were offered to him not only by producing a great deal of work, but by constantly inventing new techniques. To monochromes and monogolds he added 'anthropometries', imprints made by naked girls who smeared their bodies with blue paint, and then at Klein's direction, pressed themselves against a surface; and also 'fire-paintings', made by burning composition board with a flame-thrower.

But Klein's success was not securely based. His New York show was a dismal failure. *Art News* described him contemptuously as 'a Dalí – junior-grade'. Most of the leading New York artists rejected him – Rothko turned away without a word. And none of the paintings sold.

A crueller disaster followed. In July 1961 Klein allowed himself to be filmed making some of his anthropometries, to the accompaniment of his own one-note *Monotone Symphony*, recreating an event he had put on the previous year. Behind his back the film was mutilated: it was severely cut, its soundtrack was removed and replaced by another, and it was included as part of a sneering compilation of horrors and follies called *Mondo Cane*. Klein only discovered what had happened when he attended a preview in Cannes in May 1962. Three days later he suffered a major heart attack. This was quickly followed by a second and fatal one. He died on 6 June 1962, at the age of thirty-four.

EVA HESSE

Eva Hesse was born in Germany in 1936, the daughter of a criminal lawyer. Her parents were Jewish, and in 1938 she and her older sister were sent on a children's train to Amsterdam, while her parents went into hiding in the countryside. Though the family were soon reunited, this separation was the defining event of her life, a continuing source of depression and anxiety.

In 1939, the Hesses fled to New York, where Hesse's father became an insurance broker. Her mother did not survive this uprooting well. She was hospitalized with severe depressive illness, and in 1945 Hesse's father got remarried, to a woman whom Eva disliked. In January 1946 her mother committed suicide. This was a fresh source of anxiety for Eva, who worried that she might have inherited her mother's unstable temperament.

Though she initially showed little talent for art, Hesse was determined to become an artist. In 1952 she graduated from the High School of Industrial Arts, New York, and went to the Pratt Institute to study advertising design. Dissatisfied with the course, she left in the middle of her second year, and entered Cooper Union, from which she graduated in 1957. After this, she attended the Yale School of Art – she was at this time working as a painter rather than as a sculptor. The diaries she kept during these student years show that she constantly questioned the instruction she was receiving. One of her instructors was Josef Albers, with

Eva Hesse in her studio, *c.* 1968. Photographer unknown

The early years of her marriage were probably the happiest of Hesse's life, but the relationship was already in trouble by the early months of 1964. Later in the year, there came a diversion which preserved the union, at least for a while. Doyle was invited by a patron of his, a German textile manufacturer, to move to Germany and make use of a disused factory there, exchanging work for accommodation, materials and other help. Hesse was at first reluctant to make use of the opportunity, despite the fact that she spoke good German. When she got to Germany her nightmares returned, and she began to suffer severe pains in her legs, probably psychosomatic in origin, which sometimes prevented her from working.

Despite her ill health she and Doyle were able to travel a good deal, both within West Germany and outside it. In August and September of 1964 they made a tour which took them to Mallorca, Paris, Rome, Florence and Zurich.

Hesse had a workshop of her own in the disused factory their German patron had provided, and at the end of the year, partly in response to a suggestion made by her husband, she began making sculpture for the first time. At first she used string and other discarded weaving materials found in her studio. Doyle later showed her how to build up forms using plaster, and she also received a good deal of help from the factory workers provided by their patron from his workforce, with whom she was a popular personality. Knowing her lack of skill with tools, they did some of the basic fabricating for her.

In 1965, the couple returned to New York, via London and Ireland. By this time the marriage was clearly at an end, and in January 1966, Doyle moved out to the space across the road from their SoHo loft which he had long used as a studio. It was just at this moment that Hesse scored her first major artistic success, as one of the contributors to a show entitled *Eccentric Abstraction* curated by the critic Lucy Lippard at the Fischbach Gallery. Hesse had always had a number of close friends among the group of leading Minimal sculptors whose work had now begun to dominate the New York art scene – she was close to Sol LeWitt in particular – and her work was recognized as offering a new direction in Minimalism, with unexpected Surrealist and Expressionist overtones.

Hesse experimented with a new range of materials, first with latex (which she started to use in 1967), then with fibreglass and polyester resin. Her work in fibreglass was done at Aegis Reinforced Plastics on Staten Island,

whom she had a tense but fruitful relationship. In 1954, the year she left the Pratt Institute for Cooper Union, Hesse began a course of psychotherapy. These sessions were to last until the end of her short life.

In 1960 she moved back to New York, and took part-time employment as a textile designer. She was extremely lonely without the support offered by the student environment, and began to suffer recurring nightmares about abandonment and early death. In her diary, she spoke of the 'deeprooted insecurity which has made any relationship, [any] meaningful one, impossible.' Nevertheless in 1961 she met Tom Doyle, a sculptor eight years older than herself, whom she married in November of that year. In 1962, she made her first three-dimensional object, a costume of chicken-wire and soft jersey for a series of 'Happenings' organized by Allan Kaprow and others. Her first solo exhibition took place in a New York commercial gallery, in March 1963.

with the help of Doug Johns, who became Hesse's close friend, as well as technical adviser and assistant on all her subsequent major pieces. Sculptures made at Aegis featured in Hesse's first solo show at Fischbach in 1968. The New York critical community found it difficult, even at this stage, to understand what she was doing. Perhaps the best statement of her mature artistic intentions was made by Hesse herself, in the exhibition catalogue: 'I would like the work to be a non-work. This means it would find its way beyond my preconceptions.' Despite a slight air of mystification in the reviews, the exhibition made a deep impression, and was hailed as marking the full emergence of an important new talent.

She was not able to enjoy her success for long. Early in 1969, a brain tumour was diagnosed, for which Hesse underwent an operation in April. This was followed by a second operation in August, then chemotherapy, and a third operation in 1970. All treatment failed, and Hesse died later that year.

The story of Hesse's life, when told in bald outline, seems gloomy. Sol LeWitt, for example, wrote to Hesse in April 1965, saying perceptively: 'You seem the same as always, and being you, hate every minute of it.' Certainly she had little luck until after her death, when her work was taken up by the vigorously growing feminist movement. There certainly are feminist elements in the attitudes recorded in her notes and diary entries, such as her concern for female strength and independence,

and also in some of the techniques she invented, which combine methods taken from textile art with more familiar sculptural procedures. But her work also startles and disturbs partly because of its quirky sense of humour – contemporaries recall Hesse's lively personality and her occasionally 'juvenile' behaviour. It also bears out a proposition put forward by LeWitt: 'Conceptual artists are mystics rather than rationalists. They leap to conclusions which logic cannot reach.' Above all, there is an indissoluble bond between the work itself and the personality of the artist which makes Hesse unclassifiable stylistically, and a precursor of artistic developments in the 1970s, 1980s and 1990s.

EVA HESSE, *Sans II*, 1968

Bruno Bischofberger and
Jean-Michel Basquiat,
Zurich 1982. Photo Beth Phillips

JEAN-MICHEL BASQUIAT

Jean-Michel Basquiat, whose meteoric artistic career spanned less than a decade, was born in Brooklyn, New York, in 1960, the son of a middle-class accountant from Haiti and a mother of Puerto Rican descent. He began drawing at an early age, inspired and helped by his mother, who also took him on frequent visits to the Brooklyn Museum, the Metropolitan Museum, and the Museum of Modern Art. In May 1968 he was the victim of a serious accident – he was hit by a car while playing ball in the street: he not only broke his arm, but also had to have his spleen removed. He spent a month in hospital, and one of the presents his mother brought him there was a copy of *Gray's Anatomy*, which was to have a lasting influence on his work.

In the same year Basquiat's parents separated. Though he had always felt closer to his mother, his father retained custody of the children (he had two sisters) and in 1974 he moved them all to Puerto Rico, where they remained for two years. Basquiat was already rebellious, and in Puerto Rico he briefly ran away from home. When the family returned to New York, he transferred to the City-as-School, a progressive school designed for gifted children with learning difficulties. Here he met Al Diaz,

a participant in the burgeoning teenage graffiti movement in New York, and the two became close friends and collaborators.

Despite the liberal nature of the City-as-School, Basquiat ran away from home again, and this time remained absent for two weeks until his father tracked him down to Washington Square Park in Greenwich Village. He had spent his time there taking LSD. Returning to school, Basquiat renewed his alliance with Diaz, and the two became ring-leaders in the graffiti movement, which was now starting to attract attention from the press. Basquiat created a fictional alter ego called SAMO (Same Old Shit), the prophet of a fake religion. With the name as 'tag' or signature, Basquiat started painting gnomic aphorisms in huge decorative letters on New York subway trains.

His school attendance came to an abrupt and final end in June 1977, when he disrupted the graduation ceremonies at his school by running up to the podium and dumping a box full of shaving cream on the principal's head. A year later, with his father's reluctant blessing, he left home for good and started a period of living in the apartments of various friends, or, failing that, sleeping rough in the streets.

Basquiat, long convinced that he would become a 'star', but perhaps more committed to music than he was to art (most of his heroes were musicians), became a conspicuous figure in the burgeoning downtown club scene, noted for his stylish dress sense and wild dancing. He also began to frequent artists' and film-makers' parties – the three worlds of pop music, art, and film found a focus in the East Village Mudd Club, which Basquiat haunted assiduously. He continued to create graffiti under the SAMO pseudonym until he and Diaz had a serious falling-out over Basquiat's penchant for self-advertisement. In 1979 he formed his own band, frequently renamed, but continued to produce artworks to make some cash – postcards and T-shirts but also drawings and collages, which he sold in his old hang-out, Washington Square Park, in the SoHo gallery district, and in front of the Museum of Modern Art. He exhibited publicly for the first time in the 'Times Square Show', a group exhibition held in a vacant building at the corner of Forty-First Street and Seventh Avenue. Enthusiastically received, this event marked the emergence of a whole new generation of New York artists. The notice attracted by Basquiat's work in particular led him to quit his band and decide to become a full-time artist. It was at this moment that he was introduced to Andy Warhol who, afraid of young black men, was at first extremely reluctant to have anything to do with him.

The impact made by the 'Times Square Show' led to a further series of survey shows featuring new New York art in the following year. Basquiat was a conspicuous contributor to these, but attracted almost more attention from Europeans than from Americans. To European dealers in search of novelty he seemed a quintessential representative of the new mixed-race urban culture of the United States. In May 1981 Basquiat had his first solo exhibition at the Galleria d'Arte Emilio Mazzola in Modena, Italy. Shortly after this, Annina Nosei, an Italian with a gallery in New York, became his principal dealer.

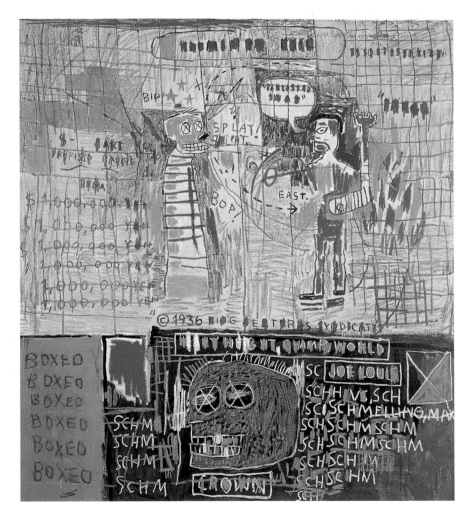

JEAN-MICHEL BASQUIAT,
Napoleonic Stereotype, 1983

In December – his real American breakthrough – he was the subject of a long, enthusiastic article in a leading art magazine, *Artforum*.

Despite his lack of seniority, Basquiat now began to be included in important international exhibitions, notably in *Transavantguardia: Italia/America* in March 1982, a show curated by the leading Italian critic Achille Bonito Oliva, where he was seen with a number of well established artists of the Neo-Expressionist movement, among them Sandro Chia, Francesco Clemente and Enzo Cucchi from Italy, and David Salle and Julian Schnabel from America. In June 1982 he was the youngest of the 176 artists invited

to participate in *documenta 7*, the great international showcase in Kassel. At the same time, however, his behaviour was becoming increasingly erratic, due to a prodigious intake of drugs.

In 1983 Basquiat was included in the Whitney Biennial, perhaps the most important index of official recognition for an emergent American artist. His relationship with the initially cautious Andy Warhol now began to blossom, and in August he moved into a studio in Great Jones Street rented from Warhol, the owner of the building. Warhol, an indefatigable party-goer, began to take Basquiat as his escort to parties and openings. The two travelled to Europe together, and at the end of

JEAN-MICHEL BASQUIAT
with Andy Warhol (left) and
Francesco Clemente, 1984.
Photo Beth Phillips

the year Basquiat, Warhol and Clemente began work on a series of collaborative works.

By this time, both Basquiat's artistic style and his pattern of life were fully established. His paintings were graffiti-like in the sense that they made use of roughly scribbled images, interspersed with words – often long inscriptions – and abbreviated signs. They made reference to popular culture, notably cartoons and comic-strip characters, and also to the art of tribal Africa, and to African American hero-figures, such as musicians and boxers. But there were also references to the 'high art' tradition of Modernism: Picasso, Dubuffet, Pollock, and Twombly are all present in Basquiat's work. He travelled frequently – to California and to Hawaii, where he had rented a ranch, as well as to Europe. He had difficulty in maintaining relationships with dealers – his longest and most stable dealer relationship was with the Zurich-based Bruno Bischofberger, who was safely away from the hectic New York scene. He continued to make heavy use of drugs, particularly cocaine and heroin, and his health began to deteriorate as a result. Predictably, after his sudden early success, the work he was now producing began to be more harshly criticized. His collaborations with Warhol were panned by many critics when they were shown in New York in September 1985, and this put a strain on their friendship.

In 1986 he made his first and only visit to Africa, where Bischofberger had arranged a show of his paintings in Abidjan, Ivory Coast. His desire to exhibit there may have been prompted by frequent criticisms from leading members of the African American cultural community, who claimed that Basquiat was not a 'real' black artist. No record of the local reaction to this exhibition seems to survive.

Warhol's sudden death in 1987 had a devastating effect on Basquiat, even though the two were now at least partially estranged. Many mutual friends saw Warhol as the only person who was able to exercize any control over Basquiat's erratic behaviour. Despite continuing drug abuse, he still produced great quantities of work, perhaps with an increasing amount of intervention from a new assistant, Rick Prol, a painter and old friend of Basquiat's from his East Village days. In the first months of 1988 he had shows in New York, Paris and Düsseldorf. Later, he travelled to Dallas, Los Angeles and Hawaii. At the end of June 1988 he returned to New York, and died of a massive drug overdose on 17 August at his Great Jones Street loft.

ZHANG XIAOGANG

Zhang Xiaogang is perhaps the best known of the artists who emerged in China in the 1990s, and who have made a special place for their nation in the world of contemporary art. The sombre-hued portraits of his 'Bloodline: Big Family' series, which brought him to international notice, speak particularly clearly about the tensions between the individual and the collective in Chinese society in the 1960s and 1970s – the turbulent final years of Mao Zedong's rule.

Zhang was born in 1958, in Kunming, the capital of Yunnan province in southern China, into a family of government officials, but subsequently moved with his parents and three older brothers to the neighbouring province of Sichuan. When the Cultural Revolution began in 1966 he was eight years old. The ensuing decade of social and political turmoil formed the background to the later part of his childhood and the whole of his adolescence. He remembers how 'people came to our house and asked my parents to make confessions about what they did wrong.' He also recalls how his parents worried that he and his brothers would get into trouble if they went out, 'so they gave us paper and crayons so we could draw at home. The first teacher was my mother.' He made drawings that imitated comic strips, and created elaborate battle scenes showing the Chinese fighting the Japanese. When Zhang's parents were sent to a 'study camp' in the countryside for several years, the four boys were brought up by an aunt. His vivid memories of the time spent in a village where the only entertainment was the music and propaganda that issued from loudspeakers have been expressed in some of his paintings.

Despite all the difficulties, Zhang's perspective on this era is not wholly negative: 'The Cultural Revolution gave me the impression that it was very fun, because I didn't have to go to school. I could always be with my friends and I could see things that a boy my age would want to see, such as weapons and people walking freely along the streets.' Zhang's interest in art increased and by the time he was seventeen he had decided that he wanted to be an artist. He found a professional teacher and began formally to study drawing.

In 1976 the Cultural Revolution finally caught up with him and he was sent to a 're-education camp' to work with the peasants. However, Mao died later that

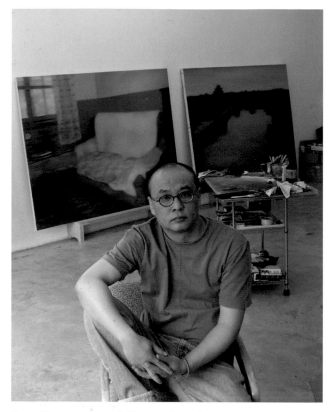

ZHANG XIAOGANG, *c.* 2008. Photographer unknown

Germany and became interested in Gerhard Richter's paintings based on photographs. The following year, on a visit to his parents, he was looking through old photographs, particularly of his mother when young, and began to consider how they touched on a larger subject: 'China is like a family, a big family. Everyone has to rely on each other and to confront each other. This was the issue I wanted to give attention to.'

The result was the family portraits that were the beginning of the 'Bloodline' series, which became his sole focus for over a decade and are now Zhang's most celebrated works. The paintings reference a tradition of family photographic portraiture that remained strong in China despite all the wars and revolutions that shook the country during the twentieth century. He makes subtle use of the conventions established by these photographs: flat backgrounds, dramatic lighting that highlights the main forms and a degree of idealization imposed by heavy retouching. He has said that he wanted 'to create an effect of "false photographs"'. He also calls on the delicate technique used in charcoal portraiture to depict facial expressions. Mostly executed in black and white, with patches of colour, the paintings have thin red lines running through them that suggest family ties.

Commentators have noted that this long series of paintings offers a uniquely subtle and nuanced reflection of a major historical drama, which makes them central to the story of the development of Chinese art in the late twentieth century. As Zhang has commented: 'Politics play a close role in Chinese people's lives. If you really want to show your perspective on life, your work will naturally reveal a political element.' He adds:

> For me, the Cultural Revolution is a psychological state, not a historical fact. It has a very strict connection with my childhood, and I think there are many things linking the psychology of the Chinese people today with the psychology of the Chinese people back then.

From 1993 onwards the 'Bloodline' paintings brought Zhang critical attention abroad and in 1995 his work was displayed at the 46th Venice Biennale. In China, the sensitivity about anything to do with the Cultural Revolution meant that in 1996 his paintings were pulled from the Shanghai Biennale. Official attitudes have changed since then, so much so that in the mid-2000s

year and the change of regime led to the re-opening of colleges. In 1977 Zhang enrolled at the Sichuan Academy of Fine Arts in Chongqing, where he trained as an oil painter, graduating in 1982. Western classical technique was re-introduced to Chinese art academies at that period and Zhang was particularly attracted to the work of Gauguin, Van Gogh, Magritte and Dalí. But he also learned to produce propaganda images on billboard scale, a skill that has re-emerged in the large proportions of many of his paintings. After college, he worked for a time designing sets and costumes for a dance troupe and returned to his alma mater as a teacher. During this period he experimented with two or three styles, painting his friends in an expressionist manner, but also went through a period of depression and alcoholism – for six years death was his primary subject and had to deal with his mother's schizophrenia. Nonetheless, this was also the time when he began to associate with other young artists who were feeling their way towards a new kind of post-revolutionary Chinese art, and when he started to achieve a small degree of recognition in group shows.

It was only in the early 1990s, however, that his mature style evolved. In 1992 Zhang made a trip to he was commissioned to paint a mural for the subway in the southern city of Shenzhen.

Memory has continued to be a theme in Zhang's series 'Amnesia and Memory', 'Inside–Outside' and 'Green Wall'. The last title refers in part to the government practice of painting the lower parts of walls green in public and private spaces in the 1960s and 1970s. Some of these paintings are landscapes and interiors but nonetheless they show that 'the memories or past are still fresh'.

In 1999 Zhang moved to Beijing, where he now lives. He has a daughter from an earlier marriage and photographs of her and his friends adorn the walls of his huge studio. He works slowly and alone, and has described his routine in this way: 'I sleep in the morning. I wake up at noon, eat lunch and then work in the afternoon until night. And then at night I eat and drink and have fun with my friends.' Although his work has fetched enormous sums in major auction rooms, he remains modest about his achievements: 'I don't know what contributions I've made ... I'm just lucky this time period selected me and then allowed me to make good progress. For me, it's luck.'

This final section features four women artists. They typify the rising tide of interest in women's art as well as signalling other important changes in the contemporary art world, such as globalization. None of the four comes from Western Europe, which was the cradle of the Modern movement in art. Only two of them inhabit the countries in which they were born – Marlene Dumas was born in South Africa, but has long lived in the Netherlands; Shirin Neshat comes from Iran but has based herself for most of her career in the United States. And only Dumas is primarily a painter – Yayoi Kusama, Judy Chicago and Shirin Neshat have practised a range of different disciplines. It is worth noting that women have often taken the lead in this process of diversification, because painting, for so long the dominant Western art form, has a history that is overwhelmingly male.

Yayoi Kusama,
*Dots Obsession –
Infinity Mirrored Room*,
2008

YAYOI KUSAMA

Yayoi Kusama, now one of Japan's best-known contemporary artists, first came to international attention in the 1960s with her paintings, soft sculptures and performance art, all characterized by her trademark polka dots. After a period away from the limelight in the 1970s and 1980s, in 2006 she received her country's Praemium Imperiale for painting – the most prestigious award Japan can offer to any painter, native or foreign.

Kusama's rise to fame has been unconventional, even by the standards of the art world of the twenty-first century, where eccentricities of all kinds pass without question. She was born in 1929, in Matsumoto, Nagano prefecture, in central Japan. Her background was upper middle-class, but her childhood was not happy; she claims that she was subjected to severe physical abuse by her mother. From the age of ten she started to experience hallucinations, in which spots, nets and flowers covered every visible surface, and she began to do pencil drawings of these motifs. She has described one such episode, when she was looking at the red flower patterns on a tablecloth:

> When I looked up, I saw the same pattern covering the ceiling, the windows and the walls, and finally all over the room, my body and the universe. I felt as if I had begun to self-obliterate, to revolve in the infinity of endless time and the absoluteness of space, and be reduced to nothingness.

A number of large environmental works, made much later, have tried to reproduce the essence of this experience.

Kusama's hallucinations have formed the basis for her art ever since, which she describes as arising 'from a deep, driving compulsion to realize in visible form the repetitive images inside of me'. 'Art,' she adds, 'is both the symptom and cause for my obsession.'

During the war Kusama worked in a parachute factory and in 1948 she spent a year at the Kyoto School of Arts and Crafts. Her desire to be an artist met with no encouragement from her conservative family, who constantly felt that her behaviour was inappropriate for a girl: 'When I wanted to get a driver's licence, my mother said that I could get a chauffeured car if I married well. When I said I wanted to be a painter, she told me to be

an art collector instead.' Nonetheless, Kusama held her first two shows at Matsumoto Civic Hall in 1952, her abstract paintings attracting the attention of figures in the Japanese art world as well as Dr Shiho Nishimaru, a professor of psychiatry, who made her work the subject of a paper at a conference on mental illness.

Eventually, in 1957, after having some trouble obtaining a visa, Kusama departed for the United States, burning much of her work before she left. She thought America would provide a more stimulating environment, and after a brief period in Seattle, she moved to New York. Here her circumstances changed because her family had difficulty in sending her money: 'It was freezing cold in the much-too-large loft with its broken windows. I had only one blanket ... Day after day I forgot my coldness and hunger by painting.' Nevertheless she rapidly – if only partially – assimilated into the lively New York art world of the time, forming friendships with Donald Judd, Frank Stella and, in particular, Joseph Cornell. Judd, at that period more widely recognized as a critic than as an artist, wrote favourably about Kusama's work in 1959: 'The expression', he said, 'transcends the question of whether [the art] is Oriental or American. Although it is something [of] both, certainly of such Americans as Rothko, Still, and Newman, it is not at all a synthesis and is thoroughly independent.'

Initially Kusama established herself with her large 'Infinity Net' paintings of fields of dots but it

YAYOI KUSAMA,
I'm Here But Nothing,
2000–2008

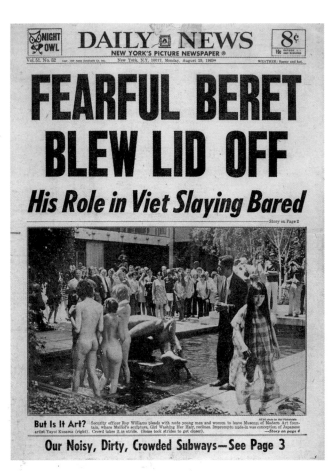

DAILY NEWS
NEW YORK'S PICTURE NEWSPAPER ®

8¢

Vol. 51, No. 52   New York, N.Y. 10017, Monday, August 25, 1969   WEATHER: Sunny and hot.

FEARFUL BERET BLEW LID OFF

His Role in Viet Slaying Bared

—Story on Page 2

But Is It Art? Security officer Roy Williams pleads with nude young men and women to leave Museum of Art fountain, where Maillol's sculpture, Girl Washing Her Hair, reclines. Impromptu nude-in was conception of Japanese artist Yayoi Kusama (right). Crowd takes it in stride. (Some took strides to get closer.)
—Story on page 4

Our Noisy, Dirty, Crowded Subways—See Page 3

was during the years she spent in New York that she pioneered the innovations that later became integral to the contemporary American art scene, garnering a good deal of notoriety in the process. She produced soft sculptures with phallic protuberances and her airmail-sticker collages anticipated the work of Andy Warhol.

Her greatest fame came as a pioneer of performance art. In 1967 she started to stage Body Festivals and Anatomic Explosions in public locations in New York. The Body Festivals were innocuous – members of the public were offered the chance to be covered in Kusama's signature polka dots – the Anatomic Explosions less so, as they involved groups of nude dancers, clad in nothing but body paint, shaking and shimmying at well-known places such as the Statue of Liberty and Wall Street. In the most notorious of these performances, 'Grand Orgy to Awaken the Dead at MoMA', naked men and women stepped into the pond of the sculpture garden at the Museum of Modern Art. The event made the front page of New York's *Daily News* in 1969. These 'Happenings',

provocative and unauthorized, were invariably broken up by the police.

Although Kusama's personality became increasingly visible to the general public – it is said that in 1968 she attracted more press coverage than Andy Warhol, then at the height of his early celebrity – this was not matched by success with New York's museums or with leading commercial galleries. Her exclusion can perhaps be attributed to both her race and her gender. But in this period she was also broadening her activities: in 1968 she made a film, *Self-Obliteration*, about her 'Happenings', and established Kusama Fashions to make clothes.

In 1972 Kusama's close friend Joseph Cornell died. She characterized their relationship as 'ideal': 'I disliked sex and he was impotent so we suited each other very well.' His death brought on a mental crisis, leading to her return to Japan in 1973, leaving much of the work she had made in America behind. The majority has since been either lost or destroyed. Her father died in 1974 and in 1975 she entered Seiwa Hospital for the Mentally Ill in Tokyo, taking up permanent residence there, at her own request, in 1977. She has lived there ever since and has found new inspiration in the institution's art-therapy programme. She goes every day to a studio only a short distance from the hospital. Dr Shiho Nishimaru notes that 'Psychiatric treatment gave Kusama what her parents had always refused – the liberty to express herself, and the liberty to be insane.' She herself says, 'If it were not for art, I would have killed myself a long time ago.'

Since her return to Japan Kusama has been strikingly prolific, making not only numerous art works, but publishing novels and poems, and working with film and in fashion design again. Her reputation as an artist gradually revived, particularly after she represented her country at the Venice Biennale of 1993. In 1998 the Los Angeles County Museum of Art originated an exhibition entitled *Love Forever: Yayoi Kusama, 1958–1968*, which travelled to the Museum of Modern Art in New York and the Museum of Contemporary Art, Tokyo. This served to consolidate her reputation as one of the most original artistic figures of the 1960s.

Kusama has been co-opted by feminist critics as a fellow feminist, but remains firmly uninterested in being placed in any category. In a 1997 interview she observed: 'Museums try to include me in their group shows of all kinds – Minimal art, Pop Art, women's art. But Kusama is Kusama, not anything else.'

YAYOI KUSAMA,
'Grand Orgy to Awaken the Dead at
MoMA' on the front page
of the New York *Daily News*,
25 August 1969

JUDY CHICAGO

For over four decades Judy Chicago has been questioning the conventional definitions of art, the role of the artist and women's means of expression. Her feminist installation *The Dinner Party: A Symbol of Our Heritage* (1974–79) is now one of the best-known art works of the twentieth century. Seen by more than one million people at exhibitions in the USA and Western Europe, this multimedia work has been permanently housed in the Elizabeth A. Sackler Center for Feminist Art at the Brooklyn Museum in New York since 2007, thereby furthering Chicago's aim of obtaining proper recognition for women's achievements.

Chicago was born Judith Cohen in Chicago in 1939, the descendant of a long line of celebrated Lithuanian rabbis. Her immediate family, however, was not religious: her father was a union organizer, who suffered for his left-wing political views in the McCarthyite era. He died

in 1953, when Chicago was only thirteen, but nevertheless he provided her with an intellectual and moral foundation that has remained important to the whole development of her work. Her father was less enthusiastic about her artistic talent – she began to draw at about the age of three – but her mother encouraged her.

In 1945, as a young child, Judy Chicago began to attend classes at the School of the Art Institute of Chicago and continued to do so until she was eighteen, also spending time looking at the Institute's superb collection of Impressionist and Post-Impressionist art. However, she moved west to continue her art studies and earned her BA (1962) and an MFA (1964) at the University of California, Los Angeles. While there she had a brief marriage (1961–63) to Jerry Gerowitz, a fellow student who died in a car crash.

In California she was plunged into a new art scene – liberated in almost everything except its attitude to women. At that time, Californian artists were interested,

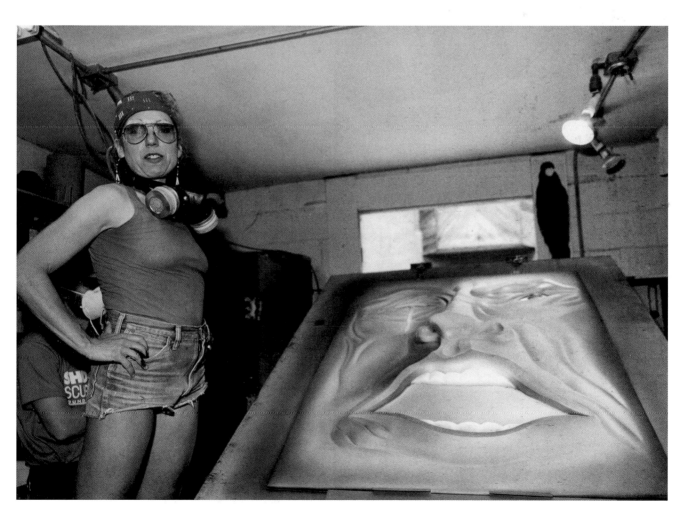

Judy Chicago.
Photo Donald Woodman

far more than their New York counterparts, in new industrial techniques, especially in those that could be used to produce an immaculate finish. After leaving college, therefore, she enrolled in auto-body school in order to learn to spray paint. She was the only woman among 250 men.

Almost immediately Judy Chicago's reputation began to reach beyond the West Coast. Her large sculpture *Rainbow Pickett* (1965, reconstructed 2004) was included in the *Primary Structures* exhibition held at the Jewish Museum, New York, in 1966 – an event that helped to define the Minimal Art movement, one of the major artistic currents of the 1960s. During this time she became known in Californian avant-garde circles for her combative personality and her loud Midwestern accent, which eventually earned her the designation 'Chicago'. In 1970 (the year following her second marriage, to the artist Lloyd Hamrol) she legally took this as her last name in a stand against male social dominance. A well-known exhibition poster of the period shows her as a combatant in a boxing ring, wearing a sweatshirt with her new name, ready to take on all comers.

On the question of having children, in a commencement address at Smith College in 2000, when she was awarded an honorary degree, Chicago recalled: 'I looked to history and discovered that those women who had achieved at the level at which I had set my sights had been childless and those that were not had suffered constant guilt at not being able to meet the demands of both their work and their children.'

Through the 1960s Chicago became increasingly aware of the sexist bias faced by women artists. In 1970 she began to pioneer feminist art education at California State University, Fresno, and the following year established the Feminist Art Program at the California Institute of the Arts, in conjunction with the artist Miriam Schapiro. This led her work towards what are now regarded as quintessentially feminist forms of expression: installation and performance art. One major result of the Feminist Art Program was the creation of *Womanhouse* in 1972. A near-derelict house in downtown Los Angeles was transformed by the two artists and their students into a series of art environments and was also used as a setting for performances.

Chicago, however, has never felt comfortable with completely ephemeral work. After *Womanhouse* she returned to painting – works in which minimal imagery is subtly shifted towards feminist connotations. In her bestselling autobiography, *Through the Flower*, published in 1975, Chicago said:

> In my work, I felt a body identification with both the images I made and the surface on which they were painted. I felt myself to be both the image/surface and the artist working on that painting simultaneously.

The imagery used in the paintings from the mid-1970s led directly to *The Dinner Party*, which nevertheless in many respects marked both a radical change of direction for the artist and for American art as a whole. The main feature of *The Dinner Party* is a massive triangular table – an emblem of the female pubis – set with thirty-nine places. The thirteen settings each side are, of course, a direct reference to the Christian Last Supper, with women as participants rather than men. Chicago sees the installation as a historical narrative:

> [It] is divided into three parts, corresponding to the three wings of the table. The first table begins with pre history and ends with the point in time when Greco-Roman culture was diminishing. The second wing stretches from the beginning of Christianity to the Reformation, and the third table includes the seventeenth to the twentieth centuries.

The story Chicago wanted to tell was that of the destruction of matriarchal societies and their replacement by patriarchal ones, leading to 'the eventual domination of women by men'.

To achieve what she had in mind, Chicago worked with a wide variety of collaborators, and used forms and materials associated with craft and the decorative arts, returning to a tradition where no distinction existed between so-called 'fine art' and other kinds of visual expression.

In March 1979 *The Dinner Party* opened to the public at the San Francisco Museum of Modern Art. Its critical reception was largely, and often savagely, hostile, and although museums in cities such as Boston, Atlanta and Houston would not exhibit it, women raised the funds to display it at other venues. Everywhere it travelled it drew vast crowds. Chicago was immediately stereotyped as an 'outsider', of more interest to the feminist community than to people who saw themselves as experts on contemporary art. The strange thing, in hindsight, is that Judy Chicago now seems very obviously part of one of the central strands of artistic development in twentieth-century America. Like the Regionalists before her, she is a populist, making ambitious art that addresses a large democratic audience, in terms that are easy to respond to. It seems no accident that her drawings have a close resemblance to those made by the great Midwestern muralist Thomas Hart Benton.

The Dinner Party was the first in a series of major projects, usually with a collaborative aspect. The *Birth Project* (1980–85) has a subject that is obvious from its title. It overlapped with *Powerplay* (1982–87), 'an examination of the gender construct of masculinity', which explores the distortion that power has when it dominates men's lives and how it affects both sexes. The *Birth Project* concentrated on textile techniques, a

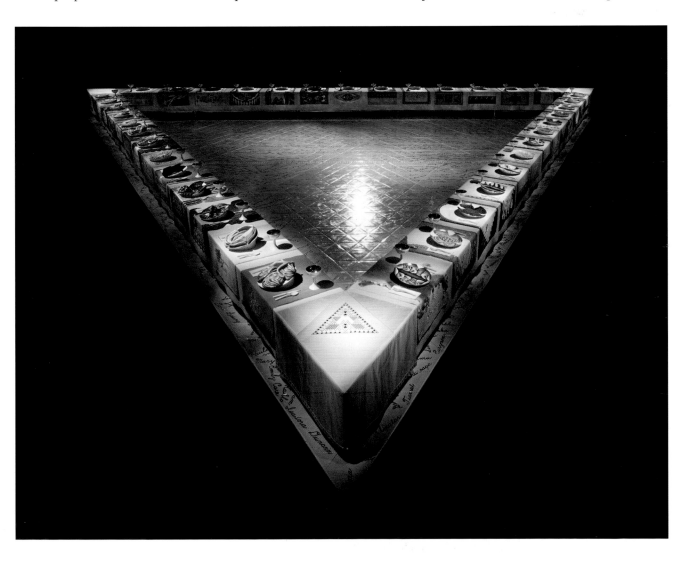

JUDY CHICAGO,
The Dinner Party,
1974–79

traditionally female way of making art, whereas *Powerplay* reverted to long-established methods of creating fine art – drawings, paintings, sculptures – and was heavily influenced by the Renaissance masterpieces Chicago saw on a visit to Italy in 1982.

The enterprise with the greatest impact, following the *The Dinner Party*, was undoubtedly the *Holocaust Project: From Darkness into Light* (1985–93), undertaken in collaboration with Chicago's third husband, the photographer Donald Woodman, whom she married in 1985. (Her marriage to Hamrol had ended in 1979.) Commentators often found it hard to accept that the *Holocaust Project* was a narrative concerning an intolerable series of events as well as an artistic expansion of, and anguished commentary upon, the story that was being told. On a personal level, the *Holocaust Project* sprang from the collaborators' exploration both of their own Jewishness and of their separate ways of making art. Many of the works in the series offer a unique blend of painting and photography.

Judy Chicago now lives in New Mexico, a state that has long been a haven for artists. She began regular visits there in 1982, living full time in Santa Fe from 1985 and moving to Belen, a small town just south of Albuquerque, in 1996. Here she and her husband have renovated a former railway hotel, classed as a historic monument, which provides them with living space, office accommodation and studios. They share their household with a tribe of cats, about whom Chicago wrote a light-hearted illustrated book called *Kitty City: A Feline Book of Hours*, published in 2005.

Since 1999 Chicago has been expanding her mission as a teacher, not only accepting one-semester appointments at institutions across America but also via Through the Flower, the not-for-profit feminist art organization that she founded in 1978. This now occupies a building in Belen across the road from where she lives and works. She also continues to explore new artistic horizons and in 2006 had her first exhibition of her exquisite sculptures in glass, which are quite unlike anything she has made previously. Chicago has received numerous awards and honours, and her work was recognized by a major survey of her career at the National Museum of Women in the Arts in Washington, D.C., in 2002.

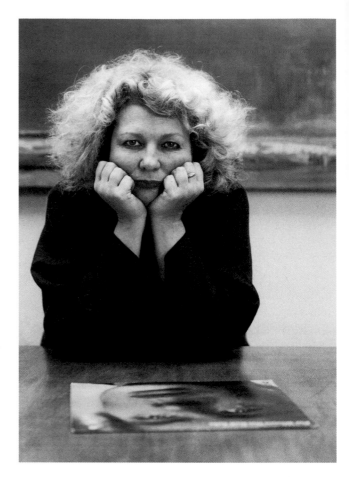

MARLENE DUMAS

Marlene Dumas is one of a new generation of painters for whom the figure is central, although her images are mostly derived from photographic sources, not done from life. Her background gave no indication of an artistic future. The youngest of three children, she was born into an Afrikaans-speaking family in the small town of Kuils River, near Cape Town, South Africa, in 1953. Her father, who died when Dumas was twelve, owned a vineyard, Jacobsdal, which is now run by her older brother Cornelis. Her other brother is a minister of religion. The family name, Dumas, indicates that they were not originally Dutch, but almost certainly of French Huguenot origin.

Dumas began to draw when she was still a child, taking inspiration from literary or print sources such as fairy tales, Bible illustrations, cartoons, comics and magazines. She grew up without television, which arrived in South Africa only in 1976. Films, however, although regulated by the apartheid regime, were an influence, and when Dumas was studying fine arts at the University of Cape Town (1972–75), she joined the university's film society, seeing, among others, Godard's and Resnais's groundbreaking films. There was the rigorous censorship of many forms of visual expression, however – from photographs in newspapers to sex scenes in films – compounded by the fact that not much classical painting, or, for that matter, European and American contemporary art, was on display in the local museums. Dumas remembers that you did not see 'the work you had to write essays about – Judd, Manet, Monet'. Her basic source of information concerning contemporary art was illustrations in art magazines.

In 1976 Dumas departed for Europe, with a scholar-ship to study art for two years at Ateliers '63 in Haarlem, an independent institute run by artists. She now says, somewhat defiantly, that her choice had little to do with her putatively Dutch ancestry. She chose to make Europe her home – rather than America, to which many other artists were emigrating – because it gave her the opportunity to familiarize herself with the great traditions of European art. Contemporary American art was, in any case, available in Dutch galleries, already famous for their wide-ranging internationalism.

Dumas has remained faithful to the institute, now located in Amsterdam and called simply de Ateliers, and she still teaches there. It had been founded by a group of contemporary Dutch artists, and Dumas was fascinated by the work of the conceptual and Arte Povera artists she encountered there: 'It looked so intelligent. It looked like modern art. Who wanted to paint a naked figure?' Nearly all of her early work comprised abstract drawings and collages incorporating fragments of text. She consciously rejected oil painting, perhaps because of its almost oppressive presence in the history of Dutch art, perhaps, too, because contemporary women artists have often tended to see painting as a male preserve.

For a young woman coming from apartheid South Africa, the absence of censorship in the Netherlands was a revelation. Dumas not only read widely about South African politics but she was also intrigued by the pornographic films readily available in Holland. She studied the masterpieces in Amsterdam's many museums, bringing home to her the difference between a reproduction and the original work, especially in painting. She began to analyse both the differences and

the common ground between abstract and figurative work: 'The abstract painters always insist on their connection with visible reality, while the so-called figurative artists (or at least I do) insist that what they really care about is the abstract qualities of life.'

Not long after she left Ateliers '63, Dumas took a course in psychology at the Psychological Institute of the University of Amsterdam (1979–80), the city in which she decided to settle. She started to exhibit in group shows and then in 1984 she made a decisive change by beginning to paint heads and figures. In doing so, she was moving broadly with the current of the times – many leading artists having started to experiment with a new version of figurative Expressionism – though her work had a conceptual edge to it, and showed a concern with portraiture, which set her apart. Her first all-painting show took place at the Galerie Paul Andriesse in Amsterdam in the following year, and it set the stylistic course she has followed ever since.

The connection with Paul Andriesse persists. Not only is he still her Dutch dealer but his first cousin, the painter Jan Andriesse, has been Dumas's partner since the late 1980s. They have lived for much of that time on a houseboat on the Amstel river in the centre of Amsterdam, and have a daughter, Helena, who was born in 1989. Dumas often paints likenesses of her, though most of her sources are images borrowed from other media, chiefly from photographs, mostly not made by her. Many of the images, in the form in which Dumas presents them, seem hauntingly familiar, resonating with the nether world of our own imaginations. Others appear almost shockingly violent and degraded, capable of both reflecting and challenging deep-rooted taboos and embedded social stereotypes.

The images are rendered using a gestural technique that owes much to the reductive abstract painting that Dumas has long admired, though she sometimes also makes jokes at her heroes' expense. A painting called *Ryman's Brides*, for example, made in 1997, shows six women in white wedding gowns, standing in a row, with arms linked. The various modulations of white in their dresses allude to the abstract painter Robert Ryman's obsession with the same colour or non-colour. He had insisted on the physical properties of paint, and while Dumas was similarly fascinated by the presence of the painting in space, she has described how she always

MARLENE DUMAS, *Ryman's Brides*, 1997

had an interest in 'the eroticism and psychology of the figures as well'.

Marlene Dumas does not consider herself a feminist artist. She argues that now, 'when the rape and abuse of women is worse than ever, and with all the official and unofficial wars that surround us, we should all be feminists as human beings. But as a painter, I don't work with any "-isms" as a primary subject matter.' She is also resistant to any directly political interpretation of her work. She says:

> It depends on what's meant by 'political'. If you define it as only relating to South Africa's apartheid politics, then I find it a hypocritical and stupid interpretation — what about American, European, and other racist and imperialist politics? If 'political' includes the fact that all aesthetic judgments are culturally biased and context sensitive, then you're getting closer.

It has been said that Dumas is obsessed with death, in two related ways. First, she frequently paints corpses or what appear to be corpses – something that seems to align her with Francis Bacon, though his figures are more often suffering than actually dead. She admits there is a certain influence, but sees it as a formal one: 'I did get things from Bacon — the fact of the figure in an abstract background. It is a figure, but where is the figure?' Secondly, she is seen as someone who is concerned with the prevalent idea of 'the death of painting'.

In fact, her ideas seem to run contrary to this. She is one of the great defenders of painting's power to produce both visual and psychological effects that can be discovered nowhere else:

> Painting is about the trace of the human touch. It is about the skin of a surface. A painting is something you have to get up close to. To see, you have to get intimate. If a painting doesn't change as you get closer, it is not a good painting.

Dumas now ranks as a major artistic figure. Her work has been exhibited extensively in Europe, including at the Kassel *documenta* and the Venice Biennale, and in 2007–8 she had major retrospectives in the US, and for the first time in Japan and South Africa. This

latter exhibition proved a particularly charged event for Dumas, not only because it took place in her native country but because the exhibition opened just a month after the death of her mother. She subsequently began work on a new series of paintings obliquely referencing this emotional upheaval, featuring images of famous women crying in public.

In 2005 and again in 2008 Dumas commanded the highest price for a living female artist at auction. Little interested in such matters, she sees the significance of her work, instead, as having been to: 'bring subject matter back into painting. I don't just want the figure back: I want to re-use the figure and portraiture to stand for all sorts of other things.'

SHIRIN NESHAT

The Iranian-born artist Shirin Neshat came to international prominence in the 1990s with a striking series
of video works that explored issues of gender and identity
in Islamic society. Born in the provincial city of Qazvin
in north-west Iran in 1957, the fourth of five children,
Neshat grew up in a warm and supportive upper middle-
class Muslim family that was not particularly religious.
Her father was a well-known physician, very progressive
and a supporter of the Shah. She has recalled:

> He fantasized about the west, romanticized the
> west, and slowly rejected all his own values; both
> my parents did. What happened, I think, was that
> their identity slowly dissolved, they exchanged it
> for comfort. It served their class.

The family's western orientation meant that initially
Neshat was educated at a Catholic boarding school in
Tehran, a difficult experience that made her anorexic.
At that period, many prosperous Iranian families wanted
their children, usually the sons, to study abroad and in
1974, at the age of seventeen, Neshat went to the USA
to attend a high school in Los Angeles: 'My father insisted
that all his children, including the girls, go to the highest
levels of education,' she has said. She moved to the
San Francisco Bay area to attend Dominican College, a
Catholic liberal arts institution, completing her BA at the

University of California at Berkeley in 1979, the year of
the Islamic revolution in Iran. With little English and
very homesick, she recalls her early years in California
as the darkest of her life:

> Psychologically, I really had a difficult time. As much
> as I didn't want to admit it, I was really lost. I was very
> young, without any support, and so most of my time
> was spent trying to survive.

Although the prosperity of her family was destroyed
by the political turmoil in her country, Neshat was able
to continue her studies at UC Berkeley, where she gained
an MA and an MFA. In 1983 she moved to New York,
with the intention of becoming an artist, maintaining
herself by working as receptionist in a hair salon, but
she felt isolated and intimidated by the city's art scene.
'I was a really bad painter. I've never been shy about
saying that. I battled with that in art school, so I left art
completely and did other things for ten years.' Nearly all
the work she made at this period has been destroyed.

Not long after she arrived in New York Neshat met
a Korean-American artist, Kyong Park, who in 1982
had founded a not-for-profit organization in downtown
New York called Storefront Art and Architecture. Still
flourishing, it is committed to exploring issues in art and
architecture and to interdisciplinary collaboration across
geographic and ideological boundaries. Neshat began
to work there as an administrator and on the curatorial
programme of exhibitions, conferences and artists' talks,
and in 1987 she married Park. Their son, Cyrus, was born
in 1990. Looking back on this period, she says: 'Working
there became my true education, mostly helping me
to mature and to begin to develop my own ideas and
methodology.'

In 1991 Neshat was able to return to Iran for the first
time in twelve years and went back each year until her
last visit in 1996, when she was detained at the airport.
She was fascinated by the changes the revolution had
brought, and in particular by the large number of visual
images associated with it. She tried to understand and
come to terms with what had happened and what she had
missed by living in the USA. This curiosity crystallized in
a photographic series called 'Women of Allah' (1993–97),
which led to Neshat's first solo exhibition in New York
in 1995 and brought her to critical attention. The
photographs, made in collaboration with Larry Barns,

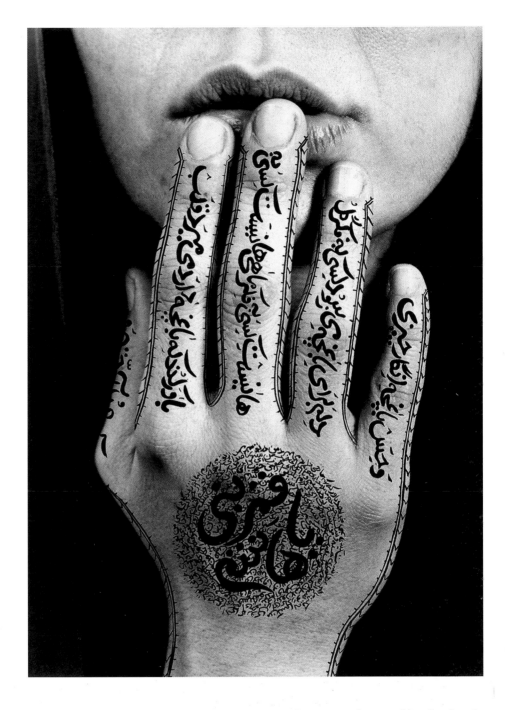

a professional photographer who lives near Neshat's country home at Westport in the Adirondacks, and sometimes featuring Neshat herself, were intended to explore martyrdom and women's part in it. She portrayed the female body, the veil and the gun, and inscribed the photographs with poems written by Iranian women who had been involved in the revolution.

Neshat now perceives that work as naïve, although she realizes it was a necessary stage in her development as an artist. It also led her to leave Storefront and her husband. She wanted to move away from overtly political subject matter to something more nuanced, that touched on universal human nature, and in 1997 she began to make the video works for which she is now best known. These have been made in collaboration with a group of largely Iranian exiles, including the filmmaker Shoja Azari, with whom she now lives in New York, the cinematographer Ghasem Ebrahimian and the singer Sussan Deyhim.

The most famous of these is a trilogy of dual-screen installations: *Turbulent* (1998), *Rapture* (1999) and *Fervor* (2000). *Turbulent* won the International Prize at the 48th Venice Biennale in 1999 and established Neshat's reputation as a star of contemporary art.

These videos have an emotional power that has made them accessible to western audiences, yet Neshat sees them, as she said in a 2000 interview with the American critic Arthur Danto, as the first things she made 'that no longer had the perspective of an artist distanced from her culture'. *Turbulent* and *Rapture* are both based on the notion of opposites, and arranged so that the viewer is caught between two projections. In *Turbulent* one screen shows a male singer performing a Sufi poem by Rumi to an all-male audience; on the other screen the camera circles a female singer who improvises her music to an empty auditorium. In contemporary Iran, women are not allowed to sing in public. When he finishes, the male singer is staring at the female vocalist. Neshat explains the scene: 'having clearly proved herself through her unbelievable performance, she appears relieved and peaceful whereas he comes across as shocked and at a loss.'

Neshat is often cited as a feminist or viewed as an oracle about Muslim womanhood but her work can be seen as much more universal. In describing *Rapture*, which depicts a group of women dressed in chadors travelling from the desert to the sea, where some of them set sail in a boat, Neshat told Danto: 'This journey, the attempt to break free, for me symbolizes bravery ... those women remaining behind symbolize the idea of sacrifice. The film questions women's nature as opposed to men's.'

Between 2004 and 2008 Neshat created a five-video cycle (*Mahdokht, Zarin, Munis, Faezeh, Farokh Legha*) loosely based on *Women Without Men*, a novel by the émigré Iranian novelist Shahrnush Parsipur that tells the story of five different women in Iran in 1953. Neshat used the same book as the basis for her first feature film, which she completed in 2008.

Neshat has been given numerous honours and awards. At the time she received the prestigious Lillian Gish prize in 2006, she said about her work: 'In art, one is able to untangle complicated ideologies, demystify group and self identity, observe humanity and interpret memory.' Even Neshat's detractors have to admit the extraordinary impact made by her videos. They rank among the works that justify the existence of video as a major art form, and as a means of expression particularly suited to the demands of our time.

Shirin Neshat, production still from *Turbulent*, 1998

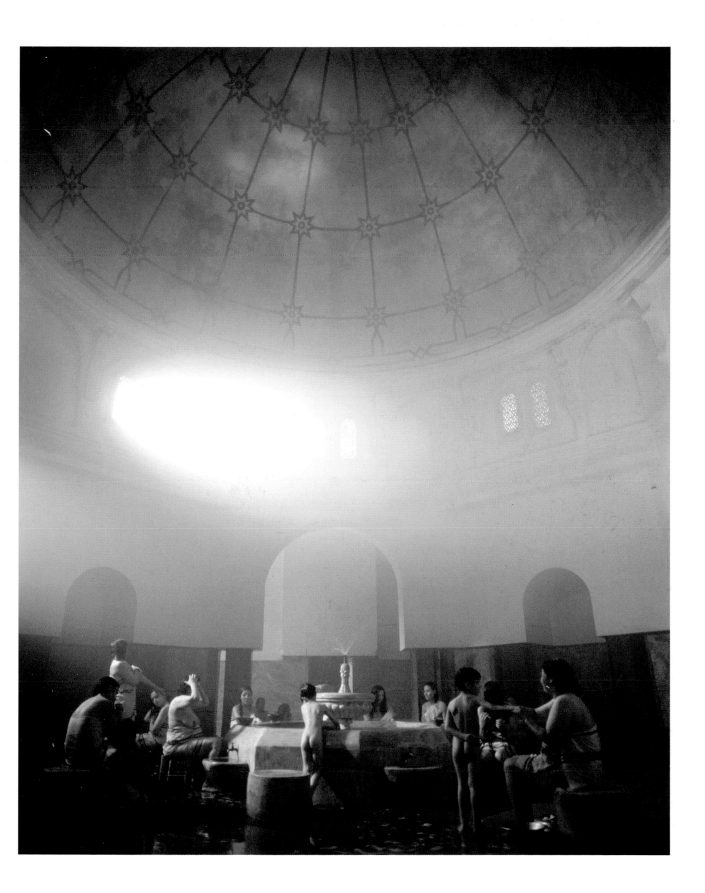

Shirin Neshat,
Untitled, 'Zarin' series, 2005

Select Bibliography

1 Towards the Modern

Edvard Munch

McShine, Kynaston (ed.), *Edvard Munch, The Modern Life of the Soul* (exhibition catalogue), Museum of Modern Art, New York, 2006

Messer, Thomas M., *Munch*, Thames & Hudson, London, 1987

Woll, Gerd, *Edvard Munch: Complete Paintings* (catalogue rasionné), 4 vols, Thames & Hudson, London, 2009

Käthe Kollwitz

Hinz, Renate (ed.), *Käthe Kollwitz: Graphics, Posters, Drawings*, Pantheon Books, New York, 1981

Kollwitz, Käthe, *The Diary and Letters of Käthe Kollwitz*, Northwestern University Press, Evanston, Illinois, 1988

Prelinger, Elizabeth, *Käthe Kollwitz* (exhibition catalogue), National Gallery of Art, Washington/Yale University Press, New Haven and London, 1992

2 The Fauves

Henri Matisse

Elderfield, John, *Henri Matisse: A Retrospective*, Thames & Hudson, London, 1992

Schneider, Pierre (ed.), *Henri Matisse: exposition du centenaire* (exhibition catalogue), Réunion des Musées Nationaux, Paris, 1970

Spurling, Hilary, *A Life of Henri Matisse*, Vol. 1, Hamish Hamilton, London, 1998

——, *A Life of Henri Matisse*, Vol. 2, Hamish Hamilton, London, 2005

Maurice de Vlaminck

Vallès-Bled, Maïthé, *Vlaminck, Critical Catalogue of Fauve Paintings and Ceramics*, Wildenstein Institute Publications, Paris, 2008

—— (ed.), *Vlaminck, un instinct fauve* (catalogue of an exhibition at the Musée du Luxembourg, Paris), Skira, Milan, 2008

André Derain

Derain, André, *Lettres à Vlaminck*, Paris, 1955

Lee, Jane, *Derain*, Phaidon, Oxford 1990

3 The Nabis

Pierre Bonnard

Bois, Yve-Alain, et al., *Pierre Bonnard: The Work of Art, Suspending Time*, Lund Humphries, Aldershot, 2006

Bonnard, Pierre, and Henri Matisse, *Bonnard/Matisse: Letters Between Friends, 1925–1946*, Abrams, New York, 1992

Bouvet, Francis, *Bonnard: The Complete Graphic Works*, Thames & Hudson, London, 1981

Hyman, Timothy, *Bonnard*, Thames & Hudson, London, 1998

Edouard Vuillard

Easton, Elizabeth Wynne, *The Intimate Interiors of Edouard Vuillard*, Thames & Hudson, London, 1989

Preston, Stuart, *Vuillard*, Thames & Hudson, London, 1985

Roger-Marx, Claude, *Vuillard: His Life and Work*, Paul Elek, London, 1946

Thomson, Belinda, *Vuillard*, Phaidon, Oxford, 1988

4 Cubism

Fernand Léger

Kosinski, Dorothy (ed.), *Fernand Léger 1911–1924: The Rhythm of Modern Life*, Prestel, Munich, 1994

Lanchner, Carolyn, *Fernand Léger*, Museum of Modern Art, New York, 1998

Schmalenbach, Werner, *Fernand Léger*, Thames & Hudson, London, 1991

Pablo Picasso

Cowling, Elizabeth, *Picasso: Style and Meaning*, Phaidon, London, 2002

——, *Visiting Picasso*, Thames & Hudson, London, 2006

Daix, Pierre, *Picasso: Life and Art*, Thames & Hudson, London, 1994

Gilot, Françoise, and Carlton Lake, *Life with Picasso*, Nelson, London, 1965; reissued, Virago, London, 1990

Green, Christopher, *Picasso: Architecture and Vertigo*, Yale University Press, New Haven and London, 2005

Hilton, Timothy, *Picasso*, Thames & Hudson, London, 1976

Richardson, John, *A Life of Picasso*, Vol. 1, Jonathan Cape, London, 1991

——, *A Life of Picasso*, Vol. 2, Jonathan Cape, London, 1996

——, *A Life of Picasso*, Vol. 3, Jonathan Cape, London, 2007

Rubin, William (ed.), *Picasso and Portraiture*, Thames & Hudson, London, 1996

Sabartès, Jaime, *Picasso: An Intimate Portrait*, W. H. Allen, London, 1948

Stein, Gertrude, *Picasso*, Batsford, London, 1938

Georges Braque

Danchev, Alex, *Georges Braque: A Life*, Hamish Hamilton, London, 2005

Mullins, Edwin, *Braque*, Thames & Hudson, London, 1968

Zürcher, Bernard, *Georges Braque: Life and Work*, Rizzoli, New York, 1988

Robert Delaunay and Sonia Delaunay

Baron, Stanley (with Jacques Damase), *Sonia Delaunay: The Life of an Artist*, Thames & Hudson, London, 1995

Bernier, Georges, *Sonia et Robert Delaunay: Naissance de l'art abstrait*, Jean-Claude Lattes, Paris, 1995

Hoog, Michel, *Robert Delaunay*, Flammarion, Paris, 1976

Robert Delaunay, Sonia Delaunay (exhibition catalogue), Musée d'Art Moderne de la Ville de Paris, 1987

Juan Gris

Green, Christopher, *Juan Gris* (exhibition catalogue), Whitechapel Art Gallery, London/Yale University Press, New Haven and London, 1992

Kahnweiler, D. H., *Juan Gris: His Life and Work*, Lund Humphries, London (new and enlarged edn), 1947

5 Futurism

Giacomo Balla

Faggiolo Dell'Arco, Maurizio, *Balla, the Futurist*, Mazzotta, Milan, 1987

Giacomo Balla (exhibition catalogue), Galleria d'Arte Moderna, Turin, 1963

Umberto Boccioni

Ballo, Guido, *Boccioni: la vita e l'opera*, Milan, 1964

Coen, Ester, *Boccioni* (exhibition catalogue), Metropolitan Museum of Art, New York, 1988

6 German Expressionism

Emil Nolde

Haftmann, Werner, *Emil Nolde: Forbidden Pictures*, Thames & Hudson, London, 1965

Vergo, Peter, and Felicity Lunn, *Emil Nolde* (exhibition catalogue), Whitechapel Art Gallery, London, 1995

Paula Modersohn-Becker

Perry, Gillian, *Paula Modersohn-Becker: Her Life and Work*, Women's Press, London, 1979

Gabriele Münter

Heller, Reinhold, *Gabriele Münter: The Years of Expressionism, 1903–20*, Prestel, Munich, 1998

Hoberg, Annegret, and Helmut Friedel, *Gabriele Münter: 1877–1962* (exhibition catalogue), Prestel, Munich, 1992

Hoberg, Annegret, *Wassily Kandinsky and Gabriele Münter: Letters and Reminiscences, 1902–1914*, Prestel, Munich, 1994

Ernst Ludwig Kirchner

Gordon, Donald E., *Ernst Ludwig Kirchner*, Harvard University Press, Cambridge, Mass, 1968

Jenderko-Sichelschmidt, Ingrid, and Karlheinz Gabler, *Ernst Ludwig Kirchner: Dokumente/Zeichnungen*, 2 vols, Aschaffenberg, 1980

Ketterer, R. N. (ed.), *Ernst Ludwig Kirchner: Drawings and Pastels*, Alpine Fine Arts Collection, London (new edn), 1995

Lloyd, Jill, and Magdalena M. Moeller, *Ernst Ludwig Kirchner: The Dresden and Berlin Years* (exhibition catalogue), Royal Academy of Arts, London, 2003

Max Beckmann

Beckmann, Max, *On My Painting*, Tate, London, 2003

——, *Self-Portrait in Words: Collected Writings and Statements, 1903–1950*, University of Chicago Press, 1997

Lackner, Stephen, *Beckmann*, Thames & Hudson, London, 1991

Rainbird, Sean (ed.), *Max Beckmann*, (exhibition catalogue), Tate, London, 2003

Selz, Peter, *Max Beckmann*, Abbeville Press, New York, 1996

Franz Marc

Hoberg, Annegret (ed.), *Franz Marc* (exhibition catalogue), Prestel, Munich, 2005

Hoberg, Annegret, and Isabelle Jansen (eds), *Franz Marc: The Complete Works, Vol. 1, The Oil Paintings*, Philip Wilson, London, 2004

Marc, Franz, and Vasily Kandinsky, *Der Blaue Reiter*, Munich, 1912

——, *The Blaue Reiter Almanac*, Thames & Hudson, London, 1974

7 The Vienna Sezession

Gustav Klimt

Metzger, Rainer, *Gustav Klimt: Drawings & Watercolours*, Thames & Hudson, London, 2005

Nebehay, Christian M., *Gustav Klimt: From Drawing to Painting*, Thames & Hudson, London, 1994

Novotny, F., and J. Dobai, *Gustav Klimt*, Thames & Hudson, London, 1968

Whitford, Frank, *Klimt*, Thames & Hudson, London, 1990

Oskar Kokoschka

Kokoschka, Oskar, *Letters 1905–1976*, Thames & Hudson, London, 1992

——, *My Life*, Thames & Hudson, London, 1974

Schröder, Klaus Albrecht, and Johann Winkler, *Oskar Kokoschka*, Prestel, Munich, 1991

Egon Schiele

Kallir, Jane, *Egon Schiele: Drawings & Watercolours*, Thames & Hudson, London, 2003

Leopold, Elizabeth, *Egon Schiele: Poems and Letters*, Prestel, Munich, 2008

Nebehay, Christian M., *Egon Schiele Sketchbooks*, Thames & Hudson, London, 1989

Whitford, Frank, *Egon Schiele*, Thames & Hudson, London, 1981

8 The Ecole de Paris

Georges Rouault

Courthion, Pierre, *Georges Rouault*, Thames & Hudson, London, 1962

Hergott, Fabrice, and Sarah Whitfield, *Georges Rouault: The Early Years, 1903–1920*, Royal Academy of Arts/Lund Humphries, London, 1993

Molinari, Danielle, *Georges Rouault 1871–1958: Catalogue Raisonné*, Musée d'Art Moderne de la Ville de Paris, 1983

Piet Mondrian

Bax, Marty, *Complete Mondrian*, Lund Humphries, Aldershot, 2001

Bois, Yve-Alain, *Mondrian* (exhibition catalogue), Leonardo Arte, Milan, 1994

Holtzman, Harry, and Martin S. James (eds), *The New Art, The New Life: The Collected Writings of Piet Mondrian*, Thames & Hudson, London, 1987

Jaffé, Hans L. C., *Mondrian*, Thames & Hudson, London, 1970

Constantin Brancusi

Chave, Anna C., *Constantin Brancusi: Shifting the Bases of Art*, Yale University Press, New Haven and London, 1993

Giménez, Carmen, and Matthew Gale (eds), *Constantin Brancusi: The Essence of Things*, Tate, London, 2004

Miller, Sanda, *Constantin Brancusi: A Survey of His Work*, Clarendon Press, Oxford, 1995

Amedeo Modigliani

Meyers, Jeffrey, *Modigliani: A Life*, Duckworth, London, 2006

Modigliani, Jeanne, *Modigliani: Man and Myth*, André Deutsch, London, 1959

Schmalenbach, Werner, *Amedeo Modigliani: Paintings, Sculptures, Drawings*, Prestel, Munich, 1990

Chaïm Soutine

Tuchman, Maurice, et al., *Chaim Soutine: Catalogue Raisonné*, 2 vols, Benedikt Taschen, Cologne, 1993

Werner, Alfred, *Soutine*, Thames & Hudson, London, 1991

9 The Russians

Kasimir Malevich

Crone, Rainer, and David Moos, *Kazimir Malevich: The Climax of Disclosure*, Reaktion, London, 1991

Douglas, Charlotte, *Malevich*, Thames & Hudson, London, 1994

Milner, John, *Kazimir Malevich and the Art of Geometry*, Yale University Press, New Haven and London, 1996

Mikhail Larionov and Natalia Goncharova
Nathalie Gontcharova, Michel Larionov (exhibition catalogue), Centre Pompidou, Paris, 1995
Parton, Anthony, *Mikhail Larionov and the Russian Avant-Garde*, Thames & Hudson, London, 1993
Tsvetaeva, Marina, *Nathalie Gontcharova: sa vie, son œuvre*, Clémence Hiver, Paris, 1990

Vladimir Tatlin
Milner, John, *Vladimir Tatlin and the Russian Avant-Garde*, Yale University Press, New Haven and London, 1983
Zhadova, Larissa (ed.), *Tatlin*, Thames & Hudson, London, 1988

Marc Chagall
Compton, Susan, *Chagall*, Royal Academy of Arts/Weidenfeld and Nicolson, London, 1985
———, *Marc Chagall: My Life, My Dream*, Prestel, Munich, 1990
Kamensky, Alcksandr, *Chagall: The Russian Years 1907–1922*, Thames & Hudson, London, 1989
Wullschlager, Jackie, *Chagall: The Dream of Life*, Allen Lane, London, 2008

Liubov Popova
Adaskina, Natalia, and Dimitri Sarabianov, *Liubov Popova*, Thames & Hudson, London, 1990
Dabrowski, M., *Liubov Popova*, The Museum of Modern Art, New York, 1991

El Lissitzky
Lissitzky-Küppers, Sophie, *El Lissitzky, Life, Letters, Texts*, Thames & Hudson, London, 1968 and 1980
Perloff, Nancy, and Brian Reed (eds), *Situating El Lissitzky: Vitebsk, Berlin, Moscow*, Getty, Los Angeles, 2003

Naum Gabo
Hammer, Martin, and Christina Lodder, *Constructing Modernity: The Art & Career of Naum Gabo*, Yale University Press, New Haven and London, 2000

Alexander Rodchenko and Varvara Stepanova
Karginov, German, *Rodchenko*, Thames & Hudson, London, 1979
Lavrentiev, Alexander, *Varvara Stepanova, a Constructivist Life*, Thames & Hudson, London, 1988
——— (ed.), *Alexsandr Rodchenko: Experiments for the Future, Diaries, Essays, Letters, and Other Writings*, Museum of Modern Art, New York, 2005

10 Dada
Francis Picabia
Camfield, William A., *Francis Picabia: His Art, Life, and Times*, Princeton University Press, Princeton, NJ, 1979
Picabia, Francis, *I am a Beautiful Monster: Poetry, Prose, and Provocation*, MIT Press, Cambridge, Mass, 2007

Marcel Duchamp
Adès, Dawn, Neil Cox and David Hopkins, *Marcel Duchamp*, Thames & Hudson, London, 1999
d'Harnoncourt, Anne, and Kynaston McShine, *Marcel Duchamp*, Prestel, Munich, 1989
Naumann, Francis M., and Hector Obalk, *Affect Marcel, The Selected Correspondence of Marcel Duchamp*, Thames & Hudson, London, 2000
Parkinson, Gavin, *The Duchamp Book*, Tate, London, 2008
Schwarz, Arturo, *The Complete Works of Marcel Duchamp*, Thames & Hudson, London, 1997

Kurt Schwitters
Dietrich, Dorothea, *The Collages of Kurt Schwitters: Tradition and Innovation*, Cambridge University Press, 1993
Elderfield, John, *Kurt Schwitters*, Thames & Hudson, London, 1985

Hans Arp and Sophie Taeuber-Arp
Andreotti, Margherita, *The Early Sculpture of Jean Arp*, UMI Research Press, Ann Arbor, MI, 1989
Arp, Hans, *On My Way: Poetry and Essays 1912–1947*, Wittenborn, Schultz, New York, 1948
Kuthy, Sandor (ed.), *Sophie Taeuber-Hans Arp*, Kunstmuseum, Bern, 1988

John Heartfield
Herzefelde, Wieland, *John Heartfield: Leben und Werk*, Verlag das Europaïsche Buch, Berlin, 1986
Pachnicke, Peter, and Klaus Honnef (eds), *John Heartfield*, Abrams, New York, 1992

11 Metaphysical Painting
Giorgio de Chirico
Crosland, Margaret, *Giorgio de Chirico*, Peter Owen, London, 1999
de Chirico, Giorgio, *The Memoirs of Giorgio de Chirico*, Peter Owen, London, 1971; reissued, Da Capo Press, New York, 1994

Giorgio Morandi
Abramowicz, Janet, *Giorgio Morandi: The Art of Silence*, Yale University Press, New Haven and London, 2004
De Salvo, Donna, et al., *Giorgio Morandi* (exhibition catalogue), Tate, London, 2001

12 Surrealism
Max Ernst
Ernst, Jimmy, *A Not-So-Still Life: A Child of Europe's Pre-World War II Art World and His Remarkable Homecoming to America*, St Martin's Press, New York, 1984
Ernst, Max, *Beyond Painting and Other Writings by the Artist and his Friends*, Wittenborn, Schultz, New York, 1948
Spies, Werner (ed.), *Max Ernst: A Retrospective* (exhibition catalogue), Tate Gallery/Prestel, London, 1991
——— (ed.), *Max Ernst: Life and Work*, Thames & Hudson, London, 2006

Joan Miró
Lanchner, Carolyn, *Joan Miró*, Museum of Modern Art, New York, 1993
Penrose, Roland, *Miró*, Thames & Hudson, London, 1985
Rowell, Margit (ed.), *Joan Miró: Selected Writings and Interviews*, Thames & Hudson, London, 1987

René Magritte
Gablik, Suzi, *Magritte*, Thames & Hudson, London, 1970, reprinted 1985
Magritte (exhibition catalogue), Musée des Beaux-Arts, Brussels, 1998
Sylvester, David, *Magritte*, Thames & Hudson, London, 1992

Salvador Dalí
Adès, Dawn, *Dalí*, Thames & Hudson, London (revised edn), 1995
———, *The Centenary Retrospective*, Thames & Hudson, London, 2004
Gala-Salvador Dalí Foundation, *Salvador Dalí: An Illustrated Life*, Tate, London, 2009
Secrest, Meryle, *Salvador Dalí: The Surrealist Jester*, Weidenfeld and Nicolson, London, 1987

13 The Bauhaus
Vasily Kandinsky
Friedel, Helmut, and Annegret Hoberg (eds), *Kandinsky*, Prestel, Munich, 2008
Hahl-Koch, Jelena, *Kandinsky*, Thames & Hudson, London, 1993
Röthel, Hans Konrad (ed.), *Kandinsky: Catalogue Raisonné of the Oil Paintings*, 2 vols, Sotheby, London, 1982–84

Lyonel Feininger
Luckhardt, Ulrich, *Lyonel Feininger*, Prestel, Munich, 1989

Paul Klee
Grohmann, Will, *Klee*, Thames & Hudson, London, 1987
Haftmann, Werner, *The Mind and Work of Paul Klee*, Faber, London, 1967
Lanchner, Carolyn (ed.), *Paul Klee* (exhibition catalogue), Museum of Modern Art, New York, 1987

László Moholy-Nagy
Kaplan, Louis (ed.), *László Moholy-Nagy, Biographical Writings*, Duke University Press, Durham, NC, and London, 1995
Passuth, Krisztina, *Moholy-Nagy*, Thames & Hudson, London, 1987

Josef Albers
Albers, Josef, *The Interaction of Colour*, Yale University Press, New Haven, 1963
Albers, Josef, and T. G. Rosenthal, *Formulation : Articulation*, Thames & Hudson, London, 2006
Weber, Nicholas Fox, and Martin Filler (eds), *Josef + Anni Albers: Designs for Living* (catalogue of an exhibition held at the Cooper-Hewitt National Design Museum, NY), Merrell, London, 2004

14 The New Objectivity
Otto Dix
Löffler, Fritz, *Otto Dix*, Holmes & Meier, New York, 1982
Otto Dix (exhibition catalogue), Tate Gallery, London, 1992

George Grosz
Flavell, M. Kay, *George Grosz: A Biography*, Yale University Press, New Haven and London, 1988
Grosz, George, *A Little Yes and a Big No*, New York, 1946
Hess, Hans, *George Grosz*, Yale University Press, New Haven and London, 1985
Jentsch, Ralph, *George Grosz: Berlin – New York*, Skira, Milan, 2008

15 The Mexicans
José Clemente Orozco
del Conde, T., *J. C. Orozco Antología crítica*, Universidad Nacional Autónoma de México, Mexico City, 2001
Elliott, David (ed.), *Orozco!* (exhibition catalogue), MOMA, Oxford, 1980
J. C. Orozco, an Autobiography, University of Texas Press, Austin, 1962
MacKinley, Helm, *Man of Fire: J. C. Orozco*, Harcourt Brace, New York, 1953; reissued, Greenwood, Westport, CT, 1971

Diego Rivera
Exposición de homenaje a Diego Rivera (exhibition catalogue), Palacio de Bellas Artes, Mexico City, 1977
Marnham, Patrick, *Dreaming with his Eyes Open: A Life of Diego Rivera*, Bloomsbury, London, 1998

David Alfaro Siqueiros
Solis, Ruth, et al., *Vida y obra de David Alfaro Siqueiros*, Fondo de Cultura Económica, Mexico, 1975
Stein, Philip, *Siqueiros: His Life and*

Works, International Publishers, New York, 1994

Frida Kahlo
Frida Kahlo and Tina Modotti (exhibition catalogue), Whitechapel Art Gallery, London, 1982
Herrera, Hayden, *Frida: A Biography of Frida Kahlo*, Harper & Row, New York, 1983
Kahlo, Frida, *The Diary of Frida Kahlo: An Intimate Self-Portrait*, Abrams, New York, 2006

16 America Between the Wars
Edward Hopper
Levin, Gail, *Edward Hopper: An Intimate Biography*, Knopf, New York, 1995
Troyen, Carol, et al., *Edward Hopper*, Thames & Hudson, London, 2007

Georgia O'Keeffe
Eisler, Benita, *O'Keeffe and Stieglitz: An American Romance*, Doubleday, New York and London, 1991
Messinger, Lisa Mintz, *Georgia O'Keeffe*, Thames & Hudson, London, 2001
Robinson, Roxana, *Georgia O'Keeffe: A Life*, Bloomsbury, London, 1990

Thomas Hart Benton
Baigell, Matthew, *Thomas Hart Benton*, Abrams, New York, 1973
Thomas Hart Benton: A Retrospective of His Early Years 1907–29 (exhibition catalogue), Rutgers University, New Jersey, 1972

Stuart Davis
Boyajian, Ani, and Mark Rutkoski (eds), *Stuart Davis: A Catalogue Raisonné*, 3 vols, Yale University Press, New Haven and London, 2007
Sims, Lowery Stokes, *Stuart Davis: American Painter*, Metropolitan Museum of Art, New York, 1991

17 England Between the Wars
Jacob Epstein
Epstein, Jacob, *Let There Be Sculpture: An Autobiography*, Michael Joseph, London, 1940
Rose, June, *Demons and Angels: A Life of Jacob Epstein*, Constable, London, 2002
Silber, Evelyn, *The Sculpture of Epstein*, Phaidon, Oxford, 1986

Stanley Spencer
Hyman, Timothy, and Patrick Wright (eds), *Stanley Spencer* (exhibition catalogue), Tate, London, 2001
MacCarthy, Fiona, *Stanley Spencer: An English Vision*, Yale University Press, New Haven and London, 1997

Ben Nicholson
Lynton, Norbert, *Ben Nicholson*, Phaidon, London, 1993
Stephens, Chris (ed.), *Ben Nicholson* (exhibition catalogue), Tate, London, 2008

Henry Moore
Berthoud, Roger, *The Life of Henry Moore*, Faber, London, 1987
Kosinski, Dorothy (ed.), *Henry Moore: Sculpting the Twentieth Century* (exhibition catalogue), Dallas Museum of Art/Yale University Press, New Haven and London, 2001
Lichtenstern, Christa, *Henry Moore: Work, Theory, Impact*, Royal Academy of Arts, London, 2008
Wilkinson, Alan (ed.), *Henry Moore: Writings and Conversations*, University of California Press, Berkeley, 2002

Barbara Hepworth
  Festing, Sally, *Barbara Hepworth: A Life of Forms*, Viking, London, 1995
  Hammacher, A. M., *Barbara Hepworth*, Thames & Hudson, London, 1987
  Stephens, Chris, *Barbara Hepworth Centenary* (exhibition catalogue), Tate, London, 2003
  Thistlewood, David (ed.), *Barbara Hepworth Reconsidered*, Tate Liverpool/Liverpool University Press, 1996

18 Abstract Expressionism
Mark Rothko
  Anfam, David, *Mark Rothko: The Works on Canvas* (catalogue raisonné), Yale University Press, New Haven and London, 1998
  Borchardt-Hume, Achim, *Rothko: The Late Series* (exhibition catalogue), Tate, London, 2008
  Waldman, Diane, *Mark Rothko 1903–1970*, Thames & Hudson, London, 1979 and 2001
Clyfford Still
  Demetrion, James T. (ed.), *Clyfford Still: Paintings 1944–1960* (exhibition catalogue), Hirshhorn Museum/Yale University Press, New Haven and London, 2001
  Kellein, Thomas (ed.), *Clyfford Still: The Buffalo and San Francisco Collections*, Prestel, Munich, 1992
Willem de Kooning
  de Kooning, Willem, *The Collected Writings of Willem de Kooning*, Hanuman Books, Madras and London, 1988
  Hall, Lee, *Elaine and Bill, Portrait of a Marriage: The Lives of Willem and Elaine de Kooning*, HarperCollins, New York, 1993
  Waldman, Diane, *Willem de Kooning*, Thames & Hudson, London, 1988
Arshile Gorky
  Arshile Gorky (exhibition catalogue), Whitechapel Art Gallery, London, 1990
  Herrera, Hayden, *Arshile Gorky, His Life and Work*, Bloomsbury, London, 2003
Barnett Newman
  O'Neill, John P. (ed.), *Barnett Newman: Selected Writings and Interviews*, Knopf, New York, 1990
  Shiff, Richard, *Barnett Newman: A Catalogue Raisonné*, Yale University Press, New Haven and London, 2004
Lee Krasner
  Landau, Ellen G., and Jeffrey D. Grove, *Lee Krasner: A Catalogue Raisonné*, Abrams, New York, 1995
Franz Kline
  Gaugh, Harry F., *Franz Kline*, Cincinnati Art Museum, Cincinnati/Abbeville Press, New York (2nd edn), 1994
  Gordon, John, *Franz Kline 1910–1962* (exhibition catalogue), Whitney Museum of American Art, New York, 1968
Jackson Pollock
  Landau, Ellen G., *Jackson Pollock*, Thames & Hudson, London, 1989 and 2005
  O'Connor, Francis V., and Eugene Victor Thaw, *Jackson Pollock* (catalogue raisonné), 4 vols, Yale University Press, New Haven and London, 1978
  Varnedoe, Kirk, and Pepe Karmel (eds), *Jackson Pollock* (exhibition catalogue), Museum of Modern Art, New York, 1999

Ad Reinhardt
  Ad Reinhardt (exhibition catalogue), Museum of Modern Art/Rizzoli, New York, 1991
  Rose, Barbara, *Art as Art: The Selected Writings of Ad Reinhardt*, Viking, New York, 1975

19 Post-War Europe
Alberto Giacometti
  Lord, James, *Giacometti, a Biography*, Farrar, Straus, Giroux, New York, 1985
  Sylvester, David, *Looking at Giacometti*, Chatto & Windus, London, 1994
Jean Dubuffet
  Husslein, Agnes (ed.), *Jean Dubuffet: Trace of an Adventure*, Prestel, Munich, 2003
Balthus
  Clair, Jean, *Balthus*, Thames & Hudson, London, 2001
  Klossowski de Rola, Stanislas, *Balthus*, Thames & Hudson, London (revised edn), 2002
  Rewald, Sabine, *Balthus* (exhibition catalogue), Metropolitan Museum of Art/Abrams, New York, 1984
Francis Bacon
  Farson, Daniel, *The Gilded Gutter Life of Francis Bacon*, Century, London, 1993
  Gale, Matthew, and Chris Stephens (eds), *Francis Bacon* (exhibition catalogue), Tate, London, 2008
  Russell, John, *Francis Bacon*, Thames & Hudson, London, 1993
  Sylvester, David, *Interviews with Francis Bacon*, Thames & Hudson, London (3rd, enlarged edn), 1993

20 The Heirs of Abstract Expressionism
Louise Nevelson
  Lisle, Laurie, *Louise Nevelson: A Passionate Life*, Summit Books, New York, 1990
  Rapaport, Brooke Kamin (ed.), *The Sculpture of Louise Nevelson*, Yale University Press, New Haven and London, 2007
David Smith
  Giménez, Carmen (ed.), *David Smith: A Centennial* (exhibition catalogue), Tate, London, 2006
  Gray, Cleve (ed.), *David Smith by David Smith*, Thames & Hudson, London, 1989
Morris Louis
  Elderfield, John, *Morris Louis*, Museum of Modern Art, New York, 1986
  Upright, Diane, *Morris Louis: The Complete Paintings* (catalogue raisonné), Abrams, New York, 1985

21 American Neo-Dada
Robert Rauschenberg
  Hopps, Walter, and Susan Davidson (eds), *Robert Rauschenberg: A Retrospective* (exhibition catalogue), Guggenheim Museum, New York, 1997
  Tompkins, Calvin, *Off the Wall: A Portrait of Robert Rauschenberg*, Penguin, Harmondsworth, 1981
Jasper Johns
  Crichton, Michael, *Jasper Johns*, Thames & Hudson, London (revised edn), 1994
  Varnedoe, Kirk (ed.), *Jasper Johns: A Retrospective*, Museum of Modern Art, New York, 1996

22 British Pop Art
Richard Hamilton
  Hamilton, Richard, *Collected Words 1953–1982*, Thames & Hudson, London, 1982
  ———, *Richard Hamilton: Painting by Numbers*, Thames & Hudson, London, 2007
  Morphet, Richard (ed.), *Richard Hamilton* (exhibition catalogue), Tate Gallery, London, 1992
David Hockney
  Evans, Gregory, *Hockney's Pictures*, Thames & Hudson, London, 2004
  Hockney, David, and Nikos Stangos (ed.), *That's the Way I See It*, Thames & Hudson, London, 1993
  Livingstone, Marco, *David Hockney*, Thames & Hudson, London (revised edn), 1996
  Stangos, Nikos (ed.), *David Hockney by David Hockney: My Early Years*, Thames & Hudson, London, 1988
  Tuchman, Maurice, and Stephanie Barron, *David Hockney: A Retrospective* (exhibition catalogue), Los Angeles County Museum of Art/Thames & Hudson, London, 1988

23 American Pop Art
Roy Lichtenstein
  Corlett, Mary Lee, *The Prints of Roy Lichtenstein: A Catalogue Raisonné 1948–1997*, National Gallery of Art, Washington/Hudson Hills Press, New York (2nd edn, revised), 2002
  Waldman, Diane, *Roy Lichtenstein*, Guggenheim Museum, New York, 1993
Andy Warhol
  Hackett, Pat (ed.), *The Andy Warhol Diaries*, Simon and Schuster, New York and London, 1989
  McShine, Kynaston (ed.), *Andy Warhol Retrospective*, Museum of Modern Art, New York, 1989
  Warhol, Andy, *The Philosophy of Andy Warhol*, Cassell, London, 1975; reissued, Penguin, London, 2007
Claes Oldenburg
  Claes Oldenburg: An Anthology, Guggenheim Museum, New York, 1995
  Gianelli, Ida, and Marcella Beccaria, *Claes Oldenburg and Coosje van Bruggen: Sculpture by the Way*, Skira, Milan, 2006
Jim Dine
  Dine, Jim, and Caroline Joubert, *L'Odysée de Jim Dine: A Survey of Printed Works from 1985–2006*, Steidl, Göttingen, 2007
  d'Oench, Ellen G., and Jean E. Feinberg, *Jim Dine Prints 1977–1985*, Harper & Row, New York, 1986
  Krens, Thomas, *Jim Dine Prints 1970–77*, Harper & Row, New York, 1977

24 The Artist Not the Artwork
Louise Bourgeois
  Morris, Frances (ed.), *Louise Bourgeois* (exhibition catalogue), Tate, London, 2007
  Storr, Robert, et al., *Louise Bourgeois*, Phaidon, London, 2003
Joseph Beuys
  Borer, Alain, *The Essential Joseph Beuys*, Thames & Hudson, London, 1997
  Mesch, Claudia, and Viola Michely (eds), *Joseph Beuys: The Reader*, Tauris, London, 2007
  Rosenthal, Mark, *Joseph Beuys: Actions, Vitrines, Environments*, Tate, London, 2004

Yves Klein
  Charlet, Nicholas, *Yves Klein*, Adam Biro, Paris, 2000
  Morineau, Camille, *Yves Klein: Corps, couleur, immatériel* (exhibition catalogue), Centre Pompidou, Paris, 2006
  Restany, Pierre, *Yves Klein: Fire at the Heart of the Void*, Journal of Contemporary Art Editions, New York, 1992
Eva Hesse
  Pollock, Griselda, and Vanessa Corby (eds), *Encountering Eva Hesse*, Prestel, Munich, 2006
  Sussman, Elisabeth (ed.), *Eva Hesse* (exhibition catalogue), San Francisco Museum of Modern Art/Yale University Press, New Haven and London, 2002
Jean-Michel Basquiat
  Hoban, Phoebe, *Basquiat: A Quick Killing in Art*, Penguin, London (2nd edn, revised), 2004
  Marshall, Richard, et al., *Jean-Michel Basquiat* (exhibition catalogue), Whitney Museum of American Art, New York, 1992
  Mayer, Marc (ed.), *Basquiat*, Merrell, London, 2005
Zhang Xiaogang
  Reckoning with the Past: Contemporary Chinese Painting (exhibition catalogue), Fruitmarket Gallery, Edinburgh, 1996
  The Revolution Continues: New Art From China (catalogue of an exhibition at the Saatchi Gallery, London), Jonathan Cape, London, 2008

25 Four Women Artists
Yayoi Kusama
  Applin, Jo, *Yayoi Kusama*, 2 vols, Victoria Miro Gallery, London, 2008
  Hoptman, Laura J., *Yayoi Kusama*, Phaidon, London, 2000
  Love Forever: Yayoi Kusama, 1958–1968 (exhibition catalogue), Los Angeles County Museum of Art, 1998
Judy Chicago
  Chicago, Judy, *Beyond the Flower: The Autobiography of a Feminist Artist*, Viking, New York, 1996
  ———, *The Dinner Party: From Creation to Preservation*, Merrell, London, 2007
  Levin, Gail, *Becoming Judy Chicago: A Biography of the Artist*, Harmony Books, New York, 2007
  Lippard, Lucy R., et al., *Judy Chicago* (catalogue of an exhibition organized by the National Museum of Women in the Arts, Washington, D.C.), Watson-Guptill, New York, 2002
Marlene Dumas
  Bonacossa, Ilaria, *Marlene Dumas*, Mondadori Electa, Milan, 2006
  Boogerd, Dominic van den, et al., *Marlene Dumas*, Phaidon, London (2nd edn, revised), 2008
  Butler, Cornelia (ed.), *Marlene Dumas: Measuring Your Own Grave* (exhibition catalogue), Museum of Contemporary Art, Los Angeles, 2008
Shirin Neshat
  Neshat, Shirin, *Shirin Neshat* (exhibition catalogue), Serpentine Gallery, London, 2000
  ———, *Women of Allah*, Marco Noire Editore, Turin, 1997
  Zaya, Octavio, *Shirin Neshat, The Last Word*, Charta, Milan, 2006

List of Illustrations

Measurements are given in centimetres, followed by inches in brackets

Wedge, 1919. Poster. © DACS 1999 **122** (below) Varvara Stepanova, cover design for *Zigra ar*, 1918. Gouache on paper 18.5 × 16 (7 1/2 × 6 1/4). Collection Alexander Lavrentiev. © DACS 1999 **123** Alexander Rodchenko, *France and England*, 1920. Watercolour and coloured ink. Private collection. © DACS 1999 **124** Varvara Stepanova, 1928. Photo Alexander Rodchenko. © DACS 1999 **125** Alexander Rodchenko, *The Pioneer Trumpeter*, 1930. Musée Nicéphore Niepce, Chalon-sur-Saône. © DACS 1999 **127** Naum Gabo, *Linear Construction in Space No. 2*, 1972–73. Perspex with nylon monofilament, H 92 (36 1/4). Private collection, Switzerland. Photo John Webb. The works of Naum Gabo © Nina Williams **128** Naum Gabo with his wife Miriam, South of France, *c*. 1936. Photographer unknown. Tate Gallery Archive Collection. Photograph © Graham and Nina Williams **129** Naum Gabo with *Head*, 1968. Photo Herbert Reid. Tate Gallery Archive Collection. Photograph © Graham and Nina Williams **130** Marcel Duchamp, *Fountain*, New York 1917 (no longer extant). Photo © Alfred Stieglitz, from the second issue of *The Blind Man*, published May 1917, by Marcel Duchamp, Beatrice Wood and H.-P. Roché. Photograph courtesy the Museum of Modern Art, New York. © ADAGP, Paris and DACS, London 1999 **131** Hans Arp's navel, Brittany *c*. 1928. Photographer unknown. Fondation Arp, Clamart **132** Francis Picabia, *Parade Amoureuse*, 1917. Oil on board 96 × 73 (37 3/4 × 28 3/4). Private collection. © ADAGP, Paris and DACS, London 1999 **135** Francis Picabia in motorcar *c*. 1930. Photo Man Ray. © Man Ray Trust/ADAGP, Paris and DACS, London 1999/Telimage, Paris **136** Marcel Duchamp. Photo Eliot Elisofon. Life Magazine. © Time Warner Inc./Katz Pictures **137** Marcel Duchamp, 1966. Photo Jorge Lewinski **138** Kurt Schwitters, 1924. Photo El Lissitzky. Photogram 11.5 × 10.5 (4 1/2 × 4 1/8). Private collection. © DACS 1999 **139** Kurt Schwitters, *Merzbau*, *c*. 1930. Destroyed. Photo Landesgalerie, Hanover. © DACS 1999 **141** (above) Sophie Taeuber-Arp, Munich 1913. Photographer unknown. Fondation Arp, Clamart **141** (below) Sophie Taeuber-Arp, *Composition with Bird Motifs*, 1927. Watercolour 38 × 26.5 (15 × 10 1/2). Private collection **142** Hans Arp in his studio, Basle, 1954. Photo Denise Colomb, courtesy Association Française pour la Diffusion du Patrimoine Photographique, Paris. © Ministère de la Culture, France **143** Hans Arp, *The Dancer*, 1925. Painted wood 146.5 × 109 (57 3/4 × 42 7/8). Musée National d'Art Moderne, Centre Georges Pompidou, Paris. © DACS 1999 **145** John Heartfield, *John Heartfield with Chief of Police Zörgiebel*, from *AIZ*, 8, no. 37, 1929. Rotogravure on newsprint from original photomontage. The Museum of Fine Arts, Houston. Museum purchase with funds provided by Isabell and Max Herstein. © DACS 1999 **146** John Heartfield *Hurrah, the Butter is Finished!*, 19 December 1935. Photomontage. Photo Akademie der Künste der DDR, Berlin. © DACS 1999 **148** Giorgio de Chirico, *Great Metaphysical Interior*, 1917. Oil on canvas 95.9 × 70.5 (37 3/4 × 27 3/4). The Museum of Modern Art, New York. Gift of James Thrall Soby. Photograph © 1998 The Museum of Modern Art, New York. © DACS 1999 **149** Giorgio de Chirico, 1929. Photographer unknown. Hulton Getty Collection/Corbis **151** Giorgio de Chirico and his wife Isabella, 1951. Photo © Philippe Halsman/Magnum **152** Giorgio de Chirico, *Portrait of Guillaume Apollinaire*, 1914. Oil and charcoal on canvas 81.5 × 65 (32 × 25 5/8). Musée National d'Art

Moderne, Centre Georges Pompidou, Paris. © DACS 1999 **153** Giorgio Morandi, *Still-Life*, 1946. Oil on canvas 37.5 × 45.7 (14 3/4 × 18). Tate Gallery London. © DACS 1999 **154** Giorgio Morandi, Bologna 1953. Photo Herbert List. © Herbert List Estate–Max Scheler, Hamburg **155** Giorgio Morandi, *Mannequins on a Round Table*, 1918. Oil on canvas 47 × 54 (18 1/2 × 21 1/4). Private Collection, Milan. © DACS 1999 **156** Max Ernst, *The Robing of the Bride*, 1940. Oil on canvas 130 × 96 (51 1/8 × 37 3/4). Peggy Guggenheim Collection, Venice. Photo Solomon R. Guggenheim Foundation, New York. © ADAGP, Paris and DACS, London 1999 **157** Max Ernst, Sedona, Arizona 1946. Photo by Lee Miller. © Lee Miller Archives, Chiddingly, England **160** Joan Miró, *Women Encircled by the Flight of a Bird*, from the *Constellations* series, 1941. Gouache and oil wash on paper 46 × 38 (18 1/8 × 15). Private collection, Paris. © ADAGP, Paris and DACS, London 1999 **161** Joan Miró at the Maritime Museum, Barcelona 1955. Photo Brassaï. © Gilberte Brassaï **164** (above) René Magritte with chessboard and body-bottle, 1960. Photos Charles Leirens, courtesy Giraudon **164** (below) René Magritte, *The Mathematical Mind* (*L'esprit de géométrie*), 1936 or 1937. Gouache on paper 37.5 × 29.4 (14 3/4 × 11 1/2). Tate Gallery, London. © ADAGP, Paris and DACS, London 1999 **166** Salvador Dalí with fly on his moustache, 1954. Photo © Philippe Halsman/Magnum **167** Double portrait of Salvador Dalí and Gala, 1937. Photo © Cecil Beaton, Sotheby's, London. © Salvador Dalí – Fundacion Gala–Salvador Dalí/DACS, London 1999 **168** Salvador Dalí, *The Enigma of Desire*, 1929. Oil on canvas 110 × 150.7 (43 1/3 × 59 1/3). Private Collection, Zurich. © Salvador Dalí – Fundacion Gala–Salvador Dalí/DACS, London 1999 **170** Vasily Kandinsky, Walter Gropius and the Dutch architect J.J.P. Oud at the opening of the Bauhaus exhibition, 1923. Photographer unknown. Bauhaus-Archiv/ Museum für Gestaltung, Berlin **171** Vasily Kandinsky with Gabriele Münter, March 1916. Photographer unknown. Photo AKG London **172** Vasily Kandinsky's Paris studio as he left it at his death in 1944. Photo © Alexander Liberman, 1954 **175** Lyonel Feininger, self-portrait cartoon in the *Chicago Sunday Tribune*, 1906. © DACS 1999 **176** Lyonel Feininger, 1936. Photo Imogen Cunningham. © 1978 The Imogen Cunningham Trust **177** (above) Lyonel Feininger, *Lady in Mauve*, 1922. Oil on canvas 100 × 80 (39 3/8 × 31 1/4). Private collection. © DACS 1999 **177** (below) Lyonel Feininger, *Church at Gelmerode XII*, 1929. Oil on canvas 100.3 × 80.3 (39 1/2 × 31 5/8). Museum of Art, Rhode Island School of Design. Gift of Mrs Murray S. Danforth. Photography by Cathy Carver. © DACS 1999 **178** Paul Klee, Wiesbaden, 1924. Photo Elain. Bildarchiv Felix Klee/Paul Klee Stiftung, Bern **179** Kandinsky and Klee posing as Schiller and Goethe on the beach at Hendaye, France 1929. Photo Lily Klee **180** Paul Klee, *The Tightrope Walker/Equilibrist*, 1923. Watercolour and oil on paper, mounted on cardboard 48.5 × 31.5 (19 × 12 1/2). Paul Klee Stiftung, Kunstmuseum, Bern. © DACS 1999 **181** Paul Klee, *Fire Source*, 1938. Oil on newspaper on burlap 69.5 × 149.5 (27 3/8 × 58 7/8). Private collection. © DACS 1999 **182** László Moholy-Nagy, early 1920s. Photo H. Künstler. Photo © Ullstein Bilderdienst, Berlin **183** László Moholy-Nagy, *Light Play: Black/White/Grey*, 1922–30. Gelatin silver print 37.4 × 27.5 (14 3/4 × 10 3/4). The Museum of Modern Art, New York. Gift of

the photographer. Copy print © 1998 The Museum of Modern Art, New York. © DACS 1999 **184** Group of students and teachers at the Bauhaus in Weimar, *c*. 1921–23. Photographer unknown. Photo AKG London **185** (above) Josef Albers, *Factory*, 1925. Sandblasted, opaque flashed glass with black paint 29.2 × 36.2 (11 1/2 × 14 1/4). Collection The Josef and Anni Albers Foundation, Bethany, CT. Photo Tim Nighswander. © DACS 1999 **185** (below) Josef Albers, study for *Homage to the Square Departing in Yellow*, 1964. 76.2 × 76.2 (30 × 30). Tate Gallery, London. © DACS 1999 **186** (above) Josef Albers in his studio. North Forest Circle, New Haven, *c*. 1960s. Photographer unknown. Photo Yale News Bureau, courtesy the Josef and Anni Albers Foundation, Bethany, CT **186** (below) Josef Albers at Black Mountain College. Photographer unknown. Photo courtesy the Josef and Anni Albers Foundation, Bethany, CT **188** Otto Dix, *To Beauty*, 1922. Oil on canvas 140 × 122 (55 1/8 × 48). Von der Heydt-Museum. Wuppertal. © DACS 1999 **189** Otto and Martha Dix, *c*. 1927–28. Photo August Sander. © Photographische Sammlung/SK Stiftung Kultur – August Sander Archiv, Cologne. © DACS 1999 **192** (left) George Grosz, *Explosion*, 1917. Oil on composition board 47.8 × 68.2 (18 7/8 × 26 7/8). The Museum of Modern Art, New York. Gift of Mr and Mrs Irving Moskovitz. Photograph © 1998 The Museum of Modern Art, New York. © DACS 1999 **192** (right) George Grosz, *Daum marries her pedantic automaton George in May 1920, John Heartfield is very glad of it*, 1920. Watercolour and collage 42 × 30.2 (16 1/2 × 12). Galerie Nierendorf, Berlin. © DACS 1999 **193** George Grosz, 1928. Photographer unknown. Photo © Ullstein Bilderdienst, Berlin **194** Portrait of José Clemente Orozco, New York, 1933. The Ansel Adams Publishing Rights Trust/Corbis **195** José Clemente Orozco, *La Evangelización*, 1938–39, detail of mural at the chapel of the Hospicio Cabañas, Guadalajara, Mexico. Photo Istituto Nacional de Bellas Artes, Mexico **198** Diego Rivera, *Crossing the Barranca*, 1930–31, mural, Palacio de Cortés, Cuernavaca, Mexico. Photo Bob Schalkwijk **199** Diego Rivera, 1923. Photo Edward Weston. AKG London **199** Diego Rivera and Frida Kahlo in San Francisco, *c*. 1930. Photo Edward Weston. AKG London **202** Diego Rivera, *Flower Day*, 1925. Encaustic on canvas 147.4 × 120.6 (58 × 47). Los Angeles County Museum of Art. LA County Funds **203** David Alfaro Siqueiros, *Portrait of the Bourgeoisie*, 1939, detail of mural at the headquarters of the Union of Electricians, Mexico City. Photo Istituto Nacional de Bellas Artes, Mexico **204** David Alfaro Siqueiros in front of the *Polyforum Siqueiros*, *c*. 1960s. Photo © Daniel Frasnay/Rapho **206** Frida Kahlo, *The Two Fridas*, 1939. Oil on canvas 173.5 × 173 (68 1/4 × 68 1/8). Museo de Arte Moderno, Mexico City **207** Frida Kahlo, *c*. 1939. Carbro print. Photo Nickolas Muray. © Nickolas Muray Photo Archives, courtesy George Eastman House, Rochester **210** Edward and Jo Hopper in South Truro, Massachusetts, 1960. Photo © Arnold Newman **211** (above) Edward Hopper, *House by the Railroad*, 1925. Oil on canvas 61 × 73.7 (24 × 29). The Museum of Modern Art, New York. Given anonymously. Photograph © 1998 The Museum of Modern Art, New York **211** (below) Edward Hopper, *Nighthawks*, 1942. Oil on canvas 82.8 × 152.4 (33 × 60). The Art Institute of Chicago. Gift of the Friends of American Art **213** Georgia O'Keeffe, 1927. Photo Alfred Stieglitz. Yale Collection of American Literature, The Beinecke Rare Book & Manuscript Library,

Yale University **214** Georgia O'Keeffe with *Pelvis, Red and Yellow*, *c*. 1960. Photo Michael Vaccaro/Image Bank. © ARS, NY and DACS, London 1999 **215** Georgia O'Keeffe, *Abstraction, White Rose II*, 1927. Oil on canvas 91.4 × 76.2 (36 × 30). The Georgia O'Keeffe Foundation, Albuquerque. © ARS, NY and DACS, London 1999 **218** Thomas Hart Benton, late 1920s. Photographer unknown. Photo Corbis/UPI **219** Thomas Hart Benton, *Independence and the Opening of the West*, 1959–62 (detail). Mural, Harry S. Truman Library, Independence, Missouri. © Estate of Thomas Hart Benton/DACS, London/VAGA, New York 1999 **221** Stuart Davis with painting *Summer Landscape*, dated 1930. Photographer unknown. The Peter A. Juley & Son Collection, National Museum of American Art, Smithsonian Institution, Washington, D.C. **222** Stuart Davis, *Pad No. 4*, 1947. Oil on canvas 35.6 × 45.7 (14 × 18). The Brooklyn Museum of Art, New York. Bequest of Edith and Milton Lowenthal. © Estate of Stuart Davis/DACS, London/VAGA, New York 1999 **223** Stuart Davis, *Eggbeater No. 1*, 1927. Oil on canvas 74 × 91.4 (29 1/8 × 36). Collection of the Whitney Museum of American Art, New York. Gift of Getrude Vanderbilt Whitney. © Estate of Stuart Davis/DACS, London/VAGA, New York 1999 **225** Epstein in his Chelsea studio in front of his Oscar Wilde Memorial, 1912. Photo © Emil Otto Hoppé. The Royal Photographic Society collection, Bath, England **227** Epstein in his studio at Hyde Park Gate among some of his works. September 1947. Photographer unknown. Photo Hulton Getty **228** Stanley Spencer on a working visit to the Clydeside shipyards at Port Glasgow, October 1943. Photographer unknown. Photo Hulton Getty **229** Stanley Spencer, *Resurrection of Soldiers* at the Oratory of All Souls at Burghclere in Berkshire, 1928. National Trust Photographic Library/A. C. Cooper, London. © Estate of Stanley Spencer 1999. All rights reserved DACS **231** Ben Nicholson, St Ives 1956. Photo Bill Brandt. © Bill Brandt Archive Ltd **233** Ben Nicholson, *White Relief*, 1935. Oil on carved board 52.3 × 73.8 (20 1/2 × 29). Ivor Braka Ltd, London. © Angela Verren-Taunt 1999. All rights reserved DACS **234** Henry Moore, Much Hadham, 1954. Photo Ida Kar/Mary Evans Picture Library **237** (above) The sculptor John Skeaping and his wife Barbara Hepworth, Hampstead, 21 March 1933. Photographer unknown. Photo Hulton Getty **237** (below) Barbara Hepworth, *Pelagos*, 1946. Wood with colour and strings, H 40.6 (16). Tate Gallery, London. © Alan Bowness, Hepworth Estate **238** Barbara Hepworth, *Assembly of Sea Forms*, 1972. White marble, mounted on stainless steel base, H 105.4 (41 1/2). Norton Simon Art Foundation, Pasadena, CA. © Alan Bowness, Hepworth Estate **239** Barbara Hepworth, 1963. Photo © Cornel Lucas, London **240** Mark Rothko, New York City 1964. Photo Hans Namuth. © 1991 Hans Namuth Estate Collection, Center for Creative Photography, The University of Arizona, Tucson **241** Photo of the opening of Franz Kline's exhibition at Sidney Janis Gallery, New York, March 1960. Photo © Fred W. McDarrah **242** Mark Rothko, *Orange, Yellow, Orange*, 1969. Oil on paper mounted on linen 123.2 × 102.9 (48 1/2 × 40 1/2). Photo courtesy Marlborough Gallery, New York. © Kate Rothko Prizel and Christopher Rothko/DACS 1999 **243** Mark Rothko, East Hampton 1964. Photo Hans Namuth. © 1991 Hans Namuth Estate Collection, Center for Creative Photography, The University of Arizona, Tucson **246** (above) Clyfford Still in his studio, 1953.

Figures in bold indicate the artist's main entry